Guns, Race, and Power in Colonial South Africa

In this book, William Kelleher Storey shows that guns and discussions about guns during the seventeenth, eighteenth, and nineteenth centuries were fundamentally important to the establishment of racial discrimination in South Africa. Relying mainly on materials held in archives and libraries in Britain and South Africa, Storey explains the workings of the gun trade and the technological development of the firearms. He relates the history of firearms to ecological, political, and social changes, showing that there is a close relationship between technology and politics in South Africa.

William Kelleher Storey is associate professor of history at Millsaps College in Jackson, Mississippi. He is the author of *Science and Power in Colonial Mauritius* (1997) and *Writing History: A Guide for Students* (1998; 2nd ed. 2003; 3rd ed. 2008), which he developed when teaching in Harvard's Expository Writing Program. He has received a research and writing fellowship from the John D. and Catherine T. MacArthur Foundation and the Abbott Payson Usher Prize from the Society for the History of Technology. In 2006, he received the Teacher's Award from the Mississippi Humanities Council.

Guns, Race, and Power in Colonial South Africa

WILLIAM KELLEHER STOREY

Millsaps College

CAMBRIDGE UNIVERSITY PRESS
Cambridge, New York, Melbourne, Madrid, Cape Town, Singapore, São Paulo, Delhi

Cambridge University Press
32 Avenue of the Americas, New York, NY 10013-2473, USA

www.cambridge.org
Information on this title: www.cambridge.org/9780521885096

First published 2008

Printed in the United States of America

A catalog record for this publication is available from the British Library.

Library of Congress Cataloging in Publication Data

Storey, William Kelleher.
Guns, race, and power in colonial South Africa / William Kelleher Storey.
p. cm. – (African studies ; 109)
Includes bibliographical references and index.
ISBN 978-0-521-88509-6 (hbk.)
1. South Africa – History – To 1836.   2. South Africa – History – 1836–1909.
3. South Africa – Colonization.   4. Imperialism – History.   5. Technology
transfer – South Africa – History.   6. Firearms – Social aspects – South Africa – History.
7. Firearms – Political aspects – South Africa – History.   8. Firearms – Environmental
aspects – South Africa – History.   9. Political culture – South Africa – History.
10. South Africa – Politics and government.   I. Title.   II. Series.
DT1828.S76   2008
305.896′0680903 – dc22   2008010659

ISBN   978-0-521-88509-6 hardback

Contents

List of Tables

List of Illustrations

ix

Preface

This book is a narrative of the spread of firearms in South Africa during the seventeenth, eighteenth, and nineteenth centuries. I recount more than the workings of the gun trade and the narrower technological development of firearms: I have related the history of firearms to ecological, political, and social changes. To accomplish this, I relied mainly on materials held in archives and libraries in Britain and South Africa. I also considered histories and sociologies of technologies set in other places to help flesh out the argument.

I argue that when South Africans discussed the gun trade and gun control, they were shaping broader aspects of colonial political culture. I make the related argument that the rise and decline of various shooting skills were related to the formation and destruction of African communities, settler communities, and indigenous wildlife. While social, political, and ecological changes occurred, the representation of guns and shooting skills became highly politicized.

I started to be interested in firearms and imperialism in 1985, when I was an undergraduate at Harvard. My tutor, Robin Kilson, introduced me to the work of Daniel Headrick. I was impressed by Headrick's book, *The Tools of Empire*, which has chapters about firearms, but Robin held that Headrick gave too much credit to technological factors in explaining European imperialism. It is to Robin's credit as a teacher that I have made a career out of trying to understand the relationship between conflict, environment, and technology. I pursued related topics during graduate studies under the supervision of Philip Curtin at Johns Hopkins, where, in 1993, I completed a doctoral dissertation on conflict over sugar canes in colonial Mauritius. In 1995, when I was a postdoctoral Fellow in Cornell

University's Department of Science and Technology Studies, I returned to the history of imperialism and firearms after conversations with my mentor, Sheila Jasanoff, and my office mate, Michael Aaron Dennis. Since that time, several institutions have sponsored my research and writing. I am particularly grateful to the John D. and Catherine T. MacArthur Foundation, which underwrote full-time research in the United States, England, South Africa, and New Zealand from December of 1997 to May of 1999. During that time, I was hosted by Saint Antony's College of Oxford University, the Department of History at the University of Cape Town, and the Stout Research Centre at the Victoria University of Wellington. Since returning to the United States, I have been a professor at Millsaps College in Jackson, Mississippi, where I have pursued this project with the support of college research and travel grants. I am also grateful for summer stipends from the Hearin Foundation in 2003 and from the National Endowment for the Humanities in 2004.

While I was writing, I received excellent advice from scholars who attended the presentations that I gave at Cornell University, Harvard University, Millsaps College, MIT, National University of Singapore, Northeastern University, Oxford University, and the University of Mississippi, as well as my presentations at the annual meetings of the American Society for Environmental History, the Southeastern Regional Seminar on African Studies, and the Society for the History of Technology. I was also able to present my ideas at two special conferences, the British World Conference, hosted by the University of Calgary in 2003, and the African Technopolitics Workshop, which was held in Ithala, Natal, in 2006, and jointly sponsored by the Society for the History of Technology, the University of Michigan, and the University of KwaZulu-Natal.

I also thank a number of individuals who have helped me as I brought this project to fruition. Sheila Jasanoff, John McNeill, and Pat Manning read drafts and proposals at various stages of the project. Christopher Saunders and Nigel Worden arranged for me to have a happy and productive stay in Cape Town, where I also had support and advice from Vivian Bickford-Smith, Patrick Harries, and Lance van Sittert. Many librarians and archivists helped me, particularly at Rhodes House, the Cape Town Archives Repository, the University of Cape Town, and the National Library of South Africa in Cape Town (formerly the South African Library). There, I especially thank Peter Coates for his work on indexing Cape newspapers, without which my research would have taken much longer. I spent two months in Wellington, New Zealand, exploring comparisons with the help of the staff at the Alexander Turnbull Library and the New Zealand National Archives. On returning home to Jackson, Mississippi, the librarians at Millsaps College helped me locate many obscure books and documents through Interlibrary Loan. I was fortunate that one of our students, Jon-Mark Olivier, and his father, Ross Olivier, were able to help me translate documents from Afrikaans. Louise Hetrick helped with the bibliography and record keeping. While I was writing, William Beinart, Saul Dubow, Shula Marks, and John Staudenmaier – plus four anonymous reviewers – made incisive comments on drafts of an article called "Guns, Race, and Skill" that was eventually published by *Technology and Culture* in 2004. I am also grateful for the thorough and thoughtful comments of the two anonymous scholars who reviewed the book manuscript for Cambridge University Press.

Finally, I add a personal note of thanks to my wife, Joanna Miller Storey, who has been a consistent supporter of my writing projects. She listened to me discuss the book, she read and commented on parts of it, and she accompanied me on research trips. These kinds of support are ordinarily acknowledged in a preface, but I believe that my wife's support was extraordinary. While she was helping me with the book, she was launching her medical career and bringing five children into the world: Ian, Andrew, Neil, Graham, and Robin. Sufficient words of appreciation cannot be said for Joanna, for the children, and also for their grandparents, Dick and Sue Miller and Bill and Mary Storey.

List of Abbreviations

BPP	British Parliamentary Papers
CO	Colonial Office
Conf. Pr.	Confidential Print
CPP	Cape Parliamentary Papers
CTAR	National Archives and Record Service of South Africa, Cape Town Archives Repository
LMS	London Missionary Society
OFS	Orange Free State
PRO	The National Archives of the United Kingdom, Public Record Office, Kew
RHL	Rhodes House Library, Oxford University
SAAR	Breytenbach et al., *South African Archival Records*

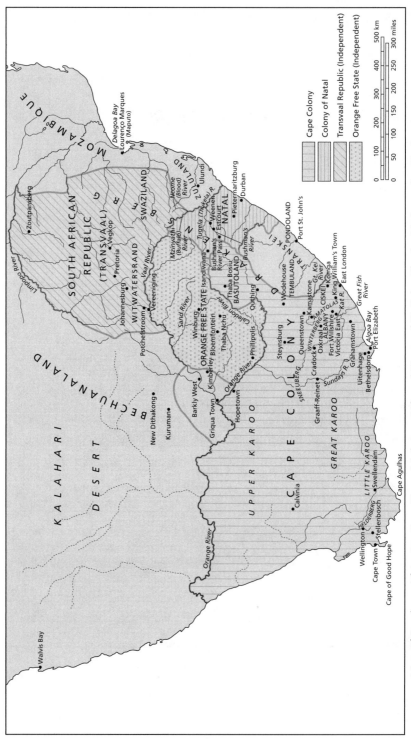

FIGURE I. Map of Southern Africa in 1872. (From Molteno, *Life and Times of Sir John Charles Molteno*, frontispiece.)

Guns in Colonial South African History

In 1971, the historians Shula Marks and Anthony Atmore wrote that during the colonial period South Africa became a "gun society." They suggested that "the role of firearms in southern African society deserves at least one major study."[1] Their challenge is taken up by the present study, which focuses on the history of South Africa prior to 1910.[2]

In South Africa, guns and colonialism went hand in hand. Starting with the earliest contacts between Africans and Europeans, guns became important commodities in frontier trade. Colonists and Africans alike – particularly the men – considered guns necessary tools for hunting and fighting. In the nineteenth century, the focus of the present study, guns were associated with the depopulation of game animals; the development of capitalism; and the establishment of new colonies, republics, and chiefdoms. Legal restrictions on gun ownership came to mark who was a citizen and who was not.

This book does more than assess the influence of guns over historical outcomes, as other scholars have done. It explores the ways in which people involved guns in changes in society, politics, and ecology. All the while, firearms were undergoing a technological revolution. The

---

[1] Marks and Atmore, "Firearms in Southern Africa," 517.
[2] Legally speaking, the country known as "South Africa" did not come into existence until 1910, when the Union of South Africa was formed from the Cape Colony, Natal, the Orange Free State, and the Transvaal. However, during the nineteenth century, which is the focus of this study, most English-speakers referred to the region south of the Limpopo River as "South Africa." This is the term that is used here. This study does not give much consideration to the other parts of "Southern Africa," such as present-day Botswana, Namibia, Malawi, Mozambique, Zambia, and Zimbabwe.

increasing lethality of guns persuaded South Africans to reconsider ideas about citizenship, institutions, and identities. People who owned guns came to support ideologies that they associated with technological changes. At the same time, ideologies were being reflected in the design of the guns themselves.

The first three chapters trace the spread of guns in South Africa during the seventeenth, eighteenth, and nineteenth centuries. Beginning in the middle of the seventeenth century, the Dutch East India Company (VOC) encouraged settlers to procure firearms and to serve in the militia. Until the end of the eighteenth century, gun ownership and militia service were encouraged and even required by the VOC, but the Boers who crossed the colonial boundaries into the African interior were forbidden from selling guns to Africans. These regulations were ineffectual yet remained in force even after the advent of British rule in 1795.

British rule transformed South Africa's economy, polity, and society. South Africa became engaged with the world's most powerful industrial economy, a process that reoriented South African markets and politics. British liberals came to have great influence in the Cape Colony, where they advocated free trade, slave emancipation, and evangelical Christianity. Thanks to liberal influences over the course of the early nineteenth century, trade became free and the slaves were emancipated. Meanwhile, Christian ideas entered into African thinking. Evangelicalism and liberalism were associated with humanitarianism. Yet in South Africa, as in Europe and the United States, evangelicals and liberals were satisfied with a kind of superficial humanitarianism that made plenty of room for an underlying utilitarianism. The liberals and evangelicals who called themselves "friends of the natives" rarely considered Africans to be their social equals. Furthermore, liberal merchants and missionaries benefited economically and professionally from dominance.

Merchants and missionaries encouraged Africans to take up firearms as a way to gain security on a violent frontier. Guns were also a means for killing game animals. In 1812, after commenting on the extraordinary animals of the South African interior, the famous English traveler William J. Burchell wished that guns would spread more extensively to help people kill off the unwanted beasts. This in turn would result in the extension of modern, productive agriculture.[3] Animals died and agriculture spread. During the nineteenth century, Africans and settlers saw

---

[3] Burchell, *Travels in the Interior*, 2:369.

guns as hallmarks of modernity, yet for most people in South Africa there was precious little security. The spread of European settlement and government caused major disruptions to African societies, even as the British colonies at the Cape and Natal, together with the Boer republics, attempted to rein in disorder. Part of their efforts involved gun control. The republics prohibited Africans from gun ownership, while the Cape and Natal imposed various restrictions on ownership and trade, including licensing and fees.

As Europeans were settling South Africa, firearms designers were spurred on by rivalries between European states as well as by the American Civil War. Firearms became much more effective. First, hunters and soldiers replaced flintlock ignition systems with percussion caps. Next, smoothbore muzzle-loaders were replaced by more accurate rifled muzzle-loaders. Then, rifled muzzle-loaders were replaced by quick-firing rifled breechloaders. The uptake of new weapons flooded world markets with secondhand muzzle-loading muskets and rifles that sold at cut-rate prices. At the same time as these weapons were becoming easily available, more Africans migrated to Cape farms and to the Kimberley diamond diggings, where they earned cash to buy guns. While Africans armed themselves, the opening of the Kimberley diamond mines and the commercialization of agriculture inspired British investors to buy South African shares, putting increased pressure on colonial governments to ensure order.

Order was endangered by armed Africans, according to settlers, who convinced the governments of Great Britain, the Cape Colony, and the Colony of Natal to implement disarmament. In 1859, Natal required all Africans to register their firearms with the lieutenant governor. This did not totally disarm Africans, but it was a crucial first step. In 1878, the Cape passed legislation allowing the governor to disarm entire districts. Disarmament occurred at the same time as Britain was attempting to unify the chiefdoms, colonies, and republics of South Africa under one form of government. Confederation became a famous failure, while disarmament became a patchy success.

Descriptions of insecurity and risk intensified during the 1870s, as South Africa's mineral revolution raised the stakes for settlers, Africans, and Britons alike. At the Cape, the governor, Sir Bartle Frere, who is most famous for starting the Anglo–Zulu War, also attempted to change opinions about the importance of guns for modern civilization. He moved to disarm Africans, claiming that "in a well-ordered community where the police protects the unarmed, the carrying of arms is entirely superfluous."

Frere and other Englishmen had come to believe that security was the concern of the state, not the individual. Orderly communities did not need individuals to carry guns.[4] Many Africans had to surrender their guns under the terms of a new Peace Preservation Act passed in 1878. This diminished their ownership of guns but it did not sever the ideological ties between the bearing of arms and the performance of civic duties. In 1898, at the outbreak of the South African War, many African and "coloured" men clamored to bear arms in the service of Britain, while plenty of Africans rode off to war in the service of the Boer commandos.[5]

During the second half of the nineteenth century, two key civic questions came before South Africans. To what extent should the colonies, republics, and chiefdoms of South Africa be independent or united, either with each other or with Great Britain? And to what degree should Africans and Asians be given the rights of citizens? Liberal ideas about citizenship sat uneasily in a racially divided South Africa. The foundations of racial discrimination were laid in the seventeenth century when the Cape Colony was founded by the Dutch East India Company. Under Dutch rule, racial divisions were given the sanction of law, mostly as a way to support slaveholding. As Europeans extended their reach into the interior, they lived among indigenous people and often placed them in relations of subordination. Servants, spouses, and slaves often happened to be African – sometimes they were Asian – but fully fledged discrimination on the basis of race did not begin to develop until the nineteenth century under British rule.[6]

At first the British continued legal discrimination. Then, in the 1820s and 1830s, British liberals limited legal discrimination and emancipated the slaves. It would be naïve to take the progressive view and say that these were early, tentative steps toward equality. The African experience of liberal colonialism was much more troubling. As the anthropologists Jean and John Comaroff have written, "Colonialism held out the promise of equality, but essentialized inequality in such a way as to make it impossible to erase; held out the promise of universal rights, but made it impossible for people of color to claim them; held out the promise of individual advancement, but submerged it within the final constraints of ethnic subjection."[7] The historian Clifton Crais has also shown, in *White*

---

[4] BPP [C. 2569] 1880, No.13, Frere to Hicks Beach, March 15, 1880, pp. 19–20.
[5] Nasson, *Abraham Esau's War*, 41–63.
[6] Newton-King, *Masters and Servants*, 232–4.
[7] Comaroff and Comaroff, "Revelations upon *Revelation*," 121.

Supremacy and Black Resistance, the vehemence of settler racism in the Eastern Cape during the 1830s and 1840s, even as liberals were gaining ground in Cape Town, in the Western Cape.

It was in the 1870s that humanitarian, liberal racists in Cape Town and the Western Cape shifted toward the more strident, utilitarian racism of the Eastern Cape. The 1870s were a time when British and European racism was becoming increasingly chauvinistic and pseudoscientific. During the discussions about confederation, racially discriminatory legislation began to be passed in the guise of laws that were intended to disarm Africans and to arm settlers. Discriminatory laws had been on the books since the days of slavery. Even after the emancipation of the slaves in the 1830s, discriminatory laws continued to regulate labor, travel, and voting. The new gun control measures of the 1870s pushed legal discrimination further: the Cape took a step in the direction of the Boer republics, which denied Africans all rights of citizenship, including the right to own a weapon. Africans could not be citizens of the republics, nor could they own weapons, although the intricate relations of paternalism included the idea that servants helped masters to bear arms.

In the 1870s, British and colonial politicians seized on the risks of proliferation as a way to reconfigure ideas about citizenship and identity and make Cape political culture resemble the political culture of the republics. "Blacks" would be disarmed at the same time as they were being disenfranchised. This conjunction of problems, the exclusion of non-Europeans from citizenship, the production and proliferation of better guns, and the desire for political unity, may have been coincidental. I argue that it was not, and that these technological and political processes were closely related.

This book brings together social, political, and cultural history with technological history, showing the richness of South African debates about technologies imported from the West and bridging the gap between historians of nineteenth-century South Africa and historians of nineteenth-century technology. The historians of technology once focused almost exclusively on Europe and the United States, believing that the countries outside of the West that adopted Western technologies did not modify or change them in interesting ways. It was also widely believed that imported technologies "transferred" with little debate. Such assumptions about the global effects of industrialization have changed a great deal in the past twenty years, as historians of technology have developed a stronger interest in European empire building. By the same token, historians of colonialism in nineteenth-century South Africa have produced important works of social, political, and cultural history without much reference to technology.

This book follows a number of recent studies that describe technological exchanges from a global perspective. Authors have paid special attention to the relationship between industrialization and imperialism in the nineteenth century, when Western countries secured global dominance by using new technologies such as breechloaders, quinine, and steamships. Technology and ideas about technology were central to the formation of new global power arrangements in which London, Paris, and other imperial capitals extended their reach to remote corners overseas.[8] And adding to the literature on technological imperialism, we now have a number of rich, local studies that describe how technical knowledge and practices circulated in more complex ways than in simple transfers from the European "core" to the colonial "periphery."[9]

Early Approaches to the Social History of Firearms in Africa

South Africa has a rich local history as well as a close relationship with the countries of Europe. There is no better illustration of this than the social history of firearms. The topic has attracted some attention from scholars already, as has the social history of firearms in other parts of Africa. Histories of firearms in Africa have generally taken the form of journal articles about particular times and places. Most of the articles discuss social and political issues thoroughly, yet show little awareness of the dynamic relationship between society and technology. This has something to do with the fact that the articles were written by Africanist scholars in the 1960s and 1970s, a time when the history and sociology of technology was relatively undeveloped. The historians of technology had few methodological insights to offer Africanist colleagues.

When African history was coming of age as a field, there were some strong early efforts in firearms history, such as R. W. Beachey's 1962 article about the East African arms trade that was published in the

---

[8] Adas, *Machines as the Measure of Men*; Drayton, *Nature's Government*; Headrick, *The Tools of Empire* and *The Tentacles of Progress*.

[9] Some representative works on science, technology, and imperialism that take into account local knowledge in the colonies: Arnold, *Science, Technology, and Medicine in Colonial India*; Dubow, *Science and Society in Southern Africa*; Fairhead and Leach, *Misreading the African Landscape*; Grove, *Green Imperialism*; Richards, *Indigenous Agricultural Revolution*; Storey, *Science and Power in Colonial Mauritius*; and Todd, *Colonial Technology*.

brand-new *Journal of African History*.[10] In 1966, Martin Legassick published an article about the ways in which Samori Touré used modern breech-loading and repeating firearms to resist the French. Legassick showed that Samori's success with guns had a great deal to do with social innovations, including changes in military formations, as well as support for local gunsmiths.[11]

In the late 1960s, the social history of guns became a central focus of the African History Seminar at the University of London. Many of the seminar papers were revised and published in two special issues of the *Journal of African History* that appeared in 1971 and that have since been cited by numerous scholars. One issue, edited by Gavin White, focused on West Africa, while another, edited by Marks and Atmore, focused on southern Africa. The articles traced the history of the gun trade in Africa in detail, arguing that guns often had significant social and political consequences. In the case of South Africa, Marks and Atmore argued that starting in 1652 the acquisition of guns, shooting skills, and martial organization played an important role in the extension of settlements and colonial rule. Under the Dutch, and later under the British, the Cape Colony became a gun society, where the balance of power reflected the possession of guns by states and societies. At the same time, the authors tended to downplay the importance of early firearms, on account of their technical shortcomings. Old muskets had their limitations, while in the early years there were some people without firearms who managed to defeat people with firearms.

The 1971 articles considered whether the possession of guns fostered imperialism or resistance. The acquisition of guns and shooting skills had a direct bearing on tactical and strategic outcomes among South Africans. During the 1970s, other Africanists began to explore the relationship between technological, social, and political history. In 1971, the anthropologist Jack Goody published a book, *Technology, Tradition and the State in Africa*, in which he argued that there was a close correlation between West African political structures and the "ownership of the means of destruction," including guns and horses. Forest states like Asante, Benin, and Dahomey tended to have private, slave armies that used guns and were closely controlled by a centralized ruler. By contrast, savannah states like Bariba, Gonja, and Oyo were less centralized and

[10] Beachey, "The Arms Trade in East Africa in the Late Nineteenth Century."
[11] Legassick, "Firearms, Horses, and Samorian Army Organization 1870–1898."

tended to deploy cavalry units. Similarly, an article and book by Joseph Smaldone explored the importance of firearms for the political history of the Central Sudan. Smaldone argued that when the states of the Central Sudan took up modern firearms in the late nineteenth century, the impact on warfare was not so great, but the impact on the feudal system was profound. Rulers bought guns and trained slave-soldiers to fight with them as a way of rendering vassals more dependent.[12] Smaldone's work, like Goody's, assessed the impact of guns on the state but had little to say about the impact of the state on guns, either in terms of regulation or in terms of technical development. The technology and the polity were seen as separate analytical categories.

While Smaldone and Goody argued for the importance of guns for politics, scholars of the Atlantic slave trade argued for the importance of guns in commerce. In analyzing the role of guns in the slave trade, they confirmed centuries of speculation about the so-called gun–slave cycle. Joseph Inikori demonstrated statistically that a gun–slave cycle did, indeed, exist. In an article he argued that guns and gunpowder were an essential component of the Atlantic slave trade during the eighteenth century. Almost every slave-seller along the Gold Coast and Slave Coast received guns and powder, among other commodities, in exchange for slaves, while those who sold other commodities to Europeans frequently did not require guns. Inikori's findings were supported by additional research published in a 1980 article by W. A. Richards, although both their findings about the importance of the gun trade for the slave trade were contradicted by Philip Curtin's study of Senegambia, where he found no correlation between the statistical evidence on gun imports and slave exports during the same period.[13]

The articles that established the existence of a gun–slave cycle in certain parts of West Africa also emphasized the impact of guns on politics, yet went beyond Smaldone and Goody to show that politics were influencing the regulation and design of guns. Inikori and Richards both presented evidence that African buyers placed orders for many different types of flintlock muskets. Designs varied depending on price as well as particular

---

[12] Smaldone, "Firearms in the Central Sudan" and *Warfare in the Sokoto Caliphate*. For gunmaking in the Western Sudan, see McNaughton, *The Mande Blacksmiths*, 35–39, and plates 28–30.

[13] Inikori, "The Import of Firearms in West Africa 1750–1807." Richards, "The Import of Firearms into West Africa in the Eighteenth Century." Curtin, *Economic Change in Precolonial Africa*, 321–25. See also Smith, *Warfare & Diplomacy in Pre-Colonial West Africa*, 80–89, 141–5.

uses. This hinted at a dynamic relationship between politics and technological design, a hint that might have been explored further had better
methodologies from the history of technology been available at the time.
For the same reason, a similar suggestion by Gemery and Hogendorn
about the role of technological innovation in the growth of the slave
trade could not have been fully explored.[14]

Instead of following the lead of the early studies of guns and slavery,
which showed a dynamic relationship between the making of economies,
states, and technologies, some scholars wrote articles that completely dismissed the technical importance of guns, crediting them, instead, with
mere symbolic importance. In a 1972 article, Richard Caulk argued that
even at the end of the nineteenth century, when reliable, potent guns
were available, firearms had a mainly symbolic importance for politics
in Ethiopia.[15] The importance of firearms as symbols was explored even
further by Gerald Berg, who wrote in a 1985 article that the rise of Ime-
rina kingdom in eighteenth-century Madagascar had little to do with the
acquisition of muskets, which did not work well enough to change the
balance of power. Even so, muskets meant a great deal, because Adri-
anampoinimerina incorporated them into the symbolism of his emerging
unitary kingdom.[16] The articles by Berg and Caulk show the ways in
which guns may be incorporated within the political culture, but one
must ask of these articles, why choose guns as symbols and not something else? Guns, even old, ineffective guns, must have had some physical
quality that "worked" in some way that they would be singled out for
special, symbolic treatment. The articles about guns in Madagascar and
Ethiopia missed the relationship between design and politics that was
touched on briefly by Inikori, Richards, Gemery, and Hogendorn.

Scholarship on the role of guns in African society and politics dried
up in the 1980s. Marks and Atmore recognized that their own article
about South Africa was "incomplete and cursory," adjectives that might
also be applied to the rest of the articles about guns that appeared in the
1960s and 1970s. There were only two scholarly books, by Smaldone
and Goody. In 1976, the empirical and analytical basis of Goody's book
was strongly called into question by Robin Law in a journal article,[17]
leaving us with Smaldone's book as the only fully fledged study of guns
in an African society and polity.

---

[14] Gemery and Hogendorn, "Technological Change, Slavery and the Slave Trade."
[15] Caulk, "Firearms and Princely Power in Ethiopia."
[16] Berg, "Madagascar's Sacred Musket."
[17] Law, "Horses, Firearms, and Political Power in Pre-Colonial West Africa."

Smaldone's book and the other, shorter studies cited above were forays in social, political, and technological history that were circumscribed by the methodological possibilities of the 1960s and 1970s. At that time, the historical and sociological study of technology was in its infancy. Most accounts of guns and other technologies were written by antiquarians, engineers, or biographers who favored taking an "internal" approach to technology, focusing on the influence of individuals over design and paying little attention to cultural, political, and social influences that were "external" to the process of invention. Much of this work was impressively detailed. In the case of South African firearms, there is one book in this genre, *Die Boer se Roer* ("The Boer's gun") written by Felix Lategan in 1974, that is still indispensable. Lategan described and catalogued South African firearms in great detail, yet like most "internal" historians of technology, he had limited interest in "external" factors, such as the relationship between technological development and economic, political, and social change. By contrast, Marks, Atmore and their colleagues were well aware of economic, political, and social developments. They did not present a detailed consideration of the technology, as Lategan was able to do, but they arrived at the important insight that guns played a significant role in South African society.

That being said, Marks and Atmore's argument that South Africa became a gun society has proven difficult to test. The concept itself has problems of definition. It may be possible to define a gun society as one in which a high percentage of people own a gun. This study will present plenty of evidence to suggest that in the eighteenth and nineteenth centuries, guns became widespread, even though gun owners were not always detected by record keepers. Yet at what statistical point can we say, with accuracy, that a gun society exists? Besides, the widespread ownership of a technology does not determine a society. Nineteenth-century South Africans owned many iron pots, but we do not say they lived in an iron-pot society. To be sure, pots have less cultural resonance than guns, which symbolized citizenship, dominance, and masculinity, in different ways to different people. Marks and Atmore did show the ways in which gun possession influenced political changes. Yet it has proven difficult to find evidence to support the claim that as a symbol or as a cultural artifact, a majority of the people south of the Limpopo made guns into a fetish. Guns were not the focus of attention at all times, but awareness of guns and the actions that could be performed with guns certainly permeated the consciousness of many South Africans. This study will show that guns were widespread enough to be important to culture, politics, and society. At the same time, this study will refrain from making arguments about a gun society that are difficult to confirm or contradict.

The Coproduction of Politics, Society, and Technology

The spread of colonial power was bound up with the spread of better guns. Yet the methods of 1971 did not foster an analysis that went beyond assessing influence. And influence is difficult to prove through qualitative or quantitative analysis. There are other reasons why, in the 1970s, making an argument for the strong influence of technology might have been problematic. No author wants to be ridiculed as a "technological determinist," in other words, a scholar who would make guns – inanimate objects – appear to have decisive influence over people. Technological determinism is a great taboo of historical scholarship. History, even technological history, is supposed to be about people first, a common belief of historians that has attenuated the exploration of the relationship between technology and environment, on the one hand, and ideology and consciousness on the other.

Today there are a variety of ways in which historians may describe the relationship between technology and the human capacity to change the course of events, or "agency." As the historians of technology Leo Marx and Roe Smith pointed out in their 1994 collection of essays, *Does Technology Drive History?* "hard" technological determinists may actually believe that technology has agency, while "soft" determinists seek the origins of technological power in human actions. In this way, technology can still be seen as a force influencing history; it is just a force whose creation and use is subject to human decisions. Marks, Atmore, and their fellow authors had to qualify their views about the influence of guns, since historians of technology were not yet providing a subtle model for understanding the ways in which technology can be both influential and subject to human control at the same time.

Since the 1970s, the historiography of technology has become rich and complex. It now engages cultural and social history more extensively, as can be seen from a cursory glance at the articles, bibliographies, and book reviews published in the flagship journal *Technology and Culture*. At the same time as the social history of technology has matured, a new, interdisciplinary field of Science and Technology Studies (STS) has come into its own, with scholarly journals, book series, and foundation support, not to mention programs and departments at major universities.[18] Most STS scholars take an interdisciplinary approach that enriches scholarly understanding of the relationship between science and technology, on the one hand, and culture, politics, and society on the other. The field's key formulation, "social constructivism," breaks down the intellectual barriers between the material and the social and explores the ways in which people articulate a relationship between the two.

An approach from STS known as the "social construction of technological systems" reveals the ways in which technologies never stand alone but receive social support from scientists, engineers, and politicians.[19] Networks of support can be both local and global, an insight that raises questions about older, Eurocentric approaches to technology and imperialism. According to the historian Jan Todd, when Australians imported European technologies such as the anthrax vaccine and the cyanide process for extracting gold from ores, there was a "coming together of technological systems." Technologies that had been developed in Europe now needed the support of local Australian networks to become credible. The credibility of these new technologies depended on promoters' mustering supportive witnesses to achieve their objectives. In Australia, British and French promoters relied heavily on the effective demonstration of their technologies before local judges and expert witnesses, who certified the originality and patentability of the new technologies. Promoters of metropolitan technologies had to persuade people to adapt new technologies to local economic, political, and social systems. Different classes and cultures in different locations came to understand the same technologies in different ways.[20]

In light of methodological refinements in STS and the history of technology, it is no longer sufficient to write about the impact – or lack of it – of a technology on politics or society. Today, the best studies examine the ways in which technology, politics, and society are mutually constituted or "coproduced," a term coined by Bruno Latour and fleshed out by Sheila Jasanoff in a recent book, *States of Knowledge*. Accounts of coproduction recognize that nature, objects, states, and societies are not separate categories that influence each other but are ideas and contingencies that

---

[18] For an introduction, see Jasanoff et al., *Handbook of Science and Technology Studies*.
[19] On the social construction of technological systems and other sociological approaches to technology, see Bijker, *Of Bicycles, Bakelites, and Bulbs*.
[20] Todd, *Colonial Technology*. The discussion of demonstrations by Todd and also by Storey in *Science and Power in Colonial Mauritius* follows the analysis of "witnessing" in Shapin and Schaffer, *Leviathan and the Air-Pump*.

evolve interdependently. Coproduction is not a theory but an idiom that helps us understand how guns became important in South Africa without attributing agency to guns and without denying the importance of guns for social and political change.

The present study about guns draws on the STS literature on coproduction as well as on a number of historical studies about South Africa that have shown the subtle interpenetration of social life and material objects. In *The Seed Is Mine*, Charles van Onselen's eloquent biography of the twentieth-century sharecropper, Kas Maine, we see the complex relationship between family life, ecological conditions, and material acquisitions, all of which are circumscribed by an advancing tide of segregationist legislation. The environmental historians William Beinart, Nancy Jacobs, and Lance van Sittert have all explored the relationship between material culture and political culture by showing the close interdependency between ecological and political regimes in such different locations as the Karoo, the Kalahari, and Cape Town.[21] And in perhaps the best-known example of scholarship that bridges the human and the material worlds in South Africa, Jean Comaroff and John Comaroff's *Of Revelation and Revolution* examines interactions between Tswana and missionaries during the nineteenth century, paying particular attention to the close relationship between ideological and material changes, on the one hand, and changes in behavior and consciousness, on the other.

The Comaroffs argue that Tswana people recognized that by accepting British dress as well as cultivation techniques and literacy they were accepting aspects of colonialist hegemony. These ranged from racial divisions to new ways of understanding the world and themselves. Perceptions of the world and the self, as well as perceptions of power, were bound up in everyday practices, just as much as they were related to professing the Christian faith and pledging loyalty to the queen.

The Comaroffs' approach gives us a good starting point to enquire what it meant, ideologically, to engage in everyday practices with guns, such as carrying them, caring for them, and storing them, as well as the less routine tasks of hunting and fighting with them. Skills with guns and their perceived and real links to political power were debated extensively in southern Africa, starting in the seventeenth century. Practices with guns as well as the representation of these practices were highly ideological, even as they became ubiquitous and apparently less interesting. This is readily

---

[21] Beinart, *The Rise of Conservation in South Africa*. Jacobs, *Environment, Power, and Injustice*. Van Sittert, "Our Irrepresible Fellow-Colonist" and "To Live This Poor Life."

apparent in the efforts of people who wished to regulate the spread of guns. Nineteenth-century settler politicians often made highly politicized claims about skill and practice. Such claims highlight the ideological nature of skill descriptions, as well as the methodological problems that historians face when they attribute skills to people in the past.

Colonial studies of technology can highlight methodological issues that are treated as a passing concern, either by historians of colonialism or historians of technology. This book will address one such issue that cropped up persistently in South Africa, the politics of skill, by drawing on the extensive literature on European firearms as well as an ethnography by STS scholars Wiebe Bijker, Harry Collins, and G. H. de Vries. The three ethnographers observed cardiologists at work and devised a way of describing skill. They distinguish two types of skills: "mimeomorphic" skills that are learned through repetition up to the point that they may be taken for granted and polymorphic or judgmental skills that involve using the technology while reacting to changing circumstances.[22] For example, balancing and pedaling on a bicycle are mimeomorphic skills, while deciding how fast to pedal or where to turn are polymorphic skills. Mimeomorphic skills are easier to replace with machinery, as would happen with guns during the nineteenth century, although in some circumstances mimeomorphic skills might be valued just as highly as polymorphic skills. At any rate, the distinction between mimeomorphic and polymorphic skills is crucial for an understanding of the use of any technology, including firearms.

The studies cited above all focus on relatively small aggregations of skill in relatively small regions. The "micro" approach is the trend in historical studies of environment and technology in South Africa, which has been especially notable in recent conference presentations and journal articles.[23] The micro study is also common in the STS literature on coproduction, but so are larger aggregations. As Jasanoff writes, "At whichever scale individual studies are framed, though, the findings help

[22] Bijker, Collins, and De Vries, "Ways of Going On." To advance the claim further that ethnographic descriptions of skill have been more successful than historical ones, it is interesting to note that in Bijker's more historical work, he has argued that skills are embedded in local cultures without fully fleshing out the point with much direct evidence. See *Of Bicycles, Bakelites, and Bulbs: Toward a Theory of Sociotechnical Change*, 4.

[23] Two conference volumes have been published: Beinart and McGregor, *Social History and African Environments*, and Dovers, Edgecombe, and Guest, *South Africa's Environmental History*. The following two journals published special issues on South African environmental history: *Journal of Southern African Studies* 26:4 (2000), and *Kronos: Journal of Cape History* 29 (November 2003).

to clarify how power originates, where it gets lodged, who wields it, by what means, and with what effect within the complex networks of contemporary societies."[24] The present study will show many connections between coproduction on the micro and macro levels.

In assessing "coproductive" debates about an evolving technology and an evolving political culture, I have arrived at an argument that is similar to one made recently by a historian of South Africa, Saul Dubow. In his book *A Commonwealth of Knowledge*, Dubow assesses debates among predominantly white Cape intellectuals that took place during the nineteenth century, primarily ones that took place in public institutions as well as civic institutions like churches, libraries, and museums. These civic institutions fostered discourse about the acquisition of knowledge of South Africa as well as the acquisition of knowledge from overseas. At the Cape, scientists studied Africans as well as the local fauna and flora, at a time when settlers were taking over the landscape. Dubow indicates that their inquisitions were closely related to their acquisitions. Yet as settlers appropriated the land and its peoples, they also found themselves "becoming African." Dubow argues that "their expertise was closely bound up with claims to be rights-bearing citizens of a country that they were consciously making their own." The records of these debates show how, over the course of the nineteenth century, a uniquely South African identity was emerging. Proponents of "South Africanism," as Dubow calls it, sought to bridge the differences between Boers and Britons, while at the same time exaggerating the differences between Europeans and Africans in order to justify racial segregation.[25]

In addition to the work of Dubow, I have relied on the labor and insights of many other historians of South Africa, especially those with expertise on particular geographical regions and population groups. My basic method of research was to read monographs, articles, and dissertations, mining them for references to firearms, and then to "follow the footnotes," checking facts and arguments against sources from the colonial era. This method is reflected in the bibliography, which lists more than four hundred works, including journal articles and scholarly books, in addition to numerous primary sources such as government documents, newspaper articles, and archival sources, mostly from Britain and South Africa. Whenever possible, I followed up reference-checking by combing through the primary sources for further references to guns.

---

[24] Jasanoff, "The Idiom of Co-Production," in *States of Knowledge*, 5.
[25] Dubow, *Commonwealth of Knowledge*, 4–6.

My approach to sources has helped me to produce a broad, qualitative study of firearms in colonial South Africa. Readers who hope for detailed studies of gun ownership in particular communities may, therefore, be disappointed in this book, although those wishing to conduct sociological studies will hopefully be helped by the guideposts set down here. This is also not a study based on extensive research in statistics. I have provided estimates of the extent of gun ownership and the volume of the gun trade based on colonial reports and on works by other historians, but I have refrained from much further statistical analysis. I believe that several factors stand in the way of arriving at truly precise figures. In colonial South Africa, many people had motives to hide guns from those who wished to count guns, while some of the guns that might have been counted were probably outmoded or dysfunctional. Both these factors were commented on by colonial officials. Colonial statistical reports such as the Blue Books contained general information about firearms that was not contested at the time. I have relied on these for an overall picture. Historians who wish to dig deeper into the statistical history of firearms will find much information in the Cape archives, yet I expect that this information will not change the substance of the story that I present here.

2

Early Colonialism and Guns at the Cape up to 1795

Gunpowder and guns arrived with the first Europeans at the Western Cape, a frontier zone where Europeans and Africans had complex, over-lapping encounters with each other during the sixteenth, seventeenth, and eighteenth centuries.[1] At the Cape, as the historians Richard Elphick and V. C. Malherbe have written, there developed three different sorts of frontiers: a frontier of trade, a frontier of "agrarian settlement," and a frontier of European and mixed-race pastoralism.[2] Guns and shooting skills were an important part of each frontier. To understand this story of the spread of people and guns, it will be important to understand how guns work, in both the technological and social sense. The possession of guns, and the skills and ideas surrounding and supporting them, helped constitute a new society at the Cape.

---

[1] Much has been written about F. J. Turner's frontier thesis and its misapplication to both North America and South Africa. Key works that helped to reconceptualize the South African frontier as a zone of cross-cultural interaction include Legassick, "The Griqua, the Sotho-Tswana, and the Missionaries," as well as the essays in Lamar and Thompson, *The Frontier in History*. These studies, in turn, have been strongly challenged by Susan Newton-King in *Masters and Servants on the Cape Eastern Frontier, 1760–1803*, a monograph that recognizes a high degree of cross-cultural interaction of a negative sort. She argues that these interactions were characterized primarily by violence, domination, and subordination.

[2] Elphick and Malherbe, "The Khoisan to 1828," in Elphick and Giliomee, *Shaping of South African Society*, 7–8.

Guns and Skill in the Early Modern Period

The story of South African gun skills begins with the very first Portuguese ships to call at the Cape, which were armed with small cannon. Sailors and soldiers were likely to have carried crossbows. Firearms that could be carried by one soldier were adopted by Western Europeans only gradually over the course of the sixteenth century, the same time when they were exploring the Cape. There were several reasons for the switch. In the fifteenth century, longbows were still more powerful than firearms and could be loaded more quickly, but the longbow required tremendous strength on the part of the archer, as well as years of practice to develop the requisite mimeomorphic skills. The crossbow took more time to reload and was less powerful than the longbow, but it was coming into wide use because firing one did not require as much strength and skill. By the middle of the sixteenth century, it became clear that crossbows were being superseded by firearms, thanks in part to advances in metallurgy and powder making. At the same time, Western European states were engaged in ever more expensive and far-ranging warfare. To save money and reduce the amount of time it took to train soldiers, they began to develop infantry tactics that were better suited to the use of firearms. These mainly involved the use of combined units of musketeers and pikemen. These units drilled and marched to make the best use of their weapons, so that the technical skills of using a firearm were supplemented by cooperative social skills.[3] It was at precisely this point in the evolution of firearms that English, French, and Dutch merchants began to show an interest in the Cape, with the Dutch becoming preeminent by the middle of the seventeenth century.

In the sixteenth and seventeenth centuries, contacts between Western Europeans and the Khoi often featured firearms. In order to understand the role of firearms in these early contacts, it is important to understand the weapons themselves and the skills that were required to use them. Skill is an issue of fundamental importance to historians because it comes at the intersection of the human and the material.

The most widely used firearm of the early and middle seventeenth century was a kind of musket called the matchlock. It consisted of a wooden stock supporting an iron barrel. The barrel was usually four feet long, while the total length of the barrel and the stock together was

---

[3] McNeill, *Pursuit of Power*, 79–95.

five feet. It was a large weapon that was so cumbersome that shooters often fired the gun while propping the muzzle on a forked stick. The firing process was complex, too. On the side of the barrel nearest to the shooter, there was a hole with a priming pan attached to it. Powder in the priming pan was ignited by a burning piece of matchcord, essentially a kind of rope that had been soaked in a solution of saltpeter and then dried. The burning matchcord was mounted on a serpentine, an S-shaped hook attached to the side of the stock. When the trigger was pulled, the serpentine flipped forward, allowing the matchcord to ignite the powder in the priming pan. The flash in the pan went through the hole in the barrel and ignited the powder.

The matchlock musket was more than just an ingenious mechanical artifact: it worked best when it was supported by certain forms of military organization. In other words, it required manual skills as well as social skills. Social skills were closely connected to the design of the technology itself. The matchlock was not particularly accurate beyond fifty meters, although it could kill at a maximum range of about 150 meters. This distance can be run by an attacker in twenty to thirty seconds, yet it took about that long to load and fire a matchlock musket. While being careful of the burning match, the gunner measured a sufficient quantity of coarse black powder (powder was measured beforehand for soldiers) and then poured the powder down the barrel. Next he dropped the ball down the barrel, letting it rest on top of the powder and securing it with wadding. Then the soldier had to fill the priming pan with powder. The musket had to be loaded from the muzzle, or front end, which meant that it was best to perform this time-consuming maneuver while standing.

To further complicate matters, the barrel's fouling made it progressively more difficult to load the weapon. A fouled barrel necessitated the use of a ramrod to push down the ball. To diminish the effects of barrel fouling, soldiers often loaded with balls that were smaller than the caliber (or diameter) of the barrel. When the ball was fired from a typical smoothbore musket, it bounced down the sides of the barrel, diminishing accuracy. To compensate for the weapon's inaccuracy, and to protect soldiers while they were loading their muskets, soldiers were drilled to load and fire in volleys. Volley firing worked well for armies, yet had little application to civilian life. Civilians who owned smoothbore muskets hedged their bets by loading with shot pellets, or by purchasing rifles, in which grooves on the inside of the barrel imparted spin to a tight-fitting ball, thus ensuring some accuracy. Rifles were even slower to load than muskets and tended to be costlier, too. For these reasons they tended to be used more by hunters than by soldiers.[4]

The slow and awkward procedure for loading a musket made the soldier vulnerable to enemy attack. To protect matchlock musketeers, sixteenth- and seventeenth-century European armies also deployed soldiers with pikes. In addition, European soldiers, most famously a Dutchman, Prince Maurice of Nassau, devised special drills for musketeers to make them more effective. Maurice broke the loading and firing of the musket down into a series of forty-three consecutive motions, each governed by a shouted command. Soldiers were taught to load and fire their muskets in unison. This had two effects on the battlefield: soldiers who were accustomed to moving in unison seemed to form more cohesive and reliable units, and a volley of musket balls pointed in the general direction of the enemy had a more lethal effect than individually aiming and firing at will. Maurice perfected drilled volley firing by teaching his troops what came to be known as the "countermarch." One line of soldiers fired a volley then began to load; a second line of soldiers advanced in front of the first line to fire their own volley. The countermarch could be performed in a number of different ways, but the principle was that successive rows of troops fired and then loaded their muskets. The military effectiveness of the matchlock musket was closely related to the social organization of the military. Social skills were combined with technological skills.[5]

Matchlock muskets became the most common firearms employed in the armies of Western Europe during the early seventeenth century. From that time, the history of early firearms is often told as a tale of progress from the matchlock to the flintlock, because armies adopted flintlocks toward the end of the seventeenth century. It is interesting to note, however, that throughout the sixteenth and seventeenth centuries, many civilians and a few soldiers, too, preferred the flintlock (and also a less common ignition system called the wheellock). After all, the matchlock could be rather awkward, especially in damp weather, and it was difficult to carry a lit matchcord while walking through the woods or lying in ambush. The matchlock was most effective when both sides of a battle agreed to fight in good weather and in open fields. Without these agreed-upon conventions, the matchlock was an unwieldy weapon. Even

---

[4] Brown, *Firearms in Colonial America*, 28–31.
[5] McNeill, *Pursuit of Power*, 128–43.

so, as long as Western European armies agreed to fight in the open, there was not such a great incentive to switch to flintlocks. Armies only did so toward the end of the seventeenth century, as the older muskets needed to be replaced. Civilians, however, often preferred the flintlock.

The flintlock was more complex and more expensive than the matchlock. The matchlock depended on a smoldering matchcord, while flintlocks achieved ignition by mechanically creating a spark. In a flintlock, the trigger connects to a hammer, or cock, that holds a flint. When the trigger is pulled, the cock springs forward and the flint strikes a battery, called a frizzen. In early seventeenth-century models, called "snaphaunces" ("snaphaans" in Dutch), the frizzen and pan cover were two separate pieces. The pan cover was mounted on a metal arm that had to be moved to the side before firing. Later "true" flintlocks combined the pan cover and frizzen in one L-shaped piece. When the hammer strikes it pushes the frizzen forward, uncovering the powder, while at the same time, the friction of the flint on the frizzen produces a spark that ignites the powder. The "flash in the pan" ignites the powder inside the barrel. In this way, the flintlock was more effective than the matchlock but it still had technical limitations. Like the matchlock, the flintlock ignition system also had to be primed by placing powder in the pan. Then the gunner would cock the hammer, aim, and pull the trigger. The procedure for cocking the hammer, aiming, and pulling the trigger was still slow, and the users of flintlock muskets remained vulnerable to wet weather as well as to enemy fire. For added protection, eighteenth-century soldiers began to attach bayonets to their muskets.

The flintlock musket remained in common use from the end of the seventeenth century to the beginning of the nineteenth century. Different gunsmiths produced different models, and different models were adopted by many armies. The best-known models of the eighteenth century were the French "Charleville" and the British "Brown Bess," which were similar in design. Here, it will be enough to describe the Brown Bess, which was more common in South Africa. It was introduced by Britain's Board of Ordnance in 1718 and modified somewhat over the course of the eighteenth century. In its original version, called the Long Land Service Musket, it was 62 inches long, with a 46-inch-long barrel. It weighed ten to twelve pounds and with a 0.75-caliber barrel firing a 0.69-caliber ball (to diminish the problem of barrel fouling). Smaller versions were used by the cavalry, marines, and navy, and by the end of the eighteenth century, even the army's "New Pattern" Brown Bess was four inches smaller and a pound or two lighter.[6] A significant risk attached to firing muskets. Muskets were made of wrought iron, which has a tendency to crack and cause the musket barrel to explode, unless it is manufactured and maintained to a high standard. Standards were enforced by "proof houses" near the main centers of gun manufacturing in London and Birmingham. Private proof houses, or testing sites, had existed in London and Birmingham since the seventeenth century. In 1813, the British government required each city's proof house to be licensed, while also requiring that only proofed weapons be sold in England and Wales. The proving test was relatively simple. Gun barrels were loaded with a double charge of powder, fired, and then inspected for defects. The weapons that passed were stamped with a crown, the monarch's initials, the year, and the manufacturer. Unproven firearms, or firearms with forged proof marks, were often sold in the African trade.[7]

The flintlock muskets of the eighteenth century were more effective than matchlocks. Even so, one British officer of the period, Colonel George Hanger, observed that flintlocks had their limits: "A soldier's musket, if not exceedingly ill-bored ... will strike ... a man at eighty yards; it may even at 100; but a soldier must be very unfortunate indeed who shall be wounded ... at 150 yards, provided his antagonist aims at him ... I do maintain that no man was ever killed at 200 yards, by a common soldier's musket, by the person who aimed at him."[8] British officers trained their soldiers to fire one shot every fifteen seconds, although few probably ever achieved such a rapid rate, especially in stressful combat conditions. Misfires were also common from damp powder and fouled barrels. Even the best units, drilled thoroughly to fire in volleys, may not have been able to hold off an attacking enemy for very long. This is why infantry flintlocks were usually fitted with a bayonet.

The flintlock was more complex and more expensive than the matchlock. It was also easier and more reliable to load and fire. The mimeomorphic skills associated with using a matchlock, such as lighting the cord, were replaced by technologies such as flint ignition. The change in mimeomorphic skills influenced the elaboration of new polymorphic

---

[6] For comparisons of the different types of Brown Bess muskets, see Brown, *Firearms in Colonial America*, 397.

[7] Harris, *History of the Birmingham Gun-Barrel Proof House*, 15–27, 45, 67, 88–95, 152–5. George, *English Guns and Rifles*, 66, 120, 225, 327.

[8] Brown, *Firearms in Colonial America*, 228.

skills. For example, without a smoldering matchcord, it became a simpler matter for hunters or fighters to conceal themselves.

By the end of the seventeenth century, most European armies were converting to flintlocks. In the colonies, the transition to flintlocks was even quicker. In seventeenth-century New England, English colonists and Native Americans discarded matchlocks in favor of flintlocks somewhat earlier than western European armies did. As Patrick Malone observes in *The Skulking Way of War*, few early New England colonists hunted, leaving the activity to Native Americans. The Native Americans, in turn, demanded flintlocks, which allowed for more spontaneous shooting than the matchlock, which would require the hunter to walk through the woods with a smoldering matchcord. The Native Americans insisted that their flintlocks have particular features, too. They preferred shorter, lighter barrels that could be brought to bear on an animal more quickly than long, military weapons. They also loaded their muskets with smaller, multiple balls, which increased the likelihood of a hit. Coincidentally, muskets that were better for hunting were also better for woodland fighting, while experienced hunters were better woodland soldiers. This became clear to colonists over the course of the seventeenth century. Colonists were relatively inexperienced with weapons; what little training they had involved volley-firing matchlocks. By contrast, Indian warriors, with experience in hunting, were often good marksmen. They fought like they hunted, employing the tactics of ambush and concealment. For these purposes, too, flintlocks were decidedly superior. This point became evident to the colonists over the course of several wars during the first fifty years of settlement. By the 1670s, New England militia, too, were using flintlocks and practicing marksmanship and concealment.[9]

Later, in the eighteenth century, American hunters ensured accuracy by purchasing rifles, whose manufacture had been perfected by Bavarian and Swiss gunsmiths. They knew that if they placed rifling, or spiral grooves, on the inside of the barrel, they could impart some spin on the ball, thus ensuring that it would fly straighter. Unlike a smoothbore musket, a rifle could hit a target at 200 meters. Even so, the procedure for rifling the barrel was skilled and tedious. The barrel had to be made perfectly straight in order for rifling to work at all, and then the gunsmith had to cut the grooves into the barrel.[10]

---

[9] Malone, *Skulking Way of War*, 59–66. Brown, *Firearms in Colonial America*, 140–1.
[10] Brown, *Firearms in Colonial America*, 28–31.

Rifles were time consuming and expensive to make, but there was another important reason why they were not widely adopted, especially by armies. Rifles took a long time to load. In order for the grooves to spin the ball, it had to fit snugly against the barrel. The soft lead ball was cast to be slightly larger than the barrel, and the ball had to be tapped down the barrel with a ramrod and a mallet. A smaller ball covered in a greased fabric patch could speed the procedure, but such a ball might be less accurate. In addition, a soldier loading a rifle would be even more vulnerable to attack than a soldier loading a smoothbore musket, who could simply drop the ball down the barrel. By the eighteenth century, only hunters and specialized soldiers were armed with rifles.[11]

Colonial American militia forces were slow to change their weapons and tactics, yet their governments were quick to regulate the gun trade with indigenous people. As early as 1619, the Virginia legislature passed an act banning the sale of weapons and ammunition to the Native Americans, and throughout the century other colonies followed suit. This was not only the case in English colonies: the Spanish authorities controlled access to guns through government monopoly on the trade. Yet strict laws were not sufficient. Most colonial laws proved ineffectual, at least in part because French, Spanish, and English traders disregarded them and partly because governments were willing to supply guns to Native American allies, whose own trade was difficult to regulate.[12]

Guns and Dutch Colonial Policy at the Cape

During the early seventeenth century, as the Spanish, English, and French attempted to regulate their American frontiers, the Netherlands was emerging as a major player in international politics. This tiny country grew powerful for a number of reasons. Its tolerant climate fostered scientific research, which supported, in turn, the development of advanced navigational technologies, which ranged from shipbuilding to optics. And at a time when many European states had authoritarian rulers, the Dutch embraced a liberal political culture. The Dutch bourgeoisie was composed of "burghers," men who were expected to behave not out of a desire for wealth but out of a sense of civic duty that was often at odds with self-promotion or greed.[13]

---

[11] Brown, *Firearms in Colonial America*, 30, 263–72.
[12] Russell, *Guns on the Early Frontier*, 10–14.
[13] Schama, *Embarrassment of Riches*.

Amsterdam was fast on its way to becoming the center of European banking, making it relatively easier for Dutch merchants to receive financing. By 1600 the Dutch controlled most of the shipping of northern Europe, with a nearly complete lock on the trade of the Baltic and the northwest Atlantic coast. The Dutch East India Company (VOC), created in 1602, began the gradual process of wresting control of Indian Ocean shipping from the Portuguese. To do so, the VOC founded Batavia, present-day Jakarta, in 1619, and within short order pushed all other Europeans out of the East Indies trade. The VOC pioneered trade with Japan, too, until the shogun imposed restrictions in 1641. The VOC was more successful than the Dutch West India Company, which nonetheless spent the first half of the seventeenth century creating colonies in the Americas.

During this period of intense development, the Dutch began to explore the Cape of Good Hope, where they encountered the Khoi. The VOC hoped to make money but did not wish to act immorally. The company's leadership instructed its employees to treat the Cape Khoi decently: they were not to be molested or enslaved. The VOC directors hoped to trade with the Khoi, who kept herds of cattle. Fresh meat, as well as fresh water and vegetables, would help VOC crews to survive their journeys between the Netherlands and the East Indies. Therefore it was in the Company's best interest to have good relations with the local inhabitants, who were difficult to understand. The Khoi were known to "steal" things, or, at least, they were known to have a different understanding of property from the Europeans.

The early Europeans at the Cape formed and transmitted unfavorable ideas about the Khoi. Some of these descriptions were quite revealing, in that they said much about what Europeans disliked about themselves and quite little about how the "Hottentots" actually behaved. Turning the Khoi into an exotic, disagreeable people was a prelude to pushing them off the land. As these unfavorable representations took shape, the Europeans ignored or dismissed Khoi skills with local materials that were actually quite impressive, given the difficult environment at the Cape. The Khoi groups of South Africa were herders, whose societies and politics were based on the accumulation and distribution of cattle. The Khoi did domesticate a few plants, such as rooibos tea, but these were not especially significant. They lived in groups of 50–200, in huts made from grass mats. From a European perspective, their material practices were curious. They dressed in leather vests and aprons (karosses) and smeared themselves with animal grease. They were similar in appearance to the

San, who practiced hunting and gathering. Modern archaeologists and anthropologists tend to downplay the differences between Khoi and San, citing evidence from Europeans at the Cape who saw Khoi who were taking up hunting and gathering and San who were familiar with aspects of herding. Even so, the historian Nigel Penn presents evidence in his book *The Forgotten Frontier* that shows how the lifeways and ideologies of the Khoi and San were distinct.

Khoi groups did migrate, like the San, but the Khoi were transhumant pastoralists who raised cattle and sheep. This was an excellent response to the "Mediterranean" Cape climate and to the absence of crop plants. Crops that might have been acquired from "Bantu" neighbors to the north, like sorghum and millet, depended on summer rainfall and dry winters. By contrast, the Cape has dry summers and wet winters, more like the Mediterranean. (Observing this, later European farmers introduced suitable crops like grapes and wheat.) The Khoi migrated seasonally, moving from one place to another according to rainfall patterns. They sometimes shared space with other Khoi groups. One group acknowledged the dominion of another group by paying symbolic tribute. Khoi groups also coexisted with groups of San hunter-gatherers, particularly in marginal mountainous areas, where San sometimes became clients of Khoi.[14]

Khoi skills for coping with their environment were impressive. So were the skills that allowed Europeans to arrive on the shores of the Cape of Good Hope. By the end of the fifteenth century, European maritime technology had advanced to a degree that allowed Western Europeans to project power globally. Western European rulers of the era also encouraged exploration and conquest, unlike Chinese rulers, who had sophisticated navies, yet abandoned any political interest in exploration in the mid-fifteenth century. And while the technologies associated with gunpowder and cannons were Chinese in origin, it was Western Europeans, in the sixteenth and seventeenth centuries, who improved gunpowder weapons and paired them with long-distance sailing ships to form "gunpowder empires."[15]

In 1652, the VOC's Jan van Riebeeck landed with his crew to establish a trading post on the present-day site of Cape Town. Trade would be conducted under the auspices of the VOC, which claimed a monopoly. The

---

[14] Penn, *Forgotten Frontier*, 16–19
[15] For a comparative history of firearms in Eurasian societies before 1700, see Chase, *Firearms*.

VOC's monopoly on trade was complemented by its efforts to monopolize power. The coproduction of trade and power was related, very early on, to the regulation of guns, one of the principal tools of violence at the Cape. Gun control began almost immediately upon the arrival of Van Riebeeck. In a way, the regulation of guns was just as fundamental, for the VOC state, as the arming of soldiers and, later, burghers. Van Riebeeck ordered "every one . . . to keep a good watch upon his arms and tools . . . so that they be not stolen or carried off from him."[16] According to this earliest regulation of frontier gun trading, arms and tools were to be kept out of Khoi hands, even as friendly relations were to be established. Gun control was one of the hallmarks of the new order.

Van Riebeeck learned very quickly that the Khoi were experienced at trade. The earliest reports indicate that they knew how to barter with the Dutch and that they had already developed an interest in certain European products, including tobacco, copper, and iron. This they had done through previous encounters with European traders. Still, they were frightened by firearms. In the midst of an early transaction for cattle and sheep that took place in 1653, a VOC corporal who was "annoyed" by the Khoi fired a pistol over their heads. As a result, "all the Saldanhars took to flight, leaving their cattle behind them, until, on being called to by our people, and on their cattle being driven towards them, it was explained to be jest."[17] Similar demonstrations occurred for the next few years, as Van Riebeeck and the VOC attempted to establish trade. When VOC parties approached groups of Cape Khoi, "they often asked our people if they had fire-arms with them, sitting by our men with the greatest fear, shaking and trembling."[18] The initial Khoi fear of guns jeopardized trade. In 1657, when Van Riebeeck sent an expedition inland, he instructed the VOC troops that "it will also be very desirable that you allow no firing whatever on the way, as these natives are much afraid of firearms – those at a distance still more than those hereabouts, as on hearing it they might take to flight."[19]

The Cape's Khoi residents quickly appreciated the strengths and weaknesses of Dutch firearms. The Company's sailors and soldiers were armed with both matchlock and flintlock muskets as well as pistols, although it

---

[16] "Extract of Proclamation," October 14, 1652, in Moodie, *The Record*, 1:16.

[17] January 7, 1653, Moodie, *The Record*, 1:28.

[18] December 11, 1653, Moodie, *The Record*, 1:41.

[19] "Extracts from the Journal of Commander Van Riebeeck," October 16, 1657, in Moodie, *The Record*, 1:109.

is not known precisely how many of each kind were owned. In one early letter to the Company, written in 1653, the administrator, Van Riebeeck, requested "1 or 2 dozen good sure firelocks for journeys through the country . . . also some flints for our fire arms which are all without flints and consequently cannot be used."[20] The Cape Khoi took advantage of the matchlock's vulnerability to dampness, but according to South Africa's leading firearms history expert, Felix Lategan, they respected the flintlock.[21]

In 1654, two years after the Dutch East India Company laid claim to the Cape of Good Hope, the area around Table Bay was still home to lions. They concerned the Dutch commander, Jan van Riebeeck, who noted in his journal that one day near the fort, a lion attacked a Khoi man. The man's calls for help were answered by his friends, who cornered the lion and moved in for the kill with their spears. A Dutchman with a musket arrived at the scene and "he very fortunately killed the lion with the first shot, to the great astonishment of the Hottentoos [Khoi], that so furious an animal could be so instantly dispatched with a single shot; this will consequently cause no diminution in their fear of our fire arms."[22]

In certain circumstances, people perceived that guns brought security. In other circumstances, they perceived enhanced risks. The early accounts by Dutch East India Company (VOC administrators indicate that when the Cape Khoi first encountered Dutchmen with guns, they were terrified. The early accounts also indicate that when the Khoi began to understand how to use the guns, they became less terrified. This process of fear lessening with acquaintance appears to have repeated itself as the VOC trading frontier moved inland. In 1689, the VOC records noted that a trading party to the interior received a mixed reaction to its firearms.

As soon as the kraal people called Sonquas perceived the party sent out by us, they placed themselves in a posture of defence, and shot briskly at our people with bows and arrows, on which our people fired two muskets at them in return, when the Hottentots fled, but quickly recovered themselves, our people seeing this, saluted them with another shot, when they fled again, but soon placed themselves in their former posture, but when some shots were fired by our people for the third time, they fled altogether, and hid themselves in the mountains.[23]

[20] Moodie, *The Record*, 35.
[21] Lategan, "Firearms, Historical," 517.
[22] "Extracts from the Journal of Commander Van Riebeeck," November 3, 1654, in Moodie, *The Record*, 1:55.
[23] February 2, 1689, Moodie, *The Record*, 1:435.

At the time people were fascinated by these stories of demonstration. We remain fascinated today. People who are naïve are shown a new technology, which solves a problem or makes an impact in some unforeseen way. The witnesses are shocked, awed, and covetous. What was the purpose of these demonstrations, and also of these Dutch stories about demonstrations? The violence of these demonstrations was rooted in a complex social context. Frontiers may be thought of as zones of social intercommunication. In them, people who are different – in appearance, custom, or language – encounter each other. They must accept one people's rules, or they must work out a new order among themselves. Order is produced, in part, through the demonstration of a new technology. The people who are shocked, awed, and covetous admit the power of the people making the demonstration. The representation of these demonstrations also helps to constitute order in an unstable situation: the people who are impressed tell stories about the demonstration to acquaintances, in part to acquaint them with the object itself, but also to inform them about new possibilities in the arrangement of power. New powers are represented, too, by the demonstrators. Telling a story about how one impressed newfound peoples with previously unimagined technologies is a way of depicting oneself as more powerful than another. A new order is made out of a demonstration.

This is not a process unique to violent frontier zones, but to all situations in which power and knowledge are subject to revolutionary challenges. A classic science and technology studies (STS) exploration of demonstration and witnessing, Steven Shapin and Simon Schaffer's 1985 book *Leviathan and the Air-Pump* describes how Thomas Hobbes challenged Robert Boyle's experiments to prove the existence of a vacuum. Boyle invented an air pump while also mustering a community of important witnesses. The stakes were high. Boyle believed that "vacuism" could be validated by learned discourse among scholars, while Hobbes, a "plenist," believed that the vacuum could not be proven and furthermore that the sovereign's authority should dictate the production of knowledge. To Boyle this was intellectual and political tyranny. He arranged for his colleagues to witness the technology of the air pump, a technique and an object that repudiated the restoration of Charles II to the throne. Witnessing a dramatic new technology was a gesture in favor of a different order.[24]

---

[24] Shapin and Schaffer, "Seeing and Believing: The Experimental Production of Pneumatic Facts," in *Leviathan and the Air-Pump*, 22–79.

Restoration England and the Cape of Good Hope were a far cry from each other, even if at both places objects were witnessed in the seventeenth century as part of experiments with knowledge and order. For the Dutch, the key difference between Western Europe and the Cape was environmental: at the Cape, the mere act of survival stretched the Dutch to their limit. This had as much to do with the Cape's environment as it had to do with cross-cultural relations. Starting in 1652, relations with the Khoi did not live up to the expectations of the VOC directors. The VOC needed beef and mutton, yet the Khoi were not interested in selling their animals in large quantities. The Khoi also did not grow fruit and vegetables. Five disappointing years passed before the VOC decided to release some of its Cape employees from their contracts and grant them land nearby so they could start their own farms. This opened the "settlement frontier."

The "free burghers," as the male settlers were called, faced many restrictions. They had to sell their produce to the Company and they also had to respect the Company's monopoly on trade. This meant that they could not trade with anybody else, European or Khoi. The free burghers borrowed money and seed to start their farms, many of which did not succeed. And to make matters worse, the Khoi resented the presence of settlers. The land that the settlers occupied in the Cape peninsula, along the valley of the Liesbeek River, lay in the midst of Khoi pastures and water sources. The Khoi moved their cattle from place to place over the course of the year, migrating according to seasonal patterns, but not in a way that was completely predictable. The Khoi took the settlement of the free burghers in the Cape peninsula to be quite provocative. Their system of transhumant pastoralism was in fundamental conflict with Dutch ideas about settled agriculture.

Company policy also shifted with regard to the fort. Initially it was supposed to be a temporary trading post, and no more. It had all the appearance of a temporary structure. Even so, in 1652 such a structure was still unacceptable to some Khoi. Soon after the construction of the fort, one group objected to its presence because it lay near traditional pasturage. Nonetheless the fort proved its usefulness to the Company. Other locations in southern Africa were less suitable for refreshing the merchant fleet, therefore the VOC invested more in the Cape. Some of the free burghers, as well as some spouses of Company employees, were supported in their efforts as tailors, surgeons, and tavern keepers. In 1666, work began on a permanent fort, the Cape Castle, symbolizing the Company's desire for a permanent presence. In 1672, the Company officially declared that it was taking possession of the Cape peninsula.

Guns and Early Warfare at the Cape

Now that the Company was encouraging a degree of permanent settlement at the Cape, relations with the Cape Khoi deteriorated and the frontier became more violent. Khoi resistance was led by a Goringhaiqua Khoi named Doman, who had spent 1657–8 living in Batavia, where he learned to speak Dutch and live like a European. Upon his return to the Cape, he reverted to Khoi ways and spoke out against Dutch oppression of people from Asia and Africa. Starting in 1659, he led a series of attacks on free burgher farms, rustling cattle and burning crops. For a year, Doman and his Goringhaiqua followers attacked farms but they were never able to attack the fort or drive out the Dutch, even though a small mutiny of Company employees took place at the fort. The Dutch, for their part, did not know the terrain well enough to capture Doman or prevent his attacks. The VOC formed the free burghers into a militia while their farming slowed to a standstill. The war fizzled out when the Cochoqua Khoi decided that instead of allying themselves with Doman, they would be better served by moving their cattle out of the Cape peninsula and into the interior. Most Goringhaiqua wanted peace with the Dutch, too. As a result, Doman became isolated. The only reason he was not killed or exiled was on account of his skill as an interpreter.

Doman did not only interpret the Dutch language for the Khoi. He also interpreted the Dutch use of guns. Initially, Dutch guns had frightened the Khoi who first encountered them. Doman's years with the Dutch appear to have afforded him the opportunity to observe musketry and possibly even to practice it himself. The Dutch commander at the Cape, Van Riebeeck, seems to have believed that Doman knew how to shoot. Describing Doman's anti-Dutch views, Van Riebeeck wrote in 1658 that "we shall have some evil turn to look for at his hand; it were much to be desired that he had never been at Batavia, or that he could be induced, by fair words, to return thither, more particularly because he has learned the perfect use of firearms, and we have enough to do to keep such out of his hands."[25] Khoi skill with guns presented risks to the colony. This is plausible enough, yet it is equally plausible that in order to make an enemy seem as risky as possible, they were to be described as dangerous, accurate shooters. Such a description was a useful adjunct to a description of one's enemy as violent. The available sources do not make it possible for us to achieve an objective assessment of Doman's skills, or, for that

[25] Moodie, *The Record*, 1:129.

matter, an objective assessment of any Dutch or Khoi skills with weapons. Even so, basic marksmanship is not so difficult. Given Doman's travels overseas, it is likely that he had become an effective shooter.

Doman's knowledge of guns became significant for the emerging conflict. When Doman and his followers made their first attack on the free burghers in May 1659, Van Riebeeck commented that Doman had "persuaded his tribe, that during rain we cannot keep our matches alight, and thus can hardly shoot." Doman's tactic was "to carry off, if possible, the cattle of the Company and the free men, in such dark rainy weather as they imagine will prevent us from shooting, while they, being provided with assagays [javelins] and bows," would be able to accomplish their mission.[26] This tactic was effective when combined with another tactic related to a technical understanding of guns: how to dodge bullets. In one attack, "our men, from the wetness of the weather, could only get 2 or 3 shots at the Hottentoos, the rogues managed to avoid the balls – as they can do most cleverly."[27] In another attack, the Dutchman ten Rhyne reported that the Khoi "shrink from getting within range of our guns."[28]

Khoi knowledge of Dutch shooting was also combined with other skills, notably those associated with cattle rustling. In several wet-weather attacks, settlers pursued the Khoi on horseback, "but they drove the cattle so quickly over the flat, that we could not once get sight of them."[29] Khoi knowledge of the terrain became important, too, on days when the weather made it easier for the Dutch to use their guns. On one occasion, Dutch burghers on horseback skirmished with Doman and a few followers. Three were wounded by gunfire and one was captured, while Doman jumped over a stream and escaped.[30]

Doman's rebellion sputtered out after a year, while Doman himself died in 1663. The Goringhaiqua made peace with the Dutch while the Cochoqua drifted away from the Cape peninsula and into the interior. So, too, did some Dutch settlers, who together with the Cochoqua impinged upon grazing lands that belonged to other Khoi groups, most notably the Chainouqua. During the 1660s, a range war simmered between the Chainouqua and the Cochoqua that drew in the Company. From 1673

---

[26] Moodie, *The Record*, 1:163. An "assagay" or assegai is a javelin.
[27] Moodie, *The Record*, 1:171
[28] Ten Rhyne, *The Early Cape Hottentots*, 133.
[29] Moodie, *The Record*, 1:170; see p. 171 for another instance. A similar description is given by Dapper, *The Early Cape Hottentots*, 13.
[30] Dapper, *The Early Cape Hottentots*, 15.

to 1677, VOC and burgher cavalry pursued the Cochoqua, in alliance with the Cochoqua's enemies. The Cochoqua lost thousands of sheep and cattle and were themselves scattered into small groups living under Dutch domination.[31] It is likely that cavalrymen would have used flintlocks or wheellocks, since matchlocks were awkward to use on horseback, although there is no direct evidence to corroborate this.

By the end of the 1670s, the Company was firmly in control of the peninsula. Khoi groups either left the Cape or lived under Company rule. Those who lived under the Company often engaged themselves as servants either to the Company or the free burghers, since it was now so difficult to live independently as pastoralists. They came to be called by their generic name, Hottentots, as the societies that they came from lost their pasturage, their water sources, and their distinctiveness. The remaining independent Khoi groups resisted colonial expansion by raiding cattle and sheep from colonists. The colonists raided back, often without the sanction of the company. When the company permitted colonists to trade cattle directly with the Khoi, the Khoi were cheated, robbed, and attacked.[32] Then in 1713 Khoi communities were hit especially hard by a smallpox epidemic, although the extent of the damage sustained during the epidemic has been debated by historians. In any case, as the historians Leonard Guelke and Robert Shell have pointed out, many Khoi made the decision to stay at the Cape, even though they no longer could control their access to land and water. By the end of the seventeenth century, no society living in the Western Cape could mount an effective resistance to the VOC.[33] Even so, it is significant that under the leadership of Doman, a skilled shooter, Khoi fighters based their resistance tactics on an understanding of guns. Resistance politics, like state politics, could also be a coproduction of ideology and technology.

Guns and the Expansion of the Cape Colony

The trading post at Table Bay, later called Cape Town, became a blend of cultures. The Dutch were joined by other Europeans, especially by French Huguenots who fled France in 1685 after Louis XIV revoked the Edict of Nantes. Europeans at the Cape began to import more African and Asian

---

[31] Penn, *Forgotten Frontier*, 32.
[32] Penn, *Forgotten Frontier*, 38–41.
[33] Guelke and Shell, "Landscape of Conquest," 807–9.

slaves. By 1731, the year of the first extensive census at the Cape, the colony had 959 VOC employees, 585 free burghers, 200 free blacks, 80 VOC convicts from around the Indian Ocean, 566 VOC slaves, and 767 private slaves.[34] Slaves came from different parts of Africa and Asia. The historian Clifton Crais makes valid points about the significance of Cape slavery for later history: slavery introduced the idea of a "racial division of labor" that came to shape all forms of colonial identity. Stereotypes about white masters and black workers became important in Cape culture. They supported forms of domestic violence, as masters, seeing themselves as patriarchs, sought to control servants. They also supported cross-cultural violence. As white hunters and farmers left the Cape for the interior, they sought to reproduce this violent, stereotypical society.[35]

The settlement frontier expanded as the population grew modestly. Free burghers began to settle to the east, in the vicinity of Stellenbosch, taking their slaves with them, while burghers with scantier resources made the "trek" into the interior and took up nomadic pastoralism. This adaptation of Europeans to local environmental conditions resembled, to a degree, the lifeways of Khoi pastoralists. The advent of European and mixed-race pastoralism represented the opening of a third type of frontier, which Elphick and Malherbe call the "trekboer frontier."

The VOC drew its military strength from its garrison, supplemented by the burgher militia. As early as 1658, Van Riebeeck was warning the new, free burghers "to keep themselves and their arms in readiness." Readiness to commit state-sanctioned violence with a gun was required of all male settlers. Any burgher who lacked a gun was required to obtain one from the Company armory, and any "who may be found on the roads alone, without fire arms," would be fined. The Company would inspect burgher arms occasionally, expecting them to be kept "in good order."[36] Even caring for a gun was a political obligation. It is interesting to note that the great civic humanist philosophers of the sixteenth and seventeenth centuries considered the bearing of arms to be one of the virtues of a republic. The VOC colony at the Cape was a far cry from a republic, but the Netherlands did have a republic. According to the precepts of republican civic humanism, burghers were obliged to serve in the militia. The civic humanist Machiavelli's very definition of virtue – summarized by historian John Pocock as "a people's ability to control

---

[34] Worden, Van Heyningen, and Bickford Smith, *Cape Town*, 50.
[35] Crais, *White Supremacy and Black Resistance*, 33–5.
[36] Moodie, *The Record*, 130.

its environment by arms" – is the sort of coproduction of politics and technology that was beginning to develop at the Cape.[37]

It appears that the Company succeeded in encouraging the settlers to arm themselves. Guelke and Shell's research in archival sources shows that between 1683 and 1753 most burghers possessed a flintlock, while many also possessed pistols and sabers. The Company required the burghers to attend militia practice, which included drilling and shooting. The militia was organized into local "commandos" comprising all men between the ages of sixteen and sixty who were responsible for supplying a horse, saddle, and provisions. The VOC continued to supply the guns and ammunition.[38] The burghers elected their own officers, who in turn reported to VOC officers, who served as overall commanders. For a time, from 1722 to 1733, "free blacks" were required to join their own militia company, too.

Settlers had informal experiences in defending themselves and their cattle on the turbulent frontier. In 1715, such retaliatory activities received official sanction, when the governor authorized the Stellenbosch burghers to form a commando to attack Khoi cattle raiders.[39] In the following decades, such commandos became the preferred method for settlers to retaliate against the Khoi and San who resisted them. The commando system allowed settlers to respond quickly to threats. It also gave the settlers in remote areas a "military capability" to take the law into their own hands and to put pressure on nearby Khoi, and eventually the Xhosa, even though the Cape's indigenous people were protected from violence by VOC regulations. As Hermann Giliomee argues, the VOC ignored abuses because the commando system saved the company the expense of keeping professional forces on the frontier. And as Nigel Penn argues, the frontier society was held together, in a highly stratified form, by the threat of commando intervention. The commando leader became quite powerful in the local community. He could punish those who did not participate in the commando, while he could also reward those who did. The rewards often took the form of gunpowder. Those who cooperated received plenty of gunpowder; those who did not were cut off.[40]

---

[37] Pocock, *Machiavellian Moment*, 271.
[38] Berkovitch, *Cape Gunsmith*, 20. After the second British conquest of 1806, VOC guns were taken away from burghers. Subsequently, burgher commandos had to supply their own guns.
[39] Penn, *Forgotten Frontier*, 50. See also pp. 299–300, n. 153.
[40] Giliomee, *Afrikaners*, 59. Guelke and Shell, "Landscape of Conquest," 810–14. Penn, *Forgotten Frontier*, 112, 115–16.

The commando system, as it evolved in the eighteenth century, was associated with tactics that combined horsemanship and marksmanship. When the commando was ready to attack an enemy, the armed horsemen formed a line and charged the enemy. Once they were within effective range of the enemy – but still out of range of the enemy's spears, stones, and arrows – they dismounted, fired a volley, and then retreated to reload. They re-formed and charged again. This is the reason why students of tactics call the commando a form of "mounted infantry." Unlike the cavalry tactics of the day, which involved flanking the enemy and then charging them with lances, pistols, and sabers, the commando traveled like cavalry but attacked like infantry. These tactics proved formidable in open country, especially against opponents who had fewer horses and guns.

The commando system helped to make possible trekboer expansion onto other peoples' grazing lands. As Guelke and Shell point out, settlers used permits from the VOC to collect salt and graze as a way to stake initial claims to lands they would eventually settle. Hunters also made significant inroads to the east of the Cape during the middle of the eighteenth century. Between 1735 and 1744 there were 102 recorded hunting trips to the East, which brought significant amounts of ivory back to the Western Cape. For example, in 1736 two expeditions each acquired 396 pounds of ivory. By the 1750s and 1760s, hunters (who also traded with the Khoi and Xhosa) had beaten a regular trail from Swellendam, their jumping-off point in the Western Cape, all the way to the Great Fish River.[41] Hunters, trekboers, and salt collectors would enter an area occupied by Khoi and pressure them to leave or become clients. Through this process of gradual, sanctioned encroachment and armed violence, settlement expanded northward and eastward. With such pressure on the land, the Khoi were either incorporated into the settlements, working first as young "apprentices" and then, at the age of majority, becoming debt peons, or they were driven to hunting and gathering like the San.

The San hunter-gatherers, called "Bushmen," began to encounter settlers, too. By the 1750s settlements were established as far east as the Karoo. By the 1770s, settlers were encroaching on lands near the Fish River, which were inhabited by the Xhosa. The upper reaches of the Fish River, the Sneeuberg, were inhabited by substantial numbers of San and Khoi refugees. They reacted by attacking settlers and their cattle. The

---

[41] Crais, *White Supremacy and Black Resistance*, 37.

settlers paid them back with a campaign that aimed to kill adult males and to enslave women and children. The fighting was especially intense during the 1770s and 1780s, when commandos ruthlessly suppressed the San. There were times when the San won temporary victories, but on the whole they were not able to stand in the way of mounted settler men armed with flintlock guns.[42] According to the French missionaries Arbousset and Daumas, among one group of San, the word for "white man" was the same as the word for "gun" – *tuntsi* – which mimicked the sound that a gun makes.[43] These San saw the invaders and the gun as one.

As the Cape settlement expanded to the north and east, settlers armed some of their Khoi and mixed-race servants, who were now deemed to be sufficiently skilled and loyal. In the 1690s, the VOC asked the "landdrost" or local magistrate of Stellenbosch, just to the east of Cape Town, to require "Hottentots who know how to use firearms" to join patrols for runaway slaves.[44] From the end of the seventeenth century to the end of the eighteenth century, loyal Khoi, skilled in the use of guns, were used to supplement the burgher militia and the forces of the VOC.[45] One letter, written in 1774 from eastern frontier settlers to the governor, described a force being assembled to drive the San out of the vicinity. Only 100 settler militiamen were available for the purpose, which made it necessary to enlist 150 "Bastard Hottentots." These men were "accustomed to the use of fire-arms" and also knew how to "clamber into the mountains and there trace the robbers to their haunts." "Full reliance might be placed" on these mixed-race, Khoi-European frontiersmen, because they displayed "fidelity." They were also skilled, having "dexterity in the use of fire-arms." If they were not armed with guns, according to the settlers, "no advantage can be expected."[46]

From an early date in the history of South Africa's colonization, settlers related loyalty to skill. Skill, in turn, guaranteed a measure of good treatment. Loyalty could not be bought with coercion and beating. Respect for skills in shooting, in herding, and in other practices helped lead to

---

[42] Guelke and Shell, "Landscape of Conquest," 814–19. Penn, *Forgotten Frontier*, 125–54.
[43] Arbousset and Daumas, *Narrative of an Exploratory Tour*, 229.
[44] Leibrandt Manuscript Précis, Cape Archives, L. M. 11, Governor to Landdrost, July 3, 1690; as cited by Marks and Atmore, "Firearms in Southern Africa," 519.
[45] Marks, "Khoisan Resistance to the Dutch," 76.
[46] "Copy of a letter from the combined Boards of Landdrost and Heemraden, and Landdrost and Militia Officers, Stellenbosch, to Governor Van Plettenberg and Council," April 19, 1774, in Moodie, *The Record*, 3:25–7.

relationships between Boers and some Khoi that resembled clientship more than slavery, even though both were held up by the same paternalistic ideology.[47] In any event, Khoi often had motivations of their own to fight in commandos. In the eighteenth-century campaigns against the San and Xhosa, Khoi herders who worked for the Boers were often on the front lines, defending their masters' farms while accumulating their own cattle.[48]

Hunting in the Early Cape Colony

Skill with guns was not only related to politics and military affairs but also to hunting, an important cultural activity. In all Cape cultures, hunting was related to the violent expression of masculinity. The Khoi and San made hunting an important part of their religions, too. And while hunting was important for culture, it was also important for the economy. Khoi and San, as well as settlers and trekboers, supplemented their diets by hunting the local fauna. They also hunted animals that posed a threat to sheep and cattle, such as lions, leopards, and jackals. At the same time, the by-products of hunting, like ivory, skins, and feathers, could be traded. These items, as well as meat, could also be used to pay for land and laborers. Hunting, usually with guns, became an important aspect of the economy of the Cape and its hinterlands.

It might be said that in addition to the trading frontier, the settlement frontier, and the trekboer frontier that Elphick and Malherbe have described, there was a hunting frontier. Animals were hunted in the seventeenth century within a short distance of Cape Town. Wild animals were killed or driven out, gradually farther and farther from Cape Town. Dutch burghers and VOC employees hunted everywhere they went to trade, settle, and trek. By the start of the eighteenth century, Dutch hunters were crossing the colonial boundary, often combining hunting with smuggling. Elephant hunters secretly brought tusks to Cape Town, selling them to ships' captains from Holland and other countries. Thus were the natural resources of the colony converted into capital.[49]

Dutch settlers, traders, and hunters destroyed the game and pushed the hunting frontier to the north and east. By the 1770s, elephants could no longer be found south of the Orange River and west of the Sundays River.

---

[47] Giliomee, *Afrikaners*, 61.
[48] Giliomee, *Afrikaners*, 63.
[49] MacKenzie, *Empire of Nature*, 85–119. Newton-King, *Masters and Servants*, 100–1.

Other game animals became scarce, too, as they were killed and rendered into meat, fat, and hide. As the slaughter unfolded, it became increasingly difficult for the Khoi and San to hunt at home. This was a disaster for the San. Not only did they depend upon animals for food, they also treated animals, especially the eland, with great spiritual reverence, as can be seen in their rock art. By the eighteenth century, their material and spiritual worlds were vanishing. As the historians Susan Newton-King and Nigel Penn have shown in their recent works, *The Forgotten Frontier* and *Masters and Servants on the Cape Eastern Frontier*, the San and the Khoi resisted these changes mightily and were subjected to terrible repression. Their homes, pastures, and hunting grounds were destroyed and they were either killed or taken captive, living in conditions that increasingly came to resemble slavery, even though, legally speaking, they were not slaves. Nevertheless, for purposes of the present study, it is important to note that the San and the Khoi had highly developed skills in hunting and tracking that their new European masters put to use. European hunting parties frequently incorporated San and Khoi as trackers and as shooters, taking maximum advantage of their local knowledge in the extraction of ivory from the hunting frontier.[50]

It has been said, by various historians, that the Khoi and the San disrupted their ecosystems less than the Europeans because Europeans had more lethal technologies. It is true that firearms enabled more killing, but there were special challenges facing the first Europeans to hunt the game animals of southern Africa. It was not enough just to have a gun. In fact, some of the early guns imported to the Cape were not up to the task of hunting the largest animals. In an early dispatch from the Cape, Jan van Riebeeck wrote of an encounter with a rhinoceros that had become stuck in a salt pan: "We fired more than a hundred shots before we killed it, so many bullets rebounded from its body, particularly from its side, that we are obliged to cut out a piece with axes, and then to shoot into its entrails betwixt the ribs, and thus we killed it."[51]

European hunters who were challenged by southern African fauna benefited from sharing skills with Khoi hunters, who came to appreciate the usefulness of firearms. In 1660, renegade Dutchmen hunted rhinos with Khoi whom they had armed with guns and taught to shoot. Sometime after the hunt, Van Riebeeck interviewed three of the Khoi hunters:

---

[50] MacKenzie, *Empire of Nature*, 59–61. Newton-King, *Masters and Servants*, 100–4.
[51] Moodie, *The Record*, 1:56.

The said 3 Hottentoos persist in saying that Harman had taught them to shoot with a gun, as appeared at the shooting of the said rhinoceros, when, after Harman had missed, one of them fired with a carbine, broke the animal's leg, and killed it with a shot from Jacob Cloeten's gun, which one of them carried on his shoulder. Item, that before the war he had also shown and instructed them and other Hottentoos, how they could to the greatest injury to our people, &c.[52]

As early as the 1670s, there were reports of a Khoi who had purchased a gun and become a professional hunter, "maintaining himself by shooting sea-cows [hippos]."[53] During the same decade, VOC officials became concerned about the arming of the Khoi. According to the Company's reports during that time of conflict,

two persons . . . had supplied 2 guns to Hottentots. . . . On account not only of the injury thus done to the game, but of the attendant danger; "for no inhabitant's life could be safe if these blacks were armed with our weapons," it was declared a capital offence to sell, give, lend, or alienate in any way whatsoever to any native any firearms, or other weapons, or any ammunition, &c.[54]

These early attempts to regulate the cross-cultural trade in guns fore-shadowed subsequent debates. Europeans sought power over Africans. This was more easily achieved if Africans were technologically over-powered. Yet it was in the interest of traders and hunters to enlist the help of Khoi and mixed-race hunters. And in frontier warfare, it was often prudent to make alliances with indigenous people and to arm them and teach them how to shoot. This was the case in colonial North America during the era of the fur trade, and it was true of South Africa, too. When it suited colonists and the state, indigenous people would be armed. They would be pointedly restricted from gun ownership when it did not suit the settlers and the state. In South Africa, the dilemmas associated with these positions would carry over into the end of the nineteenth century, by which point it was a rarity to encounter game animals near European settlements and European hegemony was no longer seriously challenged.

Guns and Conflict on the Eastern Cape Frontier

In Marks and Atmore's introduction to the 1971 *Journal of African History* special issue on firearms in southern Africa, the authors claimed

---

[52] Moodie, *The Record*, 1:211.
[53] Moodie, *The Record*, 1:357.
[54] Moodie, *The Record*, 1:357.

that "a 'gun society' existed at the Cape from the beginning of white settlement there in 1652."[55] They did not define what, exactly, constitutes a gun society, and many of the articles in their special issue actually downplayed the importance of guns. Be that as it may, if there ever could be such a thing as a gun society, the Cape under the VOC must surely qualify. Many people owned and used guns. Soldiers and civil servants possessed guns, while the government also required burghers to own guns and to practice with them. Other groups owned guns as well. Starting at the end of the seventeenth century, the Khoi people of the Cape came to possess many guns, which they used to defend or attack the settlers and the VOC. Guns became important to the economy of the Cape, too, as hunters used guns to provide ivory and other animal products, and pastoralists used guns to protect their herds from predators. Human predators depended on guns, too, in the closely related phenomena of cattle-rustling and frontier justice.

Starting in the 1730s, and possibly even earlier, colonial elephant hunters and cattle traders who ventured near the colony's eastern boundary at the Fish River began to encounter the Xhosa, who had settled as far south as the Fish River by around A.D. 1250. The Xhosa were quite different from the Khoi. Like most of the other dark-skinned Africans who lived in the coastal lowlands, they practiced a mix of cultivation and cattle herding. Households were organized in kraals, circular huts arranged in circles around the cattle pen. Kraals were dominated by chiefs or heads of households, with household arrangements forming the basis of political power. Women raised children, performed chores, gathered food, and raised crops, but did not come into contact with cattle. Boys herded cattle, under the tutelage of older boys, who also taught stick-fighting, while men milked and made "amasi," the fermented milk beverage that is either drunk straight or poured over mealie porridge. Men also did the butchering, leather making, and other chores, including some construction. Men also were involved in politics, war, as well as some ironsmithing and iron mining. Manhood was marked by initiation and training in politics and war. Men married as many wives as they could afford, depending on the amount of cattle they could pay as bridewealth. Marrying off daughters was a key way for men to conclude alliances and to accumulate cattle and labor.[56]

[55] Marks and Atmore, "Firearms in Southern Africa," 517.
[56] Crais, *White Supremacy and Black Resistance*, 16–29. Peires, *House of Phalo*, 1–44.

Xhosa society, as well as most other black African societies in southern Africa, depended on the accumulation of people and the subordination of women. In a sense, these were responses on the part of African men to environmental conditions. There was plenty of land (even if it was frequently not the best soil for cultivation) but there were never enough people. Patriarchy was central to patterns of dominance. Men's control of women ensured control over reproduction as well as key aspects of agricultural production. Household production and reproduction were in turn typically controlled by chiefs, who regulated marriage. A chief's most important function, typically, was to gather enough people under his patronage. To a large extent, patronage was based on preserving good relations with others. For this reason southeast African chiefdoms have tended to be somewhat consensual and not completely authoritarian. Since there was plenty of land available, clients and younger sons and grandsons could often just leave. Chiefdoms had to be responsive even if most of them were hereditary. Many southeast African chiefdoms that were first observed by Europeans in the nineteenth century had partially representative institutions, like the Sotho *pitso*, the Tswana *kgotla*, or the Zulu and Xhosa *indaba*, in which adult men (but not women) could gather and speak in public about their problems. Chiefs also acted as administrators of justice, often spending much time hearing cases.[57]

People joined and left chiefdoms with some frequency. Chiefdoms tended to be open polities, in the sense that anyone, even Europeans, could join. It is often mistakenly thought that in the nineteenth century, African people were loyal to ethnic or national identities: Xhosa, Zulu, and so on. This sort of identity is a retrospective twentieth-century invention. Instead, in the early nineteenth century, people tended to identify with chiefs, not with ethnicities.[58]

By comparison to the chiefly balance between authority and patronage, the VOC embodied a very different, racially exclusive approach to rule, and Boer practices were often antagonistic toward Africans. Early relations between the Boers and the Xhosa were not always good. As Bundy and Saunders have written, many of the Europeans who began to intrude on Xhosa land were "hard, unscrupulous misfits who, having cheated and bullied the Khoisan of the Western Cape out of land and

---

[57] Ross, *Concise History*, Ch. 1.
[58] Etherington, *Great Treks*, 340–6. When the present work refers to groups of people as Xhosa, Zulu, and Sotho, or various subsets of those groups, it simply means people who were loyal to the chiefs who led those groups, and no more.

cattle, tried to do the same to their new rivals in the east."[59] It is possible to see this process from the perspective of the Boers, too, who had limited opportunities at the Cape to accumulate capital, on account of the VOC monopoly. Hunting, as well as stealing, provided a relatively easy way to accumulate capital and land.[60] Hunting provided a way for power to grow from the barrel of a gun, while gun ownership enhanced the ability of thieves to rob unarmed victims.

The Xhosa were able to put up a better resistance than the Khoi. The Xhosa did not yet have firearms but they did have a denser population and they were also better organized for warfare. In the 1730s, a group of Xhosa men killed the members of one hunting and trading party. The VOC reaffirmed its monopoly, threatening severe punishment for any traders who would violate Company prerogatives and disturb the border region. This did not stop trade. Next, the typical pattern ensued, with hunters and traders displacing some Khoi and Xhosa, making them into clients. The Gqunukhwebe Xhosa, who were actually a mix of Xhosa and Khoi, lived in between the Sundays and Bushmans Rivers. They sought peace with the trekboers by helping them fight the San to the north and, in some cases, by offering to work for the trekboers. The Gqunukhwebe made peace with the Company, too, by making rent payments on their own territory. Soon trekboers began to drift into the Zuurveld (sour grass) region between the Bushmans and Fish Rivers. During the 1770s, trekboers moving east began to encounter large numbers of Xhosa who were in the process of moving west. As historian Jeff Peires has written, the Xhosa envisioned an "open frontier," much like the one that they had enjoyed with their Khoi and San neighbors. People from one group could become clients of people in another group, marriages and alliances could be formed between groups, and specialists from one group could serve members of the other group. Such an open and fluid frontier was enjoyed by a few trekboers, most famously by the family of Conrad de Buys, the Dutch pastoralist who married and traded across cultural boundaries, but the vision of an open frontier was not shared by the VOC or by most trekboers.[61]

Instead, the colony attempted to fix a boundary, and to push all Xhosa to the east of it. In 1778, Governor Joachim van Plettenburg reached an agreement with the Gwali and Dange Xhosa chiefs, fixing the boundary

[59] Saunders, Bundy, and Oakes, *Illustrated History of South Africa*, 102.
[60] Crais, *White Supremacy and Black Resistance*, 37–8.
[61] Peires, *House of Phalo*, 53–6.

on a north–south line running from the northern reaches of the Fish River to the southern reaches of the Bushmans River, cutting clear across the Zuurveld. This was confusing because the VOC had previously conceived of the Fish River as the boundary, including its southern reaches, and many trekboers continued to do so. Another problem with the agreement was that the Gwali chiefs did not represent all Xhosa. In fact, the different Xhosa chiefdoms were embroiled in a number of long-standing disputes. The Dange Xhosa were actually being pressed by the Rharhabe Xhosa to their east to move westward into colonial territory. From 1779 to 1781, cattle raiding and skirmishing broke out between the trekboers and the Gwali and Dange Xhosa.

During the war of 1779–81, each side relied on different military skills and technologies. The Xhosa were able to mass large numbers of men armed with spears and knobkerrie clubs. The trekboers organized commandos with relatively small numbers of men mounted on horses and carrying guns. One such commando, organized by the trekboer Adriaan van Jaarsveld, comprised "92 Christians, and 40 Hottentots, with guns."[62]

While the trekboers and Khoi were armed with guns, the Xhosa still were not familiar with them. In 1779, the botanist William Paterson visited the Xhosa paramount chief, Khawuta, whose Great Place lay just across the Fish River. In a typical gesture of hospitality, the chief gave a steer to the botanist, who slaughtered it by shooting it. According to Paterson, the gunshot "surprised all that were about us, which I may safely say was about six hundred, few of them ever having see or heard the report of a gun."[63] Once again, the demonstration of a gun introduced new conceptions of power.

Xhosa lack of familiarity with guns worked to their disadvantage in war. In a famous incident in 1781, Van Jaarsveld and his men met a group of Dange Xhosa men at the Fish River ostensibly to negotiate the terms of a Xhosa withdrawal. The Xhosa were dissatisfied, and as they walked away Van Jaarsveld threw gifts of tobacco on the ground. The Xhosa approached the tobacco, not realizing that they made easy targets for the trekboers and Khoi, who opened fire, killing many.[64] It was only in the decade after the war that reports circulated among colonists about

---

[62] Saunders, Bundy, and Oakes, *Illustrated History of South Africa*, 69–70. Peires, *House of Phalo*, 54–5, especially the map on p. 55. See also Mostert, *Frontiers*, 227.

[63] Mostert, *Frontiers*, 245; citing Paterson, *Cape Travels*, 132.

[64] Mostert, *Frontiers*, 230; citing Moodie, *The Record*, 3:93.

small numbers of Xhosa men who were acquiring firearms. It was said that the acquisitions were giving the Xhosa confidence, although this might have been more imagined than real.[65] Real or not, it is one of the earliest instances in which guns were said to be affecting self-perception or consciousness.

The war between the colonists and Xhosa did not produce a clear victory for either side, just a heightened potential for revenge and further conflict. As attitudes changed among the Xhosa, they began to accumulate guns. The guns were apparently introduced by Khoi refugees from the Cape. Relations between Boers and Khoi were becoming strained, on account of an increasing land scarcity. Xhosa chiefs were famously willing to accept clients from other cultures. The Gqunukhwebe, in particular, were the westernmost Xhosa group, and they had already accepted so many Khoi into their culture that it might be said that they were creoles, incorporating elements of both Khoi and Xhosa cultures. As the trekboers arrived in the Eastern Cape in greater numbers, more and more of their Khoi "servants" ran away to the Gqunukhwebe and the other Zuurveld Xhosa. Wartime instability brought Khoi servants even more opportunities to run away. When absconding Khoi joined Xhosa chiefdoms, they brought with them guns, horses, and the skills to use both for fighting and hunting. Such skills might also have been learned by Xhosa men who found temporary employment with Boer neighbors.[66]

Khoi servants ran away because they were mistreated. To improve their working conditions, and to bring more control to the Eastern Cape frontier, the Company established a new administrative district at Graaff-Reinet and appointed Honoratus Maynier as "landdrost." Maynier hoped for more humane policies toward the Khoi and the Xhosa. While he could not control the activities of the commandos, he limited their raiding by cutting back on their supply of lead and powder. He also collected VOC rents on land occupied by trekboers. And yet he was not able to end raiding, nor was he able to stop the steady drift of skilled, armed Khoi servants to the Xhosa side. He was also not able to prevent the outbreak of war again in 1793, which pitted the trekboers and the Rharhabe Xhosa of the east against the Gqunukhwebe and the Zuurveld Xhosa. Like the first war, this war also involved cattle raiding and the burning of houses. Once again, the commando tactics that succeeded so well against the Khoi and San were less effective against the more

---

[65] Marais, *Maynier and the First Boer Republic*, 27.
[66] Mostert, *Frontiers*, 246. Giliomee, *Afrikaners*, 67–9.

numerous Xhosa, many of whom were also able to take advantage of
the cover provided by nearby forests and mountains. Like the first war
it did not result in a lasting settlement of the disputed boundary. It was
different only in one respect. When the trekboers learned that the peace
settlement did not suit their interests as much as they would have liked,
they rebelled, declaring their independence. The Company reined them
in by cutting off their supply of arms and ammunition, an indication that
such an act could have serious repercussions.

In the midst of the emerging conflict along the Cape Colony's eastern
boundary, events in the Netherlands and Europe were starting to make
an impact in South Africa. In the summer of 1794, Dutch democrat-
republicans, calling themselves "Patriots," took over the Netherlands
government with the support of troops from revolutionary France. The
new Dutch republic, called the Batavian Republic, became a protectorate
of France. France was at war with Britain, which resulted in the British
navy blockading the Netherlands and seizing Dutch colonies, with autho-
rization from the exiled Dutch ruler, the Prince of Orange. At the Cape, a
small British force landed in 1795. After protracted negotiations and several small battles the Dutch East India Company (VOC) administrators
decided to surrender. British administration began, with the expectation
that the Cape would be returned to the Netherlands when France no
longer threatened British shipping.

At first the Britain's Cape administration upheld the policies of the
VOC, including its policies pertaining to guns along the frontier. The
British continued to embargo arms and ammunition to the "republican"
Boers on the eastern frontier, succeeding, by 1797, in persuading them to
rejoin the Cape Colony. As the historian Hermann Giliomee argues, the
founders of these republics had not been ideologues so much as they had
been opportunists. Plenty of opportunities remained for Boers to benefit
from the difficulties that the government faced in enforcing order. One
Boer who had defied the VOC as well as several Xhosa chiefs, Conrad
de Buys, lost his possessions on account of his contumacy, but succeeded
at gunrunning and went to live at the "great place" of Ngqika, chief of
the Rharhabe Xhosa, who was keen to acquire guns and horses. The
Boers, for their part, were keen to acquire Xhosa allies as they resisted
British and Dutch rulers installed far away in Cape Town. Multiracial
recruitment for soldiers was also undertaken by the Cape administration,
which formed a Khoi regiment to fight along the frontier. The Khoi
troops formed part of Britain's strategy for bringing order to the Eastern
Cape using Khoi troops to disarm rebel Boers. In 1799, British forces,

including Khoi troopers, took control of rebellious parts of the Eastern Cape by cutting off rebel ammunition supplies, disarming Boers, and inciting Khoi servants to plunder and then leave their masters. Between 1799 and 1803, there was a Khoi rebellion against the settlers, which succeeded, for a while, in raiding settler farms and in liberating many Khoi from debt peonage.

The state of rebellion encouraged the Xhosa to attack, thereby creating lasting resentment of British authority among frontier Boers. Cattle raiding and skirmishing increased, while overall frontier security deteriorated.[67] In such a society, the individual possession of guns was of fundamental importance. They were necessary tools for hunting and for self-defense, and at the same time there existed a strong civic obligation to own and maintain them. The commercial and political order at the Cape depended heavily on guns.

[67] Giliomee, *Afrikaners*, 75–7.

3

Guns, Conflict, and Political Culture along the Eastern Frontier, 1795–1840

British rule brought significant changes to South Africa. Many intersecting and overlapping political cultures had developed at the Cape, including those of Dutch settlers near Cape Town, Boer migrants along the frontier, and indigenous chiefdoms throughout the region. All now intersected and overlapped with British political culture, which in the early nineteenth century featured a pronounced tension between conservatives, who favored established practices in government, markets, and religion, and liberals, who supported to varying degrees free markets, slave emancipation, and evangelical Christianity.

Liberalism and Conservatism at the Cape

British conservatism made an early impact at the Cape. In 1809, the British governor of the Cape, the Earl of Caledon, introduced a law intended to ameliorate the lives of Khoi "servants" in the colony. The Caledon Code stipulated that all Khoi had to register their dwelling places with a magistrate and that all colonists who wished to employ a Khoi had to sign the contract in front of a magistrate. The British hoped that Boer farmers who were required to do these things for their Khoi servants would treat them better. Khoi who were mistreated were given the right to complain to the authorities. The law also required all Khoi traveling from their residence to another destination to carry a pass from their master. This, it was thought, would make masters more responsible, but it had the effect of forcing Khoi to work as servants. Conservative protections aimed to establish a kindlier, paternalistic system based on a highly idealized view of the English countryside in order to reinforce a system of domination and discrimination.[1]

More liberal voices began to be heard in the Cape Colony, thanks in part to the arrival of British merchants and settlers. Most significantly, the rule of law came to be established. Between 1827 and 1832, the British took away the governor's judicial powers and established a supreme court, circuit courts, and local resident magistracies. Trial by jury was instituted. English became the official language of the courts but Dutch influence was not completely abolished. In the civil law, English laws and procedures were grafted onto the Roman-Dutch law in a way that showed respect for local practices. In criminal law, the Roman-Dutch law was largely superseded by English common law, particularly through the introduction of jury trials and English laws of evidence. Criminal punishments were changed, too. Under the Dutch, punishments for rebellious slaves and servants had been directed at the body. Torture, flogging, branding, and mutilation were practiced, as were various grisly forms of execution. Under the British, capital punishment was retained, taking the form of hangings, but other punishments of the body were withdrawn. Settlers, too, could no longer inflict major punishments on slaves and servants; resentful patriarchs would have to turn over serious cases to British resident magistrates. The law, not the patriarch, would have hegemony, even on the frontier.[2]

Settler men pushed for the government of the Cape to take their voices into account. Journalists secured freedom of the press and freedom of speech. In 1826, the British created an advisory council with six official members. They met with the governor, although the governor had the authority to dismiss them. In 1834, the Cape received a new constitution, which provided for a small, appointed, bicameral legislature. The governor was required to consult with the Executive Council, the upper house of four officials. The governor also appointed the members of the lower house, the Legislative Council, which included five officials of the government and between five and seven leading citizens. The Legislative Council could initiate some legislation. If the governor declined the recommendations of either house, he had to explain his reasons to the secretary of state in London.

Over the years the continued authority of the governor dissatisfied colonists, who felt that their interests were often overridden by Britain.

---

[1] Keegan, *Colonial South Africa*, 54–5. Penn, *Forgotten Frontier*, 268.
[2] Crais, *White Supremacy and Black Resistance*, 58.

In 1853, the British government acceded to the colonists' requests and granted the Cape a representative parliament that was designed, in large part, by settlers. The parliament had two houses whose members were elected by males who either earned £50 per year or who occupied a building worth £25. This partly representative parliament was also "partly responsible." In other words, it was not a fully self-governing parliament, like the legislatures in many long-standing British colonies. A British governor was appointed by the king or queen to serve as the head of state at the Cape. The governor also acted as a "high commissioner," or ambassador plenipotentiary, to the rest of southern Africa. The governor reported to the Colonial Office, a department of the British cabinet headed by the secretary of state for the colonies. Slow communication between London and Cape Town allowed the governor a degree of latitude. The governor proposed laws and policies, acting on the advice of the secretary of state in London as well as the heads of Cape government departments. The two houses of the Cape parliament, the Legislative Council and the Legislative Assembly, had the power to accept or reject the governor's initiatives, but they did not form a government. The Cape parliament also did not control foreign relations, which remained the prerogative of the British government. The Cape could raise a militia but it had no say over the use of regular British troops. In these ways, the Cape did not achieve complete self-government, although it supposedly did benefit from the presence of British soldiers and sailors.[3]

Liberal, parliamentary reforms in the Cape Colony were linked to liberal, parliamentary reforms in Britain. Both the 1832 reform of the British parliament and the 1833 emancipation of colonial slaves helped to institute liberal reform in the colonies. But by the 1850s and 1860s, rebellions in India and Jamaica were making colonial reform less popular among Britons, while a new pseudo-scientific racism painted Africans and Asians in an unflattering light. By the middle of the century, penny-pinching officials in the British government were less likely to support costly colonial interventions for the sake of humanitarianism. Humanitarian liberals who sought universal social reforms were ultimately eclipsed by utilitarian liberals who believed that free trade and balanced accounts would benefit society as a whole, even if some fared poorly.

Cape liberalism counted, among its key supporters, evangelical Christian missionaries who held views that contradicted the core values of

---

[3] For further details, see McCracken, *Cape Parliament*. See also Davenport, "Consolidation of a New Society," 311–33.

many Boers. In 1799, the interdenominational, nonconformist London Missionary Society (LMS) began its work among the Cape Colony's Khoi by sending a Dutch veteran of the Napoleonic Wars, J. T. van der Kemp. The new missionary did a number of things that indicated his disregard for the racial order. He founded a mission community where he lived side by side with Khoi people and he even married a Khoi woman. Van der Kemp became an advocate for Khoi rights, and even had Boers brought up on charges of mistreating laborers in circuit court shortly before his death in 1811. His successors, James Read and John Philip, also advocated Khoi rights in the colony, particularly their right to settle labor disputes in court. The views of Philip and his LMS colleagues have been summarized by the historian Leonard Thompson, who writes that they put their faith in "education, Christianity, and freedom from preindustrial constraints" as a recipe for the improvement of all the people of South Africa.[4]

Settler treatment of the Xhosa and the other African people of the Eastern Cape became a major cause for colonial liberals and even for liberals in England. Realizing that local reactions were often negative and obstructive, the missionaries worked to bypass local rulers by communicating directly with powerful figures in Britain, including members of parliament, a classic pattern for activists to follow under colonialism.[5] During the early decades of British rule in South Africa, liberal philanthropists often bypassed the Cape governor and the local elites. The best-known example came in 1826, when Philip sensed he was failing to make progress in South Africa and went to London. Two years of speaking, publishing, and lobbying resulted in the implementation of Ordinance 50 of 1828, which guaranteed free Khoi and mixed-race (or Coloured) people equality before the law. The rise of parliamentary liberalism was also making slave owners uneasy. The British parliament abolished the slave trade in 1807, "ameliorated" the condition of colonial slaves during the 1820s, and emancipated the slaves between 1833 and 1840. The passage of slave emancipation was clearly linked to the passage of the Reform Act of 1832, which equalized representation among the various parliamentary districts and allowed all middle-class men to vote. In the Cape Colony, pressure for amelioration and emancipation was related to the imposition of Ordinance 50 of 1828, which granted equal rights under the law to all free Khoi. After the emancipation of the slaves in

---

[4] Thompson, *History of South Africa*, 59.
[5] Keck and Sikkink, *Activists beyond Borders*, 12–14.

1833, even more Khoi and Coloured males in the Cape became technically equal, although all women as well as "Bantu" Africans and San remained subject to legal disabilities.[6]

Many settlers perceived a threat from Ordinance 50, as well as from slave emancipation and other administrative actions that undermined patriarchy. They held these suspicions in spite of the fact that Ordinance 50 and slave emancipation were not intended to overturn settler economic power or to remedy indigenous impoverishment. Ordinance 50 did not even guarantee all free male Cape residents equality before the law. Technically speaking, nonracial, male equality was first embodied in the Masters and Servants Ordinance of 1841. This act, which was passed at the insistence of the great liberal secretary of state for the colonies, Lord John Russell, established the principle that Cape laws should be "colour-blind." Yet the ordinance made it possible for laborers who broke contracts to be punished severely. It may have been color-blind in the literal sense, but it was understood that this law was the best way to regulate the behavior of ex-slaves, none of whom were white. It is worth noting, as the historian Tim Keegan has pointed out, that the result of the legislation was to extend "proletarianisation and economic dependence among the labouring classes" so that "their chances of real freedom from servility were severely limited."[7] Liberalism had its down side: while liberals supported legal equality, they had an economic and social interest in making available a ready supply of labor.

Guns along the Eastern Frontier in the Early Nineteenth Century

Local conditions influenced important divergences between British and Cape political cultures, particularly on the related subjects of citizenship, militia service, and gun ownership. During the nineteenth century, many people in Britain and the Cape Colony owned guns. Yet there were differences in the ways that both societies approached gun ownership. Early in the century, Britons did worry about the consequences of the French Revolution and the Industrial Revolution, but the level of risk and uncertainty in Britain was nothing like that felt in South Africa. Then, over the course of the nineteenth century, Britain became more secure. The level of risk from insurrection and crime declined, while the ownership of firearms became more widespread. It was only in the late nineteenth

---

[6] Keegan, *Colonial South Africa*, 103–7.
[7] Keegan, *Colonial South Africa*, 124.

century that notions of individual rights and duties as citizens to preserve order started to be eclipsed by notions of state responsibility for security. And then it was only in the early twentieth century that serious measures were taken to reduce the number of firearms in Britain, largely in response to concerns about the possibility, again, of violent revolution.[8]

By contrast, individual and collective insecurity remained high in South Africa throughout the nineteenth century. Gun ownership remained a firm part of the political culture of Africans, Boers, and Britons alike. In fact, as indicated below, during the turbulent 1870s the government of the Cape was positively encouraging settlers to buy more guns and to take more target practice. Insecurity and gun ownership also played major roles in the political cultures of Africans. All groups of people bought guns with the purpose of defending themselves as well as their communities and their governments.

During the earlier decades of the nineteenth century, significant changes in political culture also preoccupied Africans, who comprised the vast majority of the population. Many African people were on the move, thanks in part to several factors: prolonged droughts during the 1810s and 1820s, aggressive Zulu expansion in the northeast, the arrival of European settlers in the Eastern Cape and the northern interior, and widespread raiding and trading for cattle and slaves. As people migrated, new African chiefdoms formed, as well as new Boer and Griqua republics. The historian Norman Etherington, in his book *The Great Treks*, has called attention to the importance of chiefship as opposed to tribe or ethnicity as the driving concept behind political culture.

While political culture changed significantly, the spread of guns proceeded apace. By the late 1820s, most African chiefs had heard of the prowess conveyed by guns and sought to acquire them in ever greater numbers. European traders reached farther to the north, supplying Europeans and Africans with muskets. Muskets provided economic security because hunting could be lucrative. Muskets also provided personal and collective security during a time of major conflicts. Muskets became linked to new ways of war as well as to new forms of political culture, much like they had been in Europe during the sixteenth and seventeenth centuries.

From 1795 to 1825, the colony's new British government adopted violent, authoritarian policies toward Africans, especially those along the border. For much of the eighteenth century the VOC had relied on

---

[8] Malcolm, *Guns and Violence*, 90–132. Squires, *Gun Culture or Gun Control?* 25–9.

burgher commandos to patrol the frontier. The British regarded the Cape as a low priority, but were still willing to replace commandos with regular troops, believing that professional soldiers were better able to maintain order on the frontier. The British continued to restrict the flow of arms and ammunition until most of the rebellious burghers of Graaff-Reinet accepted their authority in 1796. In 1799, the Boers rebelled again, objecting to supposedly lenient British policies toward the Xhosa. In the fighting that followed, regular British forces were joined by a newly formed Cape Corps, made up of Khoi troops who had been trained according to the standards of the British Army. A mixed British and Khoi force sailed to Algoa Bay and marched inland to Graaff-Reinet, where the force captured many of the trekboer leaders and restored British control. The British–Khoi force then turned on the Gqunukhwebe Xhosa and attempted to push them out of the Zuurveld and across the colonial boundary. The Gqunukhwebe fought the British to a standstill, with the help of their own Khoi allies. These Khoi were not only mounted and armed with guns but they succeeded in drawing Khoi servants away from the trekboers. Order collapsed in the Eastern Cape, and from the Fish River and Graaff-Reinet in the east to as far west as Swellendam, trekboers and settlers left the area.[9]

The peace treaty of 1803 ended the war between Britain and the Batavian Republic, making it possible for the Cape Colony to revert to Dutch control. When the conflict between Britain and Napoleon resumed in 1806, the British returned to the Cape and restored their administration. Soon after the British established a new colonial government, they committed themselves to restoring order on the Eastern Cape frontier. To do so, they used new tactics of total war against the Xhosa. The governor, Sir John Cradock, requested that forces under Lt. Col. John Graham drive the Xhosa east across the Fish River. On Christmas Day, 1811, Graham's troops, made up of regular British soldiers, Boer commandos, and the Khoi Cape Corps, marched and rode into Xhosa territory. The fighting that followed was marked by a new British tactic. The British, along with their Khoi and Boer allies, burned Xhosa farms and killed noncombatants indiscriminately. By August 1812, Xhosa families were driven across the Fish River, making it possible for the British to possess the Zuurveld. The location of Graham's headquarters came to be called Grahamstown. Graham's ruthless tactics involved a great deal more than

[9] Saunders, Bundy, and Oakes, *Illustrated History of South Africa*, 74–5.

hit-and-run attacks and cattle rustling. His use of skilled Khoi cavalry drew on the experience of the previous two wars.[10] These Khoi, formerly known as the Cape Corps, now called the Cape Regiment, fought successfully against the Xhosa but posed problems for colonial policy. The arming and training of these Khoi was resented by many frontier Boers. The presence of the Cape Regiment formed one of the principal grievances of the Boers, who revolted and then were defeated in the Slagtersnek Rebellion of 1813.[11]

Xhosa men were still lightly armed with firearms, using them to supplement their conventional fighting weapon, the assegai, or javelin. They did not take up guns and associated tactics wholesale. To a certain extent, the small volume and clandestine nature of the gun trade made it so. When engaging enemies who were highly skilled with firearms but outnumbered, the Xhosa men fought like guerrillas. They dispersed with their families and cattle into the Amatola Mountains, a difficult, heavily wooded terrain that was difficult for British and colonial forces to attack. There, they were able to use firearms and assegais to ambush British and colonial forces.[12] Other tactics for coping with British and colonial arms were less successful. Between 1815 and 1818, drought and poverty exacerbated accusations of cattle stealing among Xhosa men and also between them and the colonists. In some of the raids, firearms were stolen as well as cattle.[13] The firearms that were stolen, as well as the ones that were bought illegally, were put to use in raiding and fighting. Some colonial officials believed that a desire to acquire weapons sparked the Xhosa chiefs' interest in attacking Grahamstown.[14]

In 1818, the governor, Lord Charles Somerset, intervened in a dispute between the Ngqika and Ndlambe Xhosa, ordering colonial troops to confiscate 23,000 Ndlambe cattle. Six thousand Ndlambe attacked Grahamstown in 1819, led by a prophet, Nxele, who claimed that the African god would ensure that British bullets would be turned to water. Nxele's millennial claims have been analyzed by several historians. For present purposes, the battle of Grahamstown in 1819 is interesting in that it illustrates the ways in which Xhosa tactics were becoming more like British tactics. It was reported at the time that several British soldiers

---

[10] Saunders, Bundy, and Oakes, *Illustrated History of South Africa*, 103.
[11] Giliomee, *Afrikaners*, 85.
[12] Stockenstrom, *Autobiography*, 154.
[13] Theal, *Records of the Cape Colony*, 12:135.
[14] Theal, *Records of the Cape Colony*, 12:201.

had deserted to the Xhosa side, including a sergeant of the Royal Africa Corps who had become a minor chief.[15] A number of Khoi men who were skilled with firearms were also reported to be among the Ndlambe. As Nxele moved his troops into position around Grahamstown, it seemed that the Ndlambe force was marching into fixed positions in a way that resembled a European army. Even so, there seem to have been only a few muskets on the Xhosa side, and these were fired ineffectively. The warriors were still mainly armed with assegais. It appears that Nxele hoped that superior numbers would carry the town, regardless of any claims of turning bullets to water. Opposed to the 6,000 Ndlambe Xhosa, the commander, Lt. Col. Thomas Willshire, had only 450 troops and burgher militiamen, several cannon, plus eighty-two Khoi troopers from the Cape Regiment.

Willshire defended the town successfully, demonstrating the skill of British forces in marksmanship and volley firing. It helped that many of the soldiers and officers were veterans of the Napoleonic Wars, where they had honed their skills under pressure. Their victory also showed the devastating effects of light artillery and the importance of having skilled allies. When Ndlambe forces charged the town, the combination of cannon firing shrapnel shells and soldiers firing muskets in volleys was devastating. Even so, the Xhosa force was so large that it seemed, for a few moments, that they might take the town. At that moment, a force of 150 Khoi marksmen led by the well-known Khoi hunter, Boesak, arrived at Grahamstown. They joined the British ranks and began to pick off the Xhosa leadership as well as the rank and file. The Xhosa force sustained heavy casualties and fled. The British lost three soldiers.[16]

British veterans of the battle described it as a "near-run thing" in which they were almost overwhelmed. The Xhosa did charge up to the mouths of the cannons, yet the higher casualties on the Xhosa side show that the contest was lopsided. It is conventionally thought that colonial warfare became lopsided only with the introduction of breech-loading rifles, machine guns, and quick-firing artillery in the 1860s and 1870s, as Headrick argued in *The Tools of Empire*. The Battle of Grahamstown shows that earlier in the nineteenth century, the combination of hunters'

---

[15] Theal, *Records of the Cape Colony*, 12:201.

[16] Pringle, *Narrative*, 281. Mostert, *Frontiers*, 472. Mostert cites Thompson, *Travels*, 1:36, 2:199; Cory, *Rise of South Africa*, 1:390; Theal, *Records of the Cape Colony*, 12:193, 203; *Cape Monthly Magazine*, May 1876, 297–303.

marksmanship with the disciplined volley firing and artillery of regular soldiers could be quite lethal, too.

The Xhosa defeat at Grahamstown made the Eastern Cape frontier safe for settlement again. The Boers drifted back and in 1820, a British government scheme introduced 4,000 British settlers to the Zuurveld. They were promised land, but few of them realized how hard it would be to farm in this environment. Furthermore, few of them realized how much their presence was resented by the Xhosa until they were greeted by the landdrost of Uitenhage, Jacob Cuyler, who warned them, "When you go out to plough, never leave your guns at home."[17] Such a statement was a throwback to the seventeenth century, when the VOC required free burghers to have their guns with them at all times. The warning startled many British settlers, who were also surprised to learn that they were expected to join the burgher militia. Few of them had any experience of military exercises, especially by comparison to their Boer neighbors, who knew how to conduct offensive operations in a commando and how to defend themselves by circling wagons in a laager.[18]

Guns, Trade, and Warfare in Early Natal

The 1820 settlers arrived during a time of turbulence. A conflict was simmering in the Eastern Cape that they would be forced to take part in. The new pressure of migration and settlement on the land was made worse by drought. Furthermore, the rise of powerful chiefs and new chiefdoms to the northeast, including Matiwane, Shaka, and Sobhuza, provoked much fighting. These chiefs and their followers caused extensive conflicts in Zululand and Natal during the 1810s and 1820s, setting refugees in motion throughout the region, in a process that has been called the *Mfecane*, the "time of troubles." The region's societies were tightly knit around the *amabutho* system, which organized young men into age-based regiments. The men in the regiment would be permitted to marry by the chief according to the availability of increasingly scarce resources. The *amabutho* system helped to distribute resources efficiently; it also made for effective fighting forces. The system is often credited to Shaka, but it is likely that fighting in age-based regiments predates the famous Zulu chief, as the practice of *amabutho* appears to have been widespread in the eighteenth century.

---

[17] Saunders, Bundy, and Oakes, *Illustrated History of South Africa*, 98.
[18] Mostert, *Frontiers*, 668–9.

The *amabutho* acted as a kind of militia, to be called up when the chief needed them. The organization of young men into age-based regiments helped chiefs procure fighters when needed. The system also helped them organize labor for cattle raising, farming, and hunting. By the end of the eighteenth century, population pressure on limited natural resources stimulated the rise of powerful chiefs as well as competition for land. Competition for land was exacerbated by severe droughts in 1809, and again from 1820 to 1823.[19]

In addition to farming and cattle raising, northeastern African economies depended to a lesser extent on hunting. As in agriculture, there was considerable overlap between mobilization for fighting and hunting. Skill in hunting was closely related to skill in fighting. For both activities the weapons were the same: short stabbing spears and long throwing spears, used in combination with axes, clubs, and shields. Norman Etherington has pointed out that the chiefs honed their leadership skills by taking their *amabutho* on hunting expeditions. Organized hunting was especially important when the quarry consisted of large animals. Hunters spread out to locate animals and then worked together to drive them into spiked pits, or into ambushes, where they were killed by warriors wielding spears.[20]

Social and environmental conditions help explain conflict in the coastal lowlands to the northeast of the Xhosa. Historians have also examined the ways in which trade from Portuguese Mozambique, particularly the slave trade, also destabilized the region. Northeast warriors and lowland chiefs probably learned about guns first from the Portuguese at Delagoa Bay, near the colonial capital Lourenço Marques, which is today called Maputo. Yet early contacts did not result in the widespread adoption of guns. The informants of the late nineteenth-century ethnographer James Stuart told him that the Portuguese only brought trade goods, not guns.[21] The Portuguese prohibited the gun trade because they feared that muskets might make warfare in Africa more lethal. They also believed that trading guns might give added leverage to their African trading partners. There was not much trade in guns during the sixteenth and seventeenth centuries, which Etherington attributes to Portugal's success in imposing restrictions. He argues that guns entered the Delagoa trade in the eighteenth century only, when rival merchants flaunted Portuguese

[19] Guy, "Ecological Factors in the Rise of Shaka and the Zulu Kingdom."
[20] Etherington, *Great Treks*, 19.
[21] *James Stuart Archive*, 2:144.

regulations. Even then, while there were reports of lowlanders purchasing guns and horses, the trade in ivory and slaves appears to have been much more important.[22] The gun trade between Natal and Portuguese traders from Mozambique only appears to have become brisk toward the middle of the nineteenth century.

Historians have debated the extent to which trade disrupted the area that is today KwaZulu-Natal.[23] The region may have been disrupted by other factors, too. In any event, everybody agrees that the 1810s and 1820s were turbulent times in this part of Southeastern Africa. By around 1810, there were three powerful chiefdoms: Ndwandwe, led by Zwide; Ngwane, led by Sobhuza; and Mthethwa, led by Dingiswayo. These three chiefdoms came into conflict over land as well as over control of the trade routes leading to Delagoa Bay. A series of wars resulted in the Ngwane fleeing to present-day Swaziland and the Ndwandwe driving the Mthethwa as far south as the Tugela River. In 1818, the Zulu chief Shaka, who was serving as one of Dingiswayo's generals, assassinated his commander and took control of the Mthethwa. He advanced northward again, consolidating his rule by incorporating many groups into alliances and by driving out his opponents.

The Zulu were led by Shaka up until 1828, when his half-brother Dingane assassinated him and succeeded to the chiefship. Under Shaka and Dingane, the Zulu incorporated firearms into their fighting and hunting in ways that were relatively limited. At first, when the British trader Henry Francis Fynn demonstrated muskets for Shaka, the chief was skeptical. He believed that a shield "dipped into water previous to an attack, would be sufficient to ward off the effect of a ball fired when they were at a distance, and in the interval of reloading they would come to close quarters, when we, having no shield, would drop our guns and attempt to run, but, as we are unable to run as fast as his soldiers, we must all inevitably fall into their hands."[24] A later demonstration of firearms impressed Shaka more. As Fynn told the story in his famous account, one evening Shaka

amused himself by treating with ridicule the power of European firearms, urging that native assegais were far superior. I contended that with our guns, we could kill elephant, sea-cow [hippopotamus], buffalo and all other kinds of game, as

[22] Etherington, *Great Treks*, 19–20, 30–1.
[23] Cobbing, "The Mfecane as Alibi." Eldredge, "Sources of Conflict." Hamilton, "The Character and Objects of Shaka." Omer-Cooper, "Has the Mfecane a Future?" Peires, "Paradigm Deleted."
[24] Fynn, *Diary*, 81–2.

well as the birds of the air, and do so at a distance their assegais could not reach. He however persisted in his argument until I retired to rest.... About an hour later a messenger appeared to say that Shaka required our immediate presence with our guns, as a troop of elephants was close at hand. I immediately went to the King and begged him not to require us to shoot the animals as the guns we had were fit only for killing birds and small game. I told him that the one used for shooting elephants was of a larger kind. I merely got laughed at for my pains.... He insisted on our going, so off we went. Our army was eight to ten strong. We had among us only three fowling pieces, two blunderbusses, and four muskets. I must say that it was fully in expectation of being laughed at by everyone that we reluctantly set forth on this venture. We arranged among ourselves to approach to within 40 yards of the animals, then to fire a volley with no other hopes than that the elephants would turn and make off. It was evident, as we proceeded in the direction of the elephants, that the several Zulu regiments that accompanied us depended solely on our efforts, or, at least, were determined not to use their own weapons until we had failed. We had travelled about half an hour when we suddenly came upon a troop of 16 elephants. We marched slowly and cautiously towards them, but as we were manoeuvring to get within the distance we had decided upon one of the sailors suddenly fired at the nearest bull. To the astonishment of the Zulus and to our far greater astonishment, the elephant dropped dead. It was some time before we could satisfy ourselves of the fact as to how such a thing could have occurred, for in those days it was considered almost impossible to kill with leaden balls. Shaka's consternation was great, and he admitted that our weapons were superior to his own.

On examining the elephant, we found the bullet had penetrated the ear. It was a mere chance shot. The sailor was certainly not accustomed to using a gun, he had no more knowledge of shooting than sailors usually possess, nor had he ever seen an elephant before.[25]

This was, in fact, a very lucky shot. This and other hunting expeditions caused Fynn to be remembered in a Zulu praise-poem as "He who points with a stick and thunder and lightning come forth,/ Everything that he points at falls and dies," and also as a "pusher-aside of elephants so that they fall."[26] Other demonstrations to commoners made strong impressions, too. In 1826, he demonstrated how to shoot a hippopotamus with a musket. Every time he fired, a group of Zulu "fell on their faces to the ground, made a hissing noise, at the same time shaking their fingers, as they observed, to prevent the 'issebum,' or musket, doing them harm."[27]

Fynn's account has been criticized for being fanciful and self-serving. When he described Shaka's fascination with guns, Fynn plainly relished

[25] Fynn, *Diary*, 120–1.
[26] *Izibongo: Zulu Praise-Poems*, 192–4.
[27] Isaacs, *Travels and Adventures*, 1:144.

knowing something Shaka did not know. His knowledge gave him power at a time when the balance of power was held by the Zulu chief. Fynn's account was even imitated in 1885 by Rider Haggard, who described, in *King Solomon's Mines*, how the characters Curtis, Good, and Quatermain demonstrated their superiority to the "Kukuanas" by firing guns at targets.[28] As fanciful as these accounts by Haggard and Fynn may seem, the Zulu men who were interviewed by James Stuart tended to confirm Fynn's reportage. According to one informant, Bikwayo, before Fynn visited Shaka he appeared at the kraal of a lesser chief, Sinqila of the Ngati, who brought him to a higher chief, Magaye. Magaye offered Fynn the customary ox to slaughter. With Magaye, his counselors, and many of his followers watching, Fynn shot the ox. "Magaye was much impressed," and decided to report Fynn to Shaka.[29]

Shaka's fascination with guns was great, according to James Stuart's other informants. One man, Jantshi, reported that Shaka was so fascinated with guns that he considered leading a regiment to England so that they could watch guns being made.[30] Another source, Makuza, confirmed this story and said that the demonstrations impressed Shaka so much, he wanted to go to England; the only thing that prevented him was a bad prophecy.[31] The demonstration of the new technology apparently did play an important role as Shaka assessed the implications of the British arrival in Natal. It functioned in the same way as the earlier demonstrations that the Dutch did at the Cape: "shock and awe" was interesting because it revealed a disparity in power and pointed the way to the creation of a new order. One matter only makes Fynn's case different from the original VOC Dutch at the Cape: they did not wish to sell their guns, while Fynn did. His demonstration of a musket was intended to make Shaka realize the limits of his power, but it was also the demonstration of a product that Fynn probably hoped to sell, either in the present or in the future.

Shaka was impressed enough with firearms that, in a subsequent war, he directed Fynn and his associates to join the fighting. Fynn's group brought along their muskets, but could not keep up with the main Zulu force. Their Xhosa interpreter, Jacob, took a musket from Fynn's group

---

[28] Haggard, *King Solomon's Mines*, 74, 92.
[29] *James Stuart Archive*, 1:96–7.
[30] *James Stuart Archive*, 1:192, 1:200, 2:162.
[31] *James Stuart Archive*, 2:166. Another positive description of one of Fynn's gun demonstrations is given by Mayinga on 2:258.

and fired a few shots at the enemy. This demonstration may have made some impression but it had little effect on the battle's outcome.[32] Shaka still recruited Fynn and other British traders to act as mercenaries. One of them, Nathaniel Isaacs, recorded that their initial use of firearms terrified Shaka's opponents.[33] Even so, according to Fynn, after one battle in 1827 Shaka "took every opportunity of depreciating" the role of a small force of British and Khoi traders and sailors "and minimizing the value of fire-arms in the estimation of his people."[34] Fynn, Isaacs, and other British traders as well as Portuguese musketeers from Delagoa all fought occasionally in regional warfare. As late as 1836, thirty "English residents" participated in the campaign of Dingane, Shaka's successor, against Sobhuza's Swazis. Participation in Zulu wars guaranteed survival and prosperity. Initially, in the 1820s, they fought as a separate unit, but in 1836 they were joined by forty Zulu, armed with guns.[35] Word reached the Cape that British and American merchants were selling arms to Zulu men.[36]

Dingane employed mercenaries but he sensed the grave threat posed by an enemy armed with guns, horses, and artillery. He gathered intelligence from the Eastern Cape about the subjugation of the Xhosa chiefs and their losses in the face of an enemy armed with guns and horses.[37] Dingane insisted on demonstrations of firearms as late as 1830. In one demonstration, Isaacs's servant was ordered to execute two female prisoners by shooting them. Isaacs wrote, "The king and his savage warriors, from whose imprecations I am convinced this execution emanated, were astounded at the effect of firearms, for at each report they shook their fore-fingers, and simultaneously exclaimed 'Eezee!' an ejaculation in battle signifying contempt."[38] Shortly afterwards, Dingane asked Isaacs to demonstrate a small fowling piece and a larger musket by shooting into a tree. Isaacs recorded the "more they gazed, the more their wonder grew." Isaacs continued:

They were unanimous, however, in declaring that it would be impossible to fight against such weapons. The king had often asked me for a musket, and did so

---

[32] Fynn, *Diary*, 126.

[33] Isaacs, *Travels and Adventures*, 1:165–6.

[34] Fynn, *Diary*, 130.

[35] Fynn, *Diary*, 249. The existence of a Zulu unit armed with muskets was confirmed in James Stuart's interview of Mkando. See *James Stuart Archive*, 3:148–9.

[36] Campbell to Bell, November 26, 1830, in Bird, *Annals of Natal*, 196–7.

[37] Etherington, *Great Treks*, 214–15.

[38] Isaacs, *Travels and Adventures*, 2:40.

again to-day; but I told him my king would perhaps charge me with cowardice, and kill me, were he to find that I had parted with a musket. He said he only wanted one for himself to frighten away the Umtagarties, people who came near his hut; however I thought it most advisable to keep him in the dark respecting the power of muskets, as the more familiar they should become with their use, the less apprehensive they would be of their effects.[39]

According to this way of thinking, the more the Zulu became familiar with guns, the less risk they would perceive from Europeans armed with them. Isaacs was linking perception and skill, which many more people were to do in nineteenth-century South Africa. His account sheds interesting light on the thinking of the earliest Europeans in Natal, even if it has not proven to be an objective and reliable source of information about the Zulu and their neighbors.

In spite of Isaacs's hesitations, trading large numbers of guns to the Zulu appears to have started around the mid-1830s. Fynn mentioned that in 1836, a trader sold Dingane an elephant gun for the price of thirty or forty head of cattle. When other traders learned how greatly the Zulu valued guns, they followed suit and sold several more guns to the chief. One double-barrelled elephant gun sold for the price of six elephant teeth. The principal objections to these sales came from the African refugees who had sheltered under the British traders at Port Natal. According to Fynn, "at present, the minds of the natives are completely alienated." They observed "that if the whites will supply their inveterate enemy with guns, etc., for a few pounds of ivory, or a few head of cattle, how can they be assured that their lives may not as readily be bartered away."[40] Trading in guns across the colonial boundary without a government permit was illegal.

The Cape government appears to have first become aware of gun trading in Natal in 1830, when the civil commissioner in Grahamstown wrote to the governor's secretary to inform him that Nathaniel Isaacs had led an American schooner to Port Natal, where it unloaded a cargo that included muskets and powder. The commissioner expressed his concern that Isaacs was teaching Zulu men how to shoot, too.[41] The trade came to the attention of the Cape Town press, although one liberal newspaper played down the trade's seriousness, by reporting that "the traders trading with Dingane in guns and powder are becoming rich – but they have hit

[39] Isaacs, *Travels and Adventures*, 48–9.
[40] Fynn, *Diary*, 255–6.
[41] Bird, *Annals of Natal*, 1:196–7.

on a happy expedient of cheating the Chief, who has at last discovered the roguery. They sell him guns, but before delivering them they take either the mainspring out of the lock, or some screw, which renders the gun useless."[42]

It seems unlikely that such simple-minded trickery would work beyond the first instance. There were plenty of stories from all around Africa that Europeans peddled shoddy guns to Africans, yet the stories make little sense. Guns that were cheaply made could still be effective, especially when the users knew how to load them properly. The most cheaply made Birmingham muskets were designed to be fired with a low-strength powder.[43] Improperly loaded guns did indeed explode, but the self-interest of the buyer and the seller assured for the most part the quality of the merchandise. The volume of the trade was impressive, with some historians contending that "trade guns" made for African, Indian, Latin American, Middle Eastern, and Native American buyers, represent the bulk of British gunmaking between 1650 and 1900.[44] Some inferior weapons were sold, but allegations that shoddy and dangerous weapons were routinely sold to Africans have been shown to be false by Inikori and Richards, who studied West African arms sales and concluded that reports of poor-quality firearms were greatly exaggerated.[45]

It does seem likely that Dingane recognized that his warriors had much to learn about guns. When the missionary and retired naval officer Allen Francis Gardiner visited Dingane and his advisors in 1835, one advisor told the minister that the Zulu did not need to learn about "the Word." To quote Gardiner, Dingane's advisor "Tambooza observed that... such words as these they were sure they could not understand. If I would only instruct them in the use of the issibum (musket) I could stay, but these [words] were things they did not care about."[46] Dingane concurred. Over the next several years, he purchased an unknown quantity of muskets

---

[42] Fynn, *Diary*, 256–7. The newspaper article is cited by the editor of Fynn's diary: Cape Town's *South African Commercial Advertiser*, January 21, 1837.

[43] Artifex and Opifex, *Causes of Decay*, 128, reports that they were "used with a special very bright grained powder of low strength."

[44] Bailey and Nie, *English Gunmakers*, 7–8.

[45] Inikori, "The Import of Firearms into West Africa," 358–61. Richards, "West African Eighteenth-Century Firearms Imports," 52–7. See Greener, *Science of Gunnery*, 88–9, for a technical discussion of some of the weapons that were inferior.

[46] Gardiner, *Journey to the Zoolu Country*, 68. "Issibum" is obviously onomatopoetic. It is reported in several early accounts of gun trading in Natal. One of James Stuart's informants, Mcotoyi, contested the usage and claimed that the first Zulu word for gun was *isitunyisa*. *James Stuart Archive*, 3:57.

from British and American traders. This situation alarmed Gardiner, who was appointed to be a magistrate over Natal's British community in 1837, even though their settlement had not yet been formally annexed. Gardiner informed the government that

muskets have been introduced as an article of barter with the Zulus by some of the European settlers at or near the port. At present this traffic is in an incipient state; but so great is the avidity of the sovereign of that well-organized and warlike people to acquire this additional means for the extension of his territory and the subjugation of his neighbors, that I fear the very worst consequences, not only as regards the tranquillity of the settlement at Natal, but eventually of the whole Eastern frontier of the Cape, should no prompt and decisive measures be adopted to render such suicidal proceedings not only illegal but criminal.[47]

Merchants and Guns in the Eastern Cape

In Natal, as in the Cape, there was a tension between liberal ideology and the problems of disorder. Eastern Cape settlers often found themselves at odds with liberal missionaries, merchants, and officials. While liberal missionaries remained preoccupied with the treatment of Khoi and Xhosa people in the Eastern Cape, the other side of liberalism, trade, was booming. The British settlers of 1820 were supposed to become farmers. Few were originally farmers, and on account of drought, most experienced bad harvests that lasted for several years. Rules required the settlers to stay but many left anyway. Others turned to trade.

Grahamstown was turning into a major commercial hub, while along the eastern border of the colony, Cape settlers tapped into Xhosa trading networks. In order to regulate the trade, and in particular to restrict the trade in cattle, guns, ammunition, and liquor, the Cape government allowed closely supervised, weekly trade fairs to be conducted in border areas. The fairs were slow to start but some became highly successful. In 1824, 196 settlers traded at Fort Willshire in the Eastern Cape. The settlers came from lower social strata and tended to act as agents for Grahamstown merchants. Africans brought produce as well as goods like ivory, baskets, and honey, often selling their goods for beads. The sale of arms, ammunition, and liquor was forbidden, although it is possible that these were traded under the table. The Fort Willshire trade fairs were so successful that the concept spread to many different parts of the northern and eastern frontier. More trade began to occur outside of fairs, too. By

---

[47] Gardiner to Bell, March 18, 1837, in Bird, *Annals of Natal*, 1:314.

1825, trade was literally coming to the rescue of the struggling British settlements of the Eastern Cape.[48]

Growing trade changed the South African economy in a number of ways. Africans realized that European demand for animal products like ivory was extremely strong. Prices rose, making beads more expensive, thereby giving European traders an incentive to go into the interior. Plenty sold guns and powder, too, either legally or illegally. One official wrote that "the use of gunpowder is so general" that it was an imposition and an "inconvenience" to place a monopoly on it and have to keep records about it. Besides, "this restriction has not had the effect of preventing the smuggling trade in arms and gunpowder upon the frontier."[49] Others weighed in on the side of freeing up the trade, too, including liberal humanitarians and missionaries who believed that trade promoted Westernization. Freeing up the gun and powder trade would ensure that it would remain in the hands of British merchants, who feared competition from Americans, particularly in Natal.[50] The Cape government became lax in enforcing its own laws, until February 1832, when the colony officially liberalized its regulations on cross-border trade. A government "order-in-council" ended the state monopoly on powder sales, allowing merchants to import and sell it on their own account. In addition, more merchants were licensed to visit African communities to the east and north. It was still prohibited to sell guns and powder to the Xhosa and yet, as traders spread out, government supervision declined. Many Xhosa acquired firearms from merchants and farmers alike, although the specific details of this informal trade went unrecorded.[51]

Concerned by the spread of guns along the frontier, the Cape governors took action. In January 1834, the interim governor, Lt. Col. Thomas Wade, wrote to London to tell the secretary of state for the colonies that the quantity of arms and powder imported and sold by private traders had "immensely increased." In 1825, the major ports of the Cape Colony imported an annual total of 29,379 pounds of powder, while by 1833 the figure had risen to 67,148. Wade reported that the powder trade to Port Elizabeth had increased most noticeably, from 1,200 pounds in 1829 to 12,910 pounds in 1833, most of it bound for the interior towns of the Eastern Cape, and from there across into the northern frontier. The

[48] Beck, "The Legalization and Development of Trade," 167. Keegan, *Colonial South Africa*, 68–9.

[49] Theal, *Records of the Cape Colony*, 27:437.

[50] Pretorius, "British Humanitarians and the Cape Eastern Frontier," 21–2.

[51] Keegan, *Colonial South Africa*, 70–1.

powder trade had grown so brisk that most people were disregarding the old regulations on sales and safe storage. Concerning the illegal trade between colonists and Africans, Wade feared "that all classes residing near the frontier are, more or less, interested in this illicit traffic." He wrote mainly about the acquisition of guns and powder by the Boers, Baastards, and Griqua along the northern frontier, yet he suspected that should the Xhosa desire to switch from the assegai to the musket, they could do so readily. He proposed a new, extensive system of licensing traders, restricting sales, and regulating storage. He included stiffer penalties for violations, which were resisted by Cape merchants. Merchants successfully petitioned the Colonial Office to reduce the penalties. Wade's proposed ordinance was accordingly modified by the Colonial Office and put into place by his successor as governor, Sir Benjamin D'Urban.[52]

Arms sales were supported by missionaries as well as by traders. This seems ironic in light of some of the teachings of Jesus, but it must be remembered that nineteenth-century missionaries were concerned to bring the material benefits of civilization to Africans. For this reason, missions often contained trading posts that had as their object the encouragement of productivity among Africans. As Africans along the northern and eastern frontiers lost interest in beads, they sought more useful items. It was illegal to trade arms and ammunition to Africans, but some people accused missionaries of doing it anyway. For example, in 1835 rumors circulated in Cape Town that James Read (of the London Missionary Society) was involved in gun trading.[53] The rumor was plausible at least in part because missionaries had defended the rights of Africans as well as the principles of free trade.

Merchants, for their part, openly disregarded bans on the arms trade across the colonial border. Colonial officials turned a blind eye, too. In Cape Town, during the 1830s, sharp increases in gunpowder imports were noticed, yet officials did not act to staunch the flow. Restrictions might just cause Americans to gain control of the trade and shift it to another colony's port. Cape government officials were suspected of corrupt involvement in the trade.[54] And along the border, some Cape

---

[52] BPP, House of Commons Paper No. 252, June 1, 1835, Part Two, Despatch No. 31, Wade to Stanley, January 14, 1834; Despatch No. 32, Spring Rice to D'Urban, July 4, 1834; Despatch No. 33, D'Urban to Spring Rice, December 24, 1834; Despatch No. 34, Aberdeen to D'Urban, March 26, 1835, pp. 75–93. See also Lancaster, "The Governorship of Sir Benjamin D'Urban," 187–8.

[53] Philip to Kitchingman, 11 September [1835?], in *Kitchingman Papers*, 154–6.

[54] Lancaster, "Governorship of Sir Benjamin D'Urban," 186.

government officials responsible for regulating gunpowder sales were suspected of taking money under the table. Officials, settlers, and missionaries maintained that there was no risk from the trade, because Africans were technically incompetent, even though it was relatively easy to learn how to shoot a musket.[55] The Europeans who benefited from the arms trade downplayed the risks of arming Africans because further restrictions on the arms trade might undermine their profits.

By the mid-1830s, it appears that the Xhosa were purchasing more guns, most of which appeared to have been made in Birmingham, according to Captain Beresford, a British officer. They were not stolen British Army weapons, either, which meant that they must have been purchased from traders or farmers.[56] Some pointed the finger at Andries Stoffel, who worked with James Read. For such men to obtain these weapons, the early twentieth-century historian, George Cory, blamed the merchants of Grahamstown.[57]

Settlers who were involved in trade, licit and illicit, plowed their money into the establishment of commercial firms and also into agriculture. Throughout the 1830s and 1840s, the arms trade formed an important niche of settler-merchant strategies for accumulating cash. Merchants in Grahamstown, the center of frontier trade, were involved in arms trading. It was easy to get a start, since licenses to trade in arms and powder were then sold to anybody who cared to buy one. The trade was highly profitable, too. In the early days, according to Cory, one teacup full of powder worth two shillings could be exchanged for two cows worth three pounds.[58]

The pattern of trade was not changed by the new regulations. In 1838 the Eastern Cape's lieutenant governor stated that "I have not the slightest doubt that every merchant of the town is deeply concerned in this unlawful traffic."[59] The trade simply went further underground. Grahamstown storekeepers sold weapons and powder to "smouses," itinerant merchants who used numerous subterfuges, including packing guns into water barrels. The guns, which were often of a cheap description, were smuggled across the colonial boundary and sold with the help of Xhosa intermediaries. These middlemen sometimes hid the weapons in the thatched roofs of huts, waiting for their customers to appear at midnight

[55] Keegan, *Colonial South Africa*, 134–5.
[56] *Aborigines Committee Report*, 2491–8.
[57] Cory, *Rise of South Africa*, 3:52–3.
[58] Cory, *Rise of South Africa*, 3:200–1.
[59] Keegan, *Colonial South Africa*, 157.

rendezvous. The customers, in turn, bought the guns with cattle, some of which may have been stolen from the colonists, and which, in turn, may have originally been stolen from the Xhosa. The Xhosa were not the only buyers, either. In other cases, gun traders carried firearms north to the Orange River, where they sold weapons and ammunition to hunters bound for the interior.[60]

Guns and Racial Conflict

Some settlers denounced the Europeans who sold guns to Africans. Robert Godlonton, a settler politician and the publisher of the *Grahamstown Journal*, called the gun merchants "traitors" and predicted that during the next frontier war "which will surely take place sooner or later, and something more than inch-plank will be required to blockade your town and protect your stores."[61] Yet some settlers had good economic reasons for selling guns. Licit and illicit trade produced profits that financed land purchases as well as investments in merino sheep.

The conflict between the Xhosa and the Eastern Cape settlers was, at rock bottom, about access to land. Conflict over grazing rights was more or less inevitable. The best pastures lay on the border between the colony and the Xhosa. Khoi and Mfengu migrants put further pressure on Xhosa land. In 1829, the British government rewarded loyal Khoi with farmland in the Kat River valley, taking it away from the Ngqika Xhosa chief, Maqoma. He lost even more land in 1833, which caused him to resent the British and to forge alliances with the other Xhosa chiefs. At the same time as the British were confiscating Xhosa land, many Mfengu families were entering the region. *Mfengu* was a blanket term for Africans who were fleeing Zululand during the warfare associated with the rise of the Zulu state. The Mfengu refugees arrived with very little and attached themselves to Xhosa chiefs as clients. The Xhosa chiefs helped the Mfengu to build up their wealth, yet treated them as inferiors. For this reason, many Mfengu turned increasingly to the British settlers. They traded with merchants, worked for settlers, and began to convert to Christianity.

---

[60] Cory, *Rise of South Africa*, 4:336–9. Smuggling plots were occasionally uncovered: see "A Gun Powder Plot!!" *Grahamstown Journal*, August 14 and September 4, 1834, p. 3; see also "Illicit Trade in Guns," *Grahamstown Journal*, September 2, 1841.
[61] "Trade in Gun Powder," *Grahamstown Journal*, July 22, 1841, p. 2. Godlonton denounced gun trading on a number of occasions. See the *Grahamstown Journal*, July 15, 1841, p. 3; July 29, 1841, p. 3; September 2, 1841, p. 2; May 16, 1846, p. 2.

The establishment of the missionaries, merchants, and settlers – in other words, the establishment of a new order – placed considerable pressure on the Xhosa chiefs. Around Christmas of 1834, the Xhosa leadership reacted to pressure – pressure to adopt British ways of thinking as well as pressure on land and labor – by attacking the settlers. Thousands of Xhosa fighters crossed the boundary, causing Britons as well as the remaining Boers to flee to Grahamstown and other settlements. The Xhosa chiefs divided their forces, concentrating on attacking farms and killing male settlers while avoiding engagements with British troops and the Cape Mounted Rifles, the new name for the Khoikhoi Cape Corps or Cape Regiment. In the event, British forces retreated to Grahamstown, abandoning all other frontier outposts. In January 1835, Col. Harry Smith, a veteran of Wellington's Peninsular and Waterloo Campaigns, took command of the British forces and formed a militia of the British, Boer, and Khoi settlers. With them, he crossed the Fish River and attacked the Xhosa, who fought concealed in the forest. The Mfengu took advantage of the situation, stealing Xhosa cattle and occupying Xhosa land. The Xhosa fell back to the Amatola Mountains, where they continued to resist. Their assegais served them well in "bush fighting," where the javelins could be cut down and used in hand-to-hand fighting. Even so, there were numerous reports by settlers of Xhosa using muskets.[62]

It is interesting to speculate about whether or not the Xhosa would have been able to hold off the British had they fully and effectively adapted their military tactics to firearms. The Xhosa were not the only ones to believe that guns had their advantages as well as their disadvantages. In many situations, the muzzle-loading musket was not a good enough weapon to replace the highly successful regimental formations and guerrilla tactics that were associated with spears. Guns tended to be used as adjuncts to warfare and were interesting primarily for hunting. Increasingly, as the Xhosa, Zulu, and other Nguni speakers were coming into contact with regular British forces and also with Boer and Griqua commandos, they had to be able to defend against troops armed with firearms.

The war of 1834–5 came to an end when Harry Smith's troops bypassed the Amatolas and invaded the Transkei. During the campaign Smith captured Hintsa, chief of the Gcaleka Xhosa and paramount chief of all the Xhosa. Hintsa attempted escape and was killed in doubtful

---

[62] Mostert, *Frontiers*, 689–94. Moyer, "The Mfengu, Self-Defence, and the Cape Frontier Wars," 107. Bowker, "War Journal," passim.

circumstances that came to the attention of London. The Ngqika Xhosa under Maqoma and his allies surrendered to Smith, who, together with the governor, Sir Benjamin D'Urban, envisioned putting them under authoritarian rule and converting them to British ways. His ideas resonated with the previous fifty years of imperial policy, which favored despotic rule over newly subordinated peoples. To this end, D'Urban extended the boundaries of the colony eastward to the Great Kei River, dividing Xhosa lands into several territories, where Xhosa were to be governed by magistrates. Unfortunately for D'Urban and Smith, the despotic trend in imperial affairs associated with the Napoleonic era had ended around 1830, as the historian Christopher Bayly has argued in his book *Imperial Meridian*.[63] The British government was coming under the influence of humanitarian, evangelical liberals, who were appalled by Smith and D'Urban. Their plan to rule Xhosa territory all the way to the Great Kei River was overruled by Lord Glenelg, the secretary of state for the colonies, who insisted on withdrawal. He also insisted on implementing a system of treaties with the Xhosa chiefs. This move, much resented by the settlers of the Eastern Cape, sparked a growing interest in settler self-government. Yet another rule received public approval. The 1835 and 1836 treaties between the Cape and the Ngqika required disarmament. The 1835 treaty required the Ngqika to surrender "all the Musquets which may be in their possession," while the 1836 treaty, which regulated interaction between colonists and Ngqika, prohibited Ngqika from crossing the colonial border with arms. Mfengu who were settling in the vicinity were also prohibited by treaty from crossing the colonial border with arms.[64]

Concern about South Africa, as well as other frontier societies, remained high in Great Britain. The historian Alan Lester has written in *Imperial Networks* that the administrators, missionaries, and settlers in the Eastern Cape and other colonies shaped, and were shaped by, humanitarian and political discourses in Britain. In 1834, parliament created the Aborigines Committee, which met in 1836 and 1837 to hear evidence about the treatment of indigenous people in British colonies, including the Cape Colony, "in order to secure to them the due

---

[63] Bayly, *Imperial Meridian*, 8–9.

[64] The Ngqika (a.k.a. "Gaika") treaties of September 17, 1835, and December 5, 1836, were published in the Colony of the Cape of Good Hope, *Government Gazette*, October 2, 1835, and June 9, 1837. The Mfengu treaties are published in the *Government Gazette*, November 6, 1835; June 16, 1837; and June 23, 1837.

observance of Justice and the protection of their Rights; to promote the spread of Civilization among them, and to lead them to the peaceful and voluntary reception of the Christian Religion."[65] The committee had fifteen members, including Fowell Buxton, the antislavery activist; George Grey, future governor of New Zealand and the Cape Colony; and William Ewart Gladstone, future prime minister of Great Britain. The committee's hearings stirred up considerable debate about colonial policy, as members questioned the ethics of settlers and administrators, while advocating greater rights for indigenous people. The final recommendations included the strict regulation of the exchange of land and labor between settlers and natives; shifting the administration of indigenous people away from settlers and toward professional, imperial proconsuls; and moral support for missionaries in their efforts to make contacts and converts.[66]

As the Aborigines Committee delved into colonial policy, it confirmed that gun trading had become widespread. Witnesses such as Andries Stockenstrom, the former administrator of the Eastern Cape who had attempted to place limits on settler inroads upon the Xhosa, testified that the gun trade disrupted societies and stoked conflict.[67] The gun trade and the liquor trade, which were often discussed in the same breath, posed a dilemma for liberal humanitarians. Free trade was seen as one of the benefits of civilization, yet particular commodities like guns and brandy were not entirely beneficial.

As liberal humanitarians became influential in Britain, it seems that Xhosa men were probably acquiring more firearms. For several decades Xhosa had been working for the colonists, seeing, using, and buying guns. In the 1820s trade between Xhosa and colonists was becoming more brisk. Official colonial trade fairs began in 1824, open to Xhosa and colonists alike. It was forbidden to trade alcohol or guns but it is likely that significant numbers of guns changed hands. As Xhosa acquired guns and also horses, there were reports of armed, mounted Xhosa groups ranging west of the mountains and north of the Orange River, accumulating cattle as well as Khoi, San, and mixed-race followers in much the same way as the Griqua. There was sufficient concern about the Xhosa taking up arms that between 1833 and 1835, the Cape government restricted

---

[65] BPP 1836 VII (538), p. iii.
[66] Porter, "Trusteeship and Humanitarianism," 207–9.
[67] BPP 1836 VII (538), p. 242, l.2278. See also the hearsay testimony of the following humanitarian leaders: Dr. Thomas Hodgkin, p. 457, l.3902–3 and p. 638, l.5357, and the joint testimony of Mr. Dandison Coates, Rev. John Beecham, and Rev. William Ellis, p. 503, l.4335, and p. 540, l.4416.

the supply of guns and gunpowder to the Boers, who were thought to be trading with the Xhosa. Governor D'Urban's aide, Captain George Beresford, observed to the 1836 Aborigines Committee that the Xhosa were obtaining ordinary military muskets made in Birmingham, which implied the involvement of British smugglers. Another veteran appearing before the committee, Lt. Col. William Cox, observed that the smuggled weapons were inferior.[68] In 1839, the resident magistrate for Albany in the Eastern Cape investigated the gun trade, finding that the Xhosa were obtaining significant amounts of guns from local Khoi, particularly from the loyal, Christian Khoi who lived at the Kat River Settlement. Some Khoi were going into the towns to buy a few guns from merchants, then returning to the countryside to trade the guns, along with bullets and powder, for Xhosa cattle.[69]

In spite of taking up firearms, the Xhosa failed to contain the British advance. In the early 1840s, the Cape scrapped the treaty system and reverted to settling disputes by commando raiding. In 1846, the next war broke out between colonists and Xhosa. Xhosa fighters attacked settlers again, burning crops and farmhouses, and then retreated to the Amatolas. There, Xhosa resistance was tenacious. Some settlers claimed that the Xhosa were emboldened because they had bought even more muskets from Grahamstown settler-merchants.[70] Even so, there were variable reports about how Xhosa fighters used firearms. One British trooper, Buck Adams, related that in combat, the Xhosa often fired wildly from the hip. Adams claimed that they would have been better off relying simply on assegais, although there were a number of occasions when he felt threatened by Xhosa musketry. He reported, too, that the Xhosa were using Tower muskets, sturdy hand-me-down Brown Bess flintlocks discarded by the British Army.[71]

The Xhosa chiefs were forced to capitulate when, once again, the guerrilla war was fought to a stalemate and their crops were destroyed. The Xhosa men were not defeated in battle but instead their entire families were starved into capitulation. When the Xhosa leadership refused British demands to leave the lands west of the Kei River, British and Cape forces

---

[68] BPP 1836 VII (538), p. 256, l.2497–8; and p. 352, l.3240–3.

[69] BPP 1851 [424], vol. xxxviii, Despatch No. 9, Napier to Glenelg, July 12, 1838, p. 33; Enclosures to Lt. Governor's Despatch No. 40 of 1841, pp. 100–9. Etherington, *Great Treks*, 56–7. Giliomee, *Afrikaners*, 141. Peires, *House of Phalo*, 101–2, 117–18.

[70] Keegan, *Colonial South Africa*, 215.

[71] Adams, *Narrative*, 117–19, 133, 153, 183.

burned more of their crops and forced their families out. A change of administration in London, with Lord John Russell as prime minister and Earl Grey as secretary of state for the colonies, now made it possible for Xhosa territories up to the Great Kei River to come under British rule once again. Discussions about introducing a measure of settler self-rule were initiated, too. Even so, the governors who did the most in the 1840s and 1850s to introduce British rule to Xhosaland, Sir Henry Pottinger, Sir Harry Smith, and Sir George Grey, all recognized that they did not have the resources to rule directly. It was more expedient to rule indirectly, through the chiefs.

During wartime, pressure came from settlers and soldiers alike to control the spread of guns among the Xhosa. The *Graham's Town Journal*, published by the settler politician Robert Godlonton, attributed Xhosa power to the acquisition of firearms. Godlonton wrote that "the power of the . . . hostile tribes is derived in a great measure from their possession of fire-Arms, Ammunition and such Implements of War as they have obtained from certain of the Inhabitants and Traders of the Colony." The newspaper proposed that such "evil-disposed and treacherous persons" deserved capital punishment.[72] Ironically, the editor's own friends were implicated in gun smuggling.[73] This sort of hypocrisy was not uncommon, according to the lieutenant governor, John Hare. Hare wrote to the governor in 1839, describing how even settlers who clamored for more government protection were implicated in the arms trade. In fact, Hare had "not the slightest doubt that every merchant of the town is deeply concerned in this unlawful traffic, and that all are equally culpable."[74] Settlers from the Eastern Cape sent a formal petition to the Governor's Council, asking for two things to be done to make the frontier more secure: move the capital from Cape Town to the east and resume the government monopoly on the sale of gunpowder. Members of the council dismissed this idea as impractical, claiming that the government did not have the resources to administer such a monopoly. Besides, these matters alone were not likely, in and of themselves, to bring peace to the frontier. Even so, it is worth noting that settlers believed that peace might ensue if guns and powder were restricted.[75]

---

[72] *Graham's Town Journal*, May 2, 1846, as cited by Lancaster, "The Governorship of Sir Benjamin D'Urban," 189.

[73] Dracopoli, *Sir Andries Stockenstrom*, 116.

[74] Hare to Napier, February 22, 1839, A 1415 (77), Napier Collection 4:16–17, 27, as cited by Le Cordeur, *The Politics of Eastern Cape Separatism*, 102.

[75] BPP 1847 [786], vol. xxxviii, Enclosure in Despatch No. 1, Minutes of the Council of Government, pp. 7, 11, 16.

Government officials, too, took gun proliferation seriously, even if they did reject monopoly as a solution. When Sandile, the chief of the Ngqika Xhosa, was offered terms of surrender in November of 1846, the first term was that his men surrender their firearms. That came before such items as the return of stolen cattle and the retreat of the Ngqika eastward. Interestingly, though, the Cape governor, Sir Henry Pottinger, did not require the Xhosa to surrender their guns completely. He wrote to London that Xhosa men who handed in their arms were being given a "ticket to intimate that they are British subjects, and may settle down in peace." Firearms represented a danger, but registered firearms represented citizenship.[76]

Conflict broke out again in 1850. This time Xhosa fighters were joined by the heavily armed Khoi men from the Kat River Settlement. It appears that before the war, Khoi and Xhosa alike made serious efforts to increase their stock of muskets and powder. They bought from the clandestine network of merchants and smugglers, while some farmers appear to have paid them in guns. But when the war broke out, some Eastern Cape settlers began to object to the spread of guns. In 1851, more than 300 settlers signed a petition asking the governor and the legislative council to ban the sale of arms and ammunition for one year.[77]

Pressure to regulate the spread of guns also came from the Colonial Office. The secretary of state, Earl Grey, wrote to the Cape governor, Sir Harry Smith, revealing that he was concerned to learn about large shipments of guns and ammunition leaving England and arriving at Cape Town. He hesitated to ask the British government to place restrictions on exports, thinking that these would be easily evaded. He hesitated to restrict the sale of arms, too, thinking that settlers might need muskets for self-defense. He insisted that restrictions be placed on trading with "Kafirs," presumably meaning the Xhosa. The Cape Colony's collector of customs responded to Grey, noting that it was common knowledge during the war that Cape merchants were shipping arms to Xhosa buyers. Grey was incredulous. "I have always supposed," he wrote, "that almost the very first object which in every war must engage the attention of the person charged with conducting it, is that of cutting off, if possible, the enemy's supply of ammunition." In such cases, even the principles of economic liberalism and the rule of law might be put aside for the sake of security. "Even supposing that the existing law conferred upon you no legal power of interrupting the trade . . . you would have been fully

---

[76] BPP 1847 [786], vol. xxxviii, Maitland to Grey, November 26, 1846, pp. 194–6, 198.
[77] Cory, *Rise of South Africa*, 5:412–15.

justified, or rather, you would only have done your obvious duty," in shutting down the trade in arms and ammunition. Grey demanded an explanation.[78]

Under pressure from London politicians and from Eastern Cape settlers, the government responded with strict regulations to last just one year. All shipments of arms and ammunition had to be approved by the Collector of Customs. Colonial storekeepers were prevented from selling arms and ammunition, unless they had the written permission of their local resident magistrate or, if the store was far from an administrative center, a justice of the peace. Limits were placed on the amounts that could be sold and administrators and merchants were required to transmit to the government a record of all transactions. The records were published in the Government Gazette. Violators were subject to a fine of £500 and possible jail time. Those who traded with the declared enemies of the colony would be considered traitors and executed.[79]

The ban did not appear to have much effect, probably because so many guns had already crossed the frontier before hostilities began. The governor, Sir Harry Smith, still felt it necessary to send a ship to investigate the possibility that guns and powder were entering South Africa at the mouth of the Orange River, 550 kilometers up the coast from Cape Town, and then making their way by river into the interior, a geographically improbable route. No guns were found.[80]

The war of 1850–3 resulted in further losses for the Xhosa. Once again, the British Army and settlers proved impossible to dislodge. Total war resulted in Xhosa migration and starvation, and once again, surrender involved a degree of disarmament. This time, disarmament was symbolic and focused on the chiefs, whose authority the Cape government hoped to break. The Ngqika chief, Sandile, was required to surrender 100 guns, "in token of submission," while lesser chiefs were required to surrender their personal arms.[81] What remained of Xhosa strength was spent in 1856, when many Xhosa were persuaded by the young prophet Nongqawuse

---

[78] PRO CO 879/1 COCPA 19, Grey to Smith, Despatch No. 1 of November 14, 1851, and Despatch No. 2 of January 14, 1852. The word *Kafir* meant Xhosa, in this context, but could also refer to other African people. During the twentieth century, *Kafir* came to be used as a slur. I am conscious that some readers will be offended by the use of this word, yet I have decided to include it in the present work, unchanged, to give readers an accurate sense of "native policy" debates in the nineteenth century.

[79] BPP 1852 [57], vol. xxxiii, Ordinance No. 5 of 1851, pp. 101–10. The Cape of Good Hope *Government Gazettes* for 1852–3 contain all the details of legal gun and powder sales, most of which involve minor transactions between storekeepers and settlers.

[80] Cory, *Rise of South Africa*, 5:412–15.

[81] Colony of the Cape of Good Hope, *Government Gazette*, March 17, 1853.

to kill their cattle and to stop growing crops in order to ensure the resurrection of dead warriors and the defeat of the British.

As the Xhosa declined in power, the Mfengu became more influential. This is due, in part, to the way in which Mfengu men expressed their loyalty through military service. Between 1835 and 1846, the Mfengu settled and patrolled land in between the Xhosa and the colony, largely without firearms. Their main colonial contact, the Diplomatic Agent, Theophilus Shepstone, requested that able-bodied Mfengu men be armed with guns and trained to use them, but they did not receive them until several months after the outbreak of the 1846–7 war. The Mfengu literally found themselves in the middle of this war. More than a thousand enlisted in newly formed colonial forces called the "Fingoe Levies" that were officered by Europeans and prevented from entering colonial towns. The levies played significant roles as scouts, raiders, and fighters. As the British came to trust the Mfengu fighters, some were armed with muskets and trained to shoot, although in the guerrilla fighting that took place in the Amatolas, they typically reverted to "irregular" tactics. As irregulars, they began to take over roles that were historically played by the Khoi. When many Khoi rebelled during the war of 1850–3, the British began to rely even more heavily on the Mfengu levies, who were now almost all armed with guns. Guns, together with stingy rations of ammunition and shares in Xhosa land and cattle all became part of transactions in which loyalty was negotiated and recognized.[82]

It was expected that such instances of commercialization would encourage civilization, which would transform the Mfengu and Xhosa. As Sir Harry Smith told the Xhosa chiefs, their land would be "divided into countless towns and villages bearing English names. You shall learn to speak English at the schools which I shall establish for you.... You may no longer be naked and wicked barbarians, which you will ever be unless you labour and become industrious.... You must learn that it is money that makes people rich by work."[83] The establishment of civilization through commercialization and also through the undermining of the chiefs became the established "native policy" of the Cape Colony. The overall policy remained in place for the remainder of the nineteenth century. Yet where did guns fit in? Were they commodities that, if exchanged and used, would tend to increase civilization? Or were they objects that would be turned against the project of civilization?

---

[82] Moyer, "The Mfengu, Self-Defence, and the Cape Frontier Wars," 101–25.
[83] Saunders, Bundy, and Oaks, *Illustrated History of South Africa*, 133–5.

4

Hunting, Warfare, and Guns along the Northern Frontier, 1795–1868

During the early nineteenth century, the spread of guns and shooting skills helped transform the eastern frontier of the Cape Colony. The same was also true of the northern frontier. Trade and settlement patterns changed dramatically, as did human and environmental relations. People formed new states and new political identities, ranging from the new British government at the Cape, to the new Boer republics in the interior, to new African chiefdoms all around. New political cultures emerged in the midst of many conflicts and migrations.

Guns were important components of all these changes. At the beginning of the nineteenth century, guns were widespread only in the Cape Colony. By the middle of the nineteenth century, they had spread throughout the entire region south of the Limpopo River. States and chiefdoms came to depend extensively on the use of guns to generate income and maintain security. First-time gun buyers were becoming connected to a wider world of trade. They were also adopting a technology that made it more efficient to kill people and animals, thus fueling conflict and contributing to the virtual extermination of many of South Africa's most spectacular creatures. Hunting and warfare were intimately connected. Ecological degeneration put pressure on people to migrate into other people's territory, which generated conflict, while the hunt was often the training ground for war. Shooting skills that developed in one setting could be transferred to the other, while the organization of the commando resembled the organization of hunting and trading parties, as has been demonstrated in studies by the historians Martin Legassick, Susan Newton-King, and Nigel Penn.

Today, historians lament the violence that occurred during the age of imperial expansion, especially the killing of unique animals. That the slaughter was enhanced by the introduction and spread of guns shows the weapons in an especially bad light. Yet we must remember that in the early nineteenth century, Africans and Europeans saw the spread of guns and the increased efficiency of hunting as signs of progress. It was now easier for people living in remote areas to earn more money by harvesting ivory, hides, and feathers. Market expansion was encouraged by African chiefs and colonial rulers seeking to maximize their powers, as well as by Christian missionaries seeking to maximize their flocks. To buy a gun was to become modern.

Many had doubts about the benefits of guns and modernity, as the Aborigines Committee of 1836–7 revealed. Even though some British liberals and humanitarians were skeptical, in South Africa there were others who equated modernity with the uptake of firearms. William Burchell, who traveled in the interior in 1812, observed that as European trade networks reached into the interior, Africans were becoming involved in a cash economy. Many African hunters worked as clients of European traders, who relied on Africans for expert tracking and supplied them with guns and ammunition.[1] Burchell wrote that the diffusion of guns would cause the extinction of game, which in turn would incline people to pursue settled agriculture:

The great and powerful cause which will long operate to check the extension of the cultivation of grain, is the abundance of wild animals to be met with in all parts of the country; and until these shall be reduced in number or driven out of the land, it is hardly to be expected that the natives will turn to settled *agricultural pursuits.* The introduction of *fire-arms* among them would ultimately operate to the promotion of tillage, notwithstanding that their first effects might occasion the neglect of it. By hunting, this people would obtain food in a manner so much more agreeable than by agriculture, that grain would probably become but a secondary resource; but the evil would remedy itself, and the more eagerly they pursued the chase, and the more numerous were the guns and the hunters, the sooner would the game be destroyed or driven out of the country.[2]

---

[1] Burchell, *Travels in the Interior of Southern Africa*, 2:285. While Burchell was living among the Tlhaping, a man offered eight oxen in exchange for one gun, which seemed like a high price, unless one considered the value that the gun could produce by supporting hunting. Guns remained relatively rare in this part of South Africa until the 1850s.

[2] Burchell, *Travels in the Interior*, 2:369. The emphases are found in the original text. In the next paragraph, Burchell wrote that "[t]his, although an experiment not to be recommended in these regions, has actually taken place in the Cape Colony, and the result clearly proved that which has just been stated." Burchell's reservations about

Burchell was hoping for a significant transformation of the South African economy, which was, by and large, already under way by the time of his writing. Encouraged by merchants, Africans and settlers were pushing the hunting frontier far into the interior. In the seventeenth century, elephants and other spectacular quadrupeds could be found just outside of Cape Town. Since the earliest settlement, hunters had crossed the colonial boundaries in search of game that could be eaten and whose body parts could be sold for cash or could even be given to laborers as a form of payment. By the middle of the eighteenth century, parties of Boer hunter-traders were active in the Eastern Cape, along with a few settler-traders. They probably bought more game products from African people than they produced themselves.[3]

Shooting skills spread along the frontier, at least in part because hunters and settlers in need of labor hired and trained Khoi hunters to shoot game. The custom with Khoi servants was never to trust them completely and to control their access to firearms. According to a visiting botanist, Karl Peter Thunberg, one Boer settler family relied on a Khoi man to provide them and their Khoi servants with meat by shooting wild game. "The balls were counted out to him every time he went a shooting, and he was obliged to furnish the same number of dead buffaloes as he received of balls. Thus the many Hottentots who lived here were supported without expense."[4]

During the search for ivory, hides, and feathers, some of the region's game animals became endangered or extinct. One species of antelope, the blaubok, disappeared around 1800, while the Cape's most spectacular large animals were becoming quite rare. The Cape Colony introduced its first game legislation in 1822, just a few years after Burchell's visit.[5] By 1844, the hunter Henry Methuen was lamenting the disappearance of game:

The gun is employed by [the Boers] on the larger wild quadrupeds with such merciless rigour, particularly upon the elephant, rhinoceros, hippopotamus, giraffe, buffalo, and eland, that already these fine creatures have materially decreased in number. Their extirpation ... may not improbably be the event of this improvident course, and such a misfortune cannot but be dreaded alike by the naturalist and the benevolent man.[6]

ecological transformation appear to contradict his pronouncements about the superiority of agriculture.
[3] Mackenzie, *Empire of Nature*, 87–9.
[4] Thunberg, *Travels*, 94.
[5] Mackenzie, *Empire of Nature*, 89–91.
[6] Methuen, *Life in the Wilderness*, 198–9.

By midcentury, as game disappeared south of the Limpopo, only one community of hunter-traders still prospered: in Zoutpansberg, just south of the river, where the presence of malaria and tsetse fly limited white settlement and encouraged traders to employ or enslave African hunters.[7] In the rest of South Africa, ordinary farmers and traders, African and European alike, could no longer hunt animals near settlements. Some continued to hunt by traveling to remote locations. For those who did not live in remote areas, hunting had become a sport practiced mainly by the wealthy. Some scientists continued to collect specimens, yet the desire to collect and classify was turning to a desire to preserve and protect.[8]

Hunting, Skill, and Gun Design

During the early nineteenth century, South Africa underwent an economic and ecological transformation. While this process unfolded, South Africans adapted guns and skills to local circumstances. Mimeomorphic firearm skills that would appear to be universal were subject to local variation. Specific types of guns came to be used at the Cape that were well adapted to killing the local fauna. In fact, the relationship of hunting skills and shooting skills to the political, economic, and ecological transformation of South Africa can only be understood fully when we consider the ways in which South African guns were skillfully adapted to the local environment. Local adaptations are significant in that they show how the everyday practices, skills, and technologies under colonialism were not just derived from Europe and imposed on people in Africa, but were sometimes culturally and environmentally hybrid. The size of South African game animals, especially the much sought-after elephant, meant that it was best to hunt them with peculiarly large muskets. By the eighteenth century, while the Cape was still ruled by the Dutch East India Company, a distinct local pattern of firearms design was emerging that can be understood as a technological response to the region's ecology and economy.

Local settlers used a variety of weapons. In the main, these included two types of muskets: military-style flintlocks, similar to the British Brown Bess, and another musket that was even larger. The earliest eighteenth-century examples of these large guns were made in the Netherlands for export to the Cape. Some of these were "four-bore" 1.052-caliber

---

[7] Wagner, "Zoutpansberg," in Marks and Atmore, *Economy and Society*, 315–16.
[8] Mackenzie, *Empire of Nature*, 91–111. Beinart and Coates, *Environment and History*, 20–7. Beinart, "Empire, Hunting and Ecological Change," 162–86.

(26.72-millimeter) muskets that fired a ball that weighed 4 ounces (113.4 grams), and others were "eight-bore" 0.835-caliber (21.2-millimeter) muskets that fired a 2-ounce (56.7-gram) ball. These could be loaded with a charge as large as 14 drams (0.875 ounces; 24.8 gram) of powder, as opposed to the Brown Bess, which, already big at 0.75 caliber (19.05 millimeters), fired a 1.45-ounce (41.1-gram) ball with less powder. A skilled and fearless marksman could kill an elephant at short range with a well-placed shot from a 0.75-caliber musket. The larger muskets fired heavier, more destructive balls, which increased the likelihood of a kill. The larger muskets were specifically made for hunting elephants and other big-game animals.[9] Another peculiar design began to emerge that was called a Cape gun: a double-barreled gun, with one barrel smoothbore, to be used as a shotgun, and the other barrel rifled. These guns were used by hunters, while similar double-barreled guns, called Cape carbines, which had, at various times, two smoothbore or two rifled barrels, were used in the early nineteenth century by the troopers of the Cape Mounted Rifles Regiment.[10]

In the early nineteenth century, all types of muskets were imported from Birmingham and London, which were then the centers of British gunmaking.[11] Gunmakers there had a long history of custom-making both cheap and expensive firearms suited to cultural and environmental preferences in Africa, as Inikori and Richards have demonstrated in their studies of West Africa.[12] Adapting to local circumstances was a normal way for the Birmingham gunmakers to do business. Few of them actually made an entire gun; typically, one maker subcontracted all the component parts, such as barrels, locks, and stocks, to specialist makers. When the British took over the administration of the Cape Colony in 1806 and sacked the armorers of the Dutch East India Company, many of these craftsmen went into business for themselves as gunsmiths and became known for their elephant guns, as well as for their unique versions of the 0.75-caliber musket. Cape gunsmiths hybridized English guns to local

---

[9] Berkovitch, *The Cape Gunsmith*, 10–12; Tylden, "Shoulder Firearms in Southern Africa, 1652–1952," 204–6.

[10] Hinchley, "Notes on the Connection between the Birmingham Gun Trade and the South African Market," 18–20. Hibbard, "The Arms of the Cape Mounted Riflemen," 11–13.

[11] For a good summary of English gun making in this period, see White, "Firearms in Africa," 179–84. See also Bailey and Nie, *English Gunmakers*, 13–26; Goodman, "The Birmingham Gun Trade," 387–431; and the lengthy polemic by "Artifex" and "Opifex," *Causes of Decay*. On "proving" guns, see Harris, *Birmingham Proof House*, 90–5.

[12] Inikori, "Import of Firearms into West Africa," 355–61. Richards, "West African Eighteenth-Century Firearms Imports," 52–7.

conditions. They bought barrels and parts imported from Birmingham, Britain's gun-manufacturing center, and then assembled the parts together with locally made wooden stocks. Gunsmiths employed slave carpenters and blacksmiths in much of the work. After emancipation in 1834, many former slaves continued in the employ of their masters, but their children tended to find other occupations. From about the 1860s, skilled labor was so scarce that South African gunsmiths ceased assembling imported parts and began to import complete guns from Britain.[13]

The relationship of hunting skills and shooting skills to these political, economic, and ecological transformations can only be understood fully when we consider the ways in which South African guns were skillfully adapted to the local environment. Local adaptations are significant in that they show how the everyday practices, skills, and technologies of colonialism were not just derived from Europe and imposed on Africans. The size of South African game animals, especially the much sought-after elephant, meant that it was best to hunt them with peculiarly large muskets.

Hunting large and dangerous animals with a muzzle-loader required outstanding marksmanship. It was important to kill or disable the animal on the first shot. If the first shot missed, it took so long to reload a muzzle-loader that there might not be a chance of a second shot. Shooting to kill on the first shot took practice as well as knowledge of the animal being hunted. Elephants posed significant challenges. With smaller animals an eighteenth-century hunter could aim a black-powder muzzle-loader at the brain, a shot that is hard to make but instantly fatal. It would also have been possible to aim for the shoulder, a shot that is easy to make and usually disabling. In an elephant, the skull and the shoulder are so massive that they cannot be reliably targeted by old-fashioned black-powder weapons: only modern rifles firing cartridges containing high-velocity smokeless powder can be used for this kind of shot. With a black-powder weapon firing a low-velocity ball, the safest way to kill an elephant is to hit the heart, which is located farther in front than that in most animals. An elephant's heart presents a substantial target, but it can still be challenging to hit when the animal is moving. Firing a four-ounce ball through a four-bore musket gave some room for error in that it inflicted terrible damage on a wide swathe of tissue. Some hunters even used a two-bore musket firing an eight-ounce ball,

[13] Berkovitch, *Cape Gunsmith*, 34.

but the four-bore musket is generally considered the largest possible caliber to fire, painfully, from the shoulder.[14] A successful heart shot with a four-bore black-powder muzzle-loader typically results in the wounded animal running frantically for 50–200 meters before collapsing. As bad as that sounds, a shot placed a few centimeters wide can result in a flesh wound that requires the hunters to chase an animal for days over long distances.[15] Such activities seem cruel today, when we have embraced the protection of the elephant, but as the historian Noël Mostert has put it, from the perspective of the eighteenth century, the elephant hunters were "daring pioneers" and their outstanding marksmanship "was the first skill distinctive to their environment that the Cape colonists acquired" (Figure 2).[16]

Many skills, not just shooting skills, were associated with the use of the old frontier muzzle-loaders. They were made of wrought iron and so could be repaired in the field by constructing a hot fire. Fire was also used to melt lead into balls and "loopers," or shot pellets. First, powder needed to be assessed for its quality and then it could be loaded in variable quantities, depending on the game and the distance to the target. The gun had to be carried safely and stored properly when not in use. It also had to be cleaned regularly, lest moisture and black-powder residues cause corrosion.

Hunting guns occupied a special niche in South African culture. They came to be affectionately known as the *sanna*, a word derived from the Dutch word for snaphaunce, *snaphaan*, which was an early type of flintlock. They were also known as the *roer*, a Dutch word for gun derived perhaps from the sound of a shot. In South Africa these guns were designed in ways that reflected the influence of the local environment: gunsmiths made the shoulder stock unusually long and heavy with a special bend. Some called this bent stock a "fish belly," but others thought that it most closely resembled the hind quarters of a baboon, hence its nickname the *bobbejaanboud*, or baboon butt. The latter

---

[14] Tylden, "Swivel Guns, Elephant Guns – So-Called – and Large Bores," 18.

[15] There are informative descriptions by present-day hunters of what it is like to hunt elephants with four-bore and eight-bore weapons in Kirkland and Bridges, "African: Black Powder Hunting Paradise," 25–9; and in Berkemyer and Vimercati, "The Mighty 8 Bore," 17–19.

[16] Mostert, *Frontiers*, 159. Sedgwick, in "Frontier Flintlocks – Cape Colony," claims to have test-fired such weapons and has "come to the conclusion that the stories we have all heard of the fantastic marksmanship of the voortrekkers were grossly exaggerated." Yet we also know that these were the weapons used in elephant hunting, that elephant hunting required good marksmanship, and that many elephants were killed.

FIGURE 2. Engraving of Andries Africander, a hunter. In the early nineteenth century, such frontiersmen were hired to hunt and track for European ivory merchants. While the drawing is plainly a caricature, it depicts some features of large-bore Cape muskets accurately. The musket is rather large as compared with the size of the hunter; the barrel is long and the lock is a flintlock, both common features of early nineteenth-century weapons; and the stock is a classic Cape *bobbejaanboud*, carved in the shape of a baboon's hind quarters. (From Harris, *The Wild Sports of Southern Africa*, 12.)

nickname implied that the guns were naturalized to South Africa. They were also decorated according to Dutch customs. On the barrel, the gunsmith often engraved a twelve-pointed star, a Dutch folk symbol for prosperity and freedom that is known in the United States as the Pennsylvania Dutch "hex" and that was often engraved on eighteenth-century Pennsylvania and Kentucky rifles, too. At the Cape, Dutch settlers called guns decorated in this fashion the *sterloop*, or star barrel.[17]

Cape and American guns shared decorative motifs and revealed hybridity in local gun design. Cape gunsmiths blended European symbols with

[17] Berkovitch, *Cape Gunsmith*, 13–14; Lategan, "Fire-Arms, Historical," 4:520.

local environmental circumstances. Cape guns tended to be very large and powerful, on account of the importance of big-game hunting. Hunters in eastern North America tended to use smaller-caliber weapons because they hunted smaller animals, like deer, while westerners who might encounter bison, elk, or grizzly bears preferred larger-caliber weapons, although even these were rarely as large as the South African four-bore.[18] Before the 1880s, it was unusual for North American muskets and rifles to be exported to South Africa.[19]

Cape gunsmiths and their American counterparts were sensitive to the local fauna as well as to nineteenth-century technological developments. Gunsmiths adapted the percussion lock to old flintlock muskets. The length of the barrels changed significantly, from long to short. South African hunters usually hunted on horseback, firing and loading from the saddle. At first, long guns with 44-inch barrels were popular because hunters liked to stop the horse, lean over the saddle, and rest the stock on the ground while loading. Such a large gun can be awkward to manipulate on horseback, which is the reason why cavalrymen preferred shorter firearms, like carbines and pistols. Later, as gunsmiths determined that shorter guns were sufficiently powerful, hunters came to use shorter guns that a skilled rider could load in the saddle. The South African musket was adapted to riding in other ways: many required a heavy pull on the trigger to prevent an accidental discharge during a fall from a horse.[20] Horseback riding while hunting large, dangerous animals required shooters to adapt some of their techniques. To speed the loading process and to free hands for the reins, Boer hunters were known to carry musket balls or rifle bullets in their mouths. To load on horseback, they would pour powder from a horn down the barrel and then insert the moistened ball. The moisture helped seat the ball on the powder, without the use of paper wadding that would ordinarily come from a cartridge. With a few taps from the ramrod and a pinch of powder in the pan, the gun was ready to fire.[21]

The roers resembled all flintlock muzzle-loaders in that they were especially well adapted to hunting in the far interior. They used black powder, which remained available in remote areas through the end of the nineteenth century. The black powder could even be used to help start a

---

[18] For comparisons with U.S. hunting guns, see Garavaglia and Worman, *Firearms of the American West*, 33–79.

[19] Wahl, "American Percussions in South Africa," 5–6. The only North American firearm to sell well in South Africa was the Colt revolver, many of which were manufactured in England.

[20] Lategan, "Fire-Arms, Historical," 524–5. Tylden, "Shoulder Firearms," 204–6.

[21] Lord and Baines, *Shifts and Expedients*, 228.

campfire. The round, 1-inch-caliber balls, weighing a quarter of a pound, were made from melted lead that was hardened with tin in bullet molds. Molds were made of soapstone, but in the field molds could be crafted from clay or even from dirt taken from an anthill.[22] Hunters using flint-lock muskets were also known to fashion other types of projectiles. Boers were known to fire "loopers" or several smaller balls inserted down the barrel, while Africans were noted for more unusual designs. Balls were cleft down the middle so that in flight they might separate, yet remain close. Sometimes two balls were connected by a piece of wire rolled in spiral, like a spring. And in desperate situations, muskets could be loaded with bundles of tacks, or even with scraps made from iron pots.[23]

These methods applied to all flintlocks in remote areas, including roers. But roers were still special. Hunters offered rich descriptions of what it was like to use the old-fashioned large-bore muzzle-loaders. England's most famous colonial hunter, Frederick Courtenay Selous, reported that on an elephant-hunting expedition near Kuruman in 1872, he used three such guns (Figure 3). One of them appears to have been made locally, while two of them were smoothbores made in Birmingham. All of them fired a four-ounce bullet, about an inch in caliber, while the gun was loaded with twenty drams of the kind of ordinary black powder that could be found at frontier trading posts. The results impressed Selous. Over the course of three seasons, he used these guns to kill seventy-eight large animals, including many elephants. He commented that "I have never used or seen used a rifle which drove better than these common-made old muzzle-loaders." Even so, he did find the weapons challenging to use. They fired a large bullet with a large charge of powder, but the guns were relatively light. As a result, according to Selous, "they kicked most frightfully, and in my case the punishment I received from these guns has affected my nerves to such an extent as to have materially influenced my shooting ever since, and I am heartily sorry that I ever had anything to do with them."[24]

Another hunter, the administrator H. W. Struben, admired the way in which Boer "voortrekkers" could shoot so accurately with the old, long-serving "roers," even though every shot left a bruise on his shoulder.[25] To compensate for shoulder bruising, many Boer hunters were known to shoot from both shoulders. Others dismounted and used the ramrod as

[22] Tabler, *Far Interior*, 166–7.
[23] Lord and Baines, *Shifts and Expedients*, 229–30.
[24] Selous, *A Hunter's Wanderings in Africa*, 10. Taylor, *Mighty Nimrod*, 38.
[25] Struben, *Recollections of Adventures*, 62.

FIGURE 3. Frederick Courteney Selous, hunting a water buffalo in Southern Africa. Selous is armed with a large-bore muzzle-loader that is typical of the middle of the nineteenth century. The musket incorporated a percussion lock as well as a shorter barrel than the earlier model depicted in Figure 2. In spite of these changes, some shooting skills remained the same. Here, the hunter is shown approaching very close to the buffalo, which would have been done with both weapons although coming within two paces is an exaggeration. While the artist may have drawn the picture in this way to balance the composition, hunting these animals with these weapons did, in fact, require the hunter to come close. (Selous, *A Hunter's Wanderings in Africa*, 290–1.)

a stand: the shooter sat down, with knees raised forward. Then he rested the right elbow on the right knee and gripped the ramrod in the left hand. The ramrod was held up, while the left forearm balanced on the left knee. Some African hunters were known to improvise similar rests by holding two assegais in the left hand.[26] Even when these positions helped hunters control the big roers, there were other problems. Some hunters reported that the guns gave them temporary deafness. Some reported accidentally overloading their guns. In the best of circumstances, overloads resulted in the shooter being knocked backward to the ground. In the worst cases, the guns exploded, maiming, disfiguring, or killing the shooter.[27]

Of course, some preferred big guns precisely for their kick. In 1844, while leading a party of hunters in the South African interior, Methuen met the Tswana chief Sechele, who wanted to acquire a gun. Sechele

[26] Lord and Baines, *Shifts and Expedients*, 203.
[27] Tabler, *Far Interior*, 166–7.

asked to buy one hunter's four-bore, a "monster of four to the pound." He insisted on trying it, and "the gun was purposely over-loaded, that he might relinquish his attempts to buy it. Sitting down, he took a deliberate shot at an ant-hill, and hit it; a token of skill which his tribe greeted with loud acclamation. His shoulder had received a severe blow; but, imputing this to the strength of the gun, he was the more eager to obtain it, and departed very sulky at its being denied him."[28]

Guns along the Northern Cape Frontier

During the eighteenth century, a distinct frontier society was beginning to take shape in the vicinity of the Orange River, where various groups of Khoi and San mixed with Europeans and mixed-race communities. Toward the lower western reaches of the river lived the Khoi group called the Namaqua. The central region was inhabited by the Kora, also known as the Koranna. Throughout the eighteenth century, hunting drew Boer and "Bastaard" horsemen northward into the Karoo and eventually across the Orange River. The term Bastaard refers to the origins of these people, a mixture of Cape Europeans, Cape Khoi, and slaves from Africa and Asia. They lived in semi-nomadic communities, sometimes called *drosters*, or gangs, a reference to the illicit nature of some Bastaard activities, like rustling and smuggling. Over the course of the century, significant numbers of the Bastaard moved north from the Cape. These were called Oorlams, a word derived from Malay that refers to skill in riding and shooting. The Oorlams moved beyond the Orange River and divided into recognizable bands. One, led by Klaas Afrikaner and his descendants, Jager and Jonker, came to be known as the Oorlams, proper. Another group, led by Capt. Adam Kok and his descendants, came to be known as the Griqua. Further groups formed, too, including the Bergenaars and the Hartenaars. These too obtained enough arms and ammunition from Cape merchants to make themselves formidable raiders. They also received advice and support from Europeans who had fled to the frontier region in order to escape VOC law.[29]

European visitors reported that the *droster* groups were heavily armed. One traveler, George Thompson, reported that the population of the Griqua base, Griqua Town, was about 1,600 people, who possessed 500

---

[28] Methuen, *Life in the Wilderness*, 215.
[29] Penn, *Forgotten Frontier*, 157–69.

muskets that were acquired by "trafficking with the boors [Boers]," a practice that Thompson condemned out of a concern for security. The Griqua horsemen had also obtained some of their arms from the Cape government, which sought to use them as a force for stability on the northern frontier. All sides used muskets for stealing cattle from Sotho and Tswana herdsmen as well as for killing and enslaving San. Captured San and cattle alike were sold in order to buy more powder, a familiar cycle from other parts of Africa.[30]

During the 1810s and 1820s, the Griqua and other Bastaard groups enjoyed a temporary advantage over Sotho, Tswana, and other African people who lived in the vicinity. According to Rev. William Dower, the Griqua "were well provided with fire-arms and ammunition, vastly superior to the style of firearm obtaining among the Kaffirs at that time. These were mostly old tower muskets or gas pipes, skillfully manipulated in a cheap fire-arm."[31] Dower's reports were confirmed by Rev. Thomas Hodgson, who noted that one Bastaard group under Titus Afrikaner possessed eighty guns, while every Griqua commando had them. Korannas were not only well armed, but asked for more from the missionaries, who suspected the horsemen of smuggling arms across the border. At the same time, their Tswana neighbors owned but a handful.[32] Better arms, used with great skill, made the Bastaard and Griqua formidable opponents.

The advantages given by the possession of firearms and horses allowed the Oorlams to have a great deal of influence in the area, too. They had acquired numerous arms from the Boers and also, later, from English traders. Thompson claimed that two hundred out of three hundred were armed with muskets. They too used their weapons to rustle cattle and drive the San and the Nama off the land. By the 1840s, they ranged as far north as the Herero country in present-day central Namibia. Nearby, at Walvis Bay, English and European traders sold guns and powder to the Oorlams under their leader, Jonker Afrikaner. He used these arms to drive the largely unarmed Herero off much of their southernmost territory. In

---

[30] Davenport and Saunders, *South Africa*, 32–3. Thompson, *Travels and Adventures in Southern Africa*, 1:77–8; 2:69. See the following correspondence for details of the uptake of firearms by the Griquas and their neighbors: CTAR, CO 232/242/1/2, Melville to Plasket, September 5, 1825; CTAR, CO 291/16, Melville to Plasket, June 2, 1826; CTAR, CO 2695/106, Stockenstrom to Plasket, August 18, 1827.

[31] Dower, *The Early Annals of Kokstad and Griqualand West*, 43.

[32] Hodgson, *Journals*, 230, 280, 361, 373–4.

the 1840s and 1850s, the British government attempted to stop the arms trade in Namibia, but smuggling proved too easy.[33]

The trade in arms and ammunition became a central element of Bastaard politics, even if it was illegal. In order to raid and trade, the Bastaards needed guns and powder. When they crossed the Cape Colony's borders they brought with them firearms and horses as well as the commando tactics developed in the Cape Colony's early wars. As the Bastaards moved across the Orange River in the eighteenth century, they used the commando to organize fighting as well as hunting and raiding, their two principal economic activities. In order to prosper, they needed arms and ammunition. The Cape government, for its part, regulated the northern frontier by regulating the flow of arms and ammunition.[34]

Not only did the Bastaards use the weapons themselves, but they became important middlemen in the arms trade between colonists and Boers in the south and various groups of African people in the north. The arms trade became central to those Khoi, Sotho, and Tswana groups that opposed Bastaard commandos, although these people found that they had to raid for cattle and slaves and then sell them in order to purchase weapons, further perpetuating frontier instability. For example, the Griqua crossed back and forth into the Cape Colony to obtain guns and ammunition, even though it was illegal to trade across the boundary without a permit from the Cape government.[35] Cape traders complained about restrictions and in 1824 obtained easier access to cross-border permits. Gun trading remained illegal, but now it was easier than ever to conceal weapons in wagons stocked with merchandise. This probably only increased Griqua access to firearms and gave them more of an incentive to hunt for ivory and raid neighbors.

The Griqua's neighbors, in turn, also had an incentive to buy firearms. Starting in 1801, evangelical Christians from the London Missionary Society (LMS) began their work near the northern border, the Orange River. They hoped to save souls among the Griqua, many of whom were already nominal Christians, and to attach them more closely to European material culture. In some cases, getting the Griqua more interested in European material culture was a necessity: the underpaid, undersupplied missionaries relied on trade to earn a living. Many arrived in remote

---

[33] Thompson, *Travels and Adventures in Southern Africa*, 2:65–6. Vedder, *South West Africa*, 230–1, 254–5.
[34] Legassick, "The Northern Frontier to 1840," 368, 376.
[35] Keegan, *Colonial South Africa*, 170–1. Neumark, *Economic Influences*, 121–3.

areas with manufactured trade goods to barter mainly for ivory. Few missionaries grew rich on the trade, even though they had strong government support. In the early years of the mission, the Griqua were required to conduct all colonial trade through the missionaries and nobody else. For their part, the missionaries traded principally for their own subsistence, although in some cases gifts of manufactured goods were made to influential African leaders.[36]

For the next several decades, the trading missionaries also became the principal intermediaries for ideas and materials from the outside world. LMS expertise helped the Griqua expand their productivity as well as their trading networks. The Griqua did especially well in trading with the Tswana, who possessed ivory and other valuable goods and who paid high prices for colonial goods. As the Griqua made further contacts to the north, they asked the missionaries for gunpowder, which was necessary for hunting as well as for raiding. Cape policy frowned on the spread of arms and ammunition across the border, but the government relied on the missionaries to act as its agents and permitted them to supply the Griqua with weapons and gunpowder. Apparent inconsistencies in policy and theology extended the power of the Cape government into the interior, at least until 1814, when relations between the Cape and the Griqua soured and the trade in arms and ammunition was once again driven underground.[37]

While underground, the gun trade remained brisk. The Griqua and other groups, like the breakaway Bergenaars, followed the trade routes into the Cape Colony to purchase guns and powder at Graaff Reinet and even at the Bethelsdorp Mission Station, all in defiance of government bans. This illegal commerce was condemned at the highest levels of the government: the governor took up the subject with the secretary of state in London because the trade was thought to stimulate cattle raiding and conflict on the northern frontier. Senior administrators even contemplated a raid by Cape forces on the Griqua in order to disarm them, but this was rejected as impracticable. The Griqua and other groups like them, like the Bergenaars and the Kora, used their advantages in guns and horses to become the most mobile and feared warriors of the High Veld. In the 1820s, even as large groups of people from Natal migrated to the High Veld, the Griqua horsemen lost only a handful of battles. Their advantage eroded by the end of the 1820s, as other residents of the High

---

[36] Beck, "Bibles and Beads," 211–25. Legassick, "The Northern Frontier to 1840," 378.
[37] Keegan, *Colonial South Africa*, 172–3.

Veld gained access to guns and powder. Access was helped by an 1825 government policy that allowed cross-border trade. The arms trade was still prohibited, but with more traders crossing the boundary, the ban was harder to enforce.[38]

Trade picked up from the late 1820s to the 1840s, stimulated by the arrival of Boer migrants from the Cape Colony. Many Boers sold licit and illicit goods, including arms and ammunition. In the words of Timothy Keegan, the Boers were a "differentiated and dynamic" people "living on the outskirts of the exploding international economy of the nineteenth century."[39] Many Boers were involved in trade as a way of accumulating resources. Contrary to their image as independent freebooters, they maintained close ties to family, friends, and business associates in the Cape Colony. LMS converts and missionaries also became involved in the trade of the interior, often acting as middlemen and transport riders.

Missionaries almost surely continued to trade in arms and ammunition. David Livingstone reported in the 1840s that the Boers "had a great aversion to missionaries. The cause of their dislike seems to be an idea that we wish to furnish the natives with firearms" and that missionaries always took the side of Africans over Boers. While Boer fears were probably exaggerated, missionaries almost surely were involved, to some extent, in trading guns.[40] At the very least, the missionaries knew the details of local trade. There would have been sore financial temptations to participate, too, yet there is little direct evidence to support these inferences.

Much of the trade centered at Philipolis, the location of one of the principal mission stations. There was heavy trading there, with ivory, skins, and feathers moving southward and arms, ammunition, and liquor moving northward. The trade is only sporadically documented, as much of it was illegal. Even so, some sense of the trade can be gotten from court cases involving merchants who were caught. In the 1830s, for example, there were a number of cases involving merchants who were caught moving wagons from the Eastern Cape across the Orange River up into the High Veld. The traders concealed gunpowder in barrels labeled "tar" or "rice," while stashing away lead, parts, and caps, together with a handful of muskets and pistols.[41]

---

[38] Legassick, "The Griqua, the Sotho-Tswana, and the Missionaries," 283, 292, 339, 346–8.

[39] Keegan, "Dispossession and Accumulation," 191.

[40] Livingstone, *South African Papers*, 5.

[41] For examples, see CTAR, CO 3294/122, Petition of Seidenflecker to Cole, July 1830, plus the attached note from Waddell to Bell, September 22, 1830; CO 2749/94 McRosty

Trade, together with land claims and speculation, did much to transform the High Veld. The arrival of the Boer migrants and the LMS missionaries presented problems and opportunities. Lands habituated by the Griqua and Tlhaping were demarcated and sold to British and Boer speculators. The original residents who had held land in common among them suddenly found themselves living on land that belonged to Boers and Britons.[42] The Sotho and Tswana were able to hold on to their land, responding to the opening of colonial markets by producing crops. The establishment of more settled agriculture created opportunities for Griqua raiders, too. Cattle and slaves bought or stolen from the Sotho, Tlhaping, and Tswana went to pay for more arms and ammunition as well as for more alcohol. Chiefs were willing to go to some lengths to acquire arms and ammunition. The Tswana chief, Sechele, speaking in a public meeting with the LMS missionary Robert Moffat, threatened to prohibit hunting in his territory unless the Cape Colony allowed him to acquire guns and powder.[43]

Among these African groups, a consequent demand emerged for guns and liquor. Some missionaries to the Sotho, Tlhaping, and Tswana opposed the entry of illicit items, yet the very contacts that the missionaries facilitated with the Cape helped bring the items in anyway. Besides, the missionaries had entered the field to make conversions and stamp out the slave trade. Many believed that the introduction of "legitimate" commerce, even the trade in arms and ammunition, would work toward their more important ends. Some missionaries had to trade in guns and powder: in places, these were the only items that African people wanted from the missionaries. The missionary John MacKenzie reported that in 1860, when purchasing an ox near the Zouga River, north of the Limpopo, he met a man who would only accept gunpowder in exchange. "Pointing to a flint musket, he said it was of no more use than a walking-stick without powder."[44]

Guns and missionaries could bring security to frontier communities, while the lack of them could spell trouble. The Tlhaping chief Mothibi

---

to Hamilton, August 15, 1834; CO 2479/101 Burnett to Hamilton, September 17, 1834; CO 2756/77 Ziervogel to Bell, September 19, 1835; CO 2665/14 Van Felt to Bell, March 3, 1836.

[42] Keegan, "Dispossession and Accumulation," 198–200. Keegan, *Rural Transformations,* 1–9.

[43] Moffat, *Matabele Journals,* 1:168.

[44] Mackenzie, *Ten Years North of the Orange River,* 213.

was acutely aware of the relationship between missionaries, guns, and security. Since 1816, the Tlhaping had been served by the missionary James Read, who had become famous for his previous work in the Cape Colony. In the colony, Read had immersed himself in Khoi culture, married a Khoi woman, Sarah, and had, on several occasions, accused colonists of mistreating Khoi laborers. Read left the Cape to escape controversy and start fresh among the Tlhaping, where he founded the settlement called New Dithakong. Read was a pragmatist. He was a carpenter by trade, who carefully attended to spiritual and material needs. He brought with him important access to trade goods, as well as the skills to use them. When the LMS required Read to leave the Tlhaping in 1820, Mothibi was concerned about his loss of access.

Mothibi made consistent attempts to use missionaries and firearms to protect himself. After Read's departure, Mothibi pleaded with the replacement missionaries and also with the Cape administrator, Andries Stockenstrom, for access to guns and powder, claiming that his Griqua rivals obtained these items by smuggling. When Stockenstrom and the missionaries refused, resentment toward the British grew, fostered by two successive years of crop failures. Faced with insecurity, Mothibi turned to the Griqua for protection. The alliance between the Griqua and the Tlhaping succeeded until 1824 and 1825, when the Tlhaping were attacked and scattered by the Bergenaars. In 1825 and 1826, Mothibi reconstituted his authority and his people by buying guns and powder directly, and illegally, from colonist traders.[45]

The new weapons were linked to new ideas about commerce and culture on the High Veld. Interestingly, guns resonated with older ideas, too. Among the Sotho, guns were often called *tladi-ya-matsoho*, or "lightning of the hands." This name literally referred to the flash and boom of the musket. The metaphor of lightning flying from the hands also referred to the Sotho belief that sometimes death came not from God, but from "the hands" of witches, working from afar.[46] As Jean Comaroff and John Comaroff point out in *Of Revelation and Revolution*, modern European goods, such as guns, were not immediately associated by Africans with an acceptance of modern European epistemology. In the gun, there could reside more than one understanding of the material world.

---

[45] Legassick, "The Griqua, the Sotho-Tswana, and the Missionaries," 274–8, 334, 344–5, 367–9.
[46] Kunene, *Heroic Poetry of the Basotho*, 118.

Africans living in the 1820s and 1830s had to make sense of a great deal of instability and violence on the northern frontier, which was fueled by the trade in guns. Communities searched for ways of protecting themselves. When they purchased guns, they also bought into a colonial economy that required cattle, ivory, and sometimes even slaves in exchange. These goods were usually obtained by destructive means, thus furthering frontier insecurity and the demand for weapons.

Guns and Missionaries on the High Veld

Instability in the northern and northeastern parts of South Africa resulted in the emigration of the followers of powerful new chiefs like Moshoeshoe [Moshweshwe], Mzilikazi, and MaNthatisi, to new locations on the High Veld (Figure 4). The interior of South Africa, roughly bounded by the Limpopo River to the north and the Orange River to the south, had already seen decades of political turmoil. The Portuguese slave trade was beginning to affect established patterns of trade and accumulation. New and more powerful chiefdoms were forming in the coastal lowlands, most notably the Zulu and Swazi. Refugees were entering Xhosa territory, while some were joining new chiefdoms that were forming in the highlands: there were several, including Moroka's Rolong (nearby at Thaba Nchu) and Mzilikazi's Ndebele (north of the Vaal River), but the best known were Moshoeshoe's Sotho (in the Caledon River valley at Thaba Bosiu).

Moshoeshoe's followers struggled with the new circumstances to forge a new kind of order. Much earlier, in the seventeenth century, Sotho-speaking people were living in the Caledon River valley. Their settlements encompassed western areas of modern-day Lesotho as well as parts of the adjacent High Veld. They farmed their land, traded with their neighbors, and organized themselves into small chiefdoms. By the late eighteenth century, they were experiencing pressure from their Tswana, Pedi, and San neighbors, some of whom, in turn, were responding to pressure from an expanding Cape Colony. From the Cape Colony came Griqua and Boer migrants, looking for land and cattle. Drought struck more frequently than usual. And to complicate matters further, during the 1820s the consolidation of the Zulu kingdom pushed even more migrants into Sotho territory. The migrants raided Sotho cattle and crops, producing an intolerable situation. One Sotho chief's son, Moshoeshoe, forged alliances between the various Sotho chiefdoms and led them to the safety of Thaba Bosiu, a large, flat-topped mountain to the south. There, according to

FIGURE 4. Moshoeshoe. (From Casalis, *Basutos*, 47. Image courtesy of the Harvard College Library.)

the historians Sandra Burman and Elizabeth Eldredge, he forged a new nation.[47]

The Sotho nation was built largely out of a need for increased security against migrants. People needed security in order to produce food and they also needed small loans in order to increase production. Moshoeshoe helped his followers through patronage with cattle. He raided cattle from his enemies and then lent the cattle out through a system called *mafisa*. Under *mafisa*, borrowers cared for the cattle, keeping the milk and an

---

[47] Burman, *Chiefdom Politics and Alien Law*, 5–9. Eldredge, *A South African Kingdom*, 1–3.

agreed-upon number of the offspring. In this way, Moshoeshoe could have his cattle cared for by clients, while clients could feed themselves and increase the size of their own herds. The herders received protection from Moshoeshoe against raiders. When Moshoeshoe recaptured cattle from raiders, he returned them to his clients, even though he could have rightfully kept them for himself. He also lent cattle for young men who needed to pay *bohali*, or bride-price, to their future spouses' families on the condition that their daughters' *bohali* would be sent to him. As Eldredge points out, Moshoeshoe's patronage perpetuated inequalities, yet he is remembered as a ruler who was kind and supportive.[48]

Moshoeshoe was generous and flexible during his tenure as paramount chief. He employed his own sons to supervise client chiefs, who retained a significant degree of autonomy. For this reason, Burman describes the emerging Sotho nation as a "loosely-knit federation." Within this federation, men had significant freedoms. They had the right to speak freely in public meetings, called *pitso*, and there was also no standing army. Moshoeshoe was known to be inclined toward peace, and even in war he had a reputation for magnanimity.

Guns became important tools for both peace and war. Numerous chiefs attempted to contact Europeans in order to acquire guns. As far north as the Transvaal in the 1820s and 1830s, the Ndebele chief Mzilikazi recruited and protected American, British, and French missionaries in the hopes that the preachers or their trader contacts would import more firearms and instruct his people in their use.[49] Etherington points out that chiefly efforts to acquire guns were quite significant. Previously, chiefs were able to provide for their people out of the resources of their own lands. Trade was only for luxury goods. Now, trade in guns was thought to be essential. Chiefs came to depend on trade to support their uptake of guns. This presented a problem: what would they use to barter for guns? The sale of cattle diminished the herd of the chief, while hunting for ivory involved significant expenditures. It is partly on account of guns that in the 1820s, chiefs began to encourage their followers to migrate to the Cape Colony to work as farm laborers. On being paid, they bought guns and then returned home ready to defend the chiefdom, or so the chiefs hoped.[50]

---

[48] Burman, *Chiefdom Politics and Alien Law*, 10. Eldredge, *A South African Kingdom*, 34–9.

[49] Lye, "Ndebele Kingdom," 102–3.

[50] Etherington, *Great Treks*, 194–5.

During the 1840s, missionary letters and reports indicated that guns were circulating widely among the Tswana.[51] By 1849, the LMS was learning from Boer sources that the Kwena Tswana chief, Sechele, had acquired so many guns that he could arm almost every male follower. They even heard that he owned a cannon. The arms merchant, according to the Transvaal leadership, had been David Livingstone, a charge that the missionary denied. Livingstone claimed that the Kwena owned only a handful of guns. He added that Sechele did not own a cannon, only a black iron pot that had been mistaken for one. In spite of these refutations, there were a number of things about Livingstone's account that were suspicious. In his publications, he expressed disdain for the Boers, claiming that they were terrified of armed Africans. In discussing the arming of the Xhosa, he said that "ever since these 'magnificent savages' obtained possession of fire-arms, not one Boer has ever attempted to settle in Caffre-land, or even face them as an enemy in the field. The Boers have generally manifested a marked antipathy to any thing but 'long-shot' warfare, and, sidling away in their emigrations toward the more effeminate Bechuanas [Tswana], have left their quarrels with the Caffres to be settled by the English, and their wars to be paid for by English gold." Continuing in this taunting vein, Livingstone wrote that "English traders sold [to the Kwena] those articles which the Boers most dread, namely, arms and ammunition; and when the number of guns amounted to five, so much alarm was excited among our neighbors that an expedition of several hundred Boers was seriously planned to deprive the Bakwains [Kwena] of their guns." Carrying on, Livingstone added that Boers themselves sold muskets to the Kwena.[52]

Livingstone appears to have been prevaricating. Some years later, in 1885, a British official learned from some Kwena men that Livingstone had not sold arms; he had merely strongly encouraged them to buy guns and powder from merchants. Subsequently, though, the historian-anthropologist Isaac Schapera assessed Livingstone's letters and also his applications for powder permits. Schapera found that in 1852 Livingstone had indeed delivered about 375 pounds of powder and 100 pounds of lead to the Kololo chief Sekeletu, a few months after the Sand River Convention created the South African Republic and prohibited the arms trade to Africans north of the Orange River.[53] Shortly after the signing

---

[51] Livingstone, *Livingstone's Missionary Correspondence*, 32, 89, 95, 153.
[52] Livingstone, *Missionary Travels and Researches*, 38, 41–2.
[53] Livingstone, *South African Papers*, 22, 25, 30, 42, 49–59, 127–9.

of the convention, a Boer commando attacked the Kwena and demolished Livingstone's home.[54] This drastic action may not have had the desired effect on missionaries. Several years later, in 1859, the president of the Transvaal wrote to the Cape governor Sir George Grey accusing the missionary Robert Moffat of supplying the chief Mahura with three wagonloads of arms and ammunition, although Moffat denied the charge.[55]

Moffat, Livingstone, and other missionaries reported about the gun trade across the Limpopo, too, which had spread there by the 1840s and 1850s. In 1842, David Livingstone reported guns among the Shona, probably bought from the Portuguese in Mozambique.[56] In 1851, near the upper reaches of the Zambezi River, Livingstone witnessed an English trader buying ten large tusks of ivory for the extraordinary price of one thirteen–shilling musket.[57] Livingstone also noted that nearby, Portuguese traders were selling English muskets: three muskets cost thirty slaves. Demand for guns was quite strong.[58] It is on account of this early trade that in 1854, Livingstone's father-in-law, the LMS missionary Robert Moffat, reported that "Tower" muskets, much like those used by the British army, could be found north of the Zambezi River. Moffat's contacts among the Ndebele described the arms dealers as British and not as Portuguese. Their descriptions indicated that some of the traders came from the coast, probably dealing in slaves. Then, in 1857, Moffat encountered a Boer who traded guns for ivory, as well as a Transvaal official who condoned the arms trade. That year, Moffat himself presented Mzilikazi with two guns. The area north of the Zambezi remained a gun frontier through the 1850s. When Moffat visited the Ndebele chief, Mzilikazi, in 1857 and again in 1859, he found that his policy was to give guns to his followers only on rare occasions. Local knowledge of guns was so thin that on several occasions, people asked Moffat to help them fix their guns. There appear to have been only a few Ndebele who were skilled at elephant hunting. On another journey in 1858, Transvaal Boers accused Moffat of bringing hundreds of pounds of powder to Mzilikazi, although Moffat protested that the powder was being transported separately, to be used exclusively by the mission stations. Mzilikazi seems to have hoped

---

[54] Livingstone, *Missionary Travels and Researches*, 45.
[55] *SAAR Transvaal*, 4:246, 257–8.
[56] Livingstone, *Missionary Correspondence*, 17.
[57] Livingstone, *Missionary Travels and Researches*, 80–1.
[58] Livingstone, *Missionary Correspondence*, 177, 181, 183.

that Moffat would bring him more guns, a subject of some contention between them.[59]

The Ndebele adopted guns in a more widespread fashion beginning in the 1860s. Robert Moffat's son, John S. Moffat, remarked in 1862 that recently a number of traders had sold many guns to the Ndebele. The Ndebele used the guns to attack and defeat the unarmed Shona, consolidating Mzilikazi's hold over the territory just north of the Zambezi. The younger Moffat was tempted to use his skills as a gunsmith to reach out to the Ndebele, who had not accepted Christianity. He remarked that "there is no means of gaining influence so potent in South Africa as gun-mending. A good gunsmith at once takes rank, and can obtain what no one else can." He worried that his superiors in the LMS would have mixed feelings on the subject.[60]

With or without technical support from missionaries, guns became popular trade items north of the Zambezi. By the 1860s, the Shona kingdoms had followed the example of their migrant neighbors, the Ndebele, and were buying firearms from Boer, British, and Portuguese traders alike. Guns became incorporated in warfare, and also in hunting, at a time when the region to the north of the Zambezi was a center for the ivory trade. The destruction of elephants made many chiefs rich, as they sold ivory and also issued permits to Boers and others to hunt on their territory.[61]

Who else supplied the ammunition and guns to Africans? It is usually thought that merchants were the main suppliers, especially as commercial networks became stronger and spread farther throughout South Africa in the 1820s. It is likely that guns spread first along trade routes like the "Hunters' Road" that followed the Transvaal's western border.[62] Settlers blamed merchants for stimulating the gun trade, but the colonial government blamed settlers, too. In 1833 and 1834, the government restricted the supply of ammunition to settlers, culminating in an 1835 measure that restricted gunpowder to government stores. This restriction further demoralized Boers who were already feeling that the government did not give them enough respect or protection.[63]

---

[59] Moffat, *Matabele Journals*, 1:367, 2:78–9, 2:121, 2:125, 2:138, 2:159–61, 2:224–5, 2:229.

[60] Moffat et al., *The Matabele Mission*, 161.

[61] Bhila, *Trade and Politics in a Shona Kingdom*, 27–9, 206–7.

[62] Agar-Hamilton, *Native Policy of the Voortrekkers*, 54.

[63] Giliomee, *Afrikaners*, 141.

Guns and the Great Trek

Boers had been trekking out of the colony since the eighteenth century. During the 1830s, the emigration took on a different quality. The old *trekboers* had been economic migrants moving in small groups. The new Boer migration of the 1830s was characterized by the movement of large groups led by prominent citizens. The Great Trek, as it was called, culminated in the migration of about six thousand people during the 1830s. The *voortrekkers* were inspired by a mixture of cultural, economic, and political motives. Many felt that the British government at the Cape had become hostile to their interests. Ordinance 50 of 1828, the slave emancipation of 1834, and the Masters and Servants Ordinance of 1841 technically gave full rights of citizenship to men of all races. Meanwhile, it seemed to some Boers that liberal missionaries had an undue influence over the government, which was reconsidering policy on the eastern frontier. Many Boers from the Eastern Cape believed that the British were not defending frontier farms adequately. They also worried that the British would enroll Boers into a militia force and place them under British officers. Many were concerned enough about their status, and about their ability to get access to grazing land and unregulated labor, that they began to migrate out of the Cape Colony and into the interior, where they could farm using traditional, land-extensive methods.[64]

Many *voortrekkers* hoped to recreate the old racial order, although they disavowed slavery, knowing that they should not provoke the Cape administration. One trek leader, Piet Retief, wrote to the *Grahamstown Journal*, expressing his hope that the British government at the Cape would "allow us to govern ourselves without its interference in future.... We are resolved, wherever we go, that we will uphold the just principles of liberty; but, whilst we will take care that no one shall be held in a state of slavery, it is our determination to maintain such regulations as may suppress crime, and preserve proper relations between master and servant."[65]

Much later, the Afrikaner myth of the Great Trek emphasized that when the Boer voortrekkers crossed the Orange River, they entered unknown, uninhabited territory and through hard work and an independent spirit achieved autonomy. Nothing could have been further from the truth. Boer families had long relied on Khoi and San

---

[64] Giliomee, *Afrikaners*, 145–53. Davenport and Saunders, *South Africa*, 5th ed., pp. 49–54, 77.

[65] Thompson, *History of South Africa*, 88.

labor, and people from these groups continued to be recruited, sometimes forcefully. Numerous Boer hunters had already crossed into the region north of the Orange River and east of the Kei River, as had large numbers of Khoi hunters and herders. And from the east, numerous Nguni-speaking Africans were already migrating into the region, too. To other people, the trekboers' lifeways resembled the heavily armed Bastaard horsemen and herders who preceded them into the interior. They spoke the same language, the South African variant of Dutch that was evolving into Afrikaans.[66]

The Boers who trekked across the Orange River hoped to live the life that the Griqua, Kora, and other trans-frontier people were living – beyond the reach of new British laws. Thousands of wagons departed for the interior, in six major groups and many minor groups, some going as far as the Limpopo River and Delagoa Bay. They never became completely independent. Even far into the interior, they depended on merchants connected to Cape Town and Port Elizabeth for goods, especially ammunition and guns.[67]

The emigrant Boers stepped into the contested interior zone and met resistance from many people. In 1836 and 1837, trekker parties moving near the Vaal River fought Mzilikazi's Ndebele, demonstrating the superiority of organized firepower against massed numbers of fighters armed with spears. At Vegkop, waves of warriors attacked the circled wagon *laager* of the trekkers: two trekkers died compared with 430 Ndebele. And while the defensive formation of the *laager* proved impenetrable, subsequent battles showed the superiority of the offensive commando formation, not only on the High Veld, but also in the Natal lowlands. The most famous conflict happened in 1838, when emigrant Boers entered Natal and fought a series of battles against Dingane's Zulu. The Zulu did score one major victory through a surprise attack on a Boer encampment, in which they killed the leadership of one trekker party and scared many followers off. Yet in the battle that followed, the battle of Blood River or Ncome River, the Boers scored a major victory. The Boers circled their wagons in a laager and fired their guns at attacking Zulu spearmen. The battle demonstrated the superiority of guns in fighting when they were combined with practiced, suitable tactics.

The trekkers faced threats from Africans while suffering from internal divisions. While they all set off northward from the Eastern Cape between late 1835 and early 1837, they divided into six principal groups. Some

[66] Etherington, *Great Treks*, 50–3.
[67] Etherington, *Great Treks*, 340–4.

headed into Natal, others stayed in the High Veld, while some went as far north as the Limpopo River. Leadership depended, to a great extent, on personal charisma, military skill, and patriarchal authority. Numerous arguments about governance divided the groups, with some favoring autocracy, others favoring libertarianism, and still others favoring elected republican councils.[68]

In keeping with these divisions, the trekkers differed over practices and ideologies. They were all, by and large, Calvinists, yet they were divided into several different branches of the Reformed Church. They were also alienated from British culture and British rule to varying degrees. Most believed that society should be ruled by male landowners, "a free, independent, propertied class of burghers with rights, duties and privileges," in the words of Hermann Giliomee. Many Boer leaders sought "working relationships" with their African neighbors. Even as the trekkers fought African opponents, they sought treaties with African chiefdoms and labor from African workers. Their labor policies, however, were not conducive to positive, long-term development. Many trekkers continued to indenture African children as "servants," a practice that resembled slavery. Bad treatment of laborers was construed as converting them to civilization. In 1841, one trekker council, based in Natal, wrote to the Cape governor that they served as God's instruments to teach Africans about Christianity and to protect them from "murder, pillage, and violence."[69]

Tactics and guns helped Boer communities establish themselves on a turbulent frontier. By contrast, there is little evidence that Zulu warriors and hunters used firearms extensively, although there is some evidence that they adapted their tactics to defend themselves against enemies who possessed firearms. This was clearly the case in their fighting against the Boers who entered Natal in 1838. During that year, heavily armed Boer commandos lost battles to the Zulu at Thukela and eTaleni. At the latter battle, Zulu warriors hid in the long grass to surprise Boer horsemen who were employing their usual tactic of charging and then firing volleys. The Zulu won this battle and only lost at Blood River (Ncome) because the Boers were able to concentrate their firepower in a defensive laager formation.

It would have been difficult for the Zulu to completely accommodate their tactics to guns because the gun trade to Natal and Zululand appears to have been small in the 1830s and 1840s. Some sources indicate that

---

[68] Giliomee, *Afrikaners*, 163–5.
[69] Giliomee, *Afrikaners*, 163, 165–7.

Isaacs and groups of Americans smuggled low-quality muskets through Port Natal. The gun trade did not have a major impact until the 1850s and 1860s, when Dingane's successor, Mpande, allowed greater numbers of European hunters and traders to enter Zululand. By that point in time, guns were becoming not only more numerous but also more effective.[70]

The Boers formed the short-lived republic in Natal in 1839. The republic's policies toward African people reflected colonial experiences in the Eastern Cape. Cattle rustling and punitive commandos were commonplace. And one of the most common problems that needed regulation was that of smuggling liquor and horses as well as guns and powder. To supervise trade in general and the gun trade in particular, the Republic of Natal instituted trade fairs on the colonial border, along the pattern of the ones that were held in the Eastern Cape, with licenses granted to traders from the colony and from Zululand. Trading in livestock, liquor, and guns was prohibited, and the fairs were supervised by government officials. The republic also had specific rules on firearms. In 1841, to preserve their superiority in weapons, the Boers prohibited the sale of arms and ammunition to "colored people." Those who already owned guns now had to apply for special monthly permits.[71]

The republic lasted only until 1842, at which point the Cape governor annexed Port Natal as a colony. Natal Boers were given the choice of accepting British sovereignty and applying for weapons permits, or losing their weapons.[72] The new British government retained the republic's ban on arms sales to Africans, even though the Cape only restricted the sale of arms across the border. Be that as it may, the imposition of equality before the law and the strict prohibition of slavery precipitated the departure of most of the trekkers. During the 1840s and 1850s, Boers in the interior established settlements even as they met with resistance from their African neighbors and their erstwhile British rulers. In 1848, British forces intervened in conflicts between the Boers and their High Veld neighbors, particularly the Sotho. The Cape governor Sir Harry Smith even went so far as to annex the territory between the Orange and Vaal rivers. Smith's Orange River Sovereignty, as it was called, was short lived. It generated little revenue, and its existence was further imperiled by a shift in British policy, from protecting African allies from the Boers to toleration for the Boers. As a consequence, Britain ruled the area beyond

---

[70] Knight, *Anatomy of the Zulu Army*, 167.
[71] Agar-Hamilton, *Native Policy of the Voortrekkers*, 44. *SAAR Natal*, 1:31–2, 50.
[72] *SAAR Natal*, 1:289, 379–81, 391–3, 431.

the Vaal only until 1852 and the area beyond the Orange until 1854. Britain withdrew from the territory across the Orange River under pressure from a penny-pinching British government that believed the colonies should be self-supporting. The humanitarian side of the liberal imperial mission was being superseded by utilitarian principles of efficient economy.[73]

Guns and Citizenship in the Boer Republics

Britain permitted the formation of two independent Boer republics: the South African Republic (often called the Transvaal), in 1852, and the Orange Free State (often called the Free State), in 1854. In order to achieve independence, the republics had to ban slavery and also prohibit the trade in guns and ammunition with Africans, even though it had already gone on to a considerable extent. Both republics received assurances that their governments would be allowed to purchase adequate supplies of arms and ammunition from the British colonies.[74] These concessions to British policies were made but British notions of equality were rejected. The constitution of the Transvaal flatly stated that "the people are not prepared to allow any equality of the non-white with the white inhabitants, either in the Church or the State." The Orange Free State constitution was more moderate because some burghers, including some of British origin, sought eventual reunion with the Cape. Even so, the Free State constitution stipulated that citizenship would be granted to whites who resided in the republic for six months. The intransigence of the republics on racial matters alienated them from the British government. Key Afrikaner institutions in the Cape were critical, too, such as the Dutch Reformed Church, which denounced race-based church membership.[75]

In both republics, only "white" men were full citizens, with rights to own their own property, including land and guns. Africans were excluded from these and all other rights of citizenship. The early twentieth-century historian Agar-Hamilton summarized republican racial ideology:

The fundamental postulate of Boer native policy was that the native was an inferior being, absolutely precluded from receiving political privileges. The possibility of admitting him to equality, whether economic, political, or social was

---

[73] Keegan, *Colonial South Africa*, 6–7.
[74] Eybers, *Select Constitutional Documents*, 284, 358–9.
[75] Giliomee, *Afrikaners*, 176–7.

unthinkable.... Their attitude of mind was not the result of any conviction carefully argued out from evidence, nor was there any feeling of ill-will for the inferior race; the established order was accepted calmly as an absolutely unchallengeable matter of fact. In his magnificent acceptance of the principle of aristocracy of birth the Boer farmer had much in common with the nobleman of the *Ancien Régime*.[76]

Race-based gun-control measures became important to this "aristocratic" republican ideology. It is accurate to say, as Agar-Hamilton did, that limiting the spread of guns and powder to Africans became "the guiding principle of their policy," extending to external relations too. In 1840, the Natal *raad*, or council, prohibited "people of color" from owning or trading guns. A similar practice was in effect in the Transvaal, where, in 1846, the government punished traders for providing arms to the Tswana chief, Sechele. In 1848, the Transvaal *raad* prohibited Africans from possessing weapons. In 1853, after chiefs and traders ignored repeated warnings, the *raad* passed a law prohibiting the sale of weapons to Africans. Violating the law would result in confiscation of all property, plus a minimum punishment of life imprisonment or a maximum punishment of death. The powder trade was regulated, too: any traders carrying more than five pounds had to apply for a permit. In the next year, the Free State passed similar laws, prohibiting arms trading with Africans and limiting the amount of powder that could be carried by merchants.[77]

Commandos were occasionally sent out to disarm small neighboring chiefdoms. Treaty negotiations with larger chiefdoms also featured gun control. For example, in 1853 the Transvaal's South African Republic concluded a treaty with Mzilikazi that prohibited the gun trade among his Ndebele. Even so, the Transvaal could not control Mzilikazi any more than it could control the people within its boundaries.[78] The Pedi chiefdom retained a degree of autonomy within the Transvaal, retaining, as well, numerous firearms.[79] During the 1850s, Transvaal and Free State lawmakers frequently complained to their respective *Volksraad* about the proliferation of arms in the chiefdoms of Sekwati, Sechele, and Moshoeshoe.[80]

---

[76] Agar-Hamilton, *Native Policy of the Voortrekkers*, 88.
[77] *SAAR Natal*, 1:31–2, 50; *Transvaal*, 1:38–41, 62, 68; 2:156–9; *OFS*, 1:315.
[78] Agar-Hamilton, *Native Policy of the Voortrekkers*, 80–5.
[79] Smith, "Fall of the Bapedi," 238–9.
[80] See, for example, *SAAR Transvaal*, 1:102–5; 2:342–3, 364–6; *OFS*, 2:72, 252, 340; 3:34; 3:79, 98; 4:70–1.

Many independent-minded Boers flaunted the ban on gun sales. By 1858, the republican governments responded by declaring state monopolies over sales of arms and ammunition. But before then, the republican governments eased back on cross-border arms sales and began to sell or present guns to neighboring African chiefs. In 1855, the Transvaal presented powder, lead, and horses to chiefs who helped capture "coloureds," presumably enemy Griquas. In 1856, the Free State granted weapons permits to two chiefs, Moroka and Jan Bloem, and later in the decade began to arm African and Griqua enemies of Moshoeshoe. In 1857, at the request of Moravian missionaries, the Transvaal presented guns to Sechele.[81]

Arming African Hunters

Within the area controlled by the Boers, there was one way in which it was commonly understood that gun laws would not be observed: Boer masters often lent guns to their African servants. Initially, the republics outlawed this practice. The Transvaal government records indicate that in 1848 and 1850, they confiscated guns from African hunters and prosecuted Boers who lent or "hired" their guns to Africans. In 1851 the *Volksraad* considered and then tabled the matter, only to return to it in 1853, when they required that all weapons lent to Africans be collected and taken to a public office. Afterward, the government received complaints from citizens who relied on armed African servants. Many continued the practice anyway and received the sanction of law in 1857, when the Transvaal allowed Boers to apply for permits for their servants to carry weapons. Africans were allowed to hunt with guns only when a European was present. The Free State followed suit in 1858 and 1859 and even took the further step of allowing free "coloureds of good behavior" to buy weapons.[82]

African servants were allowed to have firearms so that they might protect the master's livestock and hunt with him or for him. In some northern districts of the Transvaal, like Zoutpansberg, malaria and sleeping sickness were prevalent, which meant that European reliance on African marksmen, called "black shots," was quite high. Masters routinely disregarded the laws requiring Europeans to seek permission to employ African

---

[81] *SAAR OFS*, 2:14, 4:22–5; *Transvaal*, 3:154, 174–6, 192, 418.
[82] *SAAR Transvaal*, 1:88, 325; 2:156–9; 3:247–51, 599; 5:273; *OFS*, 3:102–3.

hunters. The Transvaal government was aware of the practice, but was unable to prevent it, as many of the hunters went across the Transvaal's northern border, the Limpopo River.[83]

The practice of African elephant hunters working for European ivory traders closely resembled the practice that prevailed in Portuguese Mozambique, immediately to the north and east of the Transvaal. As the Cape hunting frontier moved northward toward the Zambezi Valley, the Mozambican hunting frontier moved westward from Delagoa Bay toward the same area, which lies within present-day Zimbabwe, Zambia, Malawi, and southwestern Mozambique. Throughout this region, the most famous elephant hunters were the *chikunda*, who were descended from the slaves held on the *prazos*, land grants to settlers in the Zambezi Valley. The *prazeiros* armed the *chikunda*, who were organized along military lines to enable them to hunt as well as to fight, a practice that began in the eighteenth century. The arming of slaves seems odd from an Atlantic or Cape perspective, but it was commonly practiced in the Muslim world, of which the Portuguese traders of the Indian Ocean had some knowledge. The *chikunda* slaves became technically free in 1858, although like their comrades, who worked for the Boers, their terms of employment included various elements of coercion. Some did, however, establish themselves as independent hunters and even had local blacksmiths make them wrought-iron muskets.[84]

It is entirely possible that the Boers who hired "black shots" derived this practice from Mozambique. Indeed, Portuguese traders from Mozambique were present in the northern Transvaal during the middle of the nineteenth century. One trader named João Albasini served as the superintendent of Zoutpansberg from 1859 to 1868, while a Portuguese community established an enclave at Schoemansdal. Both Boers and Portuguese traded and hunted between the Limpopo and Zambezi rivers. Both groups relied extensively on Tsonga people, who had been trading and migrating westward for several decades already. The historian Roger Wagner has called this a "system" based on a "workable harmony of interest" – Boer hunters based in the northern Transvaal had trade links with the Cape; these Boers engaged with Tsonga hunters who themselves were linked to coastal southern Mozambique. This

---

[83] *SAAR Transvaal*, 7:49.
[84] Isaacman and Isaacman, "Free Chikunda as Elephant Hunters," in *Slavery and Beyond*, 83–124.

system of links was tested sorely during the 1860s, when conflict broke out between Tsonga, Venda, and different groups of Portuguese traders.[85]

It did not help the system that the elephant frontier continued to recede. As the elephant hunters moved northward, African people who lived between the Orange River and the Zambezi River experienced coercion from Boers, Portuguese, and warlords during the middle decades of the nineteenth century. A lack of security provided an incentive to purchase weapons, while remoteness and weak administration made it possible to own and trade them. In a divided community, some Boer men still felt warranted in trading guns and powder to their African neighbors. James Chapman, who hunted and traded in and around the Transvaal during the 1850s, remarked that "the Boers are very suspicious of Englishmen and do not like their coming in contact with the natives, and powder or horses are strictly forbidden the latter, and though they keep such a keen lookout upon English travelers, they do not at all refrain from making a bargain now and then themselves."[86]

If Boers wanted to trade with Africans, then they had better have the guns and powder that Africans wanted. It helped Africans negotiate with Boers that the Limpopo Valley is the start of the tsetse fly belt. Boers traveling north had to dismount lest their horses die, which meant that they had to rely on African men working as scouts and porters. The northern part of the Transvaal was also the start of the malaria zone: white hunters were likely to die of fever. The Boers needed African help. In addition to hiring contractors, Boers became involved in trading and raiding for slaves, called "apprentices," north of the Limpopo, in present-day Zimbabwe. Boer and Portuguese hunters received assistance from Tsonga, Venda, and other African allies. These were often paid in guns brought from the Cape and Mozambique. The weapons increased the ability of hunters to enslave people throughout the elephant zone. Many male slaves went to the Transvaal to work as "apprentices" and afterward even to become "black shots " and return north in the employ of hunting parties. Some "black shots" recognized that the ownership of firearms evened the playing field with the Portuguese and Boers. During the late 1860s, Venda contractors refused to return their weapons. In 1853, the Ndebele chief, Mzilikazi, even sold fifty pounds of powder to Transvaal government officials. A resurgence of African chiefdoms in

[85] Wagner, "Zoutpansberg," 324–6.
[86] Chapman, *Travels in the Interior*, 1:19.

the northern Transvaal pushed the limits of white settlement southward, away from Zoutpansberg.[87]

In paying African contractors with firearms, the individual profit motive got the best of the collective desire for security. Transvaal law required any African in possession of a firearm to be supervised by a European. As Wagner has shown, these regulations were widely disregarded.[88] One partial witness to these inconsistencies, David Livingstone, remarked that

the natives know well their source of power. Guns and ammunition are purchased with great avidity, but concealed with such care, only a small number of Boers have any idea of the mine which may yet be sprung. In solemn council Potgeiter [*sic*] issued orders that no trader should be allowed to introduce these weapons, and he thinks his orders are effectual. He might as well have bolted his castle gate with a boiled carrot. Members of his own Council sell arms whenever they can do so with profit. We saw one sell two hundred pounds of gunpowder and a bundle of muskets, and laugh at the folly of his superior. When a musket is by accident discovered in the possession of a native, fearful lest he exposes one of themselves, they eagerly ask, "Did you not get it from a Missionary?"[89]

Guns and the Sotho Struggle for Autonomy

As much as contact with the Boers and their hunters produced deleterious effects, it was possible for Africans to turn a negative to a positive and use guns as tools of resistance. This was the case with the Sotho under Moshoeshoe, who lived to the southeast, in the Caledon Valley. To support peace and productivity, and possibly also to acquire guns, Moshoeshoe invited Christian missionaries to Lesotho, which was then coming to be known as Basutoland. The first missionaries to arrive in the 1830s – the Paris Evangelical Mission Society – brought new ideas about religion, politics, and economics. Like other missionaries in South Africa, they linked the spread of Christianity to the spread of European material culture. They were also willing to help Moshoeshoe negotiate with the other Europeans in South Africa. Moshoeshoe and the Sotho embraced many of the new ideas, even though many men hesitated to abolish long-standing customs that Christians disliked, such as polygamy

---

[87] Wagner, "Zoutpansberg," 330. Mavhunga, "Lowveld Firearms Diffusion," 211. *SAAR Transvaal*, 2:473–4.

[88] Wagner, "Zoutpansberg," 331–2.

[89] Livingstone, *South African Papers*, 14.

and initiation schools.[90] Moshoeshoe purchased his first horse in 1829 and his first gun shortly thereafter. He then encouraged any of his clients, who had migrated to work for Cape farmers, to return with their earnings, usually in the form of cattle, guns, and horses. In 1830, Moshoeshoe inflicted his first defeat on a band of the Griqua, demonstrating that Sotho warriors had successfully adopted their enemies' tactics and weapons.[91] The process of accumulating guns and horses continued. In 1848, British magistrates in the Eastern Cape uncovered a "regular system" of Sotho migration to work on Cape farms and to return with guns and ammunition.[92]

In the 1840s, Sotho habits of industry were making an impression on Cape liberals. The liberal newspaper *South African Commercial Advertiser* published an article praising Moshoeshoe and his subjects, noting that "not more than fifteen years ago, he had not as much as a suspicion of the existence of white nations and had never seen neither a gun nor a horse; and at this present moment, he is perhaps the chief in South Africa who is possessed of the greatest number of horses and firearms." Guns and horses were the benchmarks of civilization. The article also praised him for living in a European-style house, riding in wagons, purchasing goods with cash, and cultivating "all European vegetables and fruit trees."[93] By the 1850s, the Sotho were making their own gunpowder, with local saltpeter and charcoal mixed together with imported sulfur, which arrived in Sotho territory in spite of a ban by the Free State. An English visitor, John Burnett, reported to the Cape governor, Sir George Grey, that "this powder has been tried and found to be very good, in fact, a better quality than a great deal of that which is procured in a damp, lumpy and injured state from colonial dealers."[94] To further make themselves militarily self-sufficient, the Sotho also began to purchase and breed their signature Basuto ponies, a mix of 90 percent Arabian and 10 percent thoroughbred that was noted for being sure-footed in the mountains and also for having good qualities of endurance.[95] The Sotho became

[90] Thompson, *A History of South Africa*, 86–7. Burman, *Chiefdom Politics and Alien Law*, 11.

[91] Etherington, *Great Treks*, 194–5.

[92] Cory, *Rise of South Africa*, 5:125.

[93] "Moshesh, Chief of the Basutos," *South African Commercial Advertiser*, March 1, 1843, p. 2.

[94] CTAR, GH14/22 Burnett to Grey, July 20, 1857. See also "Letter from Our Correspondent in Bloemfontein," *Cape Monitor*, September 11, 1858, p. 3.

[95] Thornton, "The Basuto Pony."

known as innovators in agriculture, too. During the 1830s, Sotho farmers began to make the switch from hoes to plows and bought especially large quantities of plows during the 1860s and 1870s. Plow-based agriculture allowed them to expand their production of grain, especially in the early years, when organic nutrients still remained in the soil. Soil depletion, compaction, and erosion occurred in subsequent decades, while market conditions became unfavorable. As the historian Kate Showers points out in the introduction to her book, *Imperial Gullies*, Europeans were impressed by the willingness of the Sotho to adopt European ideas and technologies, such as plows, but the consequences of their adaptability ultimately became quite severe.

Moshoeshoe believed that the Sotho benefited from the presence of European missionaries, who brought knowledge and technology with them. Other Europeans – the Boers – brought knowledge and technology while challenging the very existence of the Sotho chiefdom. Beginning in the 1820s, Boers began to settle on territory claimed by the Sotho. The pace of settlement increased significantly after 1835, the year of the Great Trek. The trekboers disregarded warnings that the land belonged to the Sotho, who then approached the British government in the Cape Colony for assistance. The British offered protection to the Sotho in 1843 and 1845, as part of Britain's policy to establish what Leonard Thompson calls "client states" along the Cape's northern frontier. These clients, including the Griquas, emigrant Boers, Tswana, and Sotho, did not necessarily share the same interests, yet sought some order by affiliating with the British. By doing so, some received guns as presents. In 1843, the Cape governor George Napier sent a hundred muskets to the Griqua captain, Adam Kok, and seventy-five to Moshoeshoe, along with "a reasonable quantity in proportion of ammunition" as gifts to seal treaties of friendship.[96] In 1848, the Sotho, together with nearby Boers, came under the new colony, the Orange River Sovereignty. By the early 1850s, British policy was favoring European settlers, while becoming antagonistic toward Moshoeshoe. British forces attacked him twice, in 1851 and 1854. Moshoeshoe won, persuading budget-conscious policymakers in London and Cape Town to pull back from the region.[97]

Even though British policy was beginning to favor Boer independence, the arming of Africans on the northern frontier by the Cape government was an affront to Boer sensibilities. So, too, was the Cape's relatively

[96] BPP 1851 [424] vol. xxxviii, pp. 214–16.
[97] Thompson, *A History of South Africa*, 94–6.

relaxed approach to regulation. Throughout the 1850s, the republics complained about the brisk gun trade along the colonial boundary. In 1850, the Transvaal's commandant general, Andries Pretorius, wrote to Sir Harry Smith, the Cape governor, outlining his concerns. He ascribed the menacing behavior of Africans to their ownership of guns: "want zoodra als zy in bezit van vuurwapens zyn, houde zy op vrede te houde, en toond een moord en roofzuch [as soon as they come into possession of weapons, they breach the peace and commit murder and robbery]."[98] This is the first argument of this sort made by an official in South Africa: that possession of firearms changed the way that Africans behaved.

The Boers perceived that the gun trade was changing African consciousness, so they hoped for a change in British consciousness, too. This was more difficult to achieve. In 1852, after passing a measure pertaining to the slave trade, the Transvaal Volksraad invoked the assistance of the Almighty:

Ten 8ste schynt ons het 6de Art. zeer goed te zyn en verblyden wy ons dater zoodoende eene goede opening is om den zwarte natiën te beletten zich van vuurwapenen te kunnen voorzien, en wy hopen dat de goede God eindelyk de oogen onzer naburen – de Engelschen – geopend heft en zy betere inzichten bekomen hebben tot ons en hun geluk.

[On the 8th we approved Article 6 and we are pleased that this provides us with an opportune occasion to prohibit the black nations from being provided with guns; and we trust the Good Lord to open the eyes of our neighbors – the English – so that they may receive better understanding for both our well-being.][99]

Help from the Almighty was not enough. Several months later, the Transvaal *Volksraad* passed a measure stipulating that armed Africans found crossing into the republic from the Cape would be killed on the spot.[100]

When the Orange River Sovereignty gained its independence as the Boer republic of the Orange Free State in 1854, the Sotho found that they occupied a key geographic position between the new state and the Colony of Natal. Goods shipped between Bloemfontein and Durban passed close to Sotho territory, if not directly through it, which allowed the Sotho to buy and sell many items. The Sotho were the principal grain growers of the High Veld, and used the overland trade network to sell their supplies. In addition to grain, they dealt heavily in guns.

---

[98] *SAAR Transvaal*, 1:371.
[99] *SAAR Transvaal*, 2:326.
[100] *SAAR Transvaal*, 2:348–9.

One Free State magistrate reported in 1851 that in his district, Winburg, he had discovered wagons loaded in Natal for African residents of the High Veld. He observed that the gun trade in this area was "carried on to an extent almost incredible." The local newspaper observed that Boers exchanged guns and ammunition for Sotho grain.[101] The Boers had access to gunpowder from the Cape, which guaranteed the Free State a supply under Article 2 of the 1854 Bloemfontein Convention. This was not enough. In 1855, Free State officials approached the Dutch government for cannons and mortars. The Dutch declined, advising the Boers, instead, to build Roman-style catapults. This may have been one of the earliest efforts by a European country to advise residents of the southern hemisphere to adapt an "appropriate technology."[102]

Unlike the Orange Free State, the Sotho had no guarantees of arms and ammunition from Britain; in fact, arms trading with the Sotho was considered smuggling. Furthermore, under the Bloemfontein Convention the British agreed not to negotiate treaties with "natives of surrounding states" that might compromise the interests of the Free State. In 1854, Moshoeshoe protested this discriminatory treatment to Governor Grey, to no avail. He also continued smuggling and even encouraged the Sotho to make their own powder, which they did with limited success.[103]

The regulations did not stop Moshoeshoe from using guns and horses as well as grain production to build up his power and expand his chiefdom. His followers were now encroaching on land that belonged to African and Boer neighbors. In 1858, a range war broke out between the Sotho and the Free State, in which the Sotho gained the upper hand, only to see Free State forces bailed out by the British. Moshoeshoe dreaded the next encounter, seeing as it was easier for the Free State Boers to buy arms and ammunition.

Moshoeshoe bargained hard to obtain peace and security as well as arms and ammunition. He attempted peace negotiations with the Boers while simultaneously pursuing an affiliation with Britain. He met with

---

[101] Keegan, *Colonial South Africa*, 262, 272. "Should Native Servants Be Armed," *Friend of the Sovereignty*, January 20, 1851, p. 2; Letter to the Editor by "A. Farmer," *Friend of the Sovereignty*, August 1, 1851, p. 3; "Sale of Arms and Ammunition to Natives," *Friend of the Sovereignty*, August 18, 1851, p. 3.

[102] *SAAR OFS*, 2:167–73.

[103] Cory, *Rise of South Africa*, 6:127–8. Machobane, *Government and Change in Lesotho*, 32.

Grey and the leadership of the Free State in 1858, when he told the governor that there would be no peace unless the British gave him powder and lead. He equated refusal with abandonment, but while his efforts with Cape officials failed, within a year he was able to obtain arms and ammunition from Cape merchants.[104] In 1861, he wrote to the Cape governor, Sir Philip Wodehouse, asking to restore close ties and to place the Sotho under the protection of the queen. In doing so, Moshoeshoe linked good relations to access to guns. He wrote that "though I desire peace and much and above all things, yet, after it, I do desire also that powder and such supplies should be allowed to reach us in such measure as our conduct showed us to be deserving of confidence."[105]

Moshoeshoe's initial proposal did not go far, owing to retrenchment at the Cape and protests by the president of the Orange Free State. Border tensions flared into a second war lasting from 1865 to 1868, in which Free State forces gained the upper hand in spite of the fact that Moshoeshoe had added several eight-bore rifles with a range of 1,200 yards to his mountain defenses.[106] Over the years, Moshoeshoe had less and less success against Free State forces. Free State farmers acquired two-thirds of Sotho arable land, at the same time as new crops and cultivation techniques were causing soil to deteriorate.[107] Moshoeshoe continued to ask the British for annexation to the Cape Colony, which was not forthcoming. Without British protection, Moshoeshoe was forced to cede large portions of territory to the Free State in 1865. The Sotho position was so precarious that one of Moshoeshoe's most prominent sons, Molapo, even became a subject of the Boer republic. By 1867, Moshoeshoe was desperate enough that he began to negotiate with Theophilus Shepstone, native affairs secretary for Natal, even though Shepstone insisted on disarmament as well as the transfer of some land to European settlers. Luckily for the Sotho, the Cape governor, Sir Philip Wodehouse, was becoming more sympathetic.[108]

To stabilize the border, Wodehouse recommended to the Colonial Office that Britain annex Basutoland. Wodehouse would be the head of state, in his role as high commissioner for southern Africa, but the

---

[104] *SAAR OFS*, 3:352–3, 433–5; 4:70–1.
[105] Machobane, *Government and Change in Lesotho*, 34.
[106] Tylden, "Swivel Guns, Elephant Guns – So-Called – and Large Bores," 17.
[107] Showers, *Imperial Gullies*, 12–24.
[108] Thompson, *A History of South Africa*, 106–7. Burman, *Chiefdom Politics and Alien Law*, 14–16.

Sotho would be subject to their own laws. The Colonial Office balked at such a prospect, which they deemed to be unnecessary. Moshoeshoe then cleverly approached Natal's lieutenant governor, who was prepared to annex Basutoland. Negotiating with Moshoeshoe represented a constitutional overreach by the lieutenant governor, who was technically under the supervision of Wodehouse. Wodehouse wrote to London urging the Colonial Office to approve his own annexation of Basutoland to the Cape as a way of validating the office of the high commissioner. This argument was accepted by the Colonial Office in 1867. In 1868, Britain annexed Basutoland as a territory under the high commissioner. Wodehouse sent a small unit of the Cape Frontier Armed and Mounted Police to secure the border. He also traveled to meet the Sotho chiefs and proclaim them to be British subjects.[109]

Wodehouse was not a white knight riding to the rescue of Moshoeshoe and the Sotho. Cape rule came with a price. It was established policy along the Cape's frontier to gradually undermine the chiefs and establish "civilized" ways. During this process, guns became contested symbols, connoting many different definitions of modernity, risk, and civilization to many different African, Boer, and British leaders.

[109] Bradlow, "Cape Government Rule," 122. Machobane, *Government and Change in Lesotho*, 39–40.

5

Capitalism, Race, and Breechloaders, 1840–80

In the middle of the nineteenth century, all South Africans, even those in remote areas, were experiencing a shift in economic development. For years, South Africans had not produced much that interested the world at large, except for ivory, feathers, and hides in the interior and wine at the Cape. While demand for these goods had major effects on South Africa, total sales amounted to an insignificant portion of the world economy. In fact, the people who lived in the South African interior were chronically short of cash. Then, in the 1840s, commercial agriculture, led by sheep farming, began to generate substantial income. By the time diamonds were discovered in 1867, South Africa's economy was growing and more people were working for money.

Economic principles were affecting politics in new ways, too. Britain allowed the formation of the republics in order to save money. Underlying this decision was a shift from an earlier humanitarian imperialism to a utilitarian imperialism based on principles of economy. Such principles made it possible for settlers north of the Orange River to institute race-based republics. Settler agriculture north of the Orange River was difficult to sustain beyond the subsistence level. Yet as more productive, more capitalistic agriculture took hold in the Cape Colony, and as mining developed in the 1860s and 1870s, many Cape business leaders, as well as many British administrators, sought to emulate the racial policies of the Boer republics as a way to mobilize and control labor forces. One of the principal enticements held out to African men considering working in Cape capitalist enterprises was the possibility of earning enough money to buy guns and ammunition. Yet technological enhancements to African power were problematic for Britons and Boers who sought a discriminatory racial order.

As we have already seen, the Sotho adapted their economy to the presence of Europeans by producing crops for the market. Other African people followed the same path. In Natal and the Eastern Cape, many Africans were known to be good at European-style farming. These African farmers competed directly with European settlers, who clamored for African labor on their own farms. Many of those African farmers who were successful valued the new ways of production, to the extent that they ceased to consider themselves "traditional" members of their societies. Many African societies divided between those who considered themselves "traditionalists" and those who fancied themselves "modernizers." In the Cape, as the modernizers became more prosperous, they sought to claim political rights, like the right to vote, just at the time when racial thinking was taking stronger hold in the imagination of Europeans.

Racism has a complex genealogy among the white settlers of South Africa. In the Western Cape, the VOC instituted racial discrimination as a way to govern slaves and slaveholders, yet racism itself has deeper origins in general European chauvinism as well as in the particularities of violent contacts between Khoi and Europeans at the Cape. As Cape colonists moved eastward, they brought slaves and acquired "servants," in many cases continuing patriarchal practices as a way of extending and mimicking wealthier Western Cape patroons. Crais argues, in *White Supremacy and Black Resistance*, that eastern settlers believed that Africans embodied all the values – indolence, promiscuity, and violence – that they sought to avoid themselves (often unsuccessfully). Such characterizations of Africans as "the other" became commonplace in the Eastern Cape during the 1830s and 1840s, even as more humanitarian views tended to be espoused by white elites in Cape Town. By the 1870s, humanitarian liberalism was waning and a combination of utilitarian liberalism and racism was waxing throughout South Africa. This had partly to do with continued conflict between Africans and Europeans on the frontier and partly to do with an intensification of racial beliefs in Europe.[1]

Diamonds and Guns at Kimberley

As racism became prevalent and commercial farming spread, the discovery of mineral wealth involved even more South Africans in the cash economy. In 1867, diamonds were found on the northern frontier of the

---

[1] The origin of race and class is one of the most heavily worked topics in South African history. For an introduction, see Saunders, *The Making of the South African Past*.

Cape Colony, near Hopetown, just south of the Orange River. By 1870, more diamonds were discovered near the banks of the Vaal River, starting around the confluence of the Vaal and the Orange rivers and moving upriver to Barkly West, about 160 kilometers to the north. By 1871, the region was playing host to ten thousand miners. Then, major diamond discoveries were made at the farm of the De Beers family, near what is today Kimberley. These became South Africa's biggest diamond diggings, with fifty thousand miners at work by 1873. As in other mining boom towns, conditions were squalid. To make matters even more challenging, the railhead went only as far as Wellington, meaning that all goods had to be trucked in from Port Elizabeth and Cape Town. This continued until 1885, when the railroad finally reached Kimberley. When the boom town was connected to the railroad, the diamond region could take advantage of the communications and transportation revolution that was associated with the local development of capitalism. The telegraph, the railroad, and the steamship all made it easier to travel around South Africa. These new technologies also connected South Africa more closely to the rest of the industrializing world.[2]

Kimberley and the surrounding territory was claimed by the Cape, the Orange Free State, the South African Republic (Transvaal), and the Griqua. An official enquiry, the Keate Commission, ruled in favor of the Griqua, who were "persuaded" to ask Britain for protection. Based on this request, the British created the new, separate colony of Griqualand West in 1871, stretching from the Orange River up to the Molopo River, which forms the present-day boundary between South Africa and Botswana. Griqualand West eventually became part of the Cape in 1880. During its seven years of independence, Griqualand West followed the laws of the Cape, where *de jure* discrimination was forbidden, yet *de facto* discrimination was practiced. Many miners voiced a preference for a legal, race-based division of land and labor, along the lines of the Boer republics.

Workers migrated to Kimberley from all around the world. The European male migrants often had some experience in mining and commanded high wages, in the range of £2 per day. This compared with a rate of 10–30 shillings (there were 20 shillings to the pound) per week for African men, who were generally working as unskilled laborers. This was less than the amount that the Europeans earned, but for most African workers this was still a great deal of money. African men were migrating from as far away as present-day Mozambique and Tanzania in order to acquire cash at Kimberley, which they hoped to use in purchasing guns,

---

[2] Saunders, Bundy, and Oakes, *Illustrated History of South Africa*, 166.

tools, and cattle. Pedi men were thought to have wanted guns more than others, as a way of gaining additional security from their Boer, Zulu, and Swazi neighbors; the Sotho mine workers used cash to buy everything that was for sale. African workers usually entered into contracts, lasting three to six months, with white employers, and registered with the local magistrate. Desertion was illegal, and in the minds of the employers, it was associated with theft, which could be punished by whipping and imprisonment.[3]

Kimberley became "the cradle and testing ground of social and economic policy," to borrow words from C. W. De Kiewiet's classic study, *A History of South Africa*.[4] The Cape governor and high commissioner, Sir Henry Barkly, together with the lieutenant governor of Griqualand West, Sir Richard Southey, fought to protect small-scale miners, called "diggers," against large-scale capitalists. Southey passed ordinances prohibiting individuals from acquiring more than ten claims, yet the diggers he was trying to protect disagreed with his policy of protecting African laborers and claimholders equally under the law. As the mines went deeper, small claims became ever more difficult to work without amalgamation. A digger rebellion, together with the Colonial Office's decision to allow amalgamation, forced Southey to resign in 1875. After that, the process of amalgamation accelerated.

Mine labor and guns were closely related. Guns were among the most popular purchases by African migrant laborers, who found several shops selling guns near the diggings. That being said, guns were not the only purchases, as some contemporaries claimed. In his history of Kimberley, *South Africa's City of Diamonds*, William Worger shows that African workers were also interested in woolen goods. By 1876, they were spending more money on blankets than on guns. Cash earnings were also invested in land, livestock, plows, and wagons, at a considerably higher rate than they were invested in guns. For example, Sotho mine workers and grain merchants at Kimberley acquired more livestock than guns: guns accounted for only 2.5 percent of the property that they purchased.[5]

Guns were only a part of Kimberley's commerce, yet guns were highly visible. Near the diamond mines, merchants arranged for potential customers to witness new weapons. Product demonstrations were not restricted to utility alone. "At knock off time," recalled one miner, "our Kaffirs used to pass down streets of tented shops owned by white

---

[3] Saunders, Bundy, and Oakes, *Illustrated History of South Africa*, 169–70.
[4] De Kiewiet, *History of South Africa*, 90.
[5] Worger, *South Africa's City of Diamonds*, 76.

traders and presided over by yelling black salesmen whirling guns above their heads. These they discharged in the air, crying: 'Reka, reka, mona mtskeka.' (Buy, buy, buy a gun.)" Kimberley traders sold thousands of guns. The most popular model was the Tower musket, typically a Brown Bess that had been converted to a percussion lock. In Kimberley it sold for about £4, the equivalent of three months' wages – even though such a gun sold for £2 in Cape Town. Sometimes African men worked longer for better models, like the new £25 breechloaders.[6]

It was not completely new for African migrant laborers to buy guns. African wage laborers from the north began to migrate to rural areas of the Cape Colony during the 1840s, more than two decades before the discovery of diamonds at Kimberley. During the 1850s and 1860s, Pedi migrant laborers from the Transvaal sought work in the Cape in order to buy arms with which to fight against Zulu, Swazi, and Boers. When the Kimberley mines opened during the late 1860s and early 1870s, they attracted Pedi laborers because they offered higher wages than the farms, as well as a shorter distance to travel. Why, then, did the Pedi prefer to exchange their labor for guns, rather than cattle and grain? Grain markets were not easily accessible, ecological pressure on the land hurt farming, ivory hunting was moving north out of Pedi territory, and cattle wealth was restricted only to a few individuals. The Pedi also faced strong threats from their neighbors. By contrast, the Sotho and Tsonga who migrated to Kimberley seem to have been less pressured internally and externally. Most Sotho men went to Kimberley to supplement commodity production and acquire guns and bridewealth, while young Tsonga men seemed more motivated by the prospect of improving kinship status.[7]

The Sotho and Pedi chiefdoms, bordering on the Boer republics, had particular concerns with guns and security. From 1865 to 1869, the Sotho war with the Orange Free State revealed an emerging arms gap between Boers and Africans. At the start of the war, most Free State troops were armed with converted percussion cap "roer" smoothbores, which did not give any particular battlefield advantage over Sotho Tower muskets. Other Free Staters were armed with imported sporting guns, but as the war progressed, the Free State bought Whitworth rifled breechloaders. The Free State also added a breech-loading Armstrong cannon to its three older muzzle-loading cannons.[8] These acquisitions put pressure on the Pedi and Sotho men to buy more – and better – weapons.

[6] Turrell, *Kimberley Diamond Fields*, 61–2.
[7] Turrell, *Kimberley Diamond Fields*, 21–3.
[8] Fraser, *Episodes in My Life*, 418–19.

Some African men relied on labor migration to obtain guns. Others did not have to migrate. During the 1870s, the Zulu – who were just beyond the range of British authority – acquired large numbers of firearms from traders, most famously from John Dunn, an Englishman who had become fully acculturated among the Zulu. Thanks to Dunn and others, nearly every Zulu warrior had a gun. Most were obsolete. According to Ian Knight, who has written extensively about Zulu military history, there were about twenty thousand guns. Out of these, about five hundred were breechloaders; two thousand five hundred were recent percussion rifles, such as the Enfield; five thousand were percussion muskets; and the rest were even more obsolete flintlock muskets. In 1879, after the British defeated the Zulu at Nyezane, the *Natal Mercury* noted that

there were all sorts of guns. From Potsdam, from Danzig, Murzig, and Tulle, from "Manchester, N. H., United States," etc. The majority, however, were Tower muskets. The foreign weapons are very ancient indeed; some of them manufactured in 1835. As far as I could make out by the inscriptions, the continental weapons were condemned army ones. The sights were the most extraordinary contrivances.[9]

After the subsequent battle of Gingindlovu, a similar survey of captured guns revealed a similar collection: Tower percussion muskets mixed in with discarded foreign makes, together with a cave full of low-quality powder. Only five Martini-Henry breechloaders were found, even though the Zulu had taken one thousand at Isandlwana, where they had defeated a British force, killing more than eight hundred redcoats.[10]

Men from another chiefdom bordering Natal – the Mpondo – also armed themselves extensively from 1860 to 1880, largely on account of the arming of neighboring chiefdoms. Firearms held some appeal earlier, but high costs held back the market – in Pondoland, a muzzle-loader sold for six oxen in 1861. By 1867, as European armies made the switch to breechloaders, muzzle-loaders became inexpensive and Mpondo warriors began to buy them in large quantities. In the late 1860s, visitors to Chief Mqikela noted the presence of many armed, mounted warriors. By the 1870s, as tensions increased between the Mpondo and the colonies, the Mpondo began to arm themselves with breechloaders. According to the historian William Beinart, the Mpondo obtained many weapons from neighboring chiefdoms that were just coming under colonial authority.

[9] *Natal Mercury*, February 12, 1879, as quoted by Knight, *Anatomy of the Zulu Army*, 169.
[10] Knight, *Anatomy of the Zulu Army*, 169.

During this process, warriors were selling weapons illegally before they could be confiscated. And as in Zululand, many guns were also introduced by traders.[11]

Estimating the Volume of the Midcentury Gun Trade

The gun trade in the Cape Colony grew significantly at midcentury as European armies dumped outmoded weapons and as Africans had more ready access to cash. According to official statistics, between 1857 and 1871, an average of 4,276 firearms of all sorts were imported into the Cape in any given year, with an average of 3,603 entering for "home consumption." From 1872 to 1876, the figures jumped considerably, with total imports averaging 38,510 per year and the total "entered for home consumption" averaging 32,241. The peak year was 1873, when 64,126 were imported and 47,904 entered for home consumption. The figures declined after 1876, as new regulations were put in place. Between 1877 and 1881, Cape imports dropped on average to 9,656 per year, while 6,305 entered annually for home consumption.

Of those guns that were not entered for home consumption at the Cape, many were exported to other colonies, principally to Natal. Natal's import figures, while lower than the Cape's, follow the same overall pattern. From 1861 to 1871, Natal imported an average of 1,576 firearms per year, while an annual average of 1,541 were entered for home consumption. From 1872 to 1875, the average annual imports rose to 14,119 and the average entered for home consumption was 8,846 each year. The figures fell off after 1875. From 1876 to 1881, average annual imports declined to 1,847, while the number of guns entered for home consumption fell to an average of 1,568 per year.

In Natal, it is worth noting the discrepancy between the figure imported and the figure entered for home consumption. Between 1872 and 1877, the year before the Zulu War, 61,143 firearms were imported, while only 38,801 were entered for home consumption, leaving 22,342 to be exported. While some went to other colonies, it is strongly suspected by Ian Knight, the historian of the Zulu army, that most of these weapons were exported to Mozambique and then traded back south to the Zulu, who were not yet incorporated within the colony of Natal.[12]

---

[11] Beinart, *Political Economy of Pondoland*, 25.
[12] Colony of Natal, *Blue Books*; Knight, *Anatomy of the Zulu Army*, 169. Knight claims that 40,000 guns were reexported, with 20,000 going to Mozambique. It is plausible that

The arming of South Africa is impressive from a statistical standpoint. Between 1857 and 1881, a total of 308,512 firearms entered the Cape and Natal for home consumption. This figure does not count any firearms that entered through Mozambique, nor does it count illegal imports, which are impossible to trace. It also does not count older, outmoded firearms that arrived before 1857 and that were still in circulation. In any event, it is interesting to note that in 1870 the total European population of what is today the Republic of South Africa was 250,000, while it has been estimated that about ten times as many Africans lived there, for a total population of 2,750,000.[13] Women tended not to own guns, so for argument's sake we may reduce the number of potential gun owners by half. Another half might be removed again, to account for children and the infirm, which brings us to an estimated population of about 687,500 able-bodied men. Therefore, to make a very rough estimate, it seems that between 1857 and 1881, enough arms entered the Cape and Natal legally to arm about three-sevenths of all able-bodied men south of the Limpopo (Tables 1 and 2). Since guns entered the region legally and illegally at other points, particularly Mozambique, the real rate of gun ownership was probably more like one-half of all able-bodied men.

These rough estimates are derived from the colonial *Blue Books*, statistical volumes compiled every year by government officials. Others report higher and lower numbers. R. V. Turrell, who has written a monograph on the history of Kimberley, cites a newspaper, a magazine, and official correspondence to make the claim that from April 1873 to June 1874, seventy-five thousand guns were sold at Kimberley, while during 1875 Kimberley traders stocked two hundred thousand guns.[14] Another historian of mining at Kimberley, William Worger, has arrived at a different estimate for gun sales. He used the colonial *Blue Books* and British parliamentary papers as well as the official "gun returns" for the colony of Griqualand West to arrive at the reasonable estimate that

---

20,000 may have gone to Mozambique and then to the Zulu, because several sources comment on Zulu efforts to arm themselves. Even so, the figure of 40,000 reexported is not supported in the Blue Books.

[13] Thompson, *A History of South Africa*, 108.

[14] Turrell, *Capital and Labour*, p. 249, fn. 57, cites J. B. Currey, "The Diamond Fields of Griqualand West and Their Probable Influence on the Native Races of South Africa," *Journal of the Society of the Arts*, XXIV, 1876, p. 379; *Diamond News*, 15, August 25, 1874, Editorial, "Legislative Council debate on Gun tax" (12, 18 Aug.); and a letter from Coleman to Currey, 19 Aug. 1874, From Servants Registrar's Office, CAD, GLW 71. These sources support Turrell's claim.

TABLE 1. *Guns Imported and Entered for Home Consumption at the Cape, 1857–81*

Year	Guns Entered for Home Consumption				Total Guns Imported				Declared Value of Guns in Sterling				
	Single Barrels	Double Barrels	Pistols	Total Guns	Single Barrels	Double Barrels	Pistols	Total Guns	Single Barrels	Double Barrels	Pistols	All Imported Firearms	Average Value of an Imported Gun
1857	743	133	0	876	796	154	113	1,063	3,725	812	342	4,879	4.59
1858	607	1,119	2	1,728	703	1,149	347	2,199	4,597	9,229	1,032	14,858	6.76
1859	901	2,015	0	2,916	1,187	2,005	513	3,705	3,903	14,700	1,789	20,392	5.50
1860	1,262	2,300	0	3,562	1,277	2,351	673	4,301	4,546	15,245	2,692	22,483	5.23
1861	2,172	3,277	2	5,451	2,538	3,486	643	6,667	8,247	26,165	2,091	36,503	5.48
1862	2,650	2,471	0	5,121	3,763	3,075	527	7,365	8,039	27,557	2,029	37,625	5.11
1863	2,695	2,284	0	4,979	3,619	2,037	305	5,961	7,430	19,722	1,172	28,324	4.75
1864	1,911	648	0	2,559	1,967	587	449	3,003	4,110	4,157	1,368	9,635	3.21
1865	2,291	430	50	2,771	1,912	434	410	2,756	4,794	3,125	1,349	9,268	3.36
1866	2,507	417	0	2,924	2,865	419	217	3,501	5,054	2,883	562	8,499	2.43
1867	4,249	430	0	4,679	4,428	284	524	5,236	7,188	1,961	535	9,684	1.85
1868	2,402	329	50	2,781	3,292	230	163	3,685	5,180	2,042	415	7,637	2.07
1869	2,037	247	0	2,284	1,936	250	371	2,557	4,048	2,502	1,108	7,658	2.99
1870	3,702	317	0	4,019	3,546	295	370	4,211	7,246	2,481	911	10,638	2.53

	Guns Entered for Home Consumption				Total Guns Imported				Declared Value of Guns in Sterling				
Year	Single Barrels	Double Barrels	Pistols	Total Guns	Single Barrels	Double Barrels	Pistols	Total Guns	Single Barrels	Double Barrels	Pistols	All Imported Firearms	Average Value of an Imported Gun
1871	6,548	674	167	7,389	6,623	602	703	7,928	10,513	4,247	1,600	16,360	2.06
1872	31,378	1,784	27	33,189	34,728	1,752	606	37,086	41,162	9,022	1,230	51,414	1.39
1873	44,347	3,487	70	47,904	59,014	4,189	923	64,126	86,306	19,706	1,603	107,615	1.68
1874	22,076	2,793	0	24,869	31,244	2,533	993	34,770	74,586	15,432	1,486	91,504	2.63
1875	30,865	2,666	50	33,581	24,282	2,679	1,056	28,017	49,668	12,695	1,366	63,729	2.27
1876	19,376	2,278	9	21,663	25,134	2,332	1,089	28,555	48,563	11,838	1,543	61,944	2.17
1877	8,847	1,909	10	10,766	6,990	2,095	983	10,068	21,488	9,736	1,679	32,903	3.27
1878	7,377	1,088	176	8,641	9,306	1,090	2,759	13,155	27,527	9,141	4,711	41,379	3.15
1879	3,846	778	58	4,682	6,171	696	1,712	8,579	14,600	7,181	2,764	24,545	2.86
1880	1,959	784	99	2,842	1,980	823	1,578	4,381	8,793	7,083	2,410	18,286	4.17
1881	3,651	945	0	4,596	7,797	965	3,334	12,096	27,963	8,816	5,561	42,340	3.50
Total	210,399	35,603	770	246,772	247,098	36,512	21,361	304,971	489,276	247,478	43,348	780,102	2.56

Source: Colonial Blue Books.

TABLE 2. *Guns Imported and Entered for Home Consumption in Natal, 1861–81*

Year	Guns Entered for Home Consumption			Total Guns Imported			Declared Value of Guns in Sterling			Average value of an imported Gun
	Gun Barrels	Pistols	Total Guns	Gun Barrels	Pistols	Total Guns	Gun Barrels	Pistols	All Imported Firearms	
1861	1,218	71	1,289	1,750	72	1,822	2,222	260	2,482	1.36
1862	1,017	63	1,080	897	63	960	4,966	273	5,239	5.46
1863	1,626	177	1,803	1,475	172	1,647	7,664	873	8,537	5.18
1864	1,328	117	1,445	1,439	114	1,553	6,405	501	6,906	4.45
1865	868	126	994	875	112	987	4,843	562	5,405	5.48
1866	758	52	810	708	40	748	2,596	211	2,807	3.75
1867	634	83	717	531	81	612	2,654	350	3,004	4.91
1868	651	132	783	621	132	753	3,060	499	3,559	4.73
1869	1,102	150	1,252	1,182	141	1,323	4,958	496	5,454	4.12
1870	2,765	99	2,864	2,675	98	2,773	7,122	389	7,511	2.71
1871	3,782	127	3,909	4,031	127	4,158	8,293	410	8,703	2.09
1872	8,676	163	8,839	9,950	158	10,108	19,609	479	20,088	1.99
1873	14,582	159	14,741	19,920	159	20,079	37,933	494	38,427	1.91
1874	6,930	271	7,201	14,422	287	14,709	27,488	828	28,316	1.93
1875	4,154	451	4,605	11,129	451	11,580	22,644	1,477	24,121	2.08
1876	2,104	287	2,391	3,060	287	3,347	10,112	572	10,684	3.19
1877	846	178	1,024	1,142	178	1,320	4,520	402	4,922	3.73
1878	1,791	230	2,021	1,939	230	2,169	8,272	505	8,777	4.05
1879	1,211	531	1,742	1,526	531	2,057	5,908	1,461	7,369	3.58
1880	961	238	1,199	919	238	1,157	4,560	521	5,081	4.39
1881	836	195	1,031	838	195	1,033	3,753	470	4,223	4.09
Total	57,840	3,900	61,740	81,029	3,866	84,895	199,582	12,033	211,615	2.49

Source: Colonial Blue Books.

128

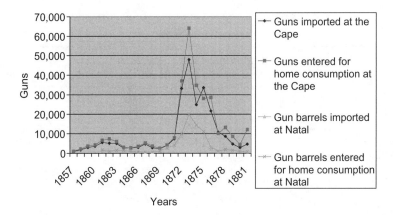

Years

between 1872 and 1877, there were seventy-eight thousand guns sold at Kimberley.[15]

It is difficult to verify or contradict the primary sources that are the basis of all these estimates, because it is likely that colonial officials did not detect a portion of the gun trade. In 1875, in the midst of the "Black Flag" revolt, a rebellion by armed white miners, the lieutenant governor of Griqualand West, Sir Richard Southey, investigated how well the diamond fields gun regulations were being implemented and discovered "a good deal of illicit trade." Southey wrote to Barkly that "there seems to have been much laxity on the part of the Officer whose duty it is to issue permits & keep a check." Southey implied that official corruption was involved, for he and other officials had been offered shares in diamond companies in exchange for favors. Corruption may obscure the figures for the gun trade, as did the system for recording information.[16] The Griqualand West records in the Cape archives indicate that permits were issued to merchants who intended to sell guns, but the records do not include information about the ultimate buyers. In most cases, guns imported into Griqualand West appear to have been sold locally, but in some cases the guns were transshipped to northern destinations.[17]

[15] Worger, *South Africa's City of Diamonds*, 74. On p. 74, fn. 23 cites CTAR, GLW 48, 53, 58, 76, 183, "Gun Returns," as well as the Cape *Blue Books* for 1872–6, and BPP XLIII (150) 709 (1878–9) "Return of All Guns and Ammunition Shipped to British and Portuguese Possessions in South Africa . . . from 1874 to 1878."

[16] CTAR, GLW 115, Semiofficial Letters, Southey to Barkly, March 25, 1875.

[17] CTAR, GLW 45, "Gun Returns, Du Toit's Pan, Kimberley, Barkly, Langford Station, 1873–1874," records four shipments totaling 852 guns to the "interior."

TABLE 3. *Volume of the Trade in Guns and Ammunition at Hopetown, 1861–73*

	Guns	Gunpowder (in pounds)	Lead (in pounds)	Percussion Caps
1861	47	2,100	9,000	20,000
1862	93	5,250	15,600	28,000
1864	302	5,400	11,000	95,000
1865	311	32,550	58,900	544,000
1866	2,110	29,000	48,800	560,000
1867	3,193	41,850	73,300	1,587,000
1868	1,104	183,100	50,500	1,56,000
1870	2,450	39,100	112,500	2,055,000
1873	12,692	72,975	55,657	7,116,750

Source: CTAR, see footnote 19 below.

Many colonial officials bemoaned the gun trade at the diamond fields. Yet official protests – and large-scale trading in guns and ammunition – were already well established in the 1860s at Hopetown, a small town in the far Northern Cape, where traders from Port Elizabeth stopped before they crossed the Orange River. During the 1860s, Hopetown's resident magistrates and civil commissioners recorded the transfer of thousands of guns, together with large supplies of caps, lead, and powder. The records are not complete and those that do exist probably understate the volume of the trade. As the resident magistrate of Hopetown, W. B. Chalmers, put it, in 1864, "there has been a great deal of illicit traffic in firearms and ammunition carried on by the traders and merchants here with the natives beyond the boundary, and as there is no police force along this boundary, there is no way of checking it."[18] Even so the records do present intriguing data about the volume and nature of the gun trade. Some years appear to be relatively incomplete. Only complete years are included in Table 3, which shows a steady rise in amounts of guns and ammunition permitted to cross the colonial boundary near Hopetown.[19]

Under the terms of the Cape governor's Circular Number 44 of 1861, guns were permitted to cross the colonial boundary but traders had to post a bond certifying that the guns would be brought back across the

[18] CTAR, CO 3073, RM Hopetown to Col. Secy., October 6, 1864. Similar remarks are made in CTAR, CO 3041, RM Hopetown to Col. Secy., March 6, 1862, and in CTAR, CO 3175, RM Hopetown to Col. Secy., February 18, 1870.

[19] CTAR, CO 2994 (1860), 3022–3 (1861), 3041 (1862), 3073 (1864), 3087 (1865), 3102 (1866), 3117 (1867), 3135 (1868), 3145 (1869), 3175 (1870), Correspondence of RM Hopetown with the Colonial Secretary's office.

border within a year's time. In November of 1865, W. B. Chalmers, the resident magistrate of Hopetown, requested that this rule be changed, on the grounds that the guns were "of such an inferior description" that they were "not worth bringing back." The government approved the suggestion in January 1866.[20] From then on, traders had to enter a bond that only required that guns and ammunition would not be delivered to the Transvaal or the Orange Free State and that the articles would only be used for hunting. Starting then, the volume of weapons and ammunition brought through Hopetown appears to have remained steady in the early 1860s, when the ostensible purpose of the guns was for hunting. Sales rose somewhat in the late 1860s, possibly correlated with the opening of the diamond diggings nearby, but probably also correlated with the war between the Orange Free State and the Sotho, which lasted from 1865 to 1869. By comparison, when gun trading reached its peak in 1873, the figures are much higher, with gun figures five times that of 1870 levels. Some guns were still destined for "the interior" or "Matabeleland" (Ndebeleland), where elephant hunting took place, but by and large the guns and ammunition were destined for the diamond fields.[21]

South African markets experienced a rise in the supply of weapons, so it is not a surprise that the average value of these weapons declined. It is interesting to note that while gun imports at the Cape and Natal rose only during the early 1870s, the value of an imported gun at the Cape began to decline in 1862. The decline became steep in the mid-1860s, which correlates with the adoption of breech-loading rifles – and the discarding of older muzzle-loaders – by the British, French, and Prussian armies. It appears that global market conditions drove down the price of guns in South Africa, more than the saturation of the regional market – although that may have become a factor, too, by the mid-1870s. In 1877, there is a notable uptick in the average value of firearms imported at the Cape, although this might be a reflection of the availability of modern, expensive breechloaders for sale (see Figure 5).

In the 1870s, most guns circulating in South Africa were still Tower muskets. These percussion-lock smoothbore muzzle-loaders cost between

---

[20] CTAR, CO 3087, RM Hopetown to Colonial Secretary, November 15, 1865; CO 3012, RM Hopetown to Col. Secy., with minute by Col. Secy., January 10, 1866.

[21] Figures from 1873 are taken from CTAR, GLW 52, Griqualand West Returns for 1873. The figures are not precise: occasionally gunpowder was counted by kegs of unspecified weight, percussion caps were weighed in pounds and not counted, and lead was counted in boxes and not pounds. Be that as it may, there was still a significant rise in the number of guns and ammunition passing through Hopetown.

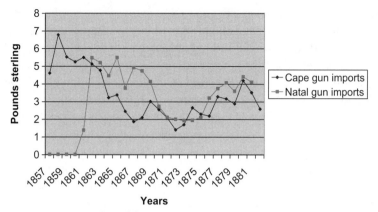

FIGURE 5. Average value of firearms imported at the Cape and Natal, 1857–81. (*Source:* Colonial Blue Books.)

two and four pounds sterling. Somewhat more expensive percussion-lock rifled muzzle-loaders were almost as common, too, like the British army's recently discarded Enfield rifles, which by the early 1870s cost between three and four pounds.[22] During the 1860s and 1870s, breechloaders also came on the market. These cost more than twenty-five pounds, yet delivered the user a great deal more firepower. The adoption of breechloaders is not fully documented in the records of the resident magistrate at Hopetown. The magistrate did not report on the types of weapons passing through to the diamond mines. The only indication we have is in the 1873 figures, which document the number of cartridges passing through Hopetown. On the South African frontier, prefabricated cartridges were not typically used in old-style percussion-lock muskets or rifles. Shooters used loose powder, wadding, and balls. Factory-made paper cartridges were used in muzzle-loading Enfield rifles, although these too could be loaded with loose powder, wadding, and minié balls. Different types of metallic cartridges were used in the Snider-Enfield and the Martini-Henry breechloaders. At Hopetown in 1873, 134,024 cartridges passed through, compared with 7,116,750 percussion caps, meaning that of all the shots fired by the customers, roughly 98 percent were fired from percussion-lock muskets or rifles that were becoming outmoded in Europe and North America.

[22] Boyle, *To the Cape for Diamonds*, 158. Doughty, *Early Diamond Days*, 184.

The Breechloader Revolution

During the middle of the nineteenth century, two revolutions took place in South Africa that related to global developments: a capitalist revolution and a breechloader revolution. Farming had been developing rapidly for decades, while mining was beginning in the vicinity of Kimberley. At the same time, firearms could now be bought that loaded from the back or "breech" end. The capitalist revolution and the breechloader revolution were related: as more Africans were drawn to migrant labor, they often spent their money on weapons. Yet this is not the only way in which the two revolutions were linked. They were also associated with deskilling: it took fewer skills to fire a breechloader than a muzzle-loader. In South Africa the breechloader revolution resembled the capitalist revolution in a certain way: African men with multiple skills, especially skills in managing cattle, might find themselves employed by settlers and miners as unskilled labor. It also took less skill to fire the new weapons.

At the individual level, interaction with the material world became less meaningful, or more alienated, as it was drained of skill. As weapons became more industrialized, shooters could not effect their own repairs and modifications, or let community members help them, either. Local specialization was no longer required, say, in making bullets or simple repairs. All shooters came to depend on highly skilled city gunsmiths, as well as on European ammunition factories.[23]

The spread of guns and shooting skills along the South African frontier is best understood in an environmental and social context. In the earlier part of the nineteenth century, people living in remote areas killed wildlife for food. At the same time hunting became one of South Africa's most important economic activities because tusks, hides, and feathers commanded high prices on world markets. Hunting could even provide more income than cattle farming, according to the famous account of the naturalist William Burchell, who traveled in the interior in 1812.[24]

---

[23] Douglas Harper makes the point that alienation and decline in skill are processes that are related to the decline in a sense of community. See *Working Knowledge*, 91.

[24] Burchell, *Travels in the Interior of Southern Africa*, 2:285. While Burchell was living among the Tlhaping, a man offered eight oxen in exchange for one gun, which seemed like a high price, unless one considered the value that the gun could produce by supporting hunting. Guns remained relatively rare in this part of South Africa until the 1850s. By the 1870s, guns were widespread, thanks in part to the availability of wage labor at the nearby Kimberley diamond mines. There, an old (but still powerful) rifled percussion musket could be bought for four pounds sterling, the equivalent of three months' wages,

Burchell observed how, as European trade networks reached into the interior, Africans were becoming involved in a cash economy. Many African hunters worked as clients of European traders, who relied on Africans for expert tracking and supplied them with guns and ammunition.

In the early nineteenth century, military and civilian firearms incorporated a number of technical improvements, changing the skill requirements of firearms considerably. Gunmakers removed the flintlock and replaced it with the percussion lock, which came into wide service by the 1840s. The percussion lock consisted of a small indentation on top of the touchhole. The indentation was designed to hold a percussion cap – a small, covered charge of explosive. When the hammer struck, the cap exploded. This in turn ignited the charge inside the barrel. This is a much more reliable means of igniting the charge than a flintlock, especially in damp weather. For the user, the percussion lock involved less skill and fewer risks than the flintlock, the reason why, by the 1840s and 1850s, most armies switched to the percussion lock. The percussion cap increased the reliability of firing and the speed of loading. These were important factors for hunters and soldiers.[25]

At around the same time, improvements in the construction of ammunition persuaded most soldiers and civilians to replace their inaccurate smoothbores with more accurate rifles. In the 1840s, Capt. Minié of the French army invented a bullet with a hollow base that expanded outward when fired. The bullet, or "minié ball," could now be slightly smaller in diameter than the rifle's bore. It could be dropped down the muzzle quickly, and then, when fired, it would expand, grip the rifled grooves, and spin its way out.[26] The most common type of muzzle-loading rifle from this period in the British Empire was the "Enfield," a 0.577-caliber weapon produced by the Royal Armories at Enfield Lock. The 1853 model had a 39-inch barrel, attached to a heavy wooden stock by three metal bands. The rifle was sufficiently accurate that the rear sight could be adjusted up to a range of 800 yards, quite a difference from the Brown Bess, which was accurate to 50 yards. In 1858, Enfield added a 33-inch version with two bands. It also made carbines of the same general pattern. These firearms were carried by the British army in the Crimean War, as

---

while a modern breechloader might cost around twenty-five pounds. See Turrell, *Capital and Labour on the Kimberley Diamond Fields*, 61–2.

[25] Headrick, *Tools of Empire*, 85–8. For an extensive discussion of the switch from flint-locks to percussion locks, see Blackmore, *British Military Firearms, 1650–1850*.

[26] Headrick, *The Tools of Empire*, 85–8.

well as by many other armies. They were used extensively by both sides in the American Civil War.

By the 1860s, further technical improvements made it possible for soldiers and civilians to switch from muzzle-loaders to breechloaders. For centuries, gunsmiths had been experimenting with guns that loaded from the back end, or breech. In the early nineteenth century, newer and better breechloaders began to gain acceptance. The main problem holding back breechloaders from widespread adoption was continued reliance on black powder and cartridges made from paper or cloth. Soft cartridges made it difficult to obtain a tight seal in the breech, which caused the ignition of the cartridge to blast hot gasses back into the shooter's face. The older breech-loading cartridges did not contain a means of ignition: a percussion cap still needed to be placed before the hammer.

Col. Edward Boxer of the British army solved these problems by placing bullets, powder, and caps in brass cartridges that were often wrapped in wax paper. These cartridges made it possible to obtain a tighter seal in the breech and eliminated the placement and removal of percussion caps from the procedures required to fire a weapon. Metallic cartridges also did a better job of protecting the powder from damp weather. Brass cartridges were the foundation of the new Snider-Enfield, adopted by the British army in 1866, and in all subsequent firearms designs.

The Snider-Enfield was a transitional technology. To make it, gunsmiths removed the back end of an Enfield muzzle-loader's barrel and added a breech block that contained a firing pin. To remove a spent cartridge, the shooter half-cocked the hammer, pulled a lever on the left side, and opened the chamber. The cartridge could be pulled out or, preferably, dumped out by turning over the rifle. The Snider-Enfield was a quick-firing, breech-loading rifle but it still had some of the deficiencies of the older muzzle-loaders. In particular, the placement of the hammer and firing pin on the right exterior of the barrel meant that the hammer had to be cocked for firing and half-cocked for loading. The procedure for unloading a spent cartridge was awkward, too. Such deficiencies were related to the fact that the rifle had been designed to be a muzzle-loader. After 1866, the Enfield factory made unconverted Snider-Enfields, but the design still reflected the weapon's muzzle-loader origins.

By contrast, the British army's next main infantry weapon, the Martini-Henry, was designed from the beginning as a breechloader. Experimental models came into use in the late 1860s. In 1871, the British army adopted it as its official infantry weapon (see Figure 6). The Martini-Henry owed its name to the Swiss inventor Friedrich von Martini,

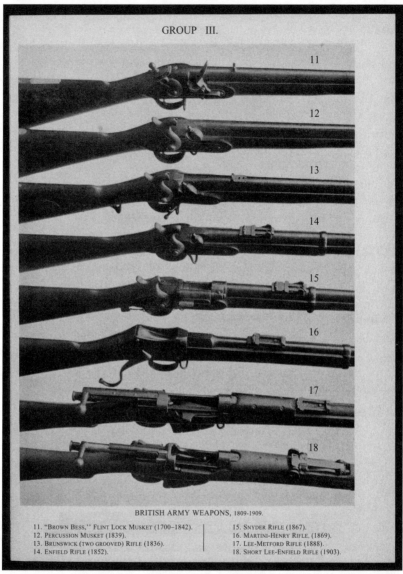

GROUP III.

BRITISH ARMY WEAPONS, 1809-1909.

11. "Brown Bess," Flint Lock Musket (1700–1842).	15. Snyder Rifle (1867).
12. Percussion Musket (1839).	16. Martini-Henry Rifle, (1869).
13. Brunswick (two grooved) Rifle (1836).	17. Lee-Metford Rifle (1888).
14. Enfield Rifle (1852).	18. Short Lee-Enfield Rifle (1903).

FIGURE 6. A side-by-side comparison of the British army's principal shoulder firearms of the nineteenth century. (From Blanch, *A Century of Guns*. Image courtesy of the Harvard College Library.)

who designed the breechblock, and the Scottish inventor Alexander Henry, who designed the rifling pattern in the barrel as well as the cartridge. The cartridge was essentially a variant of Boxer's brass cartridge that contained a longer, narrower 0.45-caliber bullet. The reduction in bullet caliber had to do with the relatively new understanding at the time that a smaller bullet could fly harder and flatter than a larger one. The main innovation, though, was Martini's breechblock. His design did away with the external hammer. Instead, a spring-loaded firing pin was placed on the inside of the breech. And to make it easier to load and unload, Martini placed a lever behind the trigger. The shooter pulled the lever, which opened the chamber and made it easier to remove and insert cartridges. When the breech was closed, the rifle cocked automatically.[27] By the late 1880s, breechloaders were using smokeless powder, which fires bullets at higher velocities and helps soldiers and hunters conceal themselves.

The technological development of firearms is a story of technical innovation and also of changing skills. The mimeomorphic skills involved in loading and aiming muzzle-loading flintlock smoothbores were replaced over time by better bullets, better ignition, and better materials, coupled with better overall design. Shooters could possess fewer of the old mimeomorphic skills and, using the same polymorphic skills, still succeed in damaging their targets. With some shooters, the elimination of the elaborate mimeomorphic skills involved in using muzzle-loaders may have made it easier to enhance their polymorphic skills. By the same token, gunsmithing now involved increasingly complex skills and equipment.

The rapid technological development of firearms between 1840 and 1880 had serious global consequences. Fast, continual upgrades made it difficult for armies to develop commensurate tactics. In the United States, for example, soldiers began the Civil War of 1861–5, using tactics that had evolved in the era of muzzle-loading smoothbores, including infantry marching across the field of battle in rows. This was in spite of the fact that during the 1850s, American soldiers had begun to adopt muzzle-loading rifles, such as the Enfield and the Springfield, which had greater

---

[27] Historical firearms hobbyists have placed excellent commentary, illustrations, and technical information about the Snider-Enfield and Martini-Henry on the Internet. See especially "British Firearms," http://www.researchpress.co.uk/firearms/britain/index.htm (June 6, 2007) and Jason Atkins, "Martini-Henry Rifles and Carbines," www.martinihenry.com (June 6, 2007).

range and accuracy than the old smoothbores. By 1863, all combatants carried rifles. The high casualties of the war can be attributed, in part, to the slowness with which social institutions like the Union and Confederate armies adapted tactics to rifles. Armies experimented with new offensive tactics, including advancing in small units and taking cover, but these were difficult to coordinate for large numbers of troops in the days before radios and telephones facilitated distant "command and control." Attacking a fortified position in rows could still work, provided that the attackers outnumbered the defenders by a ratio of three to one. Rifles favored the defense.[28]

As historians Michael Geyer and Charles Bright have shown, the years 1840–80 saw an upsurge in violent conflict all around the world. The American Civil War and the Taiping Rebellion were the bloodiest in terms of raw numbers of casualties, but other wars, such as the German and Italian wars of unification, were also comparatively lethal. All in all, counting major wars and minor rebellions, there were 177 significant violent conflicts around the world in these years. Geyer and Bright characterize this situation as a "general state of affairs" in which "warfare was dispersed, decentered, and mostly of low-intensity yet capable of threatening the survival of whole ethnes." This was certainly the case in South Africa, a region they barely mention. They go on to write that "there was no grand design or central nervous system that linked these conflicts," even though the "global outburst of violence" so "thoroughly reshaped the world."[29] One commonality might include the uptake of new weapons. The breechloader revolution did not significantly affect the Taiping Rebellion, which was the bloodiest conflict of the period, but in other conflicts the uptake of rifles and the slow adaptation of tactics may have had bloody consequences.

Gun manufacturers made clear technical progress during the nineteenth century, working closely with the support of states. Powerful industrial states poured money into the development of weapons at Enfield, Springfield, and Krupp, while even the small chiefdoms of South Africa recognized the importance of good decision making in purchasing weapons. The praise poem of Khama III, chief of the Ngwato Tswana in 1872 and again from 1875 to 1923, shows how the selection of up-to-date weapons became bound up with a chief's authority. Khama had to fight a rival, Macheng, for the chiefship. During the quarrel, Khama's

---

[28] McPherson, *Battle Cry of Freedom*, 474–7.
[29] Geyer and Bright, "Geopolitics of War," 629–30.

praise poem remembers that he "remained behind and examined the rifles; he picked out those shooting far, he picked out carbines and breechloaders."[30]

Breechloaders may seem superior to muzzle-loaders, but in the 1860s and 1870s there were still reasons for gun owners to continue to keep the old models in use. It is interesting to note that many hunters in South Africa, including famous ones like Frederick Courteney Selous, were hanging on to their large-bore muzzle-loaders. A prominent guidebook of the time recommended that if hunters had to choose one gun, they should carry a double-barreled 11- or 12-gauge smoothbore percussion gun, about the same size as the old Brown Bess musket but with a shorter barrel. The guidebook, written by the hunting experts W. B. Lord, an artillery officer, and Thomas Baines, a landscape painter, recommended this weapon because it was simpler and more reliable than a breech-loading rifle. Breechloaders, especially the later models, required special cartridges that might be hard to find in remote areas, while muzzle-loading hunters could procure lead, powder, and percussion caps at most frontier trading posts. An ordinary hunter could repair a muzzle-loader, too, even out in the field. When breechloaders broke down, repairs were more likely to be made by a professional gunsmith.[31] Lord and Baines noted that some breechloaders were quite reliable. Even so, they recommended that hunters carry a steel block that could be dropped down the barrel to convert the gun from breech-loading to muzzle-loading. They expressed the hope that in the future, the manufacturers of breechloaders would make it easier to convert the rifles to muzzle-loading.[32] Other sources reported that African blacksmiths also converted breechloaders to muzzle-loaders.[33] Muzzle-loaders were more reliable and adaptable weapons, especially out in the field.

There were other reasons why old guns held their appeal slightly longer than they did in other parts of the world. The old, big guns killed well enough (in skilled hands) that both African and European hunters carried

---

[30] *Praise Poems of Tswana Chiefs*, 204. The editor, Isaac Schapera, notes that these lines might be referring to Khama choosing an armed commando of Kwena allies, rather than firearms themselves, although this is not clear from the text or the context.

[31] Wrought-iron guns are easier to repair than are steel guns, especially in the field. Steel guns (and all guns, some would say) are best repaired by a professional gunsmith. Even so, it is possible for intrepid amateurs to repair steel guns with basic tools that may be bought from a hardware store. Chapel, *The Complete Guide to Gunsmithing: Gun Care and Repair*, 213–52.

[32] Lord and Baines, *Shifts and Expedients of Camp Life*, 8–10, 231–2.

[33] *James Stuart Archive*, 1:154.

them well into the late nineteenth century, even as most of the world's hunters and soldiers were switching to breech-loading rifles. The old black-powder hunting guns, such as the *roer*, fired a heavy round ball that moved relatively slowly. Such a bullet produces more shock to tissue than does a fast-moving, conical bullet. The old muzzle-loaders could be loaded with different kinds of ammunition and could be repaired easily in the field, too. They were a more adaptable and "flexible" technology than the new rifles, and happened to be less expensive, too.[34] Their power, their flexibility, and the fact that many people were familiar with them ensured that hunters kept the old weapons in circulation. In the Ashanti War of 1873, the British forces under Sir Garnet Wolseley armed their local allies with the Brown Bess flintlock.[35] But black-powder weapons, such as flintlock muskets and percussion-lock, muzzle-loading rifles, remained on sale in the world's remoter regions until the early decades of the twentieth century.

Breechloaders, Skill, and Game

In the late nineteenth century, guns improved, game disappeared, and skills declined. This is a progression that contradicts cherished myths about South African frontiersmen being natural marksmen that persist to the present day. The uptake of the brass-cartridge breechloader, the Martini-Henry, marked the demise of guns that were uniquely adapted to South Africa. Yet the adoption of the Martini-Henry cannot be explained simply by reference to technological progress in Europe. Any explanation must also take into consideration the ecological transformation of nineteenth-century South Africa, particularly with regard to game animals. Throughout the eighteenth and nineteenth centuries, people living in the South African interior carried large muzzle-loaders in order to hunt

---

[34] It should be noted that systematic statistical data on the costs of ammunition, in other words, the costs of using older and newer weapons, are difficult to calculate. In Cape Town, according to the customs figures in the colonial *Blue Books* from the middle of the nineteenth century, the price of gunpowder remained at around 1 pound sterling for every 20 pounds of powder, with variations based on quality and supply. From Cape Town, the powder would have had to have been shipped variable distances and would have arrived in variable conditions, making it difficult to estimate average costs on the frontier. In 1881, at the time when breechloaders would have been coming into wider use, the Blue Book estimates a value of £9,356 for 2.9 million cartridges, or £0.003 per cartridge, but without saying what types of cartridges they were or how much they would ultimately sell for.

[35] *Cape Argus*, November 20, 1873, p. 2.

game. Boer frontiersmen gained a reputation as highly skilled marksmen. In 1898, one British hunter, George Nicholson, who had a long experience in South Africa, wrote that "a formidable amount of aggregate skill in the use of their weapons was a noticeable characteristic of the period I allude to (say, twenty years ago), and at the time of the Boer war with us [the 'First Boer War' of 1880–1881] all the middle-aged men, and a good many of the youngsters, were as a rule, and as compared with trained soldiers, very efficient shots." Nicholson added that as late as the 1890s, some of the best shots still preferred to use primitive flintlock muzzle-loaders over modern breechloaders.[36]

Even so, by the 1870s, rural settlement was proceeding apace and game animals were growing scarce. In 1894, H. A. Bryden chronicled the disappearance of game south of the Limpopo. He attributed the disappearance of game to two different sorts of people. One sort, sport hunters, could be blamed for slaughtering thousands of animals, including some, like the rhinoceros, that were slow to breed. In one hunt alone, held in the Orange Free State in 1860, Prince Alfred and his hunting party shot more than six thousand animals that were enclosed and driven. Other famous midcentury sport hunters, like Gordon Cumming and W. C. Harris, killed thousands of animals, too. Their activities were sporadic compared with another sort of hunter, the Boer merchant-hunters, who ranged the Orange Free State and the Transvaal during the middle of the nineteenth century. According to Bryden, "Soon after 1850 the Boers of these pastoral republics awoke to the fact that the skins of these myriads of game were marketable commodities. For years they were hard at it working out their mine; but the end came at last, and since 1880 there has been little animal life left in these territories." Bryden found that Boer hunters adapted their skills to the marketplace: "The Boers became perfect adepts at skin-hunting, putting in just sufficient powder to drive the missile home, and carefully cutting out their bullets for use on future occasions." Their skilled harvest was immense, at first. "So lately as 1876, when I first wandered in Cape Colony, I well remember the wagons coming down from the Free State and Transvaal, loaded up with nothing but the skins of blesbok, wildebeest, and spring bok." By the 1880s, the animals were almost gone.[37]

Bryden attributed the slaughter to a number of factors. He himself was a sportsman, who understood that when "the profusion of animal was so

[36] Nicholson, *Fifty Years in South Africa*, 238–9, 241.
[37] Bryden, "Extermination of Great Game," 543–4.

great, the temptation [was] so overpowering. No one who has not been in the presence of great game, mounted and armed, can understand how difficult it is to stay one's hand at such a time." Bryden was especially forgiving of British sportsmen, because "these early explorers were men of perfect truth, honesty, and fairness, from whom the natives early formed an excellent impression of the English character." Other nationalities and other hunters were not so impressive. Bryden singled out African and Boer hunters as venal and thoughtless. To preserve the game from such men, he proposed strict game laws, which had succeeded to some extent in the Cape Colony, coupled with the creation of a vast, 100,000-acre wildlife reserve in Shona territory.[38]

Bryden also called attention to the destructiveness of the new firearms of the mid-nineteenth century:

In the days of matchlocks, and even of flint guns and smooth bores, the destruction proceeded, of course, much more slowly than at present. But with the introduction of percussion-caps a great change came quickly in the annual bill of slaughter. Improvements in rifling and precision rapidly followed, and finally came the modern breech-loader to complete the work of destruction.[39]

With the disappearance of game, young Boer men were relying less on their guns to earn a living and were therefore practicing less. As a result, the old percussion-lock muskets and rifles lost much of their appeal. Even though they were cheaper to use and easier to repair, they also required the gunner to have more skill than modern breechloaders did. With a large-bore muzzle-loader, every shot could be adjusted to the circumstances, but every shot had to count: guns had to be fired at close range, and it took so long to reload that a missed shot could result in the shooter being gored or trampled by the quarry. By contrast, a breechloader could be fired from far away and reloaded so quickly that accuracy was no longer a matter of life and death. Nicholson noted that:

With the virtual extermination of the larger kinds of game in the Transvaal, the Boers in a great measure ceased the pursuit of the scattered remnants of the survivors, and soon became but little interested in keeping up their efficiency as riflemen.

As a matter of fact, since the general introduction of long-range, breech-loading weapons, their shooting powers have steadily deteriorated, and from having been as a rule fairly good rough performers, the younger members of this generation

---

[38] Bryden, "Extermination of Great Game," 547, 551.
[39] Bryden, "Extermination of Great Game," 538–9.

have ceased to take any interest in field sports, and as regards rifle shooting are mere duffers. . . .

The extreme ease with which breech-loading rifles can be loaded, and the long range of these weapons, contributed largely to the deterioration of their original skill by inducing habits of carelessness as to distances, and a preference for pumping a stream of lead into the "brown" [game animals] without much regard to aim.[40]

The demise of game had been an ideological goal of Burchell and others who wanted to replace game animals with settlers. Over the course of the nineteenth century, settlers and sportsmen used guns to kill game, and yet, according to Nicholson's late nineteenth-century observations, killing off the animals ultimately reduced the amount of practice and skill that shooters had. It is difficult to prove the extent to which people in the past were skilled or unskilled. Even so, it does appear that Boer shooting skills were diminishing at the same time as many settlers were turning toward farming and wage labor.

Deskilling, like skill itself, is an understudied topic. There are a few studies of technology that go beyond the labor historians' concern over the deskilling of industrial laborers. Douglas Harper's *Working Knowledge*, an ethnographic study of an upstate New York mechanic named Willie, provides us with some insight. Willie does not only fix cars and tractors: like the people who lived in remote parts of nineteenth-century South Africa, Willie is deeply aware of the properties of materials, allowing him great scope for improvisation and bricolage. While working with different materials, he appears to have an intuitive, kinesthetic sense. At the same time, Willie's seemingly preindustrial work habits help bind together a community experiencing postindustrial malaise. Harper makes the point that the deskilling that goes along with the advance of capitalism has a tendency to alienate the members of communities from one another. Harper's point is demonstrated by the case of South Africa, where, in the 1870s, the spread of muzzle-loading percussion rifles as well as breechloaders was associated, in many different ways, with the rise of capitalism and imperialism and the decline of long-established communities.

[40] Nicholson, *Fifty Years in South Africa*, 240–1.

6

Guns and the Langalibalele Affair, 1873–5

In nineteenth-century South Africa, there were plenty of guns and plenty of skilled shooters, or so it seems. Shooting skills were good enough along the frontier that by the 1870s, many indigenous animals were nearly wiped out. At that time, British and Boer settlement was extending further north and east, while Africans were earning cash at the diamond mines and on settler farms and then buying guns.

During the 1870s, debates about gun control formed a large part of an emerging struggle over land and citizenship. Why did gun control emerge as a significant issue at this time? The breechloader revolution seemed to make the owners of guns more dangerous; a shift in British racial thinking paved the ideological way toward a more ambitious imperialism; and the mineral revolution raised South Africa's profile in the eyes of imperialists and investors in Britain. At the same time, the opening of the diamond mines made it easier for Africans to acquire weapons, while the spread of more powerful weapons made it easy for South Africa's anti-African politicians to manipulate ideas about the risk of guns in order to construct a more intensively racist regime that regulated Africans more closely. This is not to say that the proliferation of new weapons did not, in fact, increase the risk of shooting deaths in South Africa, although at the time humanitarian liberals sought to downplay those risks in order to preserve old, cherished notions of race-blind citizenship. Such ideas were becoming less and less tenable.

Langalibalele's Defiance

Discussions about gun control were related to broad ideological shifts in Britain and the colonies that were related to industrialization. They also had their origins in specific local circumstances that involved ideological and material changes. One particular case about gun control came to have broader significance for the South African debate about land and citizenship: the 1873 rebellion and trial of a Natal African, Langalibalele, chief of the Hlubi.

The Hlubi originally lived near the Zulu, on the Mzinyathi or Buffalo River. Around 1819, regional conflict and a succession struggle split the Hlubi into several groups. Some Hlubi joined Shaka, while others crossed the Drakensberg as refugees. One group, led by Mpangazitha, crossed over to the Caledon River valley and then back into the area that was to become the Estcourt District of Natal, near the source of the Thukela River.[1] Langalibalele was born near there in 1818 and in the 1830s became chief of this particular group of Hlubi (Figure 7). His name, which means "the sun is killing," referred to his reputed prowess as a rainmaker. He used rainmaking, marriage alliances, and military reorganization to strengthen his authority, to the point where the Hlubi began to concern the Zulu chief, Mpande.[2] In 1848, Mpande, pressed on all sides by Swazi and Boers, attacked the Hlubi in order to steal their cattle and territory. The Hlubi weathered the attack, but Langalibalele perceived that he needed to deepen his relationship with the new British colony of Natal. The government granted him permission to move his people across the Mzinyathi River and settle in the colony's northern reaches.[3]

Natal was annexed as a British colony in 1843. In 1845, it became an administrative district of the Cape and then in 1856 it became a separate colony, ruled by a lieutenant governor who reported to the governor and high commissioner in Cape Town. From Natal's very beginning, its "native policy" was under the influence of Theophilus Shepstone, a colonial administrator who had grown up in the Eastern Cape, the son of a Wesleyan missionary. Shepstone spoke fluent Xhosa and Zulu, skills that helped him secure a number of important jobs as an interpreter. In 1835, he had acted as Sir Harry Smith's interpreter during his Eastern

---

[1] Etherington, *Great Treks*, 91, 128, 161.
[2] *James Stuart Archive*, 2:11–41, Interview with Mabonsa ka Sidhlayi, January 27, 1909, File 59, Nbk.29, pp. 1–8.
[3] Wright and Manson, *The Hlubi Chiefdom*, 32–9.

FIGURE 7. Photograph thought to be Langalibalele. (From the Killie Campbell Library, University of KwaZulu-Natal, Durban. A50–006. Used by permission.)

Cape campaign, and as the historian Thomas McClendon demonstrates, Shepstone absorbed Smith's imperious style as well as his taste for ceremonies. In 1845, at the inception of the colony of Natal, Shepstone was named "Diplomatic Agent to the Native Tribes." In that role, he worked out a plan for a new system of "native administration" that was well suited to a situation in which Africans outnumbered Europeans to a significant degree. He allowed for the establishment of "native locations," areas that were set aside for chiefdoms – although the most important chiefdom, the Zulu, remained independent. Chiefs who came under Shepstone's administration were required to collect taxes, based on the number of huts in a kraal. This was a colonial imposition, but by and large, chiefs would govern their followers according to custom. European magistrates would be assigned to each location and Shepstone, as the chief magistrate, would hear appeals as a self-styled "supreme chief." Shepstone hoped that the security brought by this hybrid system of rule would allow African farmers to develop materially, morally, and politically.[4]

Shepstone's system of colonial rule through the chiefs proved controversial with ardent advocates of the Cape's "civilization" policy, who trusted in the superiority of European administrative methods. In Natal, European settlers who coveted African locations disliked the way in which Shepstone's system legitimated and perpetuated chiefly sovereignty. For this reason, Shepstone feared the development of "responsible" government by colonial settlers. His system depended on the perpetuation of an unrepresentative colonial government dominated by a lieutenant governor appointed from London. He also depended on the appointment of the right sort of lieutenant governor. The first lieutenant governor to supervise Shepstone, Martin West, was generally supportive. In 1850, a less sympathetic lieutenant governor, Benjamin Pine, was appointed. Pine developed a close relationship with the settlers and supported their opposition to Shepstone's scheme to reserve extensive lands for Africans. Pine called for reducing the size of locations, in order to alienate land to Europeans and force Africans to work on their farms. Pine and Shepstone were at loggerheads until Pine's departure in 1855, although Shepstone's system was kept largely intact.

The genius of Shepstone's system was that in an era of budgetary restraint and colonial conflict, the colonial government could rely on the chiefs to preserve order. To manage such a system, Shepstone acted as a "supreme chief" managing lesser chiefs. African political practices became incorporated into British colonial governance, a practice that several historians have noticed and that is most fully fleshed out in an article by Thomas McClendon. McClendon argues that in early disputes between the colonial government and chiefs, Shepstone punished chiefs by "eating them up" (deposing them and removing their cattle). They were punished in this way because this is what superior chiefs did to lesser chiefs who disrespected their authority. Such African practices reveal the ways in which the colonial government of Natal leaned heavily on African precedent in order to persuade new African subjects of its claims to legitimacy.[5]

The strengths and weaknesses of Shepstone's system had a significant impact on the Hlubi. When the Hlubi entered Natal in 1848, they settled

---

[4] McClendon, "Man Who Would Be *Inkosi*," 350–2.
[5] McClendon, "You Are What You Eat Up." See also Hamilton, *Terrific Majesty*.

on one of Shepstone's locations and began to prosper as farmers. The Hlubi adapted well, perhaps too well, to the emerging commercial economy of Natal, producing livestock and vegetables to sell on the Natal sugar plantations and the Kimberley diamond mines. Their independent wealth and connections to markets raised the hackles of settlers, who feared competition and were hungry for labor. To encourage the Hlubi to work on settler farms, the colonial government imposed a hut tax and a marriage registration fee on residents of the location, hoping that location residents could be persuaded to work for cash wages on settler farms. Still, many Hlubi preferred to farm their own lands or rent European lands rather than work as agricultural wage laborers. They found ways to preserve a modicum of independence, even as they became incorporated within the settler economy.[6] The settlers, for their part, not only were jealous of Hlubi success, but were nervous about being outnumbered by Africans. The historian Norman Etherington has shown that during the late 1860s and early 1870s, Natal's colonists were fixated on the possibility of white women being raped by black men, even though virtually no such rapes had occurred.[7]

In the 1870s, at a time when settlers were fearful and jealous, a number of young Hlubi men crossed the mountains to work in the Kimberley diamond mines. In Griqualand West, as in the Cape, permits to buy guns were issued by resident magistrates, who were to determine whether or not the applicant was loyal enough and "fit" enough to own a gun. Griqualand West was actually somewhat stricter than the Cape Colony. In the Cape Colony, permits could also be issued by unsalaried justices of the peace, which was not the case in Griqualand West. In any event, the administration of gun regulations was somewhat decentralized in the Cape Colony and Griqualand West. By contrast, according to Natal's 1859 gun statute, the applicant for a license to own a firearm came to the office of the resident magistrate, who kept the gun and forwarded a request for a license to the lieutenant governor. If the lieutenant governor granted the request, he communicated his permission to the resident magistrate, who registered the gun and marked it. Technically speaking, Natal's law was color blind, but magistrates and the lieutenant governor had latitude to deny licenses to Africans and to grant them to Europeans. Few Africans received licenses, except for chiefs and other prominent

---

[6] Etherington, "Why Langalibalele Ran Away," 7–9. Wright and Manson, *The Hlubi Chiefdom*, 43–50. Guest, "Colonists, Confederation, and Constitutional Change."
[7] Etherington, "Natal's Black Rape Scare."

men.[8] During the early 1870s, white Natalians sojourning in Kimberley opposed Lt. Gov. Southey's laissez-faire attitude toward gun sales and his humanitarian liberal views on racial matters.[9]

When visiting other colonies, Natal's settlers opposed the proliferation of firearms. But at home they revealed themselves to be hypocrites. The Natal government hoped that the Hlubi would protect the colony from San raiders and even presented Langalibalele with some guns. Admittedly, Natal had stricter gun-control laws than did Griqualand West, where migrant diamond miners purchased rifles more easily. It was also not a secret that two of Theophilus Shepstone's sons were among the Natal and Cape merchants who recruited laborers for the mines by offering them guns, although one of the sons denied this charge vehemently. For a long time, the Natal government turned a blind eye to the activities of arms merchants who used Durban as a staging point in the coastal gun trade. Sir Benjamin Pine, who was reappointed lieutenant governor of Natal in 1873, was on record condemning the arms trade as a "trade in blood" but he still granted permits for arms merchants to transport guns across Natal to the diamond fields.[10]

No one has been able to establish whether Langalibalele encouraged young Hlubi to obtain guns at the mines. The settlers believed he did. By contrast, one of James Stuart's informants, John Kumalo, had a subtle view of Langalibalele's role. Kumalo indicated that Langalibalele "was not in any way the person who instructed them to buy guns," but that once the young Hlubi men bought guns, Langalibalele did not report them.[11] There are not reliable figures on Hlubi gun ownership, either, and those Hlubi who had guns may have simply acquired them across the border

---

[8] Testimony of G. M. Rudolph, *South African Native Affairs Commission, 1903–1905*, 3:322, 1.22, 462–22, 469.

[9] Turrell, *Capital and Labour on the Kimberley Diamond Fields*, 57–8. *Cape Argus*, November 18, 1873, p. 2; November 29, 1875, p. 2.

[10] BPP [C. 1141] 1875, pp. 8–9; *DOL*, 25. J. W. Colenso's report was published officially in the British Parliamentary Papers as Command Paper 1141 of January 1875, entitled "Langalibalele and the Amahlubi Tribe; Being Remarks upon the Official Record of the Trials of the Chief, His Sons and Induna, and Other Members of the Amahlubi Tribe, by the Bishop of Natal." At the end of 1874, Colenso also arranged to have his report published privately in London. See J. W. Colenso, *Defence of Langalibalele, with Additional Evidence and an Appendix Bringing Down the History of the Case to the Latest Date* (London: n.p., 1874). It is here abbreviated as *DOL*. I have used the autographed copy that belonged to his daughter, Frances Colenso, who added marginalia and corrections to her father's book. It is available at the Houghton Library, Harvard University.

[11] *James Stuart Archive*, 1:218, 260.

in Zululand. In any case, in 1873 Langalibalele became embroiled in an argument with the colonial government about gun control. Natal required Africans to register their weapons by leaving them for a short while with the local magistrate. Settler fears of armed Hlubi men led the colonial government to send a directive to local magistrates to enforce gun registration strictly. The magistrate for Weenen County, John MacFarlane, had been responsible for the Hlubi since the late 1850s. Hlubi relations with MacFarlane were apparently good, while relations with local settlers tended to be strained.[12] In early 1873, MacFarlane decided that the time had come to register Hlubi guns.[13] He dispatched an African policeman named Mtyityizelwa to perform the task.

Later, Mtyityizelwa provided an account of his failed mission. His story was possibly unreliable, and it was certainly self-serving, but it indicated the thorny problems of sovereignty and authority that gun control produced among the Hlubi. When Mtyityizelwa learned that five Hlubi men had returned from the Kimberley diamond fields with rifles, he went out with three assistants to find them and register their weapons. One Hlubi man recalled that his neighbors heard rumors of guns being taken to be registered but never being returned. When Mtyityizelwa came, people said, "What is to become of our earnings, we having spent our strength for guns, if they are taken away."[14] Mtyityizelwa heard gunfire and smelled powder near the settlement of one particular family. He summoned the senior man of the family, Sibanda, to meet with him. While waiting, Mtyityizelwa noticed a boy cleaning two guns. Mtyityizelwa attempted to remove the guns, telling the boy, "I am to take you and the guns to the Magistrate, in order that the guns may be registered." Mtyityizelwa grabbed one of the guns and the boy shouted, "If that is

---

[12] Etherington, "Why Langalibalele Ran Away," 7–9. Lambert, "Chiefship in Early Colonial Natal," 280.

[13] Wright and Manson, *The Hlubi Chiefdom*, 51–2.

[14] BPP [C.1119] 1875, Testimony of Ngcamane, February 3, 1874, p. 23; *KRN*, 61–2. The official record of Langalibalele's "trial," or "enquiry," is cited here from two sources, the British Parliamentary Papers, Command Papers 1025 of 1874 and 1119 of 1875, and also the separate Natal publication, "Court of Enquiry: Langalibalele's Sons and Indunas," in *The Kafir Revolt in Natal in the Year 1873, Being an Account of the Revolt of the Amahlubi Tribe, under the Chief Langalibalele, and the Measures Taken to Vindicate the Authority of the Government, Together with the Official Record of the Trial of the Chief, and Some of His Sons and Indunas* (Pietermaritzburg: Keith & Co., 1874), which is abbreviated as *KRN*. The transcript published in the *Natal Witness*, February 6, 1874, summarizes only Ngcamane's testimony. It confirms that he discussed how the Hlubi believed that gun registration would result in losing their guns, but it does not confirm the specific words of his testimony.

your mission, our guns shall never be registered; we are taking them to Langalibalele; in fact, he has sent a message saying we are to take them to their owner, Langalibalele." The boy refused to let go and a fight broke out, with the two clutching the gun and dragging and hitting each other. The boy's mother joined in, pulling on Mtyityizelwa.[15]

The boy's father, Sibanda, arrived on the scene with several more of his sons. They separated Mtyityizelwa from the boy. Sibanda agreed with his son about the proper way to register firearms, saying that "these guns have been sent for by Langalibalele, their owner, and if you require them to be registered, you must go to him; and if he chooses to have them registered, he will send them in." Sibanda wished to have the chief as his sovereign; if the colonial government required gun registration, then Langalibalele, who was responsible for negotiating with the colonial government, would act as middleman.[16]

The statements of the boy and his father, as related by Mtyityizelwa, indicate that some Hlubi associated the sovereignty of the chief with his ability to regulate such possessions as firearms. As the anthropologist Sally Falk Moore has written, people experience the law most frequently in the guise of day-to-day regulations, not in dramatic courtroom confrontations. When people obey common rules, such as having to register newly acquired weapons, they accept the authority of the rulemakers. Everyday regulations help people perceive the social and political order.[17] The boy did not object to registering his rifle: he insisted that Langalibalele be the one to register it. Indeed, granting permission to carry and use arms was generally considered to be one of the hallmarks of a chief's authority, along with the authority to regulate witchcraft and impose capital punishment.[18]

The conflict over who was to register the Hlubi guns was not simply a case of African resistance to colonial authority. The struggle closely related to internal conflicts among the Hlubi. Mtyityizelwa related the problems of firearms regulation and sovereignty to generational conflict.

---

[15] BPP [C.1119] 1875, Testimony of Mtyityizelwa, February 10, 1874, pp. 26–7; *KRN*, 63. The transcript published in the *Natal Witness*, February 13, 1874, summarizes only this part of Mtyityizelwa's testimony. It confirms that he struggled with the boy, but it does not confirm the specific words of his testimony.

[16] BPP [C.1119] 1875, Testimony of Mtyityizelwa, February 10, 1874, pp. 26–7; *KRN*, 63–4. The transcript published in the *Natal Witness*, February 13, 1874, confirms this part of Mtyityizelwa's testimony, but gives a slightly different translation.

[17] Moore, *Social Facts and Fabrications*.

[18] McClendon, "You Are What You Eat Up," 259.

After the scuffle, he sat down with Sibanda, the father, to discuss how they might resolve their differences. The boy refused to cooperate and started loading his gun. Mtyityizelwa said to Sibanda, "See, one of your boys is loading the gun." The boy taunted the policeman, "If you want this gun you can come and get it, and I will put you to rights." Mtyityizelwa said to Sibanda, "You had better seize that boy, discharge the gun, and bring it to me, that I may take it to the Magistrate's Office and get it registered; he will not hurt you – his father – but he will fire at me." The father replied, "I dare not go; he would shoot me; I have no control over him; the boys have no respect for me. I am nothing to them."[19]

A second brawl ended inconclusively and Mtyityizelwa failed to obtain the rifles. After the policemen left, they learned that Langalibalele sent one of his own messengers to collect the guns. The police then traveled to the chief's kraal to demand satisfaction. Mtyityizelwa appealed to Langalibalele to help him register the rifles of Sibanda's sons. The chief gave him no assistance, stating that "what sort of a man do you and your father, the Magistrate, think that I am? You first of all, after hearing where these guns are, go and rouse these people, and when they have become wild beasts, you come and ask me to arrest them. I don't know where they are; they are wild animals. You should have come to me in the first instance, and allowed me to seize them first, and not have put them on their guard."[20] Langalibalele preferred to regulate the Hlubi himself.

Langalibalele wanted to preserve his control over Sibanda, so he stalled Mtyityizelwa's attempts to register their rifles. This angered the local magistrate, MacFarlane, who fined Sibanda and relayed impatient messages to Langalibalele via Mtyityizelwa. Langalibalele avoided him, which led Mtyityizelwa to demand a formal audience with the chief and his advisors. At first the chief suggested that Mtyityizelwa address a general meeting of the Hlubi by himself. Langalibalele probably did not wish to be associated with the pronouncements of the colonial authorities, whom Mtyityizelwa represented. When Mtyityizelwa threatened not to deliver the message

[19] BPP [C.1119] 1875, Testimony of Mtyityizelwa, February 10, 1874, pp. 26–7; *KRN*, 64. The transcript published in the *Natal Witness*, February 13, 1874, confirms this part of Mtyityizelwa's testimony, but gives a slightly different translation.

[20] BPP [C.1119] 1875, Testimony of Mtyityizelwa, February 10, 1874, pp. 26–7; *KRN*, 64. The transcript published in the *Natal Witness*, February 13, 1874, summarizes only this part of Mtyityizelwa's testimony, but it confirms the overall gist of the specific words in the official transcript.

at all, Langalibalele relented. The chief's advisors convened a meeting, sitting in a semicircle. Mtyityizelwa and his men sat facing the advisors in their own semicircle. Langalibalele arrived and sat himself down in the middle of the circle, with his back facing the government messengers. He asked one of his advisors to tell why he had convened the meeting, so that he might deal with the government messengers at a remove. The advisor invited Mtyityizelwa to speak. Once again he demanded to register the weapons of Sibanda's sons and complained that Langalibalele had not done so himself, as he had promised.[21]

Then, the chief challenged the authority of the colonial government to regulate firearms. Langalibalele argued that the young men had earned the weapons fairly at the diamond fields. He remarked, "I did not send them to the Diamond Fields.... It is the white men who scratch about the ground and look for diamonds. I do not; and I will not take away a gun from any man who has been to the Diamond Fields and worked for it fairly. The white people take the men there, they work there, and then the white people wish to take away the guns they have earned."[22] The colonial government hoped that African laborers would work in capitalist enterprises. Now Langalibalele used the economic side of colonialism to counter the political claims of colonial state regulation. He recognized that guns had acquired value among the Hlubi not only because they were useful technologies, but because the young Hlubi men had exchanged so much to acquire them.

Langalibalele realized that the colonial authorities were selectively applying gun-control regulations to the Hlubi. Other people in the vicinity of Natal were equally involved in the firearms trade but went about their business undisturbed. With his back still turned, Langalibalele said to

---

[21] BPP [C.1119] 1875, Testimony of Mtyityizelwa, February 10, 1874, p. 28; *KRN*, 65. *Natal Witness*, February 13, 1874. The local African custom was to greet newcomers indirectly. This meant that instead of shaking hands and exchanging greetings and good wishes, two groups meeting each other might sit in separate, nearby places and slowly enquire about the nature of the visit. It seems that in the case of Mtyityizelwa's meeting with Langalibalele, the old chief, by turning his back on Mtyityizelwa, was insulting the messenger; however, the record is not so exact to exclude completely the alternative interpretation that Langalibalele was enough of a traditionalist that he wished to avoid a direct greeting.

[22] BPP [C.1119] 1875, Testimony of Mtyityizelwa, February 10, 1874, pp. 28–9; *KRN*, 66. The transcript published in the *Natal Witness*, February 13, 1874, confirms this part of Mtyityizelwa's testimony, but gives a slightly different translation.

Mtyityizelwa, "Your fathers, the magistrates, are cats; they do not interfere with Faku, King of the Pondas, or Cetshwayo, King of the Zulus,
but they come to us, who are like rats, who have come trusting to their
protection, and annoy us."[23] Langalibalele believed that the colonial government was regulating firearms among the weakest African chiefdoms
that had formally submitted to Shepstone and that had been incorporated
with the system of locations. The chief stood up and walked away, never
glancing back at the messengers. That night, when Mtyityizelwa came to
say good-bye, Langalibalele called him a spy. The chief indicated that he
expected a confrontation with the Natal authorities in which the Hlubi
would lose all their cattle, the source of their wealth and the symbol of
their prosperity. This is what Shepstone had done to three previous chiefs,
who had resisted colonial authority. Mtyityizelwa returned to headquarters and reported to MacFarlane that the young Hlubi men still refused
to register their weapons. For all his efforts, he managed to register only
one gun.[24]

Langalibalele's challenge provoked the colonial government. In April
and May 1873, MacFarlane instructed Langalibalele to travel to the capital, Pietermaritzburg, where Theophilus Shepstone, the secretary of native
affairs, would deal with him directly. Langalibalele claimed that a leg
injury prevented him from traveling so far, but government officials suspected that he was shamming. When the local colonists heard about
unrest in the Hlubi location, they started to become uneasy. In June, the
colony's settler militia held its annual muster near Hlubi territory, raising suspicions of an attack. Shepstone spent July through September of
1873 in Zululand, where he was busy orchestrating the coronation of
Cetshwayo as paramount chief. Shepstone's absence gave the Hlubi time
to cool off, but when the secretary for native affairs resumed his duties
in October, Langalibalele was still recalcitrant.[25]

Langalibalele's continued defiance caused MacFarlane to worry about
two things. Informers told him that Langalibalele was contemplating
an escape to Basutoland, while settlers were beginning to panic. One
landowner, F. W. Moor, was giving alarmist speeches, while some Boer

[23] BPP [C.1119] 1875, Testimony of Mtyityizelwa, February 10, 1874, p. 28; *KRN*, 65.
Natal Witness, February 13, 1874.
[24] BPP [C.1119] 1875, Testimony of Mtyityizelwa, February 10, 1874, p. 29; *KRN*, 66–7.
The transcript published in the *Natal Witness*, February 13, 1874, confirms this part of
Mtyityizelwa's testimony, but gives a slightly different translation.
[25] Etherington, "Why Langalibalele Ran Away," 11–13. Manson, "The Hlubi," 21–3.
Guest, *Langalibalele*, 36–7.

settlers were already sending away their cattle.[26] Langalibalele and the Hlubi were apparently making themselves ready for a fight. According to the reports Mtyityizelwa heard, the Hlubi prepared differently than before. Hlubi forces used to be divided into age-based regiments. Now, Langalibalele ordered his army to form two divisions, one with guns and one without. The soldiers gathered at Pangweni, where a religious leader blessed them. He charmed and sacrificed a cow and then gave the flesh to the gun-owning division to eat. Those without guns did not partake of the sacrifice. Mtyityizelwa related how the gun-owning soldiers derided the gunless as good-for-nothings.[27] Langalibalele enrolled guns into the religious life of the Hlubi in order to support new military tactics. In the process, possession of unregistered firearms gained another form of social support that could challenge potential regulators.

The politics of the chiefdom changed significantly as the Hlubi moved closer to a confrontation with the Natal authorities. After several years of generational tensions, the young Hlubi men seized power from their elders. Two German missionaries on the location observed how a group of young men dissuaded Langalibalele from traveling to Pietermaritzburg. The chief usually turned only to his elders for advice, but now the elders seem to have been asking local European missionaries to intercede on their behalf with the colonial government.[28]

Langalibalele had one last chance to avert warfare, but he remained opposed to meeting Shepstone. Natal's lieutenant governor, Sir Benjamin Pine, sent an African messenger named Mahoyiza to visit the chief. Great uncertainty surrounds their meeting. Langalibalele mistrusted Mahoyiza so much that he had him partially stripped and searched for weapons. Langalibalele was concerned about colonial officials because he remembered an 1859 meeting between John Shepstone, the brother of the secretary of native affairs, and Matshana [Matyana], a neighboring chief, who was defying colonial authority. When the meeting began, Shepstone drew a concealed revolver and attempted to take Matshana prisoner. In an ensuing melée between Matshana's followers and colonial forces, the

---

[26] Etherington, "Why Langalibalele Ran Away," 12–15.
[27] BPP [C.1119] 1875, Cross-examination of Mtyityizelwa, February 10, 1874, p. 30; KRN, 65. *Natal Witness*, February 13, 1874. The record shows that Mtyityizelwa used the word *impara*. This is a colonial transcription that does not exactly correspond to modern transcriptions. The word is likely to have meant either *mpatha*, which means ignorant and untrained, or *i-phatha*, which means a useless person. Doke, *Zulu-English Dictionary*.
[28] Manson, "The Hlubi," 23.

chief escaped. Langalibalele was present at this incident and probably drew the conclusion that he should be wary of government messengers. He also knew that Matshana was deposed and his followers dispersed to work on settler farms. Langalibalele knew the likely punishment for defying colonial magistrates.[29]

MacFarlane and Theophilus Shepstone decided to deal with the Hlubi by arresting their chief, confiscating their cattle, and dispersing them. Langalibalele began to lead two or three thousand male followers out of the colony in the direction of Basutoland. MacFarlane learned about the migration, and also about how the Hlubi were hiding their cattle with the neighboring Ngwe. An angry MacFarlane punished the Ngwe by confiscating all their cattle, too, effectively ruining them.[30] Like the Ngwe, any Hlubi who stayed behind bore the brunt of colonial vengeance. Many of them were elderly or infirm, but this did not stop colonial troops from burning their homes, stealing their cattle, and even killing many of them. Six years later, Frances Colenso alleged that Hlubi women and children, plus men who were too elderly or infirm to travel, hid near their reserves in caves and other seemingly secure places. It was thought that British troops would not harm women and children – the British would allow them to catch up to the men later. That was probably a correct prediction about the behavior of regular soldiers of the British army, but that was not the type of soldier that the colony of Natal sent to attack the Hlubi. Instead, it was settler volunteers and African auxiliaries who arrived in the vicinity. They smoked the women, children, and infirm men out of caves and even fired rockets at them. Numerous noncombatants, including children, were killed and even tortured and mutilated.[31]

The migration of Langalibalele and the Hlubi men began to attract widespread attention in South Africa, with coverage appearing in all the major newspapers. Much attention also focused on the gun trade at the Kimberley diamond mines, a story that the *Cape Argus* had been covering throughout 1873, particularly as it affected trade and customs revenues at the Cape.[32] White Natalians who worked at the mines sent deputations to the Cape, the Orange Free State, and the South African Republic to

[29] McClendon, "You Are What You Eat Up," 269–71.
[30] Etherington, "Why Langalibalele Ran Away," 15–17, 20–1.
[31] Colenso, *History of the Zulu War*, 29–33.
[32] *Cape Argus*, March 27, 1873, p. 2; April 1, 1873, pp. 2–3; April 25, 1873, p. 3; May 3, 1873, p. 2; May 10, 1873, p. 3; June 19, 1873, p. 4; September 2, 1873, p. 4.

ask their governments for more vigilant gun regulation. On December 2, 1873, the *Cape Argus* printed the positive response that the Natalians received from President Brand of the Orange Free State.[33]

As word of the Hlubi migration spread throughout South Africa, Lt. Gov. Pine personally led a force of more than eight thousand British, colonial, and African troops to apprehend them. They left Pietermaritzburg on October 29, 1873, the same day that Pine signed a permit for a Natal merchant to convey one hundred breech-loading rifles to Kimberley.[34] Langalibalele's Hlubi escaped across the mountains into the territory of the Sotho. Crossing Bushmans River Pass, they fought a skirmish against Pine's force, killing three colonial soldiers and two African auxiliaries.

Langalibalele and his followers crossed into Basutoland, where they sought to take up residence in the territory that the Cape government had allocated to Molapo, son of Moshoeshoe. Molapo had difficult relations with the colonial authorities, who clinched his loyalty by offering the chief 150 cattle should Langalibalele be taken alive and 100 if he were taken dead, plus all the cattle that belonged to the Hlubi. The Hlubi soon learned that they had misplaced their trust in Molapo. Molapo's son Jonathan located Langalibalele and some of his followers and persuaded them to surrender to the Cape administration. A separate body of Hlubi was attacked by Molapo's other son, Joel, who forced them to surrender and then relieved them of their cattle. The Hlubi prisoners marched from Basutoland to Pietermaritzburg, where the colonial government put Langalibalele on trial. The colony's efforts at regulation moved from the countryside to the courtroom.[35]

Langalibalele's Trial

On December 31, 1873, settler cavalrymen delivered Langalibalele and fifty of his followers to the Pietermaritzburg jail. He spent the next two

[33] *Cape Argus*, December 2, 1873, pp. 3–4, reprinting articles from the *Diamond Fields News*.

[34] Permits signed by Pine for Parker Wood & Co., October 17 and 29, 1873, included in CTAR, GLW 45, "Gun Returns, Du Toit's Pan, Kimberley, Barkly, Langford Station, 1873–1874." The permits came to the attention of the lieutenant governor of Griqualand West, Sir Richard Southey, who forwarded them to Barkly. See CTAR, GLW 113, Semi-Official Letters, Southey to Barkly, February 20, 1874, pp. 23–4.

[35] Burman, *Chiefdom Politics and Alien Law*, 62–3. Testimony of Sitokwana, January 30, 1874, "Court of Enquiry: Langalibalele's Sons and Indunas," *The Kafir Revolt in Natal in the Year 1873*, 43–5.

FIGURE 8. John William Colenso, photographed by J. E. Mayall, 1864. (From the Killie Campbell Library, University of KwaZulu-Natal, Durban. A50–001. Used by permission.)

weeks in solitary confinement, reportedly dejected and refusing to eat.[36] While Langalibalele stared at the walls of his cell, the Anglican bishop of Natal, John William Colenso, prepared to defend the imprisoned chief (Figure 8). Colenso was no stranger to controversy. He was well known in South Africa and England as a liberal theologian who was willing

[36] Colenso, *History of the Zulu War*, 39. Herd, *The Bent Pine*, 47. *Natal Witness*, January 2, 1874.

to allow African converts to incorporate local practices into Christian beliefs. Colenso was excommunicated by the conservative bishop of Cape Town, although his ability to do so was the subject of some debate. Colenso still retained many friends and supporters among Natal's African and British population, among them both Langalibalele and Theophilus Shepstone.[37]

Colenso believed that the government of Natal was violating Langalibalele's rights, a state of affairs that could only harm mission work. Colenso decried the trial of Langalibalele in speeches, publications, and private meetings with influential people. He wrote to his lawyer in England, hoping that he would make the Aborigines Protection Society aware of the brutality of the campaign against Langalibalele and the Hlubi. A few days before the trial, he wrote to the *Times of Natal*, protesting how the newspaper's premature condemnation of Langalibalele contradicted fundamental notions of English justice. But what, then, was justice in this unprecedented case, in which a government attempted to regulate guns across the cultural and political boundaries that Shepstone's system entailed?

Immediately, a question arose: under which body of laws would Langalibalele be prosecuted, judged, and punished for, defying gun-control regulations and rebelling against the colonial government? The court believed that it had to choose from three alternatives: the hybrid of English law and Roman-Dutch law that had evolved in Britain's South African colonies; the so-called customary or native law that was itself produced and recorded under colonial supervision; or a mixture of both colonial and customary law, as might fit Shepstone's system of government. It was difficult for the court to define exactly what any of these supposedly separate, culturally bound laws meant in this unprecedented situation, in which regulations were being imposed across sovereign and quasi-sovereign boundaries as well as cultural divides. In order to try Langalibalele for his transgressions, it was necessary for the court to move from the particularities of regulation and rebellion into the overall construction of the legal order.

The legal system was considerably more ambiguous than the categories of "customary," "colonial," "English," and "Roman-Dutch" would seem to suggest. As historians Richard Roberts and Kristin Mann have argued, many Europeans believed that African customary laws were grounded

37 Guy, *The Heretic.*

in unchanging traditions, when in fact it had been colonial encounters that defined them. When colonial officials codified customary laws, they tended to favor laws that supported African collaborators. Colonial law and customary law actually had a great deal in common. They defined power relationships, particularly those that involved access to land and labor.[38] In the case of Langalibalele, what began as a dispute over the regulation of arms ended as a wholesale expropriation of Hlubi land and labor. The trial presented the government with an opportunity to solve a persistent problem: European settlers resented the way in which the unrepresentative colonial government restricted their access to African land and labor, and many among them hoped for a new constitution that would limit the authority of Shepstone and the lieutenant governor. If the Hlubi were guilty of rebellion, then Shepstone and the lieutenant governor could feel justified in redistributing their location to land-hungry settlers. If the Hlubi lost their land, they would be more likely to seek employment with labor-hungry settlers.

Three decades of colonial history constrained the choice of laws in the Langalibalele trial. The colonial magistrate in charge of each "location" had the power to intervene in disputes among Africans, while hereditary chiefs of each "tribe" retained the right to administer customary law among their subjects. Theoretically, litigants could appeal decisions of chiefs and magistrates to Shepstone, who ruled according to colonial law subject to local customary modifications. And Shepstone, the secretary for native affairs, answered ultimately to the lieutenant governor, also known as the "supreme chief," although Shepstone made most of the important decisions. Legal ambiguity opened the door for despotism, but at least the possibility of appeal to the lieutenant governor of Natal, to the governor of the Cape Colony and high commissioner, and to the secretary of state for the colonies, and even the queen, also existed.

The colonial legal system derived from both local and imperial power. London sat in final judgment over colonial cases, but in the case of Langalibalele, British laws provided limited guidance. From the sixteenth century to the nineteenth century, the crown and parliament restricted firearms ownership based on class, ethnic, and religious identity. The English Bill of Rights of 1689 guaranteed Protestant subjects the right to own firearms so that they might protect themselves against autocracy, but the parliament retained the power to pass restrictions. During the

---

[38] Roberts and Mann, "Introduction," *Law in Colonial Africa*, 3–5.

eighteenth and nineteenth centuries, legislators and jurists confirmed the right to bear arms. Identity ceased to play such an important part in gun control, but Westminster remained conscious of its ability to restrict access to arms.[39] Besides, British rule did not necessarily provide British rights for Victoria's African subjects. For example, British law recognized certain rights associated with property ownership, but Britain's colonial proconsuls did not extend these rights to people they deemed "uncivilized." As Chanock has demonstrated, colonial authorities might guarantee land rights to loyal indigenous rulers and through them to their clients, but not to people who might be hostile to colonial rule.[40] In Britain, rights protected the people against autocracy, but in the colonies rights might impede progress and civilization. The issue of whether or not colonial governments should be run on behalf of settlers or indigenous people had been a steady topic of public and legal discourse ever since the trial of the East India Company's governor general, Sir Warren Hastings, which took place between 1788 and 1794. Recently, Shepstone had instructed the Zulu that customary authorities should exercise judicious restraint in meting out punishment. The likely dispossession of the Hlubi and the execution or banishment of their chief would help define colonial notions of restraint.

The trial began on Friday, January 16, 1874, in a tent pitched on the front lawn of the lieutenant governor's mansion. Lt. Gov. Pine, styling himself as the supreme chief, could have tried the case in a courtroom, but if he was going to try Langalibalele according to customary African law then he preferred to try the case on his own front lawn. Even so, Pine's choice of location indicated some ambiguity in the colony's law; a tent in front of the lieutenant governor's mansion was hardly the kraal of an African chief. He sought to try the case by appealing to both African and English legal traditions, but as the trial proceeded the ambiguities of his choice only deepened.

Pine entered the tent, accompanied by the members of the court. They were a mix of British administrators and African advisors, many of whom had been involved in the campaign to capture Langalibalele. Pine himself had led the troops. Theophilus Shepstone, the secretary for native affairs, sat on the tribunal as the lieutenant governor's legal advisor, even though he had a long-standing and prejudicial involvement with Langalibalele.

---

[39] Malcolm, *To Keep and Bear Arms*.
[40] Chanock, "Paradigms, Policies, and Property," in *Law in Colonial Africa*.

Even more prejudicial, from Langalibalele's standpoint, was the appointment of John Shepstone as the prosecutor. This was the magistrate who had treacherously concealed a revolver in order to capture Matshana. The other four English magistrates had either participated in the campaign against Langalibalele or had lost close relatives in it. Theophilus Shepstone also arranged for the court to include six Africans to make it a believable cross-cultural tribunal. Three of the Africans styled themselves as chiefs and three were *induna*, or advisors, to the colonial government. The *induna* had also participated in the campaign against Langalibalele. They may have been credible to Shepstone, but few Africans from the locations had reason to trust them.

Pine opened the trial by addressing the sizable audience, composed of Africans and Europeans. He charged Langalibalele with many crimes, proclaiming that "rebellion is the greatest crime that can be committed, because it involves all other crimes; murder, robbery, and every other possible crime are committed under the cloak of rebellion." He declared that the court would try Langalibalele according to African law. Pine argued that under African law, Langalibalele's crime of rebellion would already be considered proven and the prisoner would already have been executed. However, the lieutenant governor said, "We are Christian men, and live under a Christian dispensation, and do not like to put men to death if we can possibly avoid it; and, even then, not without giving the accused a fair and impartial trial."[41] This statement indicated Pine's confusion about all forms of the law. The Natal Ordinance No. 3 of 1849 set down guidelines for trials under "Natal Native Law," but it did not give the lieutenant governor the power to execute criminals. In fact, the ordinance stated that "Native Law" should be invoked in cases involving only Africans. Pine said that this was to be a kinder and gentler African trial, tempered with notions of Christian justice and mercy, a statement that would have been consistent with the ordinance. However, throughout the trial Pine threatened Langalibalele with execution.

When Pine finished his preamble, the prosecutor, John Shepstone, read the indictment against Langalibalele. It included several charges, including contumacy toward the supreme chief's magistrates, rebellion against the colonial government, and the encouragement of young Hlubi to violate colonial gun regulations. The court and its English audience may

---

[41] BPP [C. 1025] 1874, Opening statement by Sir B. Pine, January 16, 1874, pp. 48–9; *KRN*, 2. The *Natal Witness*, January 20, 1874, gives a slightly different transcription of Pine's statement.

have expected a prosecutor and an indictment, but colonial customary African legal proceedings did not have either. The form of local African law that was codified as customary law did allow defendants to have legal representation, just like they would under English law, but in this case Langalibalele was not represented. The charges and procedures combined customary English law and African law in such a way as to defeat the presumed purposes of both.

Langalibalele did not resist the court, but he did not cooperate either. In the court's tent, Langalibalele never quite fit any role that could have been assigned to him: prisoner, chief, or criminal. He responded variously to the court and undermined the script of the tribunal by not defending himself fully. He had more than twenty years of experience in advocating his position before colonial magistrates, so he might have been expected to mount a vigorous defense. It is possible that the proceedings simply confused him, but it is also possible that he chose not to suit the court's expectations for debate, whether they were African, English, or simply autocratic.

The trial engaged the particularities of gun control and rebellion as well as the general construction of the legal order. While trying such an ambiguous defendant in a poorly defined legal situation, Pine and Shepstone drew on diverse witnesses, amateur theatrics, and selective amnesia to strengthen the believability of the court. As Pine and Shepstone made their case, they realized it was crucial to stabilize the government's narrative of the dispute over gun registration that they had with Langalibalele. Over the course of six days, Africans loyal to the colonial government as well as British officials testified against Langalibalele. Sometimes during the trial Pine wore a British helmet; other times he wore a Zulu chief's headring and feather. Shepstone even tampered with the trial transcript to persuade his audiences that he had a strong case against Langalibalele. This presents a conundrum for historians. When Shepstone edited the transcript to stabilize his narrative, he introduced considerable uncertainty into the historical record. Fortunately, it is possible to compare the official transcript with alternative accounts to show how colonial officials manipulated trial transcripts as part of their overall strategy to stabilize firearms regulation and colonial law.

Theophilus Shepstone recorded events in order to narrate Langalibalele's transgressions against gun-control laws and the government representatives. Much of his transcript is confirmed in other accounts, but it is readily apparent that Theophilus Shepstone employed tendentious editing to smooth out the most controversial moments in the trial.

Immediately after Lt. Gov. Pine and John Shepstone read the confusing collection of charges, Langalibalele responded and Theophilus Shepstone translated. The official version of the trial gives a summary of Langalibalele's response. The chief "admitted that he had certainly done what was charged against him" and "admitted that he had treated the Messengers of the Supreme Chief with disrespect," but he pleaded extenuating circumstances. Others influenced his decisions and he feared the government messengers. The official transcript also states that "he did not answer the charge of encouraging the young men to arm themselves for purposes of resistance, but denied that they had procured the guns in consequence of an order from him, or with any purpose whatever."[42]

The official transcript offers a clear version of Langalibalele's plea, but the verbatim transcript reported in a local newspaper, the *Natal Witness*, reveals that the trial's events were not so cut and dried. Newspapers are not always paragons of accuracy, but nobody contested the *Natal Witness*'s version of events. By contrast, Bishop Colenso demonstrated that the first version of the official transcript, contained in the colonial *Blue Book*, varied suspiciously from newspaper accounts. In his words, "It is thought to exhibit in many places strong signs of an official pen."[43] Shepstone had access to the official transcript. He also had a motive to alter it: he wanted to present the trial in the best possible light to audiences in South Africa and Great Britain. In the courtroom, Shepstone attempted to assemble a credible narrative of Langalibalele's transgressions and gun-control violations. Shepstone failed to tell a credible story in court, but he wanted to portray himself in the best-possible light before the public in South Africa and Britain, with the result that he undermined future efforts to reconstruct an accurate narrative of the trial's events. As legal and literary scholars Paul Gewirtz and Peter Brooks have suggested in their book, *Law's Stories*, trials can be seen as a contest between different narrations with the same characters. Success in a trial can depend on the crafting of a superior narrative, an insight that Shepstone understood, too, in the trial of Langalibalele.

Despite Shepstone's efforts to craft a tendentious narrative, a comparison of the official account with the newspaper account sheds some light on what may have actually happened on the Hlubi location and in the courtroom. In the *Natal Witness* transcript, Langalibalele answered Pine's blanket charges of violating gun registration laws, rebellion, and

---

[42] BPP [C. 1025] 1874, Langalibalele's plea, January 16, 1874, pp. 49–50; *KRN*, 3.
[43] BPP [C. 1141] 1875, "Preface," pp. iii–v.

contumacy by stating that he was confused. He said, "I do not understand the nature of the charge, to a certain extent; that is, I do not know that I have committed murder, or burglary." When Shepstone edited the official transcript, he wanted to make the government's charges credible; therefore, he eliminated the chief's request for an explanation.[44]

Shepstone did more than just manipulate the official record to produce a credible trial that would stabilize both gun control and colonial law. He called on numerous African witnesses to ensure that Langalibalele, who had pleaded guilty, was indeed fully culpable. But even when it came to recording the testimony of government witnesses, he doctored the transcript to make it as damning as possible. On the first day of the trial, Shepstone's six African "chiefs" confirmed Langalibalele's guilt and commended colonial justice. The official transcript of the chiefs' testimony resembles the *Natal Witness* transcript, but the official transcript contains omissions, additions, and translations that tend to exaggerate Langalibalele's guilt. The newspaper transcript of the testimony of Teteleku varies on one key point. This "chief of the Amapumiza Tribe" stated that "everyone knows it is a crime to possess a gun without having obtained the license of the Supreme Chief." Even if Langalibalele had not conspired with his men to buy guns, he must have known that they possessed them and should have had them registered. Earlier, the *Natal Witness* recorded that Langalibalele advised the young Hlubi men not to purchase guns, while the official transcript recorded that he did not answer the charge of encouraging the young men to buy guns. The same contradiction appeared in Teteleku's testimony. The *Natal Witness* reported that Teteleku said that "Langalibalele advised his young men not to buy guns," while the official transcript substitutes the word "desired" for "advised," portraying the chief's active attempt to regulate firearms as a mere passive wish.[45] Therefore, he had violated the colonial government's gun-control measures. When Teteleku and the other chiefs concluded their testimony, the court adjourned for the day.

The next morning, Saturday, January 17, another large audience assembled for the second day of the trial. John Bird, the magistrate for Pietermaritzburg County, began the proceedings with a short

---

[44] *Natal Witness*, January 20, 1874. Compare with BPP [C. 1025] 1874, Langalibalele's plea, January 16, 1874, pp. 49–50; *KRN*, 3.

[45] BPP [C. 1025] 1874, Testimony of Hemuhemu, Teteleku, Nondonise, Mafingo, Zatshuke, and Manxele, January 16, 1874, pp. 51–2; *KRN*, 4–6. *Natal Witness*, January 20, 1874.

statement. The court had already established that Langalibalele was guilty of rebellion, contumacy, and violating gun laws, even though his plea was confused; it only remained to ascertain the magnitude of the crimes. He called the two government messengers, Umnyembe and Mahoyiza, to testify that Langalibalele and the Hlubi had disrespected them when they came to persuade the chief to come to Pietermaritzburg to discuss gun registration. Mahoyiza told a story about how the Hlubi hesitated to give him access to Langalibalele. The official transcript and the newspaper reports vary slightly, but it seems that the Hlubi asked Mahoyiza what difference it made whether the government killed Langalibalele in Pietermaritzburg or on the Hlubi location. The official transcript of Mahoyiza's testimony reported that the Hlubi "all said it would be as well to die (i.e., to resist the government) for two days, and on the third day to beg for peace," while the *Natal Witness* contains no such statement. Once again, key passages in the official transcript portray the Hlubi in a less favorable light.[46]

Mahoyiza continued his damning testimony against Langalibalele, telling another story of how guns influenced relations between Africans and the government. Mahoyiza said that the Hlubi menaced him and they provided no food. They carried out orders from Langalibalele to strip the messengers naked so as to reveal any concealed firearms. Mahoyiza told the court that Langalibalele gave these orders because John Shepstone had once drawn a concealed pistol on Matshana. Consequently, Langalibalele feared all government messengers. But according to the logic of the colonial government, anyone who stripped a government messenger may as well have been stripping the lieutenant governor himself. The colonial legal system did not give Langalibalele the authority to regulate the ways in which the lieutenant governor's representatives could use their guns.

Lt. Gov. Pine allowed Langalibalele a brief opportunity to challenge the messenger's story of the search for hidden guns. Once again the official transcript portrays the chief less favorably than does the newspaper. The official transcript summarizes the lieutenant governor's question and the chief's answer: "The Supreme Chief asked the prisoner why he had allowed the Messengers to remain undressed, when he found they had nothing? The prisoner evaded the question; but said the Messengers were in the hut, and they were afterwards allowed to put on their clothes again." In the *Natal Witness*, the lieutenant governor asked Langalibalele,

---

[46] BPP [C. 1025] 1874, Testimony of Mahoyiza, January 17, 1874, p. 57; *KRN*, 10–11. *Natal Witness*, January 20, 1874.

"According to their statement the object of your stripping them was to see if they had any weapons on them; why did you not return them their clothes when you found they had none?" The chief replied in a matter-of-fact fashion: "They were in a hut and did not require them. They were allowed to put them on afterwards." Langalibalele seems not to have evaded Pine's question, as the official transcript suggested. The chief may not have even made a point of "allowing" the messengers to remain undressed. Instead, the *Natal Witness* indicates that Langalibalele gave Pine a direct answer: the messengers simply had no reason to put their clothes back on. It was not unusual to hold an indoor meeting partially clothed.[47]

Bishop Colenso found the government's case against the chief utterly unconvincing. On Sunday, January 18, Colenso confronted his friend Shepstone personally, accusing him of violating English principles of fairness: by law the lieutenant governor heard appeals and was not supposed to preside over trials. The bishop was also appalled by the way in which the court denied Langalibalele access to legal counsel. Furthermore, Colenso checked the testimony of the government's African witnesses against the accounts of other Africans and found them inconsistent. In particular, he found the testimony of Mahoyiza, the messenger, to be unreliable. Langalibalele had never had the contumacy to order Mahoyiza to strip naked; he had only removed his coat and shirt. That afternoon, Shepstone examined Colenso's witnesses and dismissed their accounts. This was natural enough, seeing how the witnesses laid the blame for Langalibalele's mistrust of government messengers squarely on the shoulders of Shepstone's brother John. With Theophilus Shepstone hearing the case against Langalibalele and with John Shepstone prosecuting the case, it was doubtful that this information would influence the outcome of the trial.[48]

Although Theophilus Shepstone ignored most of Colenso's arguments, the bishop's appeal to notions of English justice did strike a responsive chord. On Monday, January 19, Lt. Gov. Pine opened the third day of the trial by saying that he would allow a European attorney to represent Langalibalele in the court. He insisted that the presence of a defense

---

[47] BPP [C. 1025] 1874, January 17, 1874, p. 59; *KRN*, 14. *Natal Witness*, January 20, 1874. Frances Colenso wrote that "he had nothing on him but his *umutya* (tail-piece) when he entered the hut, & probably the chief himself was in the same predicament, as UmPande, the Zulu king, was, when I went to visit him in his hut, this being the usual native costume." Marginalia in the Houghton Library's copy of *DOL*, 15.

[48] Guy, *Heretic*, 206–8.

attorney should not be taken as a precedent for future trials under customary African law. He was allowing a defense attorney in this case of gun control and rebellion because of the "enormity of the crime, and the importance attached to it by the public."[49] After hearing the testimony of several witnesses, the governor asked Langalibalele whether he would prefer an African or European attorney. The chief answered that he preferred for the governor to decide. The official transcript recorded that Langalibalele said that he had "no choice," a statement that the *Natal Witness* did not report.[50] Perhaps Shepstone preferred to remind people that he could regulate the lives of Natal's Africans as autocratically as he wanted. The prisoner's guilt was not in question, but Pine adjourned the court for two days so that the defense attorney could prepare a case.

Outside the tent, the newspapers pounced on the court for listening to Colenso, in spite of the fact that they had no real reason to worry about the trial's outcome. The government brought in a Durban attorney named Escombe, telling him that he could do little more than cross-examine government witnesses. Under these circumstances, Escombe declined to represent Langalibalele. When the court reconvened on Friday, January 23, the lieutenant governor declared that the trial would proceed anyway, without anyone to represent Langalibalele. Pine believed that the chief had already pleaded guilty to rebellion and that African custom did not call for a defense attorney. He invited any members of the court to speak on behalf of the prisoner if they wished and then called the next witnesses.[51]

When the court denied Langalibalele a defense counsel, it seems that some of the colonists were troubled, but they were not troubled because they wanted the chief to have a fair trial. The focus of the trial was shifting from the particularities of a gun-control case to the general construction of the legal order. Settlers feared Africans with guns, but they also wanted colonial laws to be as forceful as possible when it came to the colony's Africans. One anonymous settler wrote to the *Natal Witness* that Langalibalele ought to be condemned for treason even if the court was far from perfect. Still, he derided the African jurists: "I omit the farce of the Native Chiefs; these would have bawled their approbation if the 'great man' had said he was a church clock, and tried to chime the hours." The author,

---

[49] BPP [C. 1025] 1874, Opening statement by Sir B. Pine, January 16, 1874, pp. 48–9; *KRN*, 15. Pine's statement is largely confirmed in the *Natal Witness*, January 23, 1874.

[50] BPP [C. 1025] 1874, January 19, 1874, p. 63; *KRN*, 18–19. The dialogue is largely confirmed in the *Natal Witness*, January 23, 1874.

[51] BPP [C. 1025] 1874, Statement of Gov. Pine, January 23, 1874, p. 64; *KRN*, 21. The statement is largely confirmed in the *Natal Witness*, January 27, 1874.

calling himself "Your Stout Contributor," criticized the government for not appointing a defense counsel for Langalibalele. Denying a prisoner an adequate defense "may be one way of proving the superiority of our race, but to the famous intelligent Zulu it must appear a sign of weakness, for he will reason to himself that we are afraid to hear our own laws argued in the defence of a black man."[52]

At this point, it seems that the members of the court began to shrink from publicity. Perhaps they believed that their efforts to stabilize a new kind of law were failing. The fourth day of the trial proceeded before a substantially smaller audience. Few people knew when the trial would recommence, according to the *Natal Witness*. It is not clear whether the lieutenant governor simply happened to reconvene the court at the spur of the moment. In any event, the court shored up its authority by calling its strongest-possible witness, Theophilus Shepstone, himself a member of the tribunal. Shepstone read a copy of a letter that he had sent to Langalibalele on October 4, 1873. In the letter, the secretary for native affairs requested that the chief of the Hlubi come to headquarters in Pietermaritzburg for an interview. Shepstone was not only annoyed that Langalibalele was resisting MacFarlane's efforts to register the Hlubi guns. In the letter, he accused Langalibalele of lying to avoid a meeting.[53]

With such a powerful witness appearing for the prosecution, Langalibalele knew that there was little he could do to contest the court's version of events. After Shepstone read the letter, Pine asked the chief, "You have heard what the secretary for native affairs has said: have you any questions to put to him upon his statement?" Langalibalele answered, "I have nothing to say in reply. I am simply awaiting the decision of the Court, and when that decision is arrived at, I would wish for an order to send and collect my children, who are scattered about, I know not where." Langalibalele kept to his own priorities. While he could predict the outcome of the trial, he worried about the fate of his family. Pine repeated his insincere invitation for Langalibalele to question Shepstone. The chief replied, "I have sinned against the Government, and can have nothing to say." Langalibalele refused to act according to the court's script.[54]

---

[52] *Natal Witness*, February 20, 1874.
[53] *Natal Witness*, January 27, 1874. BPP [C. 1025] 1874, "Message from the Secretary for Native Affairs to Langalibalele," October 4, 1873, submitted in evidence on January 23, 1874, pp. 64–5; *KRN*, 21–3.
[54] *Natal Witness*, January 27, 1874. The official transcript merely summarizes the conclusion of Langalibalele's statement: BPP [C. 1025] 1874, January 23, 1874, pp. 65–6; *KRN*, 23.

It fell to Theophilus Shepstone, then, to characterize the Hlubi dispute with the Natal authorities over gun registration. Pine questioned him about the origins of the troubles. Shepstone bent his answers to show himself, his brother John, and the magistrate MacFarlane in the best-possible light. Pine asked, "Then I understand the principal dispute between the prisoner and his Magistrate was as to the registration, and not as to the possession of firearms by his men." Shepstone answered, "Yes; that was the question at issue." Pine asked, "And the proposal for registration was resisted by Langalibalele?" The secretary for native affairs replied, "Yes; guns were found in the location, as also a great number of Diamond Fields tickets. The guns have not been registered in the colony at all. It was the question of registration generally that was disputed."[55] Had Langalibalele wished to question Shepstone, he might have pointed out the inconsistencies in this testimony. Yes, the dispute between Langalibalele and MacFarlane had been about registering firearms, not possessing them. The government bound gun control to colonial sovereignty. However, Shepstone did not mention that the young Hlubi also feared how MacFarlane might damage or confiscate their weapons if they brought them in for registration.

Nobody challenged Shepstone, who moved from telling half-truths to inventing lies. Pine asked Shepstone whether Langalibalele had grounds to fear a meeting with him: "Do you think that in the conduct he [Langalibalele] has pursued he was influenced by fear of the consequences if he came to the city?" Shepstone answered, "I suppose he must have been to some extent. But I have no idea that he had any just ground for fear." Pine reminisced about Shepstone's long years of service as an administrator and then asked, "Do you recollect a case ever happening in which a Chief responding to the call of the Government has ever come to any harm through it?" Shepstone lied, answering, "No, not in my experience." After confirming the Shepstone brothers' stories, Pine surveyed the chiefs on the tribunal, asking them if they ever feared to meet with representatives of the government. None did.[56]

Next, the lieutenant governor recalled Mahoyiza, the messenger who claimed to have been strip-searched for guns, but whose testimony stood contradicted by Colenso's witnesses. Although Shepstone rejected any

---

[55] *Natal Witness*, January 27, 1874. The official transcript varies from the *Natal Witness* in detail but not in substance: BPP [C. 1025] 1874, proceedings of January 23, 1874, p. 66; *KRN*, 24.

[56] *Natal Witness*, January 27, 1874. The official transcript varies from the *Natal Witness* in detail but not in substance: BPP [C. 1025] 1874, proceedings of January 23, 1874, pp. 66–7; *KRN*, 24–5.

testimony against Mahoyiza, it seems that he at least mentioned possible inconsistencies to Lt. Gov. Pine. The court reexamined Mahoyiza, intending to deflate Colenso's criticism. The messenger changed his testimony to suit Shepstone, but he took revenge on Shepstone for forcing him to eat crow. After Shepstone had just finished lying to protect his brother, John, Pine requested "some further description from Mahoyiza as to the extent to which he was stripped by Langalibalele's men." Mahoyiza answered, "When they told me I must take off my clothes, to show I had not a gun as Mr. John Shepstone had when he apprehended Matyana, I opened my coat, and said, 'You can search me and see that I have no gun.' While I was speaking, the men came up to me and took my clothes off." Pine asked, "Did they strip you of everything?" Mahoyiza responded, "They intended to strip me altogether, but I told them I had no other dress, and they must at least let my trowsers remain on. They took off my gaiters, shirt, and coat, leaving me nothing on but trowsers and boots."[57] There is a noticeable difference between being asked to remove some clothes and being asked to strip naked. After all, it was a search for a revolver, a large and obvious object.

One of the key prosecution witnesses was admitting to perjury, which indicated that Pine and Shepstone's case was unraveling. Mahoyiza had also suggested that Langalibalele might have had a good reason to try to regulate the guns of colonial messengers. The chief fled the colony because he feared lying and bullying civil servants who brought hidden pistols to meetings. Langalibalele's rebellion was looking less and less contumacious. Luckily for the court, the prisoner, deprived of counsel, had already pleaded guilty of contumacy and rebellion. The prosecution had bungled the case completely, without even the challenge of a defense attorney or an argumentative prisoner. Immediately after Mahoyiza's testimony, Lt. Gov. Pine moved to end the trial. He asked Langalibalele if he had anything further to say. The chief said, "I have nothing to say, beyond thanking Mr. John Shepstone for what he has said in my behalf, as it is perfectly correct that I acted under fear of the Government, and was urged on by Mabuhle and others to do what I did."[58]

Pine ignored Langalibalele's backhanded compliment to John Shepstone. He promised to render a judgment by the next week. With the

---

[57] *Natal Witness*, January 27, 1874. The official transcript varies from the *Natal Witness* in detail but not in substance: BPP [C. 1025] 1874, proceedings of January 23, 1874, p. 68; *KRN*, 26.

[58] *Natal Witness*, January 27, 1874. The official transcript varies from the *Natal Witness* in detail but not in substance: BPP [C. 1025] 1874, proceedings of January 23, 1874, p. 68; *KRN*, 26.

case in a shambles, he thanked the tribunal's African chiefs for the statements they made after Langalibalele confessed his guilt. Pine defended the chiefs against charges of bias, arguing that "according to Kafir custom and usage, the trial was over then." Pine then explained the proceedings that followed, saying that they were "in conformity with our own ideas of justice."[59] It is not clear whether "our" referred to the entire court, to its British members, or to British jurisprudence generally. When the trial began the supreme chief insisted on a customary African approach, but when judgment approached he struggled to explain himself.

While the court was out of session, Bishop Colenso offered to provide four Africans to testify that Mahoyiza lied about the search for hidden guns. Shepstone arranged for a private meeting in his office so that Colenso and his witnesses could confront Mahoyiza before some of the members of the court. Colenso's witnesses confirmed that the Hlubi did not require Mahoyiza to strip naked. Furthermore, Langalibalele provided the messengers with plenty of food and beer, contradicting their earlier testimony that they had been starved. Even Mafingo, one of Shepstone's African advisors, concluded that Mahoyiza was lying.[60] Shepstone himself began to mistrust Mahoyiza. When the messenger offered to provide witnesses to bolster his account, the secretary for native affairs simply laughed at him. Shepstone's African advisors agreed to hear Mahoyiza's witnesses, but they too decided that the messenger and his associates lacked all credibility.[61]

Now Shepstone had his back up against the wall. There was more at stake in this case than just the innocence or guilt of a rebel who resisted colonial gun registration. Not only was Shepstone using the Langalibalele trial to build a new kind of law, but for almost thirty years he had been building a system of segregated "locations" in the face of opposition from the European settlers. Ironically, Shepstone could not rely on colonial governors like Pine, who often fell under the influence of settler agitators. The Langalibalele trial should have been a showcase for Shepstone's African administration. Instead, his effort to regulate firearms drew out all the ambiguities of the system. It also caused him to lose key supporters like Colenso.

---

[59] *Natal Witness*, January 27, 1874. The official transcript varies from the *Natal Witness* in detail but not in substance: BPP [C. 1025] 1874, proceedings of January 23, 1874, p. 68; *KRN*, 26.

[60] BPP [C. 1141] 1875, "Mahoyiza's Falsehoods Exposed in the Office of the S. N. A.," January 27, 1874, pp. 109–15; *DOL*, final appendix, 16–26.

[61] BPP [C. 1141] 1875, "Mahoyiza among the Chiefs and Indunas," January 29, 1874, pp. 115–7; *DOL*, final appendix, 27–31.

Shepstone began a rearguard action to save the trial. First, he shored up the charge of rebellion and avoided the issue of gun registration altogether. On January 30, Shepstone put Langalibalele's sons and advisors on trial in a different kind of court. He presided over the court himself, with the help of two European magistrates and seven subordinate African chiefs and advisors. He charged the prisoners with rebellion, the charge that was beginning to come apart in the trial of Langalibalele. The court met in a storeroom of the Civil Engineer's Department, hardly a public location. The court made itself accessible only by publishing its proceedings in the local newspapers. The court proceeded in a business-like manner, without any philosophical disquisitions about combining European and African law. Over the course of three weeks it gathered substantial evidence about the rebellion from Langalibalele's sons, advisors, and subjects, as well as from the employees of the colonial government. The causes of the rebellion may have been complex, but at least there could no longer be any doubt that a rebellion had taken place.

Shepstone also arranged for Pine to reconvene the Langalibalele trial and to take up, once again, the mixed charges of rebellion, contumacy, and gun-control violations. On Wednesday, February 4, the proceedings resumed, with the magistrate John MacFarlane in the witness-box. He testified extensively that Langalibalele and the Hlubi had behaved disobediently "for a long time before the rebellion broke out." MacFarlane had some difficulty collecting fees for marriage licenses, but the Hlubi gave him the most trouble over gun registration. He described how he registered guns: first, he took possession of them and registered them locally and then wrote to the lieutenant governor to obtain colonial permits. He held the guns in his office until the lieutenant governor gave permission. Beginning in early 1873 Langalibalele and the Hlubi began to resist this procedure, at which point MacFarlane contacted Shepstone. MacFarlane found it particularly disturbing that Langalibalele refused to meet with him.[62]

Langalibalele rose to contradict the government's narrative of how he had violated gun registration laws. The chief argued that MacFarlane "made no allusion to the guns which were taken in for registration but never returned." MacFarlane claimed that he only kept the guns because he was awaiting instructions from the capital on how to approach this latest dispute with the Hlubi. Langalibalele reminded MacFarlane

---

[62] *Natal Witness*, February 6, 1874. The official transcript varies from the *Natal Witness* in detail but not in substance: BPP [C. 1025] 1874, Testimony of MacFarlane, February 4, 1874, pp. 69–70; *KRN*, 29–30.

that he did not meet with him because he was sick and then asked, "Did I not send in to the Weenen [MacFarlane's] Magistracy for some medicine to cure my leg?" MacFarlane mocked the chief, responding that "the prisoner often sent in to the office for a bottle of rum to be taken as a medicine, and I believe it was always sent. I fancy, also, that on one occasion I sent him a box of pills." Langalibalele shot back, "Mr. MacFarlane's memory is very convenient. He only thinks he sent me the pills. I know positively that the guns which were not returned were sent in before the disturbance." The court paid no attention to Langalibalele's objections and even excised his most pointed remarks from the official transcript.[63]

MacFarlane and Langalibalele continued to snipe at each other about the guns and the rebellion, but the official transcript attributes only one colorful line to the chief. MacFarlane accused Langalibalele of obstructing a government flunkey who was thought to be "poisoning" the magistrate's mind against the chief. Langalibalele knew that MacFarlane's mind was indeed poisoned against him. He retorted, "Is it not true, am I not here, am I not now dead?"[64] The *Natal Witness* transcript does not record this response at all. MacFarlane agitated Langalibalele to the point of defensiveness, but the official transcript portrays the chief as being appropriately resigned to his fate.

Pine interceded in the debate to change the subject completely, from MacFarlane's efforts to register Hlubi guns back to Langalibalele's efforts to search colonial messengers for guns. The *Natal Witness* reported how "the Supreme Chief mentioned that evidence had been taken elsewhere which would throw some doubt on the statement of Mahoiza in regard to the stripping. The other members of the Court disagreed, thinking it was clearly proved that the messengers of the Supreme Court had been insulted, and that it was unnecessary to re-open this question." The court would now try to restore faith in the messenger Mahoyiza's testimony by calling an expert witness, Homoi, "an old Kafir experienced in Native Law." The old man testified that according to local custom, stripping a messenger would usually be considered an act of war. The court substantiated Mahoyiza's testimony by recourse to authority: Shepstone did not allow Colenso's witnesses to contradict the old man, either in court or in the official transcript. He wanted to make sure that no ambiguity

---

[63] *Natal Witness*, February 6, 1874. Compare with BPP [C. 1025] 1874, Proceedings of February 4, 1874, p. 70; *KRN*, 30-1.

[64] BPP [C. 1025] 1874, Proceedings of February 4, 1874, p. 71; *KRN*, 31.

surrounded his narrative of how it was inappropriate for African chiefs to control the weapons of colonial representatives.[65]

Afterward, the court called more witnesses to testify that Langalibalele had rebelled against the government and violated firearms regulations. This time, they brought quantitative evidence to bear. Shepstone's clerk made it known that he registered forty-eight guns from the Hlubi, while a military officer stated that his troops had seized 111 guns after they captured Langalibalele. After this final reminder that gun control lay behind the charge of rebellion, Pine closed the case. Any further evidence would be taken in the trial of Langalibalele's sons and advisors.[66]

The lieutenant governor and his secretary for native affairs stage-managed the trial to their own advantage. Under the tent, only Langalibalele challenged the court's credibility, doing so by alternating silence with defiance. Everyone else agreed to the government's way of setting the terms of the debate between gun-control regulators and violators, loyalists and rebels. Two simultaneous discourses occurred during the trial. On one level, Pine and his officials hoped that the trial would focus on issues of power and technology. They gathered facts and arguments about Langalibalele's violations of gun-control laws and acts of rebellion. On another level, Langalibalele and the other participants in the trial had to evaluate the risks involved in presenting specific facts and arguments to the court. If Langalibalele had accepted the terms of the trial and defended himself fully, then he would have accepted a common set of questions to debate with the colonial government.[67]

On Monday, February 9, the hybrid court pronounced Langalibalele guilty of violating firearms regulations and rebelling against colonial rule. The government could punish Langalibalele in two ways, according to the colonial version of customary South African laws. The government could execute the chief and it could also take away his property. The court punished Langalibalele differently, more in accordance with the desires of the colonial settlers than anything else. Lt. Gov.

---

[65] *Natal Witness*, February 6, 1874. The official transcript varies from the *Natal Witness* in detail but not in substance: BPP [C. 1025] 1874, Proceedings of February 4, 1874, p. 71; *KRN*, 31.

[66] *Natal Witness*, February 6, 1874. The official transcript varies from the *Natal Witness* slightly but the figures match each other: BPP [C. 1025] 1874, Proceedings of February 4, 1874, p. 71; *KRN*, 31.

[67] This line of analysis, following a trial's economy of silences and interventions, inside and outside of the courtroom, owes much to Cohen, *The Combing of History*, 46–7, 75, as well as to Cohen and Adhiambo's *Burying SM*.

Pine made a show of sparing Langalibalele from execution, but he also banished the chief for life to Robben Island, a punishment that was completely inconsistent with colonial conceptions of local African laws.

Appealing the Judgment Against Langalibalele

During the Langalibalele trial, the court's attention moved from the particularities of gun registration to the broader construction of the colonial legal order. Shepstone and Pine failed to make their narrative of the trial credible, even as word of the trial spread farther and wider. Eventually, the case reached a more powerful audience, the British parliament. In Westminster, imperial lawmakers became concerned with the particularities of the case because, in the wake of Gov. Eyre's brutal repression of Jamaica's 1865 Morant Bay Rebellion, many Britons were keeping a close eye on the colonial judicial system. In addition, Disraeli's new government sought to strengthen imperial rule in South Africa. After the Langalibalele trial, Colenso, Shepstone, and Pine all found it necessary to articulate their positions to audiences in Britain who viewed the case from an imperial perspective.

During the first year of Langalibalele's exile, Colenso dedicated himself to publicizing the injustice of the conviction. First, he sent information about the violent suppression of the Hlubi and the trial of Langalibalele to the Aborigines Protection Society. In turn, members of the society put pressure on the parliament and the Colonial Office to conduct an investigation.[68] Then, at the end of 1874, Colenso published a book in London, *The Defence of Langalibalele*, that brought to light the procedural inconsistencies of the trial, as well as the more general inconsistency of the colonial administration. Colenso attacked the cynicism of colonial gun-control laws. He agreed that the Hlubi and other Africans obtained numerous unregistered firearms, but argued that they did not do so in order to defy the government. He wrote that "not a particle of proof has been produced to show that [Langalibalele] 'conspired' with his young men to procure fire-arms – still less that he did so with the purpose and intention of resisting the Government." In his book, Colenso argued that colonial gun-control laws were subject to customary variations in interpretation. He pointed out that even in England, tensions existed between customary and written laws. Colenso asked, "Are there not in this, as

---

[68] BPP [C.1025], nos. 44, 49, 51.

in other countries, things known to be 'contrary to law,' which are yet passed over lightly, or even connived at, by the authorities, unless brought specially and formally under their notice, like the game-laws or excise-laws of England?" Among Africans making a transition from oral to written culture, contemporary consensus about the spirit of the colony's laws was still quite important, particularly on the subject of gun-control laws. Colenso also suggested that the Natal government, and MacFarlane in particular, had not kept up with the increasing flow of guns into the colony. According to Colenso, who investigated the matter, "Some years ago, no doubt, when the law in question was passed, a gun was comparatively a rare article in the hands of a Kafir, and the law was strictly enforced. Now not only has the Government allowed many natives to have guns, but it is highly probable or rather certain that numbers of unregistered guns are possessed at this time in many other tribes besides Langalibalele's."[69]

Colenso presented important problems to the imperial government as well as significant opportunities, especially for those, like Carnarvon, the secretary of state for the colonies, who hoped for the uniform administration of all the colonies of South Africa. Carnarvon conducted a full investigation into the irregularities that surrounded Langalibalele's capture, trial, and punishment. The results of the investigation were published in five parliamentary command papers over the course of late 1874 and early 1875.[70]

Colenso's reports on the Hlubi rebellion and the Langalibalele trial were calling attention to the ambiguities of Shepstone's policies toward Africans at the same time as Carnarvon was seeking allies in his quest to build a federated South Africa. Shepstone had such extensive local knowledge that he had the potential to become an important ally, even though he might have to improve his relations with colonial settlers. In late 1874, both Colenso and Shepstone visited England and met on several occasions with Carnarvon. Colenso's criticism had to be dealt with, but Shepstone became a valuable friend.

---

[69] DOL [Colenso, *Defence of Langalibalele*], 24. The quotation cannot be found in the corresponding section of BPP [C.1141] 1875, on p. 9, which suggests that before DOL was published as a parliamentary paper, Colenso removed it. It is possible that he did not think that the British parliament, which was responsible for legislating for a far-flung empire, would be persuaded by arguments about local variations in the law.

[70] United Kingdom, *Hansard Parliamentary Debates*, 3rd ser., vol. 123, April 12, 1875. The five parliamentary papers are BPP [C. 1025] 1874; [C. 1119] 1875; [C. 1121] 1875; [C. 1141] 1875; [C. 1187] 1875.

Colenso's philanthropy, Shepstone's machinations, and Carnarvon's ambition all ensured that Lt. Gov. Pine took the fall for the Langalibalele fiasco, even though Shepstone bore such a heavy responsibility for it. Between March and December of 1874, Carnarvon and Pine carried on an extensive correspondence. The secretary of state asked questions and demanded evidence, while the lieutenant governor rebutted criticism and produced testimonials, all of which were published in the parliamentary command papers. Finally, on December 3, 1874, Carnarvon wrote a long letter to Pine, blaming him for a miscarriage of justice in the Langalibalele case. Carnarvon took as evidence the unnecessary administrative misunderstandings of 1873, the procedural irregularities of the trial, and the harsh punishment of the chief and his people. He recognized that firearms registration "was represented to be the immediate cause of the late disturbances," but he believed that Pine erred when he charged Langalibalele with encouraging the Hlubi to obtain unregistered firearms. Carnarvon blamed Pine for the trouble, but unlike Colenso, the secretary of state was not acting out of humanitarian concern. He concluded his letter by outlining his policy objectives in South Africa: "The system under which the natives are governed has, in fact, depended too much upon the maintenance of friendly relations, and too little upon a firm enforcement upon the Kafirs of the obligations of individual citizenship. If, as I hope, I am able hereafter to propose some material improvements in the system of Native Administration, I shall do so in full reliance upon the ready co-operation of the Legislature and people of the colony."[71] Carnarvon and Shepstone were turning Colenso's efforts to their own purposes. Pine paid the price for his involvement: Carnarvon forced him to resign and replaced him with the reformer and army hero Sir Garnet Wolseley.

Still, the Langalibalele affair remained in the public eye. On April 12, 1875, the case was discussed in the House of Lords. Earl Grey applauded the way in which Lt. Gov. Pine had suppressed Langalibalele's rebellion and argued that Natal should retain its legal and administrative system. Grey was prepared to overlook the irregularities and particularities of the Langalibalele case, arguing that he would not "enter into the details of the circumstances which had created these doubts" in the mind of the

---

[71] BPP [C.1121] 1875, Carnarvon to Pine, December 3, 1874, nos. 26–8, pp. 86–95; quotations are from p. 87 and p. 91.

colonial government about Langalibalele's loyalty.[72] Carnarvon responded by focusing his arguments on the particularities of the Langalibalele case, including the registration of firearms. According to Carnarvon, the Hlubi rebellion had "a variety of causes.... But it arose in greater measure, I believe, from ordinances passed for the registration of guns."[73] Both Carnarvon and Grey recognized that guns were part of a broader set of social problems, and also that the overall body of laws arose from particular cases; to change the status quo, Carnarvon raised the particularities of gun control, while to preserve the status quo Grey did not mention them. Gun control opened up a host of legal and administrative issues that Carnarvon was about to use to his advantage in an upcoming move to strengthen imperial rule.

There remained the awkward question of what to do with Langalibalele. Carnarvon's investigation and the firing of Pine vindicated the chief, to a degree, which meant that he ought not to be relegated to Robben Island. In November 1874, when Carnarvon presented the results of his investigation to Queen Victoria, her secretary, Henry Ponsonby, informed the secretary of state that the queen wished Langalibalele to receive clemency. "The Queen feels sure that you have given full consideration to both sides of the question," wrote Ponsonby, "and it would appear that a grievous wrong has been committed on Langalibalele, who has been unjustly treated."[74] Yet Carnarvon and the colonists sought order, above all, which might be hampered by the return of a vindicated rebel chief. Carnarvon arranged for Langalibalele to be transferred to more pleasant quarters at Uitvlugt, a farmstead on the Cape Flats, near the present site of Ndabeni, which Colenso's daughter, Frances, visited and described as a "desolate and unfruitful piece of ground." Langalibalele was permitted to live there with his family and to keep his own animals under conditions of relative freedom.[75] The move itself was the subject of controversy in Cape Town, where settlers and officials resisted.

---

[72] United Kingdom, *Hansard Parliamentary Debates*, 3rd ser., vol. 123, April 12, 1875, pp. 667–8.

[73] United Kingdom, *Hansard Parliamentary Debates*, 3rd ser., vol. 123, April 12, 1875, p. 683.

[74] RHL, Papers of J. C. Molteno, MSS. Afr. S23/3, Ponsonby to Carnarvon, November 28, 1874, copy inserted in letter of Brownlee to Molteno, n.d. July 1875, ff.14–15.

[75] CPP [A. 17] 1875, "Draft of Proposed Rules and Regulations to Be Observed in Connection with the Location of Langalibalele and Malambule at Uitvlugt." Colenso, *History of the Zulu War*, 73.

Carnarvon got his way, but his public dispute with the Cape government opened the whole case to public scrutiny once again.[76] After much controversy, Charles Pacalt Brownlee, the Cape secretary for native affairs, came to bring Langalibalele news of the move. Instead of rejoicing at leaving Robben Island, Langalibalele asked why he could not return to Natal.[77]

At Uitvlugt, tourists came to visit Langalibalele, who allowed them to pose with him for photographs, in exchange for a fee. The novelist Anthony Trollope, who visited Langalibalele in 1877 as part of a tour of South Africa, reported that the Hlubi chief appeared "stalwart." Trollope wrote in his book, *South Africa*, which was read widely in Britain and South Africa, that "the prisoner himself was very silent, hardly saying a word in answer to the questions put to him, except that he should like to see his children in Natal."[78] In 1887, the colonial authorities did allow the old chief to return to Natal, where he died two years later.

The significance of Langalibalele's case was apparent to Trollope. The novelist reflected, "It is not too much to say that the doings of Langalibalele have altered the Constitution of the Colony; and it is probable that as years run on they will greatly affect the whole treatment of the Natives in South Africa. And yet Langalibalele was never a great man among the Zulu and must often have been surprised at his own importance."[79]

Langalibalele was, indeed, an important figure in South African history for his unwillingness to acknowledge changes in the laws about guns and also about changes in the overall legal order. As Science and Technology Studies scholar Sheila Jasanoff argues, court cases "function as a medium for constructing and stabilizing particular orderings of science and technology in society." According to Jasanoff, "general claims and principles emerge from the particularities of specific cases and controversies . . . constructions of science and technology in the legal system invariably redraw the lines of power and authority."[80]

The Langalibalele case began as a dispute over technological regulation: who was the proper authority to control the Hlubi guns? As the case

---

[76] BPP [C.1158] 1875, Barkly to Carnarvon, January 5, 1875, plus enclosures, pp. 1–5; Carnarvon to Barkly, February 15, 1875, pp. 5–6.

[77] RHL, Papers of J. C. Molteno, MSS. Afr. S23/3, Brownlee to Molteno, n.d. July 1875, ff.14–15.

[78] Trollope, *South Africa*, 1:244.

[79] Trollope, *South Africa*, 1:237.

[80] Jasanoff, *Science at the Bar*, pp. xv, xvi. See also Jasanoff's discussion of the Cruzan and Quinlan cases on pp. 183–203.

moved from the Hlubi location to the colonial capital and from there to London, judges, litigants, and lawmakers called attention to the ambiguities of colonial Natal's legal system. Local debates about technological regulation brought about a miscarriage of justice that helped initiate a movement for legal reform. Over time, the Langalibalele case was less and less about guns and more and more about legal principles and the ordering of a new type of society.

The significance of Langalibalele's case was also apparent in his praise poem, collected by James Stuart at the end of the nineteenth century. The poets who memorialized Langalibalele sang:

> Chief who has the wounds of a spear,
> Who is clothed with arms like heart-fat;
> Those of the clever one [Lieutenant-Governor Pine] came with black hearts,
> And said they would take his arms as they desired,
> Thinking he was powerless and without eyes,
> Whereas it was he who had keen eyes . . .
> . . . Starer with wide open eyes,
> Who looks at a person as if he were staring right into him.
> He who crossed over to the other side [Basutoland];
> Great one who is black and also his kraals.[81]

He was not remembered as a defeated exile. He looked powerless, but his powers of discernment were such that he could see into the "black hearts" of the government men who came to disarm him. While some power came from guns, other sorts of power came from the ability to interpret a crisis. Many people in South Africa portrayed arms proliferation and arms regulation as a crisis. Its interpretation and representation had a close bearing on who would have power and who would not.

---

[81] Stuart, *Izibongo: Zulu Praise Poems*, 134–5. It is hard to know the context in which this praise poem was performed. See the methodological discussion in White, "Power and the Praise Poem."

7

Guns and Confederation, 1875–6

As the gun trade was growing and guns were improving, a shift took place in official discourse about guns. Stricter controls were proposed by British imperialists and colonial settlers. By the end of the 1870s, members of these groups were seeking to disarm Africans as part of an emerging ideological tendency to regulate African land and labor. Conservatives in Britain had a plan to confederate the South African colonies and make their "native policies" uniform, while Eastern Cape settler politicians were beginning to persuade other constituencies to adopt racial discrimination. Such proposals tended to be opposed by liberals, including missionaries, traders, and philanthropists, ideologically disparate groups that nonetheless occasionally shared some political objectives. Various liberals who believed in free trade also tended to oppose disarmament. Guns were a material component of their differently defined versions of "civilization." Guns also helped "civilized" Africans protect their communities from the "uncivilized" and from the Boers.

Liberals believed in civilizing Africans by encouraging them to adopt European material culture in the form of guns, clothing, housing, cookware, and so on. Midcentury liberals who considered themselves "friends of the natives" hoped that if they offered fatherly and motherly guidance to Africans, then eventually South Africans would all share the same culture. In politics, liberals hoped to gradually undermine the rule of African chiefs. Gradually, it was hoped that Africans would become citizens. Until then, they could be kept at arm's length. Liberalism's turning point came in the 1860s and 1870s, when it began to seem as if significant numbers of Africans were adapting to European culture. Quite a few African men were meeting the Cape's property qualification for the franchise. In some parliamentary constituencies, non-European voters constituted substantial minorities – substantial enough to influence elections. The growing number of non-European voters vexed paternalist Cape liberals and led many to lean toward racial discrimination. They had never embraced non-Europeans as equals, and now it seemed that non-Europeans might begin to wield political clout.[1]

At midcentury, many of the same Cape liberals called for a responsible government. In response, the British government insisted that the Cape shoulder further responsibilities and annex the Ciskei, which it did reluctantly in 1865. The Ciskei, which had a substantial Xhosa population, had to be represented in the Cape parliament. (The Transkei was not fully incorporated by the Cape Colony until 1885.) The desire for responsible government proved greater than the fear of African influence in the parliament. In 1871, an increase in the Cape government's revenues persuaded a bare majority of the members of parliament that the Cape could stand on its own feet and that the time had come to ask for more self-government. In the following year, the British government allowed the Cape to have a responsible government led by a prime minister, following the Westminster system. The British governor remained as head of state and retained his powers as high commissioner for southern Africa. The governor was now supposed to rule according to the wishes of the parliament. And the "native question" began to play a more prominent role in Cape politics. Liberals in particular shifted their views. Previously, liberals were inclined to support the gradual civilization of Africans. The chiefs were to be undermined slowly and European cultural practices were to be introduced carefully so as to avoid expensive conflicts. With responsible government – and with greater government revenues – liberals worried less about the expenses of conflict and came to expect rapid civilization. Those Africans who resisted outright or who dragged their feet were deemed worthy of being dominated. The new, impatient liberalism rationalized racial domination more openly than the old, gradual approach.

The slow transformation of Cape liberalism and the steady rise of racism and jingoism bore some relation to ideological developments in Britain, too. There was a sense in Britain that the country was becoming weaker relative to France and Germany. British conservatives began to advocate economic nationalism, which involved the weakening of free-trade policies and the building of closer economic and political ties to the

[1] Davenport, "The Cape Liberal Tradition to 1910."

colonies. Many colonial settlers advocated economic nationalism, too, as they elaborated new identities for themselves. The identities of white settlers have been explored extensively in histories of Australia, Canada, and New Zealand, where impulses toward self-government have never completely extinguished feelings of loyalty toward Britain, the monarchy, and British political culture more generally. Yet historians of South Africa have not yet fully explored the ways in which British settlers articulated loyalty to Britain. Ideas about loyalty to Britain have not been explored much in histories of Africans, Afrikaners, and Indians, either. In a recent preliminary study, Andrew Thompson points out that members of all these groups professed loyalty at different times, for different reasons. Some felt personal loyalty to the monarchy, while others expressed loyalty to real and imagined kinsmen in Britain. For some, particularly Africans and Indians, close ties to Britain helped guarantee their freedoms against impositions by settlers.[2]

It was in the interest of the British government to protect subject populations against settlers, as protections were thought to keep the peace – and keep down expenses. From 1868 to 1874, the liberal government of William Ewart Gladstone cut back on some of Britain's overseas responsibilities. The parliaments of New Zealand and the Cape Colony obtained "responsible" government and the Canadian colonies were confederated. Britain did gain several territories in Africa, Asia, and the Pacific, but the new colonies were acquired somewhat reluctantly. Under the "reluctant imperialist" prime minister, Gladstone, the British government did, indeed, hope that the Cape Colony's move toward responsible government would save Britain some administrative and military costs. Yet many Britons and colonists believed that settler self-government conflicted with humanitarian policymaking.

The regulation of guns might be seen as humanitarian so long as the regulations did not discriminate on the basis of race. Yet the sort of regulations that imperial policymakers began to discuss in 1873 were discriminatory and were therefore opposed, initially, by liberal humanitarians. In order to achieve more comprehensive controls on guns, leading officials were preparing to modify two important liberal tenets: free trade and racial equality before the law. As the terms of citizenship and subjection were redefined, policymakers had to make decisions about access to guns. Would all citizens and subjects have equal access? Or, would certain citizens and subjects be allowed access, while others had their

---

[2] Thompson, "Languages of Loyalism."

access restricted? Policymakers in Great Britain and South Africa debated the creation of a new state with new terms of citizenship at the same time as they debated whether or not all should have the right to buy, sell, and use guns.

The debate was exacerbated by the arrival, in the 1860s and 1870s, of breechloaders, which were much more effective than the old muskets and which caused greater concerns about risk. And finally, the opening of the Diamond Fields near Kimberley stimulated the gun trade, as African migrant workers earned cash to buy guns. The new industry, the new rifles, and the new citizenship were all taken up or rejected by different people at different times. Were there technological limits to political rights, or political limits to technological rights? Ideas about economy, technology, and state stimulated each other in such a way that it is best to describe them in terms of interdependence or coproduction.

Imperial Perspectives on Disarmament

The debate about the intercolonial regulation of guns opened in London, in September of 1873 – just as trouble was brewing on the Hlubi location – when Gladstone's secretary of state for the colonies, Lord Kimberley, exchanged memoranda with Earl Granville, the foreign secretary, about whether or not Britain should negotiate with France and Portugal to restrict the gun trade in West Africa. The object of such an agreement was to "mitigate" the "destructive wars which desolate the interior of Africa." This conceptualization linked the gun trade to warfare. The end of such wars would lead to greater prosperity and higher colonial revenues. These, in turn, would pay for any expenses associated with enforcement. The new regulations would not cost anything, an important point for the liberal Treasury. Even so, the colonial governments would still find it "necessary to import arms for the use of tribes under [their] protection or control." In other words, select "tribes" would be useful enough and easy enough to control that they could, in fact, possess firearms. This position indicated a tendency toward utilitarian arguments when it came to firearms. And thinking pragmatically, enforcement would also be difficult: some parts of the West African coast were more tightly controlled than other parts. These problems were thorny enough that the Colonial Office undertook to consult with the colonial governors of West Africa.[3]

---

[3] PRO CO 879/5 Conf. Pr. (Africa) No. 2 in No. 3, CO to FO, September 27, 1873; Conf. Pr. (Africa) No. 37, FO to CO October 6, 1873, No. 3.

The responses of the two different governors merit close scrutiny. One was Sir Garnet Wolseley, the greatest military hero of the mid-Victorian period. Having just won the Ashanti War, he was now "Major-General and Administrator" of the Gold Coast – he would hold the same position in Natal in 1875 and again in 1879. The other governor, Sir George Strahan, was the administrator of Lagos. He was to be the interim governor of the Cape Colony from September 1880 to January 1881, a short period that nonetheless encompassed much of the Sotho Gun War. Strahan's and Wolseley's comments in 1873 are interesting partly because of their later involvement in South Africa and partly because of the way in which their differing positions anticipated their involvement in South African debates about gun control.

Strahan raised one of the classic objections to colonial gun control: it was bound to be "ineffectual as regards the end in view." It would be difficult for Europeans to clamp down on the gun trade along the entire West African coastline. Furthermore, prohibitions on the gun trade would tend to affect friendly Africans living within or near the colony. The strict regulation of the gun trade would have the undesirable side effect of making it easier for unregulated enemies to attack, especially enemies who lived outside the colonial boundaries. Strahan noted that "such a prohibition would be looked upon by the Egbas and Jebus as an act of hostility on the part of this Government." Attacks on the colony, and the anger of resident Africans, were likely to disrupt all trade.[4]

Strahan was wary of disrupting trade, claiming that he wanted to help resident Africans protect themselves. Wolseley took the opposite position. In his opinion, the gun trade exacerbated conflicts, including wars that were conducted in order to kidnap slaves:

But what is it that furnishes alike to the internal and to the maritime Slave Trade the material on which it feeds? The answer is well known to you. It is the incessant warfare carried on throughout Africa by means of the weapons of war which are imported from Europe and from America.[5]

His appeal to antislavery was a clever ploy. While Strahan hoped that resident Africans would defend themselves, Wolseley enrolled antislavery, one of Britain's prime humanitarian causes, on the side of disarmament.

[4] PRO CO 879/5 Conf. Pr. (Africa) No. 37, No. 8, Strahan to Berkeley, December 10, 1873.
[5] PRO CO 879/5 Conf. Pr. (Africa) No. 37, No. 5, Wolseley to Kimberley, November 15, 1873.

He made this plea for regulation in spite of the long association between antislavery and free trade, that is, free trade in all things except for people. Wolseley was not concerned with the Colonial Office's suggestion that it might still be necessary to import arms to sell to resident Africans. He favored restricting access of all Africans to firearms: "The question is too large, too, important, for such considerations to be taken into account." In stopping the West African gun trade, he believed "that a step will have been taken which will hereafter be reckoned one of the most important in the progress of mankind and in the advance of civilization."[6]

Wolseley was attempting to overcome the Colonial Office's concerns about gun trade restrictions by linking controls to lofty causes, such as civilization and antislavery. In doing so, he hoped to shift colonial policy away from a laissez-faire approach. The Colonial Office's concerns about protecting resident Africans did not persuade him. Soon, a new Conservative government in London would pay closer attention to Wolseley's arguments.

From 1874 to 1880, the Conservative government of Benjamin Disraeli supported imperial expansion more openly than the previous Liberal administration of Gladstone. While Gladstone had been reluctant to expand the empire, Disraeli won the election of 1874 by campaigning on a platform that was openly imperialist. His arguments were appealing for a number of reasons. The Indian rebellion of 1857 and the Jamaican rebellion of 1865 resulted in the British public taking a harsher view of "other" races. Racism was on the rise, along with militarism and nationalism, while media and education, the two principal means of disseminating such ideas, were becoming more widespread. The historian Saul Dubow has noted that during the 1870s, *The Cape Monthly Magazine* – the leading periodical for educated, English-speaking South Africans – became increasingly racist toward Africans. Even Boers became the subject of racial stereotyping, although in their case English-speaking authors presented contrary opinions.[7]

At the same time as racial views were becoming prevalent, many Britons developed a heightened sense of risk. In South Africa, colonists worried about "the native question." In Britain, many people sensed that their country's naval and industrial dominance was slipping. The best way to defend against further slippage was to expand and consolidate

---

[6] PRO CO 879/5 Conf. Pr. (Africa) No. 37, No. 5, Wolseley to Kimberley, November 15, 1873.

[7] Dubow, *Commonwealth of Knowledge*, 111–15.

the empire.[8] Disraeli appointed an ardent imperialist, Lord Carnarvon, as secretary of state for the colonies. During Carnarvon's tenure, which lasted from 1874 to 1880, he supported the confederation of all the South African colonies and republics. One reason for doing so was to create a "uniform native policy" modeled on the Boer republics, where Africans faced more extensive legal disabilities than they did in any British colony. In the Transvaal and the Orange Free State, Africans could be compelled to work and they were not allowed to possess guns.[9] As we have seen, the Boer republics took a flexible, pragmatic approach to the enforcement of these laws. They armed their African allies when necessary and allowed Boer landowners to arm African servants. Such instances of pragmatism were never mentioned by British settlers and politicians who sought stricter gun laws at the Cape. Ignorance of republican realities did not interest ideologues at the Cape, many of whom found the idea of strict labor laws and gun control to be congenial. Likewise, confederationists in Britain and the Cape ignored the lack of republican enthusiasm for a union dominated by Britain.

Humanitarians on the Defensive

Each colony and republic had different gun-control laws, which did, in fact, present regulatory problems. In the Langalibalele affair, which began at around the time of Strahan's debate with Wolseley, the government of Natal protested the apparently lax regulations in Griqualand West. The gun trade at the diamond mines became related to conflict in the Orange Free State. Free State burghers were dismayed to see African laborers leaving their farms to work at the mines. Police officers and armed parties of burghers patrolled the road that connected Kimberley to the north, harassing workers. There were even cases reported of burghers kidnapping workers and confiscating their hard-earned guns.[10] The *Cape Argus* reported that in the Free State, it was rumored that two thousand guns had been taken from returning mine laborers.[11]

One such incident in November of 1872 raised larger questions about the relations between the Free State and the Cape. A "large" party of

[8] Cope, *Ploughshare of War*, 85–8. MacKenzie, "Empire and Metropolitan Cultures," in *Oxford History of the British Empire* 3:270–93.
[9] Cope, *Ploughshare of War*, 83.
[10] Cope, *Ploughshare of War*, 90.
[11] *Cape Argus*, February 22, 1873, p. 4.

armed Sotho men affiliated with the chief Jonathan Molapo left Kimberley bound for Basutoland. When they crossed into the Orange Free State, they were surrounded and threatened by a party of twenty-five burghers led by a police inspector. The Sotho migrants took cover and began to shoot. The Free Staters shot back, killing one Sotho man. The standoff continued into the night, when the Sotho snuck away.

The new lieutenant governor of Griqualand West, Sir Richard Southey, reported the incident to his superior, the Cape governor, Sir Henry Barkly. In the letter to Barkly, Southey noted that at heart, the conflict had been caused by a misunderstanding of intercolonial regulations. Officials in Griqualand West had granted the Sotho miners permits to carry their guns home to Basutoland, but the Sotho men did not realize that they needed an additional permit from the Orange Free State to transit the republic's territory. Southey instructed his magistrates to inform future migrant laborers that they needed to abide by republican rules, too. Southey made an additional, prescient observation: "I daresay there is no sufficient check upon the [arms] trade at the [Diamond] Fields, & the whole question will require careful investigation."[12]

Southey could not communicate directly with the government of the Orange Free State because it did not officially recognize the existence of the British colony of Griqualand West. The Free State did recognize the role of the Cape governor as high commissioner for southern Africa, which led Gov. Barkly to follow up on Southey's report by protesting the conduct of the Free State burghers. Barkly made the point that technically the burghers had been within the boundaries of Griqualand West. The Free State's government did not recognize the existence of Griqualand West, claiming it for themselves. A colonial boundary issue became linked to the regulation of firearms.[13] African men responded by traversing the area in even larger armed parties. The Free State burghers continued to harass them. A *Cape Argus* article of July 14, 1874, described the process: "It has been established on conclusive proof that a system of fraud has been for some time practiced upon the Basutos in several ways. In some instances their guns have been taken away from them by some field cornet or other dignitary and returned on payment of a heavy fine. A victim of

---

[12] CTAR, GLW 110, Semiofficial Letters, Southey to Barkly, January 18, 1873, pp. 29–33.

[13] *Cape Argus*, February 1, 1873, pp. 2–3; February 4, 1873, pp. 2–3; March 8, 1873, p. 2. The issue of arms along the boundary between the Orange Free State and Griqualand West was taken up again by the two governments in 1875. See *Cape Argus*, February 15, 1875, p. 3.

this robbery proceeds on his journey secretly rejoicing that he has secured his precious gun when lo! At the next village or field cornet's farm, he is again arrested and this time despoiled of his gun and the balance of what savings he may have on his person. And if happily he escapes further punishment, he goes into his country empty-handed and with the old hatred of the Free State still more embittered."[14]

Claims to regulate guns originated in specific circumstances, such as the Free State border incident, as well as in imperial ideological shifts. Participants in debates about South African guns, who were able to articulate local problems with broader imperial concerns, made a rhetorical move that aided the creation of a new regime of gun control as well as a new regime for South Africa. Powerful figures in London, such as Wolseley and Carnarvon, recognized that settler concerns about ordering transactions in guns, land, and labor had to be overcome in order for the colonies to "develop," a term first applied to colonies by Conservatives of this era. Speaking before the House of Lords in July of 1875, Carnarvon claimed that the reform of Natal was "essential to the prosperity of the colony in its development." Without reform and development, "you would end by having a black colony, which means decay of its resources, the absence of prosperity, and general falling away of its means of subsistence." Reform required a more orderly approach to ruling Africans:

There has not in my opinion been that control over Native affairs which is required by the public interest. The result is that there has been a stagnation, so to speak, of many of the industrial interests of the Colony. There has been – as I think Sir Garnet Wolseley pointed out to the Legislature – that want of internal security which leads in the long run, to a want also of external confidence – which hinders emigration and which prevents the real development of the Colony.[15]

The broader orderliness of the colonies was bound up with the proper regulation of guns. The initial correspondence about the gun trade focused on making colonial and republican regulations uniform. As early as April 24, 1873, correspondence from Natal persuaded Gov. Barkly of the Cape Colony to mention, in his opening speech to the Cape parliament, the need for "serious attention" to be paid to the intercolonial regulation of guns.[16] Others attempted to pull Barkly in the opposite direction. Richard

---

[14] *Cape Argus*, July 14, 1874, p. 3.
[15] As quoted by Cope, *Ploughshare of War*, 92. On the use of the term "development" in late nineteenth-century colonial policymaking, see Storey, "Plants, Power, and Development."
[16] *Cape Argus*, April 25, 1873, p. 3.

Southey, the lieutenant governor of Griqualand West, wrote to Barkly in November 1873 to report a meeting that he had with two Natalians who led the "Diggers' Committee." The two worried about the sale of arms, because guns were implicated in Langalibalele's rebellion. The concerned miners urged Southey to prohibit the sale of arms to Africans, which he refused to do. Southey reported to Barkly: "That for the present, I was not disposed to legislate at all, unless there was an urgent necessity for it; and that if I did legislate, I could not do so for only one class of the community." Southey stuck to older liberal racial principles and to free-trade principles, too. He added, "Of course a Proclamation might be issued prohibiting the sale to any one, except upon a special Certificate signed by some particular individual, & that individual might refuse to grant a certificate to natives; but, it would be unfair to the dealers who have got stocks of guns here." It was not the case that Southey supported an unregulated gun trade: in the same letter he bemoaned the coastal arms trade, in which ships from Port Elizabeth delivered guns at Delagoa Bay to be transshipped to Zululand.[17]

Southey hoped Barkly would recognize that the arms question involved much larger questions about citizenship. He wrote that one of the delegates from the "diggers" "is an admirer of the Natal policy of making distinctions between 'Black & White,' & of depriving the former of privileges enjoyed by the latter. He still more admires the policy of the Free State & S. A. Republic, which regards natives more like the lower animals than human beings." Southey was quick to point out the hypocrisy of such diggers, who had, after all, used guns to lure Africans to the mines. Even so, the most important point that Southey hoped to get across to Barkly was that racially based citizenship was wrong. He was a firm believer in the liberal policies of the Cape, which encouraged Africans to assimilate to European civilization and capitalism.

I fancy I have told you before, that I am no admirer of Natal native policy, and have long expected resistance to the exceptional laws under which the natives are governed. I consider that there are two ways in which it is safe to deal with the native population. One, that which the Cape Colony has adopted, of having one law for all: black & white, & endeavouring, by the aid of suitable agents, to keep them straight, & ease them in the scale of civilization; and, above all, of encouraging individual acquisition of property, that cannot be driven into the bush, & undermining the power for mischief of the Chiefs.

[17] CTAR, GLW 112, Semi-Official Letters, Southey to Barkly, November 15, 1873, pp. 42–4, 47.

The other, that adopted by the Republics, of gradually annihilating & exter-
minating the coloured races.

This latter policy could not be permitted in a British Colony, & Natal has
endeavoured to steer a middle course, which may hold together while Shepstone
lives, but will surely fail after his death.[18]

Given Southey's liberal position on guns and trade, it is interesting
to note that one of the best-known historical studies of settlers on the
Eastern Cape, *White Supremacy and Black Resistance in South Africa* by
Clifton Crais, lists Richard Southey as a "leading conservative." Southey
did, indeed, resemble many other settlers of the Eastern Cape, in that he
owned large sheep farms. Like other settlers, he had fought in the wars
between the Cape Colony and the Xhosa. In the 1835 war, he commanded
a unit of guides, including his brother, George, who famously killed the
Xhosa paramount chief, Hintsa, when he attempted to escape captivity.
Richard Southey served as Gov. Sir Harry Smith's private secretary from
1847 to 1849, during which time he led negotiations with the Boers and
the Sotho about the fate of the territories across the Orange River. As
a member of the partially responsible legislature, Southey held a succession of posts, culminating in his service as colonial secretary, or prime
minister, from 1864 to 1872. During that time, he played a key role in
promoting the annexation of territory on the eastern frontier. And yet,
despite Southey's long association with colonial expansion, he did believe
that the best way to ensure good government for settlers and Africans was
to preserve strong ties with Britain. As colonial secretary, he worked to
extend imperial control over Basutoland and Griqualand West. He also
opposed fully responsible self-government for the Cape, believing that a
settler government would not act for the greater public good. He did not
get along with Gov. Barkly, who was appointed in 1872 with instructions
from London to make responsible government work.[19]

Southey was a settler who served the government in various positions
and who had good and bad relations with several governors. It is difficult
to fit him – and many other settlers who served as colonial officials –
into easy political categories. At Kimberley, Southey governed according to some select conservative principles. For example, he created and
enforced laws that restricted the number of claims a company could purchase. This protected small diggers and discouraged big businesses from
buying up small claims and amalgamating them. Southey resisted the lib-
eralization of claim purchasing and was ultimately overruled by Cape

[18] CTAR, GLW 112, Semi-Official Letters, Southey to Barkly, November 15, 1873, p. 46.
[19] *Dictionary of South African Biography*, 695–8.

Town and London. The liberal lifting of restrictions on claim purchasing made possible the rise of consolidators like Cecil Rhodes.

In the case of the mines Southey resisted liberalism, but in other cases he defended it. He was particularly keen to defend the legal equality of all races, particularly the right of all races to purchase firearms and obtain licenses. Southey's position on guns highlights the ideological complexity of settlers, who have been stereotyped in some of the scholarly literature as uniformly opposed to rights for Africans. Crais, for example, places Southey together with Robert Godlonton, the publisher of the *Graham's Town Journal*, who was the mouthpiece of a "conservative cause" vehemently opposed to African rights. Crais writes that "the elite" of the Eastern Cape who dehumanized Africans through a racist "discourse of the Other were also at the head of agrarian capitalist development in the Eastern Cape."[20] While there is much to be said for the analysis of racist discourses that enabled capitalist development, in the case of Southey this interpretation flattens out a story that contains ideological variety. Shades of British conservatism could be found in South Africa's settler communities, but mainly settlers embraced types of liberalism that were thought to bring economic and social progress. Liberals identified themselves with a range of economic and social approaches that ranged from egalitarian humanitarianism to racist utilitarianism.

Like Southey, Barkly walked a fine line between defending liberal principles and appeasing worried colonists. In January 1874, Barkly sent a memorandum to the Cape premier John C. Molteno, indicating that he was taking complaints by Natalians, as well as by miners at Kimberley, quite seriously. He hoped to stop "the trade in diamonds from becoming a trade in blood." Barkly had heard claims alleging that the enforcement of gun regulations was lax in all colonies and republics. Even in the republics, where Africans were prohibited from owning guns, there were allegations that government officials themselves were involved in the gun trade. He pledged to investigate both intra- and intercolonial regulation while expressing the concern that real enforcement of the gun laws would require the colonies and republics to pay for more police, at a cost that might be greater than the cost of a war.[21]

Barkly believed that the total regulation of the trade was impossible. He also believed that the Natal government overestimated the extent of

---

[20] Crais, *White Supremacy and Black Resistance*, 134.
[21] RHL, Papers of J. C. Molteno, Mss. Afr. S23/2, Barkly's "Memorandum on the Correspondence with the Government of Natal as to the Acquisition of Fire-Arms by the Natives," ff.326–55.

the gun trade, which may have led to proposals for impractical measures, such as marking or registering all guns, new and old. Even so, Barkly did believe that Cape regulations could be made more uniform. He proposed to allow only resident magistrates to license weapons to publish the amount of weapons and ammunition that was bought and to tighten restrictions at the border.[22] Molteno and his attorney-general, Simeon Jacobs, disagreed. They preferred to keep Cape laws in effect, only to enforce them more strictly. They accepted only one of Barkly's recommendations: that border controls be tightened by specifying the destination of the arms as part of the terms of the merchants' bond.[23]

Molteno and his ministry did not share Barkly's or Pine's concerns about the gun trade. They did see a possible link between gun control and confederation. In Molteno's opinion, "The fact is that the trade in firearms is not to be controlled, but the danger, whatever that may be, must be met on the part of different states of S. Africa by a well-organized force with arms and accoutrements so far superior to any that natives can obtain as to make them feel that any attempt on their part to override the white population would be useless.... This question of defence is one of those which would form a strong argument and basis for the so much talked of defence."[24] Controlling the gun trade was hopeless. The "danger" could be met, not by regulation, but by a confederated armed force. The answer to proliferation was not disarmament, nor was it regulation: it was escalation, coordination, and efficiency. Once again, discourse about guns became discourse about broader state policies.

The Colonial Office in London was already advancing the idea of confederation, but was more receptive to Barkly's approach, which involved states that did a better job of regulation. In June of 1874, Carnarvon instructed Barkly not to take any action on the Sotho border incident, but instead requested that the lieutenant governor of Griqualand West, Richard Southey, report on "the whole subject of the sale of firearms" in the colony.

Southey articulated a liberal response to gun control that was rather different from the ones advanced by his fellow liberals, Molteno and

---

[22] RHL, Papers of J. C. Molteno, Mss. Afr. S23/2, Barkly's "Memorandum on the Correspondence with the Government of Natal as to the Acquisition of Fire-Arms by the Natives," ff.326–55.

[23] RHL, Papers of J. C. Molteno, Mss. Afr. S23/2, Minutes by Jacobs on Barkly's "Memorandum on the Correspondence with the Government of Natal as to the Acquisition of Fire-Arms by the Natives," ff.371–2.

[24] RHL, Papers of J. C. Molteno, Mss. Afr. S23/2, Molteno, "Trade in Firearms, etc., with Natives," f.373.

Barkly. Southey's response was also rather different from that of Carnarvon: Southey sensed danger in gun control. He had already written a long letter to Barkly in April 1874, responding to criticism from Natal that it was too easy for Natal's Africans to purchase guns at the diamond mines. He used this letter to outline his concerns. He reminded Barkly that Griqualand West's gun-control laws were actually stricter than the laws of the Cape Colony, contrary to any reports about lax regulations. In the Cape, any justice of the peace could issue a permit to someone to "deliver" arms and ammunition, whereas in Griqualand West only a resident magistrate or an assistant resident magistrate could do so. In Griqualand West, there was an additional tax of 2s. 6d. on each gun imported. Then, there was a further duty of 10s. placed on each gun sold. The colony even enforced the duties with a detachment of mounted border police.[25]

Southey's letter went well beyond defending his colony's regulations, which had been criticized by the government of Natal during the Langalibalele affair. Southey discussed the relationship between gun control and "native policy," especially as it pertained to "civilization" and citizenship. He wrote scathingly about Shepstone's "native policy" in Natal, where the colony's Africans lived under the customary authority of chiefs, who were, in turn, supervised by the lieutenant governor acting as "supreme chief." According to Southey, this was a policy that might "retard the advancement of the native people towards civilization," which, in turn, endangered the "white population of the country" and the "peace of South Africa generally." The Langalibalele affair highlighted the flaws in the Shepstone system:

A policy under which people who desire to leave the country with their wives and children and stock, because they regard the exceptional laws to which they are made subject, as oppressive and intolerable, and who, whilst endeavouring to carry their desire into effect peaceably, may be pursued by armed forces, may have all their property seized and confiscated, their women and children captured and placed in forced servitude with their white fellow subjects, and be themselves

---

[25] PRO CO 879/6 Conf. Pr. (Africa) No. 59, Southey to Barkly, April 11, 1874, Enclosure No. 5 in Barkly to Carnarvon, August 24, 1874, paras. 3–6; also printed in CPP 1881 – A.68. Barkly was well aware of the difference between the gun laws of the Cape, Natal, and Griqualand West, as we can see from RHL Papers of J. C. Molteno, Mss. Afr. S23/2, Barkly's "Memorandum on the Correspondence with the Government of Natal as to the Acquisition of Fire-Arms by the Natives," ff.326–55. The governor got only one thing wrong, according to Molteno: Barkly incorrectly believed that farmers would be fined heavily for giving weapons to farmworkers, but that was true only when the gun went unlicensed. It is not known whether or not Southey realized that the governor had a good knowledge of colonial gun control.

thereafter tried for rebellion, under savage instead of civilized laws is, to my mind, a most objectionable policy and one which should be superseded as quickly as possible.[26]

Natal's "native policy" troubled Southey. He also believed the Natalians were spreading false information about the gun trade at the diamond fields. He pointed out that African laborers were not paid in guns, but in cash, about ten shillings per week. If Africans wanted to purchase a gun at the end of their stay in Kimberley, they had to apply for a permit. In any case, Southey claimed that most workers did not come from Basutoland or Zululand, so Natalians could not blame their own gun problems on Griqualand West. Most of Kimberley's workers came from the north and they had good reasons for acquiring guns.

The main object of the natives of the interior have in acquiring guns is one of legitimate trade; the guns are used, not as Sir B. Pine supposes, merely for the shedding of human blood, but in shooting elephants, ostriches, and other large animals whose teeth, skins, and feathers are sold or bartered to European traders, at present almost exclusively British subjects, who in return supply the natives with British manufactured goods. This trade is both lucrative and important, not only to the individuals directly engaged in it, but to the British Empire.[27]

Southey believed it would be foolish to meddle with the interior trade, which he valued at one million pounds per year. The trade benefited Africans and Britons alike. It also helped advance "civilization," a long-standing objective of humanitarian imperialists. By contrast, it seemed that the Orange Free State and the South African Republic were working toward the opposite goal. Southey feared that any association with the Boer republics would lead to injustice. In fact, he believed that the "native policies" of the republics were "so tyrannical and unjust" that they were in violation of the conventions with Britain that established the republics on the condition that they prohibited slavery. Judging by the Boer practice of keeping "apprentices" and "black shots" in the Transvaal, he was correct. Southey could see no reason in signing agreements on gun control or native policy with states that did not work for the advancement of "civilization."[28]

---

[26] PRO CO 879/6 Conf. Pr. (Africa) No. 59, Southey to Barkly, April 11, 1874, Enclosure No. 5 in Barkly to Carnarvon, August 24, 1874, paras. 9–11.
[27] PRO CO 879/6 Conf. Pr. (Africa) No. 59, Southey to Barkly, April 11, 1874, Enclosure No. 5 in Barkly to Carnarvon, August 24, 1874, paras. 16, 17, 21.
[28] PRO CO 879/6 Conf. Pr. (Africa) No. 59, Southey to Barkly, April 11, 1874, Enclosure No. 5 in Barkly to Carnarvon, August 24, 1874, paras. 12–14, 21.

Southey used this letter about the gun trade to reaffirm liberal human-itarian objectives in South Africa. In his opinion, Africans should be civi-lized and then treated as fellow British subjects. He wrote that "I have no sympathy with those persons who regard the dark races of this continent as the natural enemy of the white man. I believe that they are capable of being made true friends and loyal fellow subjects." As evidence, he pointed to the experience of the increasingly assimilated Mfengu, who were becoming the most successful farmers in the Eastern Cape. In his opinion, it would be folly to restrict the trade in arms to a loyal group of Africans who were now stakeholders in the colony.

The question naturally arises, should we be justified in adopting measures cal-culated to create distrust and dissatisfaction in the minds of our native fellow-subjects and friends, in order to cultivate more friendly relations with the neigh-bouring Republics, whose native policy is a barbarous policy, which does not encourage, and, indeed, scarcely admits of the education of the native races or the spread of Christianity among them.[29]

Southey was concerned about the problem of restricting arms from "loyal natives," in the same way that Strahan had opposed restrictions on resident Africans in Lagos. There was a clear connection, in the minds of liberals like Strahan and Southey, between gun ownership, "civiliza-tion," and citizenship. Yet the liberal notion that there should be linkage between gun ownership, civilization, and citizenship in "native policy" was one that met with increasing resistance in official circles. Barkly sent Southey's letter to Sir Benjamin Pine, still the lieutenant governor of Natal, for his comments. Pine responded scathingly: "I can find nothing in Mr. Southey's despatch to shake the assertion made by the Natal Gov-ernment that at the Diamond Fields Kafirs can purchase fire-arms on the certificate of their master or employer, which is no check whatever on their acquiring such weapons." The gun trade at the Diamond Fields was not regulated well enough, which posed a problem for Pine. He believed that Natal's Africans had only one purpose of buying guns: they "rarely shoot game, indeed, there is little now to shoot. They acquire arms solely for purposes of defence or aggression." He ignored Southey's claim that most diamond mineworkers came from the far interior.[30]

---

[29] PRO CO 879/6 Conf. Pr. (Africa) No. 59, Southey to Barkly, April 11, 1874, Enclosure No. 5 in Barkly to Carnarvon, August 24, 1874, paras. 24–6.

[30] PRO CO 879/6 Conf. Pr. (Africa) No. 59, Pine, "Memorandum on Lieutenant-Governor Southey's Despatch of April 11, 1874," Enclosure No. 8 in Barkly to Carnarvon, August 24, 1874.

Barkly forwarded this entire correspondence to Lord Carnarvon, who had written in June 1874 asking for information about the gun trade in Griqualand West. Southey also wrote an official response to Carnarvon's request, in which the frontiersman reiterated his earlier opposition to tightening controls on the gun trade. The second letter, written in August 1874, provided more details and made further arguments against restrictions. Southey viewed strict controls on the gun trade as impracticable. He cited the example of the Cape Colony, which had previously attempted to prevent merchants from selling guns to Africans: "This restriction could not be enforced, and it was after a time abandoned." He also claimed that the Boer republics never complained about the open arms trade until Britain claimed the diamond fields, implying that the republics were using the gun trade as an excuse to advocate the repossession of previously undervalued territory.[31]

Barkly forwarded copies of Southey's letters to Carnarvon, along with Pine's letter and a letter from J. C. Molteno, the prime minister of the Cape Colony.[32] Molteno argued against restrictions because he thought they were impracticable, expensive, and annoying.[33] Barkly tended to agree with Molteno and Southey. In his own letter to Carnarvon, he recognized that gun control was an important problem. He mentioned the Langalibalele affair, "the immediate cause of which was the attempt of [Natal] to enforce the registration of the guns with which Langalibalele was, without its permission, arming his followers."[34]

Carnarvon and the officials at the Colonial Office tended to agree with Southey's liberal approach, too, although some remained skeptical. Barkly's letter of August 24, 1874, inspired one official to minute that Southey's dispatch showed "a mixture of good sense & bad temper." Even so, he wrote that "it is of the highest importance in the case of a trade like that of firearms in Griqua Land to keep it in the hands of respectable dealers & not frighten it into the hands of smugglers." Another wrote that "the gun license has probably a useful effect upon the natives, in

---

[31] PRO CO 879/6 Conf. Pr. (Africa) No. 59, Southey to Barkly, August 13, 1874, Enclosure No. 9 in Barkly to Carnarvon, August 24, 1874.

[32] The prime minister of the Cape Colony was officially known as the colonial secretary. I have chosen to avoid this title and to use "prime minister" instead in order to avoid confusion between this office and that of the secretary of state for the colonies, the British cabinet member who was in charge of Britain's colonies, except for India.

[33] PRO CO 879/6 Conf. Pr. (Africa) No. 59, Molteno to Erskine (Col. Secy., Natal), March 5, 1874, Enclosure No. 1 in Barkly to Carnarvon, August 24, 1874.

[34] PRO CO 879/6 Conf. Pr. (Africa) No. 59, Barkly to Carnarvon, August 24, 1874.

keeping them reminded that the Government knows about their armed strength." Carnarvon agreed, "Mr. Southey's criticism of Natal policy & his vindication of the freedom of trade is the ablest paper that I have yet seen of him & seems to me far less open to objection than the personal and irritable reply of Sir B. Pine." Even so, on the subject of gun traders entering into a bond to transport but not to sell guns beyond the Cape Colony's boundaries, Carnarvon minuted that "I cannot be party to such a measure." Better regulation of the intercolonial gun trade was needed.[35]

Preliminary Efforts to Regulate Guns

The Langalibalele affair focused settler concerns about the gun trade and African migrant workers. A heightened sense of risk caused the upper house of the Cape parliament to take up the intercolonial regulation of guns. In the Legislative Council meeting of July 27, 1874, two members from the Eastern Cape, George Wood and Robert Godlonton, initiated a discussion about preventing "the continuation of selling firearms to the natives." They expressed concern about the numbers of guns imported, which they estimated to be eighty-four thousand. Several colleagues on the council objected, noting that the magistrates already had powers to be selective in awarding gun permits. Others pointed out that restrictions on all "natives" amounted to "class" legislation – in other words, legislation targeting one group exclusively – which was forbidden by Ordinance 50 of 1828 and, technically speaking, by the Masters and Servants Ordinance of 1841. The member, George Wood, used the issue of the gun trade to argue in favor of class legislation, saying that "they should adapt their laws to the people."[36] Thus began an effort on the part of some settlers to use the issue of the gun trade to break down equality before the law, the cornerstone of the older humanitarian strain of Cape liberalism.

Some liberals responded by pressing for added restrictions that would affect all gun buyers. The lieutenant governor of Griqualand West, Richard Southey, presented his Legislative Council with a proposal to raise duties on imported firearms and ammunition.[37] Other liberals pressed for fewer restrictions, not more, suggestions that ran counter

---

[35] PRO CO 48/470, Barkly to Carnarvon, confidential, August 24, 1874, plus enclosures and minutes.

[36] *Cape Argus*, July 30, 1874, p. 3.

[37] *Cape Argus*, August 27, 1874, pp. 2–3.

to the 1870s trend. In January of 1874, members of the Chamber of Commerce discussed the benefits of fewer, not more, restrictions on the gun trade, citing the impracticality and inconvenience of many regulations.[38]

A wide gulf emerged between politicians from the east and west. Settlers in the Eastern Cape began to protest the extent of the gun trade. One settler wrote in a letter to an Eastern Cape newspaper, the *Kaffrarian Watchman*, that "I see, sometimes, remarks about the gun trade in the colonial papers and smile in my sleep when I think about how little is really known about the extent. Many Europeans have become gunsmen and many are also dealers in guns. Talk about guns, there is no scarcity in Kaffirland."[39] Others complained in the newspapers about the problems of enforcing restrictions on the gun trade. In a story about a group of Boer and African smugglers caught crossing the Kei with seventy-one weapons, the *Cape Argus* noted that "if guns are stopped at the Kei, it is pretty certain that they will be gotten into Kaffraria through St. John's River and other channels."[40] Customs controls would improve the enforcement of the gun laws. So would higher duties and fees, according to some. In August 1874, the Legislative Council of Griqualand West considered raising licensing fees on guns, only to be persuaded by merchants that such an approach would be ruinous.[41]

The remedy was thought to be new and improved regulations. In the Cape Colony, permits to purchase firearms could be issued by unsalaried justices of the peace as well as by salaried resident magistrates. The resident magistrates had further powers to regulate guns; they were the only officials who could issue permits to gun traders to cross the colonial boundary. These rules may not have been well understood by the Cape government itself, a situation that produced trouble on the eastern frontier, at precisely the time when gun control was most controversial. In 1874, the Cape government issued "Circular Number 4," which further instructed resident magistrates to issue gun permits only to Africans who were "fit" to possess guns, without defining how, exactly, to determine fitness. Justices of the peace received no such instructions.

The resident magistrate of Cradock, located in the interior on the Fish River, issued numerous permits to Sotho migrant workers whom

---

[38] *Cape Argus*, January 6, 1874, p. 3.
[39] Reprinted in the *Cape Argus*, September 29, 1874, p. 2.
[40] *Cape Argus*, October 6, 1874.
[41] *Diamond News and Griqualand Government Gazette*, August 15, 1874, p. 3.

he thought to be "loyal British subjects, who would not use the arms against Government." This troubled the Basutoland administration, which objected to the sales.[42] In Queenstown, located to the east of Cradock, across the Kei, settlers met to protest how a justice of the peace allowed a Tembu man to buy a gun and fifteen pounds of powder, when he intended to travel to Xhosa territory. His permit to travel was issued by W. B. Chalmers, resident magistrate of Cradock. Previously, in the 1860s, Chalmers had served to the north of Cradock in Hopetown, where he had overseen and even facilitated the cross-border gun trade. Now settlers accused Chalmers of helping to arm the Xhosa, who were thought to be preparing for war. Chalmers defended his actions by stating that if a justice of the peace thought an African was "fit" to possess a gun, then on what grounds could he restrict the gun-owners' movement? Furthermore, the government had not yet provided any guidelines for determining who, exactly, was "fit" to possess arms. It was a difficult question for a colony that needed to entice African migrant laborers to work on farms and public works.[43] In one case, in 1874, the Cape government had paid an agent to recruit a thousand Africans in the Transvaal, including payments for a hundred guns that were intended as presents for obliging chiefs. The railroads, in particular, needed to attract laborers, but gun purchases by workers in Port Elizabeth proved controversial, especially to the chief engineer, whose complaints resulted in the resident magistrate making a new requirement that migrant laborers obtain a certificate from their own district's officials, to certify that they were fit.[44]

While new regulations were contemplated, merchants asked the Cape and Natal governments to make regulations more uniform. In September 1874, the Cape governor, Sir Henry Barkly, exchanged letters with Thomas Burgers, the president of the Transvaal, on the subject of regulating the gun trade, particularly the trade from Delagoa Bay. In October 1874, Barkly visited Natal in his capacity as high commissioner for southern Africa. A deputation of merchants involved in the gun trade requested

---

[42] CPP [A.23] 1877, Brownlee to Chalmers, October 4, 1876, pp. 23–4. CTAR, NA 273/87 Griffith to Molteno, July 9, 1875; NA 273/90, Griffith to Molteno, July 14, 1875; NA 273/101, Griffith to Molteno, August 19, 1875; NA 273/10 April 18, 1876, Griffith to Brownlee; NA 273/16, Griffith to Brownlee, May 10, 1876.

[43] The letters pertaining to permits issued by Chalmers are contained in CPP [A.23] 1877, pp. 6–8, 24–33.

[44] CPP [A.56] 1880, "Correspondence between the Commissioner of Crown Lands and Public Works and the Chief Resident Engineer, Port Elizabeth, 1876, Relative to the Issue of Permits for the Purchase of Arms to Workmen on the Eastern Railways, &c.", pp. 1–7.

that he work on developing a "common policy" for the entire region. They highlighted the problems of developing a common policy when all local regulations could be bypassed by trading through Delagoa Bay in Portuguese Mozambique. There, the extent of the trade was not known officially, but newspaper reports indicated that both British and foreign merchants, many of them American, were actively involved. The quantity of weapons passing through Delagoa Bay into Zululand was estimated at ten thousand, while the quality of the weapons was supposed to be high.[45] In an 1873 letter to the Colonial Office, Barkly sketched the difficulties of regulating this trade by relating the story of one ship. One Union Company steamer, *American*, arrived in Port Elizabeth, where it loaded 346 packages of "warlike stores" on board the Union Company steamer, *Basuto*. A few days later, another Union Company steamer, *European*, then called at Port Elizabeth and transshipped 350 barrels of powder to the *Basuto*. The *Basuto* then proceeded to Delagoa Bay, where it delivered its cargo to a Portuguese trader "who may for ought I know be a reputable merchant, or a slave-trader designing to use it for the most nefarious purposes." Barkly suspected that these shipments were bound for Zululand but he did not have the authority to intervene. One frustrated Colonial Office official read Barkly's letter and minuted, "This shows that the British merchant will ship to any place where arms are to be bought, and it is a matter of indifference to him into whose hands these arms come." The secretary of state for the colonies, Lord Kimberley, reaffirmed liberal principles in his own minute: "I do not believe in the possibility of preventing the trade in arms to Africa. If you stop one channel of ingress, it will merely flow with unabated strength through another."[46]

The traders reported their frustration in dealing with Sir Benjamin Pine, Natal's lieutenant governor. Pine responded to the delegation by favoring restrictions on cheap firearms, which he considered dangerous to the users. He favored higher-quality imports, even if it meant relaxing restrictions on the trade to the Boer republics, who would consequently need better weapons too. Yet he also repeated his stock denunciation of the gun trade, calling it a "trade in blood." Describing this meeting, the *Cape Argus* pointed out that "as usual, Sir Benjamin Pine does not appear to have displayed much wisdom." By comparison, Sir Henry Barkly was

---

[45] *Goldfields Mercury and Lydenburg Advertiser*, May 24, 1877, p. 2. *Diamond News and Griqualand West Government Gazette*, August 15, 1874, p. 3.

[46] PRO CO 48/466 No. 114, Barkly to Kimberley, November 27, 1873.

more consistent. Faced with the challenges of intercolonial and international regulation, he began to sense that "it being impossible to keep guns out of the land, it was better that the trade should not be an illicit one." Doubt over regulation caused him either to throw up his hands or to fall back on the free-trading principles of classical liberalism.[47]

As a consequence of these controversies over laborers' guns in the Eastern Cape, the Cape Colony's secretary for native affairs Charles Brownlee was forced to clarify government policy. Brownlee had recently published an article in the colony's leading intellectual journal, *The Cape Monthly Magazine*, entitled "Present State and Future Prospects of the Kafirs," in which he sought to find middle ground between the humanitarian and settler views.[48] In his correspondence about gun control, he sympathized with the settlers, but came down on the side of African freedom to purchase arms. He believed this because any restrictions on African gun possession might call into question broader rights of British subjects in South Africa. Brownlee supported Chalmers and Southey because efforts to control African gun ownership would "do more harm than good." If the British were to call Africans fellow subjects, then they should treat them as such. Treating them as something less would "go a long way in weakening our strength, influence and rule in their estimation." Already, Africans wanted to know "why if they are really British subjects we should be so anxious that they should not possess guns." Gun control would make Africans wary of British rule, thereby conflicting with British objectives in South Africa. Brownlee noted that

it is not by preventing their having guns that we will succeed in making the natives who are under our rule peaceful and contented fellow-subjects. Our doing so will only have the contrary effect, and will only instil into their minds ideas which will result in plotting and planning schemes which they would otherwise not have dreamt of. It is only by ruling them fairly and justly and allowing them these privileges and advantages which they consider themselves as British subjects entitled to that we shall succeed in establishing peace and contentment amongst them.[49]

Gun Control, Citizenship, and the Confederation Debate

Carnarvon did not respond to Barkly for some time. He next mentioned gun control in the letter that he sent on May 1875 – a letter that touched

---

[47] *Cape Argus*, October 15, 1874, p. 2; November 12, 1874, p. 3.
[48] Dubow, *Commonwealth of Knowledge*, 111.
[49] CPP [A.23] 1877, Brownlee to Chalmers, November 8, 1876, pp. 27–8.

on the larger issue of confederation. Carnarvon proposed that a conference of delegates from all the colonies and republics of South Africa should meet to discuss "a more uniform course of action" in policymaking with regard to Africans. He cited the Langalibalele affair as an example of the problems of disunited policy. Disunity posed a threat to white settlement, because it encouraged aggression by Africans. He hoped that the delegates would discuss ways to make "native policy" more uniform, especially as it applied to gun control. He also sought uniform regulations for the extradition of criminals as well as further negotiations over the boundaries of Griqualand West. He added that he would welcome a discussion of "a possible union of South Africa." He even proposed a list of attendees: his friend, the famous imperialist historian J. A. Froude, would represent Britain; Barkly would chair the meeting; Shepstone would represent Natal; Southey would represent Griqualand West; Molteno would represent the Western Cape; John Paterson, a well-known Eastern Cape politician, would represent his home region; and the Boer republics would choose their own delegates.[50]

Carnarvon hoped to convene the conference as soon as possible. To this end he named Froude as his delegate and dispatched him to the Cape. When Froude arrived in Cape Town on June 19, he discovered that Carnarvon's proposal was meeting with strong opposition. The Cape Colony's prime minister, J. C. Molteno, would have nothing to do with it, nor would most of the other politicians from the Western Cape. Carnarvon's opponents at the Cape believed that any confederation would require the colony to shoulder the burden of additional administrative costs. They resented Carnarvon's interference in their affairs so soon after gaining responsible government in 1872. Molteno believed that any proposal such as confederation should have been initiated by the Cape parliament and the other colonial governments. And finally, the politicians of the Western Cape disliked how Carnarvon was dividing them from the easterners. For decades, the English-speaking easterners had expressed their resentment over the political influence of the more secure westerners. These differences had become less pronounced after the institution of responsible government in 1872. The new parliament was divided equally between easterners and westerners, and the prime minister himself, Molteno, embodied reconciliation. He was sixty-one years old in 1875, an immigrant from England who had made a fortune

---

[50] BPP [C.1399] 1876, No. 1, Carnarvon to Barkly, May 4, 1875, paras. 4–5, 8, 16. Also printed in CPP [A.20] 1875.

as a sheep farmer and wool trader in the Karoo. He represented Beaufort West, the Western Cape's easternmost district. Molteno had also served as a militia commander during the 1846 war against the Xhosa. In other words, Molteno was about as "eastern" as a westerner could get. Yet Carnarvon's proposal exacerbated the old differences between east and west. Molteno was to represent the west, while Paterson, a well-known proponent of separate government, was to represent the east.[51]

Carnarvon's proposal proved controversial. In June, the Cape Legislative Council – the upper house of the parliament – voted nine to seven against participation. Then, in September, Molteno and his ministers drafted a memorandum to Carnarvon that explained their opposition in detail. They did not want a uniform "native policy." The present system, even though it was irregular, still made it possible to be flexible in administering different kinds of African people. The ministry believed that the Cape's African subjects were content with the system. And no law could prevent Africans from acquiring guns. It was simply an impractical idea. Finally, the ministers objected to the continued presence of Froude in South Africa. He held no office, yet he was traveling throughout South Africa, giving speeches that were critical of liberalism and that tended to support the easterners and the republics over the westerners. Froude did stop short of offering a wholehearted endorsement of Carnarvon's plan for confederation.[52]

Froude believed that before confederation could take place, "the native question" needed to be answered. Froude offered a bleak vision for South African "natives" that was consistent with his general support for the views of Thomas Carlyle. Froude indicated to South African audiences that Africans were so hopelessly backward that the best thing would be to make them into full-fledged proletarians and to regulate them uniformly. Such racial misanthropy struck a chord with many settlers in the Eastern Cape as well as with many Boers in the republics. Froude expressed his admiration for the discriminatory legislation of the Boer republics, especially the laws that restricted African rights to vote and to purchase arms and property. In January 1876, Froude wrote to Carnarvon that "in neither of the two Republics are coloured men allowed to exercise the franchise, or to possess arms, without a license, or to acquire real

---

[51] BPP [C.1399] 1876, Molteno, "Cabinet Minute of 7 June 1875," Enclosure in No. 3, Barkly to Carnarvon, June 14, 1875, p. 5. Also printed in CPP [A.20] 1875.
[52] BPP [C.1399] 1876, "Memorandum to Accompany Minute of Ministers," September 14, 1875, Enclosure No. 2 in No. 29, Barkly to Carnarvon, October 20, 1875, pp. 30–3.

property. But the evasion of the property law is already connived at, and the formal disqualification will soon be removed; the arms restriction is a prudent precaution which might be wisely imitated throughout South Africa." The ownership of firearms was once again conflated with the other hallmarks of citizenship – property ownership and voting rights. Froude sympathized with the Orange Free State, whose government banned African ownership of guns. He admired the Orange Free State's efforts to disarm Africans who passed through the republic on their way from Kimberley in the south to their homes in the north and east.[53]

According to Froude, the Eastern Cape settlers appeared to be vulnerable. He echoed frontier concerns about the potential for "native" rebellions. In his view, the residents of the Western Cape lived far from contested areas. Their liberalism and constitutionalism was a luxury. By contrast, in the Eastern Cape and Natal, settlers felt threatened. Western Cape merchants who traveled east to sell guns had little stake in preserving peace on the frontier. And as for the Africans who bought the guns, "Contact with civilization has partially altered their habits, but without materially improving their character." The widespread possession of arms among Africans might trigger a conflict on the frontier. "If for nothing else," he added, "a Conference between the South African states is necessary to provide some consistent check on the supply of arms and ammunition to the native tribes."[54]

Froude received widespread support from the settlers of the Eastern Cape and also from Sir Garnet Wolseley, who replaced Pine as lieutenant governor of Natal and served briefly in that role from February to October 1875. Wolseley concluded his term of office by traveling from Durban to Cape Town. For half of the journey, he traveled with Froude, who appears to have absorbed some of Wolseley's ideas on the subject of gun control. Froude cited the famous general's opinions in his letter to Carnarvon: "Sir Garnet Wolseley has expressed an opinion that the general possession of guns by the natives is most dangerous."[55] Wolseley's views appear to have changed little since his days in West Africa. As his fame spread, his opinions carried even more weight.

[53] BPP [C.1399] 1876, No. 50, Froude to Carnarvon, January 10, 1876, pp. 59–60, 63. Background information on Froude is drawn from Dubow, *Commonwealth of Knowledge*, 126–7.

[54] BPP [C.1399] 1876, No. 50, Froude to Carnarvon, January 10, 1876, pp. 75–6.

[55] BPP [C.1399] 1876, No. 50, Froude to Carnarvon, January 10, 1876, pp. 75–6.

Even with the added support of Wolseley and Froude, the Eastern Cape settlers who supported restrictions on African gun ownership made little headway in the Cape parliament during the 1876 session. The eastern settlers did challenge the government to increase its scrutiny over magistrates who were granting permits, but they failed to introduce a new system of regulation. The prime minister, J. C. Molteno, and several cabinet ministers agreed that the present system was flawed but could not agree to change anything. For this, they were challenged by the editors of the *Cape Argus*. The newspaper was usually on the side of the ministry, but in this case the editors deplored the irregularities in gun regulation, citing the case in which the resident magistrate of Cradock was accused of issuing permits too liberally. The paper joined the easterners in insisting on more stringent enforcement, yet observed that "it is Eastern men who sell guns to the natives on the frontier."[56]

Froude and Wolseley's support for confederation was not enough to persuade the Cape parliamentarians to endorse Carnarvon's proposed conference on confederation either. In August of 1876, a scaled-down version of the conference met in London. The Cape parliament sent the prime minister, J. C. Molteno, as its delegate, but instructed him that he could discuss only the boundaries of Griqualand West. This limitation forced Carnarvon to reduce his ambitions for the conference, which achieved few practical objectives. The delegates did not reach any agreement on intercolonial gun control, or on any other matter. Yet it is significant to see how Carnarvon and the delegates placed gun control high on the agenda, relating it closely to efforts to create a new confederated state in South Africa. At the very least this shows how gun control was becoming a significant element of the Conservative plan for state building in South Africa.

In opening the conference, Carnarvon restated his reasons to seek a unified "native policy" among the colonies. Uniform laws were needed on basic issues of citizenship, including the franchise and property rights. He also backed uniform pass laws and vagrancy laws. According to Carnarvon, uniformity would bring expediency and would also advance "civilization." For the same reason, gun-control laws had to be made more uniform. He claimed that the arms trade was "very large and increasing and practically uncontrolled." He estimated that Africans possessed "hundreds of thousands" of arms and, in a reference to the

[56] *Cape Argus*, June 1, 1876, pp. 2–3.

availability of guns in Kimberley, noted that guns were "a dangerous form of wages." He criticized the Portuguese for allowing arms to pass through Delagoa Bay on their way to the southern African interior.[57]

Carnarvon's comments about the importance of gun control echoed those of earlier advocates, like Wolseley, who was attending the conference. He recognized the importance of gun control in building a united South Africa. Most historical works on imperial politics in the 1870s portray Carnarvon as a superficial thinker, yet it seems that Carnarvon did appreciate some of the complexities of new forms of gun control. In his opening speech to the conference, he discussed how to control the supply of guns and he also showed some understanding of the demand side. He understood that some Africans perceived a threat to their security from the Boer republics and for that reason Africans sought arms. He criticized the government of the Transvaal for "aggravating the difficulties of this case by stirring up a war" that gave Africans "a very practical proof of the importance of becoming possessed of these dangerous weapons." In his view, it was "unfair to the natives to deprive them of their means of self-defence." He may even have thought that a confederated government of South Africa could regulate guns more effectively by regulating the actions of the states of South Africa. After all, this was a conference on confederation, and he was accusing the government of the Transvaal of reckless policies toward Africans.[58]

The conference discussed the arms trade again on August 7, without Carnarvon. It only passed a tame resolution: "That the indiscriminate sale of arms should be generally restricted, but that it will be impossible to do so until all the Colonies and States of South Africa agree on the subject. The members present to-day consider it, therefore, essential that Mr. Molteno should be earnestly invited to take part in discussing with them this very important subject." Molteno would not, even after Carnarvon made a special request for him to come and discuss gun control. In light of Molteno's refusal, the conference passed the further resolution "that the Conference is of opinion that no law for the restriction of the sale of firearms and ammunition to natives will be effective, unless it is adopted and enforced by all the European Governments in South

57 BPP [C.1631] 1876, No. 65, "Speech of the Earl of Carnarvon at the Conference on South African Affairs on the 3rd August, 1876," pp. 64–5. Also printed in PRO CO 879/10 Conf. Pr. (Africa) No. 102.
58 BPP [C.1631] 1876, No. 65, "Speech of the Earl of Carnarvon at the Conference on South African Affairs on the 3rd August, 1876," pp. 64–5. Also printed in PRO CO 879/10 Conf. Pr. (Africa) No. 102.

Africa, and that the co-operation of all such Governments be invited by Her Majesty's Government."[59]

Molteno declined to participate in any discussion of intercolonial gun control, nor would he participate in any of the other discussions about "native policy," including property rights, education, pass laws, and the regulation of liquor. In this way, Molteno and his Western Cape backers in the Cape parliament effectively sabotaged Carnarvon's conference. They were arguing the constitutional point that under responsible government, legislation was supposed to be introduced by the Cape parliament and not by the governor or the secretary of state. They felt that the Cape, not London, should coordinate any efforts toward confederation. They worried that if the move to confederation were directed by London, the Cape would pay the costs without reaping any benefits. Molteno and his allies won this battle but confederation remained a viable proposition, partly because its advocates linked it to proposals for restrictions on African possession of firearms.

[59] PRO CO 879/10 Conf. Pr. (Africa) No. 102, Minutes of the South African Conference, August 7 and 11, 1876, pp. 7–9. BPP [C.1631] 1876, No. 77, Molteno to Carnarvon, August 10, 1876, p. 76.

8

Risk, Skill, and Citizenship in the Eastern Cape, 1876–9

South African discussions about loyalty, guns, and citizenship took place in a wider context of settler fears of Africans. In June 1876, the British settlers of the Eastern Cape began to protest what they perceived to be irregular restrictions on African gun ownership. These irregularities became broadly significant for South African politics. The prominence of these debates, in parliament and in newspapers, highlighted the importance of skills with guns as well as the everyday carrying of guns. In June 1876, the Eastern Cape settlers failed to get the government to pass new regulations, but they did manage to persuade the Cape parliament to authorize an official Colonial Defence Commission to investigate eastern preparedness against attack. The commission dwelt extensively on the spread of guns among Africans, as well as on the reorganization of settler militias. Throughout these debates, settlers indicated that they perceived a close relationship between citizenship, risk, and gun ownership.

The commission was officially appointed by Gov. Barkly on August 7, 1876. It was not a coincidence that the nine members began their work at the same time as settlers were complaining about the ease with which Africans obtained guns, and also at the same time as Carnarvon's confederation conference was failing in London. Settler politicians in the Eastern Cape worried about the security of the frontier, even as they sought provocative restrictions on Africans. The concerned settlers were led by a rising star in politics, John Gordon Sprigg, who represented East London in the Legislative Assembly (Figure 9). Sprigg was a stubborn, abstemious Baptist who, during his youth in England, had reported on the British parliament for a stenography service. He moved to South Africa

FIGURE 9. Photograph of John Gordon Sprigg. (From *Men of the Times: Old Colonists of the Cape Colony and Orange River Colony*. Image courtesy of the Harvard College Library.).

in 1858, settling on a farm in a remote part of the Eastern Cape, near the foothills of the Amatolas. He learned how to farm while becoming involved in politics. He was a new kind of liberal. He admired Africans who were willing to become completely "civilized" and supported their right to vote. Yet Sprigg detested Africans who did not civilize themselves immediately and supported harsh treatment for them. For example, early in his career he supported a bill to allow magistrates to flog Africans who did not dress "decently." Africans were either "with him" or "against him" – there was no middle ground and no room for gradual change. He held these views unwaveringly throughout his long political career, as his biographer James Perry Vanstone has demonstrated. This may surprise students of South African history. During and after the South African War of 1899–1902, Sprigg became famous as an elder statesman and defender of the Cape constitution, including the franchise for non-Europeans, but this only meant that he supported rights for non-Europeans who behaved exactly like Europeans.[1]

Sprigg was joined on the Colonial Defence Commission by four fellow members of the Cape parliament as well as by other men affiliated with the colonial and imperial armed forces. They received the endorsement of the governor, Sir Henry Barkly, who gave the commission official status. Sprigg presided over commission hearings in the Eastern Cape towns of King William's Town, East London, Queenstown, Fort Beaufort, and Grahamstown, from September 14 to October 20, 1876. Over the course of these hearings, the commissioners interviewed traders, settlers, soldiers, and administrators to canvass their opinions on the subject of colonial defense. The commissioners also sought the opinions of several Africans.

The questions of the commissioners and the testimonies of the witnesses were published as an official report in early 1877. The report and the discussions that followed it provide us with a window into colonial debates about security, with particular attention paid to the relationship between gun ownership and citizenship. The commission took up many of the same questions about gun control that had been on the colonial and imperial agenda since 1874. As in earlier debates, the discussion of armament was bound up with the discussion of citizenship. But now, much of the discussion focused on how best to form a colonial defense force. The commission considered whether or not "loyal" Africans like the Mfengu were loyal enough to be entrusted with arms and enrolled in a colonial "burgher force," or militia. They also considered the militia's potential enemies, especially the Xhosa, and whether or not they ought to be subject to more stringent gun control.

The commission explored the relationship between loyalty and gun control. One of the first people to give evidence was Commandant J. H. Bowker, a well-known veteran of the Xhosa wars of the 1830s, 1840s, and 1850s, who was himself a member of the commission. His fellow commissioners asked him about the loyalty of the Mfengu and the possibility of them serving in a colonial militia. He gave a lukewarm

---

[1] Vanstone, "Beginnings," in "Sir John Gordon Sprigg," 8–93.

endorsement while pointing out that under current regulations it was easier for the supposedly hostile Xhosa to purchase guns than the loyal Mfengu:

Are they [the Mfengu] well supplied with arms? – No. Unfortunately they cannot get arms with the same facility as Kafirs do.

How do you account for that, if they are a loyal people? – A Fingo told me the other day that the Fingoes were not as well armed as the Kafirs, and my question was, How is that? He replied, "If I go into a trader's shop and say I want a gun, the trader looks at me and says, you are a Fingo, you must get a permit from your Magistrate; but while I am talking a Kafir comes and gets a gun without any permit whatever."

Are the Fingoes anxious to arm themselves? – Yes, to a man if they could.

Do you think it would be advisable to arm those Fingoes whom you believe to be so loyal? – I would throw facilities in their way, but not make it known publicly that they were to be armed. Any Fingo producing a certificate from his Magistrate or Headman should be allowed a gun.[2]

The commissioners and witnesses debated whether or not "loyal" Africans ought to be armed. One settler, Daniel Hockly, proposed that loyal Africans be enrolled in the burgher militia. One of the commissioners, Commandant Lonsdale, responded by saying, "You are aware that in the last war there was a force known as the Kafir Police, who all deserted to the enemy at the beginning of the war?" Hockly responded, stating that "we are much more mixed up with the Natives now than we were at the last war. They have not the back country to go to now." He suggested that all Africans with certificates of citizenship should be enrolled in the militia and that if they did not participate, or acted disloyally, they should lose their certificates. Citizenship would act as a check on loyalty.[3] As one long-serving administrator pointed out, many African people sought certificates of citizenship.[4]

Such a proposal to link African loyalty to the performance of militia duties was unusual. Most witnesses opposed the arming of Africans. One settler, John Frost, a leading farmer of the Queenstown area and a member of the legislative assembly, expressed his doubts about arming the Mfengu near Oxkraal. Even though he believed that "they would be true to us," he still stated that "I am not in favour of arming them

---

[2] CPP [G.1] 1877, *Minutes of Evidence, Colonial Defence Commission*, King William's Town, September 14, 1876, l. 45–50. In the nineteenth century, the Mfengu were known to English speakers as the "Fingoes."

[3] CPP [G.1] 1877, *Minutes of Col. Def. Comm.*, King William's Town, September 14, 1876, l. 106–10, 117.

[4] CPP [G.1] 1877, *Minutes of Col. Def. Comm.*, Grahamstown, October 17, 1876, l. 5785. Testimony of C. M. Huntley, civil commissioner and resident magistrate of Albany.

at present. I would rather see white men armed."[5] Others were just as reluctant to arm the Mfengu.[6] Richard George Tainton had commanded some Mfengu troops against the Xhosa and still believed that "it would be a dangerous thing to put arms into the hands of any body of Natives in this Colony and teach them drill." He indicated that "loyal Fingoes" might be asked to muster annually, to make sure that they were ready to help the government. Even so, his fears of an uprising were so great that he suggested disarming all Africans.[7] Some settlers agreed with Tainton's original idea to drill the Mfengu once each year.[8] Robert Godlonton, a famous settler politician and proponent of confederation, agreed that the Mfengu "might be organized, but it should be under certain restrictions that they should be armed, if they are armed at all."[9]

It was possible that some Mfengu might be considered loyal. One long-time resident of the Eastern Cape, George Gray, suggested that the Mfengu would be loyal because "there is a certain amount of gratitude towards the Government, and a certain amount of fear towards the Kafir. I think the latter is most powerful." For this reason, he believed that there was not a "sufficient guarantee" against Mfengu disloyalty.[10] Other witnesses were also skeptical about African professions of loyalty. They mentioned famous acts of "disloyalty" by colonial subalterns, like the Kat River Rebellion of 1851 and even the Indian rebellion of 1857.[11]

Some suspected that the Mfengu would be loyal only so long as it appeared that the settlers were more powerful than the Xhosa.[12] According to one settler, William Stanton, the Mfengu could only be trusted

[5] CPP [G.1] 1877, *Minutes of Minutes of Col. Def. Comm.*, Queenstown, September 29, 1876, l. 2722.

[6] CPP [G.1] 1877, *Minutes of Col. Def. Comm.*, Queenstown, October 2, 1876, l. 3222; October 3, 1876, l. 3505.

[7] CPP [G.1] 1877, *Minutes of Col. Def. Comm.*, King William's Town, September 14, 1876, l. 171, 189–90.

[8] CPP [G.1] 1877, *Minutes of Col. Def. Comm.*, King William's Town, September 15, 1876, l. 499; Queenstown, September 28, 1876, l. 2358.

[9] CPP [G.1] 1877, *Minutes of Col. Def. Comm.*, Grahamstown, October 14, 1876, l. 5376.

[10] CPP [G.1] 1877, *Minutes of Col. Def. Comm.*, King William's Town, September 19, 1876, l. 1308, 1377.

[11] CPP [G.1] 1877, *Minutes of Col. Def. Comm.*, King William's Town, September 19, 1876, l. 1208; September 22, 1876, l. 1821; Queenstown, September 28, 1876, l. 2128; Fort Beaufort, October 6, 1876, l. 4004.

[12] CPP [G.1] 1877, *Minutes of Col. Def. Comm.*, King William's Town, September 22, 1876, l. 1942; Queenstown, September 28, 1876, l. 2113.

not to rebel so long as the British had the upper hand. "They cannot be trusted any further." He urged the government to prevent "natives" from settling in "fastnesses" and obtaining arms and ammunition. According to him, Africans needed to be "treated as children" and "ruled with a rod of iron."[13] Another settler, Thomas Brown, agreed that the Mfengu were loyal out of self-interest, but pointed out to the commissioners that it would never be in the Mfengu interest to allow the Xhosa to defeat the British. He speculated that "if the Kafirs were to get the upper hand, the Fingoes would all be made slaves of, as they were before."[14] The Mfengu had, in fact, served as dependents of the Xhosa after their flight from Zululand. Another settler, John Ogilvie, used the same reason to support arming the Mfengu. The chairman, Sprigg, asked him, "Do you think that enrolling the Fingoes would be rather gratifying to them than not?" Ogilvie replied, "Yes, I think it would; because the Fingoes and Kafirs will never amalgamate." Even so, the Mfengu could not be fully trusted. He continued, "But, at the same time, I look upon the Fingo as a perfect Jew; and, if he saw any chance of plunder, he would avail himself of it."[15]

Some thought that self-interest alone would bind the Mfengu to the British cause. This might be reason enough to permit them to drill occasionally, if not to be armed all the time. Others categorically rejected the idea of arming the Mfengu or any Africans. One settler, Benjamin Booth, had been farming in the Eastern Cape since 1840. When asked if he favored arming Africans in peacetime, he claimed that he had "never known more than one loyal Kafir during the whole of that long period [1840–76]." He had no faith in the Mfengu, or "in the loyalty of any man who has a black skin."[16] Some of the most blunt testimony came from regular officers of the British army who were stationed in the Eastern Cape. One captain of the Thirty-Second Light Infantry recommended that a militia comprise only whites (except for Cape Malays, who might be enrolled as unarmed workers in the commissariat). He would not arm any Africans. When he stated this unequivocal position, a fellow captain interjected by saying that "I would not trust a man with a black face."[17]

---

[13] CPP [G.1] 1877, *Minutes of Col. Def. Comm.*, Fort Beaufort, October 7, 1876, l. 4451–2.
[14] CPP [G.1] 1877, *Minutes of Col. Def. Comm.*, Queenstown, September 29, 1876, l. 2619.
[15] CPP [G.1] 1877, *Minutes of Col. Def. Comm.*, Fort Beaufort, October 6, 1876, l. 4087, 4141.
[16] CPP [G.1] 1877, *Minutes of Col. Def. Comm.*, Fort Beaufort, October 6, 1876, l. 4004–5.
[17] CPP [G.1] 1877, *Minutes of Col. Def. Comm.*, King William's Town, September 22, 1876, l. 1801–5.

This lack of confidence in the Mfengu was echoed by most witnesses, who tended to believe that all Africans should be excluded from militia service. According to Richard George Tainton, a settler and a former commander of Mfengu "levies," "It would be a dangerous thing to put arms into the hands of any body of Natives in the Colony and teach them drill."[18] Another witness even thought that the Mfengu already thought that the time had come to join Sarili's Gcaleka Xhosa.[19] Yet, some did speak in favor of African participation in colonial defense. Jesse Shaw, a trader to the Xhosa, thought the Mfengu to be "thoroughly faithful" and advocated enrolling them in a militia.[20] One settler, J. P. Mansel Weale, a farmer, journalist, and naturalist, advocated enrolling every citizen in the militia, even Africans. All citizens should drill together, without bringing their arms home. The commission reiterated its point that an armed detachment of "Kafir Police" had proved disloyal. Weale responded that these police, unlike the Mfengu, lived "apart from Europeans," and ought not to have been trusted to take arms home or to have the franchise. A commissioner then asked, "How are we to prove the loyalty of an individual before we give him the rights of free citizenship?" Weale responded by saying that "if you give a man the right of an elector it is his duty to defend you."[21] Civic duties came with civic privileges.

Another advocate of full citizenship for Africans was Percy Nightingale, the civil commissioner and resident magistrate of Victoria East. He was a career civil servant who had fought as a volunteer against the Xhosa in 1851. When asked if the Mfengu should be allowed to be armed and be enrolled in a militia, he gave an unequivocal "yes." He said, "I think that the Fingo landowners ought to be armed in the same way as we propose to arm the Europeans. I would assess native locations in the same way as I would assess Municipalities, where the natives are Fingoes." The commission expressed surprise; no other witness had "spoken up for" the Mfengu in that way. He explained, simply, that during his wartime service, he had found the Mfengu "levies" to be loyal. "We had Levies of them and they protected the whole District. I was out with

---

[18] CPP [G.1] 1877, *Minutes of Col. Def. Comm.*, King William's Town, September 14, 1876, l. 171.

[19] CPP [G.1] 1877, *Minutes of Col. Def. Comm.*, Grahamstown, October 14, 1876, l. 5229–30, 5319.

[20] CPP [G.1] 1877, *Minutes of Col. Def. Comm.*, Fort Beaufort, October 7, 1876, l. 4485–90.

[21] CPP [G.1] 1877, *Minutes of Col. Def. Comm.*, King William's Town, September 22, 1876, l. 1896, 1909–19.

them and under fire with them many times, and they always behaved loyally." Since that time, his occasional contacts with Mfengu people had persuaded him that they had not "made so much progress as they might have done if they had been more looked after. They are left too much to themselves," with limited government contacts, and little in the way of schools. "The consequence of all this," according to Nightingale, "is that the people have not advanced in civilization lately."[22]

Liberal policies of civilization implied that Africans might be trusted to serve in the militia. Trustworthiness might be determined by evaluating either collective or individual degrees of civilization. The liberal, humanitarian administrator Joseph M. Orpen was asked by Sprigg how best the Cape might administer African people. He responded by saying, "I think the natives should be treated with fairness, justice, and truth. These three things exist together, and depend upon each other. I think we have been deficient in them in our native policy."[23] Orpen advocated arming loyal Africans, and even considered some to be more loyal than settlers. The commission pressed him:

[Commissioner Sprigg]: *In the letter you addressed to me you recommend the arming of the native population, to what extent would you carry that?* – [Orpen] I think the Government might have all the natives that may be trusted with them.

[Commissioner Burger]: *Are there any such natives?* – [Orpen] I think so.

[Commissioner Pringle]: *Can you mention any tribe?* – [Orpen] I am not speaking of whole tribes but of natives.[24]

Orpen's position – that Africans be considered as individuals rather than as tribes – flew in the face of much colonial thinking. He believed that as individuals Africans might be trusted to defend the colony. Trustworthiness was to be measured materially. According to Orpen, "natives who have European houses" in "Kaffraria" (Transkei) and "Basutoland" ought to be accorded representation in the Cape parliament. When a commissioner asked Orpen about the loyalty of the Mfengu, he stated that they were loyal: "I know no reason why they should not be loyal, on the contrary there are many reasons why they should. They are

---

[22] CPP [G.1] 1877, *Minutes of Col. Def. Comm.*, Fort Beaufort, October 7, 1876, l. 4308, 4316.

[23] CPP [G.1] 1877, *Minutes of Col. Def. Comm.*, Grahamstown, October 16, 1876, l. 5500–2.

[24] CPP [G.1] 1877, *Minutes of Col. Def. Comm.*, Grahamstown, October 16, 1876, l. 5530–43, 5564–6.

accumulating a large amount of property, which I consider to be a guarantee of their good conduct."[25] The more property that Africans acquired, the more they advanced, and the safer the colony would be. As Rev. William Impey, a Wesleyan missionary, stated to the commission, the acquisition of property by the Mfengu was "one of the greatest protections we can have."[26] Guns were property and were often bought with wages. In the eyes of some people, they too may have distinguished the "civilized" from the "uncivilized."

Race and Shooting Skills

By this point, the South African debate about interracial and intercolonial gun control had been going on for some time. Participants in the debate linked gun ownership to broader policy debates about civilization, citizenship, and trade. These debates continued to be linked to gun control for some years to come.

As South Africans quibbled over guns and confederation, the debate took a peculiar turn. In 1875 and 1876, whites in South Africa began to debate whether or not Africans could shoot well. On the face of it, such a debate seems absurd. For more than two centuries, people in South Africa had been using guns to hunt and fight. Besides, Africans would appear to have the same inherent abilities, on average, as Europeans. Basic marksmanship is not so difficult to master, even if it is challenging to become a top-notch shooter. In the Cape Colony, settler perceptions of the risks of armed Africans were linked to their descriptions of Africans as skilled with firearms. The very same settlers portrayed Africans as racially inferior, yet racism appears to have been trumped by thinking about risk.

Ideologically motivated descriptions of skill reveal a methodological problem for historians. Historians tend to overlook the methodological challenges of describing skill, which is often discussed without much analysis. For example, historians of industrialization in Europe and North America have written about the ways in which the loss of worker skill was related to the loss of worker power. High-status workers fought to preserve old workplace skills, even as industrialists introduced new

---

[25] CPP [G.1] 1877, *Minutes of Col. Def. Comm.*, Grahamstown, October 16, 1876, l. 5585–6.
[26] CPP [G.1] 1877, *Minutes of Col. Def. Comm.*, Grahamstown, October 17, 1876, l. 5848–50.

technologies that relied less on worker skill.[27] Were worker and capitalist descriptions of skill so heavily freighted with ideology that they were misleading to historians? Only a few historians have raised the possibility that perceptions of technological skill may reflect perceptions of order.[28] Seemingly neutral descriptions of skill may harbor ideologies. One of the most neutral descriptions of African shooting skill in our period comes from a British officer, who hosted two unnamed sons of Letsie, the Sotho paramount chief, during his visit to Cape Town in the early 1870s. The officer, General Sir Arthur Cunynghame, reported that "I took them to the shooting grounds at Wynberg, and placing rifles in their hands requested them to compete with ourselves. We were all astonished at their success. The eldest beat all but two of their competitors, at a range of five hundred yards."[29] Why was Cunynghame astonished that the sons of a Sotho chief could shoot well? On the previous page of his account, he even described how well the Sotho fought. One of the only accounts of a side-by-side competition between African and European shooters contained racially motivated suppositions.

What is real and what is myth when it comes to skill? As far as South African shooting skills are concerned, the sources contain many contradictions. Enemies were described as skilled and risky; friends were described as unskilled and safe. Such contradictions highlight a significant methodological problem. If descriptions of skill are ideological and biased, then how can historians use old sources to assess technological skill? Must skill actually be witnessed to be described accurately?

There is little awareness of this methodological problem in the historiography of technology. More specifically, it is not recognized in the historiography on firearms and colonialism, either. In the best available study of shooting on a colonial frontier, *The Skulking Way of War: Technology and Tactics among the New England Indians*, Patrick Malone describes how European settlers introduced guns to New England, pointing out that Native Americans adapted them most skillfully to the local environment. The Native Americans learned shooting skills and combined them with older forest warfare skills, whereby they gained a

---

[27] Rydén, "Skill and Technical Change in the Swedish Iron Industry, 1750–1860," 386–7. Rydén cites the well-known study, Braverman, *Labor and Monopoly Capital*; a similar point is made by Scott in *The Glassworkers of Carmaux*.

[28] Lerman, "Preparing for the Duties and Practical Business of Life;" Evans, "*The Labyrinth of Flames*," 71–3.

[29] Cunynghame, *My Command in South Africa*, 89.

temporary advantage in warfare, at least until English colonists learned how to fight with guns in forests, too. Malone's study is based largely on colonial sources, though, and he does not raise the possibility that English descriptions of Native American skill with guns may have been aimed at portraying the Native Americans as more dangerous than they really were. This type of description would have furthered colonial aims to dispossess Native Americans.

In the South African context, there is only one place to find a scholarly discussion of shooting skills: the 1971 issue of the *Journal of African History* that addressed the social history of firearms. Here, the authors reached unexamined, contradictory conclusions about skill. Using colonial sources, the authors reported that the Khoisan and Griqua were skilled with weapons, which enabled them, at first, to resist colonialism. The Xhosa were both good and bad marksmen, while the Mfengu were skilled and dangerous. The Sotho were "indifferently armed and were poor shots" before the 1870s, when they became "crack marksmen." The Zulu never integrated firearms completely into their military tactics, but by the Anglo–Zulu War of 1879, some Zulu shot well, supposedly, according to a British government source, because Zulu fighters received instruction from redcoat deserters.[30]

Discussions of skill and community in South Africa predate the industrial era, but not by much. In the Eastern Cape, there had been some discussion of race and skill as far back as the 1840s, when some settlers were portraying the arming of Africans as risky. Crais demonstrates repeatedly in *White Supremacy and Black Resistance* that the European settlers of the Eastern Cape stereotyped blacks as violent in order to justify regulating them. These early stereotypes of violent Africans became linked to guns. In 1841, a letter writer to the *Grahamstown Journal*, who called himself "Candidus," opined that

Some of your traders, Mr. Editor, may say that a gun in the hands of a Kaffir is useless; but I tell you no such thing. They have a *strong nerve and a steady arm*, far different from many of your English brandy drinkers, who weaken their strength and shatter their nerves by intemperance. I have seen a Kaffir shoot a monkey perched on top of a high key with a single ball, and have bought ducks with them that have, in the same way, been brought down with a bullet. But in all events, the worst shot amongst the many who are actually armed with guns

---

[30] Marks and Atmore, "Firearms in Southern Africa," 518–19, 523–4; Atmore and Sanders, "Sotho Arms and Ammunition in the Nineteenth Century," 539, 542; Guy, "A Note on Firearms in the Zulu Kingdom," 560.

would be able to creep behind a rock and hit *a regiment of soldiers* on their march through the Fish River bush, or shoot into an encampment and *hit a tent.*"³¹

The author of this letter hoped to show that while some Africans were highly skilled shots, others were at least competent, which meant they compared well with the settlers. Even so, the skill, or lack of skill, on the part of Africans and settlers did not emerge as an important topic of public discussion until the 1870s.

In retrospect, the 1870s debate about race and shooting skills seems ironic. The most racist voices argued that Africans had become skilled and dangerous shooters, even though many doubted that Africans were apt participants in "civilization." Equally ironically, the liberals who were encouraging "civilization" and a free trade in guns were expressing doubts about African marksmanship.

Froude, one of the best-known conservatives, had some revealing thoughts on the beliefs of liberal merchants. He wrote to Carnarvon that "the Cape merchants – themselves at a safe distance – refuse to lose the opportunity of a profitable trade, and shelter themselves behind a pretence that the natives are less dangerous when armed with guns than with assegais, an opinion in which soldiers, who will have to deal practically with them if the danger becomes real, are not inclined to agree."³² One regular officer of the British army, Lt. Col. Crossman of the Royal Engineers, agreed with Froude. In a confidential report to Carnarvon about labor in Griqualand West, he argued that only long-serving Africans ought to be permitted to purchase guns. "For my own part," he continued, "I would not allow guns to be sold to the natives at all. They do not purchase them for hunting but for purposes of war. They are not satisfied with the common exported article, but endeavour to obtain the best rifles they can purchase, saying 'that as the red [British] soldier uses good rifles they also must have them.' Many of them become expert shots, and whatever civilians may say, a Kafir with a rifle is a far more dangerous opponent than a Kafir with a bundle of assegais."³³

It is difficult to determine whether any particular group of people in the past has been more or less skilled with weapons, given the lack of reliable, direct evidence. One may reasonably assume that many Africans and Europeans could, and did, learn how to use guns skillfully. When

---

³¹ "Trade in Guns," *Grahamstown Journal*, September 23, 1841, p. 3.
³² BPP [C.1399] 1876, No. 50, Froude to Carnarvon, January 10, 1876, pp. 75–6.
³³ PRO CO 879/9 Conf. Pr. (Africa) No. 96, "Report of Lieut.-Colonel Crossman, R. E., on the Affairs of Griqua-Land West," June 1876.

considering the relationship between discussions about guns and discussions about native policy, it is more useful – and more possible – to assess the relationship between descriptions of skill and pronouncements on gun control. Why were settlers and administrators were making such curious public statements about African skill?

This question about race and skill has been addressed in some of the literature on technology and imperialism. In one well-known study, *The Tentacles of Progress*, Daniel Headrick argues that Europeans who held racial biases tended to import technologies into their colonies without establishing much local technical education.[34] Michael Adas makes a similar point in his own well-regarded book, *Machines as the Measure of Men*. He shows that by the late nineteenth century Europeans were arguing that their superior technologies reflected the innate superiority of their civilization. According to Adas, "a tautological relationship developed: scientific and technological achievements were frequently cited as gauges of racial capacity, and estimates of racial capacity determined the degree of technical and scientific education made available to different non-Western peoples." Adas makes the further point that these racist beliefs had diverse origins: in pseudoscientific racism and also in European backlash against rebellious colonial subjects. These beliefs about the inherent difficulty of transferring technical skill multiplied by the middle of the nineteenth century, so that by the 1870s, they were beginning to be enacted into policies. Colonial subjects might never be fully assimilated to European ways, but might be kept at arm's length, as associates in their own domination.[35]

Adas and Headrick drew evidence to support these points largely from discourse about educational policy. The discussions about gun-control policy in South Africa tend to complicate their findings. In the 1870s, many settlers sought to keep Africans at arm's length, to deprive them of land, and to turn them into pliant laborers. This much is consistent with the findings of Adas and Headrick, yet the South African case differs from their cases in one key respect. In order to deprive Africans of their rights and build a new political order, colonial settlers and officials portrayed Africans as so sufficiently skilled with guns that they posed a risk to the new order. Some settlers were using scare tactics to

---

[34] Headrick, *Tentacles of Progress*, 304–9.
[35] Adas, *Machines as the Measure of Men*, Chap. 5, "The Limits of Diffusion." The quotation is taken from p. 275.

build a new kind of racially exclusive state in South Africa. By contrast, liberals who adhered to the old model of trying to "civilize" Africans tended to argue that Africans were not fully skilled. They did so partly to allay concerns about the risks of armed Africans, and partly to lay the groundwork for their broader argument that Africans were not yet fully "civilized," and needed more help. The Colonial Defence Commission of 1876 took up the question of whether or not Africans were skilled in the use of their weapons. In the eyes of most of the settler commissioners and witnesses, skill did not indicate civilization as much as it indicated risk.

There were some people who took a compromise position on skill. Some of the witnesses who favored militia service for "civilized" Africans also had doubts about African skills. The settler Daniel Hockly believed that African citizens were "not so well acquainted with the use of arms as the Burghers" and ought to be enrolled and drilled in the militia. One commissioner objected to this line of reasoning and asked, incredulously, "Do you not think that if these Natives were drilled they would make use of that knowledge against us?" Hockly responded that drilling might serve to inculcate feelings of loyalty among African citizens. He also mentioned that the Xhosa, the perennial bogeys of the colony, were becoming more skilled with guns. Perhaps Hockly was suggesting that this threat might be mitigated by the training of loyal Africans. In any event, he sought to put a stop to the current availability of arms and ammunition to Africans. He hoped that guns might be stored by the government and handed out to militiamen during drills and emergencies.[36]

As the commission explored questions of skill, virtually the only sensible and nonideological testimony came from the Mfengu "headman" William Dima. He testified that most Mfengu in the Transkei were armed, mostly with single- and double-barreled muzzle-loaders. They did not buy new guns for shooting game – there was none left to shoot. They bought guns out of fear of a Xhosa uprising – Dima and other Mfengu had the same fear as that of the settlers. Yet according to Dima, the Mfengu lacked powder and were no more likely to practice with their guns than they were to practice with their assegais. That being said, one commissioner enquired whether or not the Mfengu would fight better with guns than with assegais. Not surprisingly, Dima thought they would fight better with guns. Mfengu armed with guns could be taught how to use a

---

[36] CPP [G.1] 1877, *Minutes of Col. Def. Comm.*, King Williamstown, September 14, 1876, l. 72, 107, 152–7.

gun fairly quickly. In a previous war, according to Dima, "Fingoes that had not practised soon got it up."[37]

One English officer of the Frontier Armed and Mounted Police, E. B. Chalmers, thought that the Mfengu ought to be trusted to bear arms in a colonial militia. He supported the way in which the government "allowed them every facility for getting arms." By contrast, he thought that the Xhosa were quite poorly skilled with guns. Chalmers claimed that he "would rather face a Kafir with a gun than with an assegai." The Xhosa were "wretchedly bad" marksmen. "I have seen [Chief] Gange-lizwe himself trying to pot a crow at ten yards, and miss it." To make matters worse, the Xhosa had "no idea of keeping their guns clean" and thought that practicing was a waste of ammunition. According to Chalmers, the Xhosa carried guns largely for "show." "They think that if they have a gun it will frighten away the enemy." He did not fear a Xhosa attack.[38]

By contrast, most settlers testified to the commission that they feared an attack and that the Xhosa were skilled with guns. When the commission asked one settler, Frederick Martin, whether the Xhosa were "more to be dreaded with a gun or with an assegai," he responded, "A gun, decidedly, and they will become more accustomed to the gun every day. In those times [the wars of 1835 and 1846] they were very indifferent shots, and the guns were very inferior." But now, he implied that the Xhosa were becoming more skilled and were using better weapons.[39] Other settlers tended to agree, as did some of the soldiers who were stationed in the Eastern Cape. In addition to Martin, fourteen settlers testified to that effect before the commission, while three disagreed.

For some, it was not easy to admit that the Xhosa might be skilled. The commission asked one magistrate, John Hemming, if he thought the Xhosa were more dangerous with guns. He answered, "Of course they are more formidable with guns; but they are bad shots."[40] Assess-ments of skill reflected colonial ideology, even the assessments that were positive. The chair of the commission, Gordon Sprigg, had heard

---

[37] CPP [G.1] 1877, *Minutes of Col. Def. Comm.*, King Williamstown, September 15, 1876, l. 328–77.

[38] CPP [G.1] 1877, *Minutes of Col. Def. Comm.*, King Williamstown, September 16, 1876, l. 679–93.

[39] CPP [G.1] 1877, *Minutes of Col. Def. Comm.*, East London, September 18, 1876, l. 856–8.

[40] CPP [G.1] 1877, *Minutes of Col. Def. Comm.*, Queenstown, September 30, 1876, l. 2977.

that some Africans owned Winchesters, the advanced multiple-shot, lever-action rifles used most famously in the western United States. He expressed surprise that Africans could use such weapons: "how would they manage for ammunition for guns of that sort! They could not use pot-legs for them?"[41] (In remote areas, some African hunters loaded their muskets with any scraps of iron that could be found, including "pot-legs."[42] This clever adaptation to geography and poverty was derided as ignorance.) Others took an even dimmer view of Xhosa capabilities. One settler, A. N. Ella, stated that "the Kafir does not understand a gun." He also stated that "the Kafirs understood the old flint-lock musket" and could do more damage with it than with the new guns. Yet, he saw fit to propose stricter regulations on African gun ownership. According to him, guns themselves did not make Africans more dangerous. The "possessor of it [a gun] gets thoughts into his head which might not otherwise get there." He did not think that Africans bought guns with the idea of attacking Europeans, but said that "when a lot of men with guns get together they might get ideas of that nature into their heads."[43]

Settlers claimed that guns changed African thought and behavior. A superficial analysis of these settler claims would dismiss them as "deterministic." And yet, if we consider the Comaroffs' claim that the everyday material practices of colonialism were associated with hotly contested changes in people's understanding of themselves and the world around them, then these settler claims take on added significance. As part of the settlers' effort to dispossess and disenfranchise Africans, they were debating the relationship between technical skill, everyday practices, and colonial modes of thought. Ideas about the use of guns became instrumental to racial politics.

Settlers with racist views portrayed Africans as generally incapable, yet as easily influenced by new technologies. In the era of the breechloader revolution, another important question would help settlers determine the level of risk from Africans: what types of guns were Africans using? As Major Anderson of the Thirty-Second Light Infantry put it, "The great question is what sort of guns they have."[44] This was an urgent

---

[41] CPP [G.1] 1877, *Minutes of Col. Def. Comm.*, Queenstown, September 28, 1876, l. 2395.

[42] This practice is confirmed by Lord and Baines in *Shifts and Expedients*, 229–30.

[43] CPP [G.1] 1877, *Minutes of Col. Def. Comm.*, Queenstown, October 2, 1876, l. 3056, 3084, 3127.

[44] CPP [G.1] 1877, *Minutes of Col. Def. Comm.*, King William's Town, September 22, 1876, l. 1831.

question during the 1870s because muzzle-loaders were being replaced by breechloaders. Those who still possessed only muzzle-loaders were at a distinct disadvantage. Yet there was little reliable information about the precise type of weapon that Africans owned. The commission heard testimony from two gun traders John Grainger and J. T. Morris, who stated that mostly they sold Africans "a cheap description of gun," designed for firing bird shot and not musket balls. They also believed in a free trade in muskets and might naturally downplay the effectiveness of their wares to a commission that was considering further restrictions on arms sales.[45] A. N. Ella thought that Africans at the diamond fields were buying muskets "which were not so good as the original musket." By the "original musket" he meant the old "Tower" musket, the smoothbore muzzle-loader that the British army used in the early nineteenth century. According to Ella, the muskets being sold in Kimberley were made in Belgium and were prone to bursting.[46] William Dima testified that most Mfengu were armed with single- and double-barreled muzzle-loaders, but not with breechloaders.[47] Percy Nightingale, the magistrate, had actually carried out an inspection of Xhosa and Mfengu weapons some years before in Victoria East. He claimed that some owned inferior old muskets, while some owned "new ones."[48] Frederick Martin, the settler, considered some of these muzzle-loaders to be "splendid guns" that potentially endangered settlers.[49] Another settler, John Webb, claimed that many Africans owned Enfield muzzle-loading rifles, the basic military weapon of the late 1850s and early 1860s. This worried him, even though the Enfield had been surpassed by breechloaders.[50]

Settlers described African skill with guns in order to warn the Colonial Defence Commission about perceived threats to frontier settlements. Who, then, was to blame for the arming and training of Africans? The government railway works received a large share of criticism, along with

---

[45] CPP [G.1] 1877, *Minutes of Col. Def. Comm.*, King William's Town, October 17, 1876, l. 5977–9.

[46] CPP [G.1] 1877, *Minutes of Col. Def. Comm.*, Queenstown, October 2, 1876, l. 3056; A. N. Ella to Col. Def. Comm., October 3, 1876, in *Col. Def. Comm. Appendix.*, pp. xlii–xliii.

[47] CPP [G.1] 1877, *Minutes of Col. Def. Comm.*, King William's Town, September 15, 1876, l. 328–9.

[48] CPP [G.1] 1877, *Minutes of Col. Def. Comm.*, Fort Beaufort, October 7, 1876, l. 4232.

[49] CPP [G.1] 1877, *Minutes of Col. Def. Comm.*, East London, September 18, 1876, l. 877.

[50] CPP [G.1] 1877, *Minutes of Col. Def. Comm.*, Grahamstown, October 14, 1876, l. 5306.

the diamond fields and smugglers. One settler who had commanded a burgher unit from Komga blamed "the armed rebel Hottentots" for arming and training the Xhosa.[51] Dutch and English merchants from Cape Town were singled out for criticism by A. C. Bissett, a settler who had lived in the Eastern Cape since 1820. According to him, the Cape merchants were "arming the Kafirs to destroy us."[52] By far the most extraordinary claim about merchants was made by Gordon Sprigg, the chair of the commission. While questioning one witness, he stated, "Probably you know that the majority of guns are not sold by English people, but by Germans and Jews?"[53] While there were some German and Jewish traders who sold guns on the frontier, the gun trade did tend to be a multicultural affair, with English settlers represented heavily in applications for trading permits. Again, racial ideologies and stereotypes pervaded these discussions of risk.

There was only one way in which the commission's investigations overturned a stereotype. Throughout the English-speaking world, settlers on the frontier were supposed to be heavily armed and skilled with weapons. And yet, during testimony before the Colonial Defence Commission, it came out that settlers in the Eastern Cape were lightly armed and unskilled. This is somewhat surprising. As we have already seen, plenty of people in South Africa owned guns, while the available studies indicate that in nineteenth-century Britain, the settlers' country of origin, firearms ownership was still widespread.[54] There were a number of conditions prevailing in the Eastern Cape that may have caused settlers to give up on guns: there was precious little game to hunt and burgher militia service was not popular.

In 1876, as fear of a Xhosa attack mounted, some settlers and soldiers fretted about whether the Europeans living in the Eastern Cape were trained well enough in the use of firearms. E. B. Chalmers of the Frontier Armed and Mounted Police testified that few Eastern Cape settlers had guns.[55] Several other settlers called attention to the same matter.

---

[51] CPP [G.1] 1877, *Minutes of Col. Def. Comm.*, King William's Town, September 19, 1876, l. 1202.

[52] CPP [G.1] 1877, *Minutes of Col. Def. Comm.*, East London, September 18, 1876, l. 878.

[53] CPP [G.1] 1877, *Minutes of Col. Def. Comm.*, Queenstown, September 30, 1876, l. 2775.

[54] Malcolm, *Guns and Violence*, 130.

[55] CPP [G.1] 1877, *Minutes of Col. Def. Comm.*, King William's Town, September 16, 1876, l. 709.

According to two witnesses, fewer than half of the settlers owned guns, although many more knew how to use them and more of the young men were learning.[56] According to another witness, "farmers and their sons" not only lacked arms, but had lost the skill of riding while carrying a gun.[57] It took a great deal of time to manage a farm or to work at a craft, and time was not often available for hunting increasingly rare animals or even just for target practice. This was a predicament for settlers that Patrick Malone has also noted in his study of weapons and tactics in colonial New England.[58]

Some Eastern Cape settlers still thought themselves to be superior fighters. Their skills were innate, and only needed training to bring them out. As one settler, A. N. Ella, argued, "The European Colonist is perfectly at home on horseback, and with a breech-loading rifle and trained shooting horse . . . nothing native in Africa can stand against him" if he were "well led."[59] Such skills could be demonstrated to Africans during peacetime. One of the older settlers to testify, John Sweetman, believed fervently in the superiority of farmers as irregular soldiers, even when questioned about their slipping skills. He encouraged the government to supply arms to European farmers, and the farmers to hold public shooting demonstrations: "I think that getting up rifle corps and practicing shooting, and showing ourselves in force among the natives would have a good effect." When one commissioner asked if such activities would be overly provocative, he responded, "No, I do not think it would. I remember we used to have meetings for rifle practice at the Winterberg, and the Kafirs used to come and see us shooting, and it had a good effect upon them."[60]

Settlers had been fascinated by demonstrating weapons since the start of the VOC settlement at Table Bay in 1652, when guns were demonstrated to reinforce the demonstrators' sense of superiority to reveal a new order. Yet Sweetman's proposal to demonstrate settler shooting skills came at an awkward time: settler marksmanship was no longer what it used to be. A better way to redress the imbalance between a perceived

---

[56] CPP [G.1] 1877, *Minutes of Col. Def. Comm.*, Fort Beaufort, October 6, 1876, l. 4028; Grahamstown, October 17, 1876, l. 5807–9.

[57] CPP [G.1] 1877, *Minutes of Col. Def. Comm.*, Queenstown, September 28, 1876, l. 2303–4.

[58] Malone, *Skulking Way of War*, 60.

[59] CPP [G.1] 1877, *Minutes of Col. Def. Comm.*, Queenstown, October 2, 1876, l. 302.

[60] CPP [G.1] 1877, *Minutes of Col. Def. Comm.*, Fort Beaufort, October 6, 1876, l. 3769, 3773–4.

decline in European skills and a perceived increase in African skills was to impose new regulations on guns. Some witnesses proposed to eliminate gun sales to Africans altogether. Others proposed the introduction of heavier fees for gun licenses. The usual objections were raised to such proposals: they might be thought provocative, and besides, guns were easy to hide and smuggle. Others thought that the existing gun laws might be modified. One proposal was endorsed by the liberal magistrate J. M. Orpen and the settler politician J. M. Peacock: let the government monopolize the sale of gunpowder and ammunition, just as the Orange Free State did and as the Cape Colony had done in the past.[61] Yet such a plan could be undermined by smugglers, too, as was pointed out by W. M. Fleischer, the resident magistrate of Steynsburg. According to him, it was futile to attempt to restrict the gun trade. He favored a completely free trade in weapons and ammunition.[62]

Such a classic liberal proposal fell on deaf ears. In early 1877, the commission recommended a package of proposals for new regulations in two key areas: militia service and gun control. Both areas were closely related, albeit lapsing, in English political culture, yet remained vibrantly connected in the Boer republics, where all young men took turns serving in commandos and where Africans were excluded from gun ownership, a hallmark of their secondary political status. Following the Boer republics, the commission asked the Cape parliament to pass sweeping legislation. Such measures were justified, because, in the words of the commissioners,

The conviction has deepened during the progress of the inquiry that the Colony is living as upon a mine, that may at any moment be sprung beneath its feet. Different opinions prevail as to the extent of the danger; but all are agreed that our present position is perilous in the extreme, and that if we are to avert the calamity of war, we must immediately place the country in a defensive position.[63]

The risks from the Xhosa were thought to be so significant that the commission recommended the establishment of a larger colonial defense

---

[61] For Peacock's testimony, see CPP [G.1] 1877, *Minutes of Col. Def. Comm.*, King William's Town, September 23, 1876, l. 1989. Orpen had proposed a monopoly at least a year and a half earlier. See CPP [G.21] 1875, "Report of the British Resident in St. John's Territory," March 1875, *Blue Book on Native Affairs*, pp. 111–12.

[62] CPP [G.1] 1877, *Minutes of Col. Def. Comm.*, Queenstown, October 3, 1876, l. 3589–91.

[63] CPP [G.1] 1877, *Report of the Col. Def. Comm., 1876*, p. 3. There are two versions of the report with slightly different pagination. The first version, cited here, is one page ahead of the second version. Thus, p. 3 in the first version is p. 4 in the second version, and so on.

force. The Frontier Armed and Mounted Police were to be increased in number from 940 to 1,500 and to be given better training, especially in marksmanship. The second line of defense would be formed by new "burgher and volunteer" forces. All the European men between the ages of sixteen and sixty living in frontier districts were to be enrolled as burghers and would be required to drill regularly. This would create a force of about twenty thousand men between the ages of eighteen and fifty, of whom only ten thousand might be called up in a frontier war. The government would be empowered to enroll Europeans in the Western Cape, too, in cases of dire emergency. A separate force of volunteers would be armed by the government and trained more extensively, in exchange for being exempted from burgher duty. And schools would be required to drill young boys. All this was estimated to cost £76,808 per annum. The cost was to be borne by a poll tax on all those who did not serve in the burgher force, including westerners and Africans.[64]

The new burgher and volunteer forces were to provide additional security against "the national enemy." So were new gun-control laws. The commission recommended that arms should not be sold to African laborers on the public works at Cape Town and Port Elizabeth; even though it was never established that the government was selling the guns, the commission implied that this was certainly the case. Permits to own and trade guns should only be issued by resident magistrates and not by justices of the peace. Smuggling should be discouraged at Port St. John's, which still remained under the jurisdiction of the Mpondo. And finally, since guns were already so widespread, the government should turn away from liberal trade policies and monopolize the sale of ammunition.[65]

The commission made a number of other recommendations too. The telegraph and railroad lines of the Eastern Cape should be improved. "Native administration" should be more extensive, and administrators should be better paid. This would make it easier to advance the cause of civilization. Xhosa law was to be codified, and at the same time the authority of the chiefs was to be undermined by allowing individuals the right of land ownership. Medical doctors should be sent to replace "witch

---

[64] CPP [G.1] 1877, *Report of the Col. Def. Comm., 1876*, pp. 5–14.

[65] CPP [G.1] 1877, *Report of the Col. Def. Comm., 1876*, pp. 15–16. Independent Pondoland, with its coastline and its location between Xhosa and Zulu territory, had been an important location for smuggling since the 1850s. See PRO CO 48/407, Currie to Grey, March 18, 1861, Encl. in Grey to Newcastle, April 13, 1861.

doctors," dowries would be limited to first wives as a way to encourage monogamy, and children should be sent to "industrial schools." Such recommendations echoed liberal hopes for civilization, even while employing a harsh, punitive tone. The commission sought to "put down some of the heathenish customs so offensive to civilized men." The "natives" were said to "simply exist amongst the colonists in the same ways as wild beasts exist. They are left to their own devices, and those devices are mainly evil, and fraught with danger to the Colony." The commission singled out the Mfengu as an "industrious race" but did not feel "justified in recommending that they should be entrusted with arms." Arms could not be entrusted to Africans. Instead, dangerous Africans would be made civilized and industrious.[66]

Frontier Defense and Gun Control

While the Colonial Defence Commission was meeting, the imperial push for confederation was still proceeding. In August 1876, after Molteno's ministry had blocked confederation, Carnarvon devised other means to fulfill his ambitions. At that moment, it was beginning to seem possible that the government of the South African Republic might lose control of the Transvaal to Sekhukhune's Pedi, who appeared poised to attack. Historian Richard Cope suggests that Shepstone, who was in London attending the conference, probably advised Carnarvon on the implications of Boer collapse in the Transvaal, none of which were good for confederation. The Pedi might consolidate their authority or the Zulu might even invade the Transvaal. Transvaal's British settlers might be greatly helped by confederation.[67]

On September 14, Gov. Barkly suggested action, even though he disapproved of Carnarvon's confederation scheme. Barkly sent a telegram to London, warning that Sekhukhune had defeated a Boer force and that the Transvaal's Volksraad, or parliament, might ask Britain to take over the territory. Carnarvon replied by asking Barkly to pursue the annexation of the Transvaal. Shepstone warned that Barkly had poor relations with Thomas Burgers, the president of the Transvaal. Shepstone offered to return to South Africa to negotiate the annexation himself. On September 22, he reembarked for South Africa, as a special commissioner empowered to annex the Transvaal. When Shepstone returned to Natal four

---

[66] CPP [G.1] 1877, *Report of the Col. Def. Comm., 1876*, pp. 17–19.
[67] Cope, *Ploughshare of War*, 103–5.

weeks later, he found that the threat from the Pedi was not so dire, but that the republic's finances were dismal. The government had bankrupted the treasury by borrowing heavily in order to build a railway to the coast. Shepstone negotiated with the Transvaal leadership for several months. During the talks, he indirectly threatened the republic by saying that he alone was preventing the Transvaal from being overrun by the Zulu. The negotiations failed, yet the government was so weak that Shepstone annexed the Transvaal by proclamation on April 12, 1877. With the British and Zulu armies poised on the border, resistance was futile, at least for the moment.[68]

Carnarvon took further steps to advance confederation. Carnarvon and the confederationists believed that Barkly was too close to Molteno, even though the two had disagreed on numerous occasions. Carnarvon appointed a new governor Sir Bartle Frere, a leading administrator from India (Figure 10). Frere had been a brilliant pupil at Haileybury, the training college for the Indian Civil Service. On arriving in Bombay (now known as Mumbai) in 1834 (after an adventuresome journey through Arabia) he began to master Hindi, Gujarati, and Marathi. From the late 1830s until the mid-1860s, he had played an important role in various aspects of the government of the Bombay Presidency. He was particularly talented at finance and diplomacy. His talent as an administrator virtually assured his appointment as governor of the Bombay Presidency in 1862. He retired in 1867 and returned to England, where he sat on the Indian Council and wrote about imperial affairs. His friendships with members of the royal household and the aristocracy kept him in the limelight, as did his scientific interests: he was a Fellow of the Royal Society as well as past president of the Royal Asiatic Society and the Royal Geographical Society. Frere's expertise and connections persuaded Lord Carnarvon that he would be a good replacement for Barkly. Carnarvon appointed Frere as governor of the Cape Colony and high commissioner for southern Africa, hoping that the policy of confederation might yet be salvaged by a skilled administrator. Frere arrived in Cape Town in March 1877 with a mandate to bring about a closer union of the South African colonies.

In addition to Frere's many accomplishments, he had a significant record in regulating firearms. From 1851 to 1859, he served as commissioner of the recently annexed province of Sind on the northwest frontier of India. Frere organized the administration of the province, built a

[68] Cope, *Ploughshare of War*, 104–5, 113–5, 126–8.

FIGURE 10. Sir Bartle Frere. (From Martineau, *Life and Correspondence of the Right Hon. Sir Bartle Frere*. Image courtesy of the Harvard College Library.)

strong defense force, and implemented a policy of licensing firearms and restricting the arms trade. Frere's strategy appeared to work. During the Indian rebellion of 1857, Sind remained tranquil. In fact, troops from Sind were sent to other provinces to quell the rebellion. At that time, the viceroy promulgated an Arms Act throughout India that instituted licenses for gun owners and placed restrictions on the arms trade, much like Frere's policy in Sind. But in 1860, when the Arms Act came up for renewal, the chief justice, Sir Barnes Peacock, proposed to disarm the entire population. Frere, who had been promoted to the viceroy's council, offered a significant critique: "I do not approve of any general attempt to take away arms from the people, for I believe it will be made everywhere, but especially in the North-West and Punjab, an instrument of frightful oppression, and be quite ineffectual, except to make rebels." Peacock responded by proposing that Europeans, Americans, and Eurasians be exempted. Frere would not countenance such discriminatory legislation, calling it unjust. He persuaded the council to reject Barnes's revisions and to keep the existing restrictions in place.[69] In 1878, well after Frere's departure, the Indian government's new Arms Act did exempt Europeans. It only allowed arms to be possessed by Indians who could demonstrate their loyalty and pay a fee to a magistrate. In practice, magistrates were expected to grant very few licenses. This was the policy of Lord Lytton, who governed India as viceroy from 1876 to 1880. Lytton is remembered today as the most aggressive Conservative viceroy. His views on gun control reflect a surge in British racism and jingoism during the late 1870s, yet his restrictive policies were retained until 1959, twelve years after independence, when some modifications were put in place. Decades later, Indian gun laws remained quite restrictive.

Frere's views of gun control in India varied from his views of gun control in South Africa. Either that, or he had changed his mind since his retirement from service in India. Soon after he arrived at the Cape, he made clear his views. During a visit to the Eastern Cape settlement, King William's Town, he recommended the complete disarmament of the Cape's African population. At this point, the governor was far ahead of even the most vociferous settler politicians, like Sprigg, who did not yet advocate disarmament, just tighter controls.[70] Previously, Froude had

[69] Martineau, *Life of Sir Bartle Frere*, 328–9.
[70] Speech of Saul Solomon, Cape Legislative Assembly, August 25, 1879, *Cape Argus*, August 28, 1879. Speech of J. Gordon Sprigg, August 29, 1879, *Cape Argus*, September 2, 1879.

FIGURE 11. Saul Solomon. (Portrait by W. H. Schröder (1883), reproduction by A. W. Turton (1988). Collection of the Parliament of South Africa. Used by permission.)

been the only person of stature to advocate the complete disarmament of Africans.

When the parliament began its session in late May 1877, two months after Frere's arrival, the report of the Colonial Defence Commission had only just been published. Ordinarily, government documents were published in Cape Town by a press that belonged to Saul Solomon (Figure 11). In addition to owning a press and the *Cape Argus* newspaper, Solomon was also a member of the Cape parliament. Solomon was a dwarf whose talents as an orator earned him the nickname "the Little Giant." He also happened to be one of the colony's most vocal advocates of rights for Africans. Sprigg arranged for the commission's report to be printed by another printer in Grahamstown, so that he might supervise the work himself. Sprigg released the commission's conclusions as a separate document some weeks before parliament met.[71] On June 21, the Cape parliament again discussed the irregularities in Eastern Cape gun regulations. Once again, members cited the liberal approach of the resident magistrates and justices of the peace in eastern districts. One member from the Eastern Cape, Patrick Gould, went so far as to recommend that the Cape follow the lead of the colonial authorities in Ireland, where the government had the power to disarm disloyal subjects.[72]

Gould's position echoed Frere's position that Africans should be disarmed. Sprigg and his allies did not yet share this view, at least not publicly. Instead, Sprigg's efforts to diminish risks from Africans tended in the direction of creating a militia. Sprigg was proposing that residents of frontier districts should be enrolled in a burgher force subject to the governor's command, that residents of other districts should contribute funds to it, and that Africans should be excluded from service. When the Legislative Assembly took up these recommendations, called the Burgher Force Bill, on June 25–27, it was already late in the session. The members of Molteno's coalition hesitated, claiming that they needed time to consult with constituents. They offered an alternative bill, in which all able-bodied men of the entire colony were required to serve.[73]

Some members thought that drilling might needlessly provoke Africans. The attorney general, Simeon Jacobs, argued "that it was a bad policy to parade an armed force before the natives, and hold out to them a menace, as it were." In the words of John X. Merriman, the commissioner of public works, the policy of "civilizing" the natives was working to create a sense of community between Africans and settlers. It would be foolish to alienate Africans who were acquiring property, abandoning "witchcraft," and discarding chiefs. The secretary for native affairs, Charles Brownlee, stated that "the Government wished to discourage, as far as possible, the indiscriminate issue of arms to the natives," but that the Mfengu could be, and were being, trusted to bear arms to defend the

---

[71] *Cape Argus*, July 21, 1877, p. 2.
[72] *Cape Argus*, June 21, 1877, p. 3.
[73] *Cape Argus*, June 28, 1877, suppl.; June 30, 1877, p. 3 and suppl.

colonial border. The ministry proposed that the new bill should be sent to a subcommittee so that it might be debated, revised, and then voted on in the next year's session.[74]

Sprigg was indignant. A burgher force had to drill in order to be effective, "so that the Kafirs themselves may see that the country is prepared to resist an outbreak." Drilling was important because "large numbers of our young men are not accustomed to the use of fire-arms as they were in times past." Skill with weapons had to be improved and then demonstrated, so that Africans might appreciate the risks involved in antagonizing settlers. Sprigg commented that "a body of men properly armed and equipped the Kafirs could see and would respect, and every Kafir servant all over the colony would tell his fellows how the white men were practising rifle-shooting, and a wholesome dread of us would follow."[75] Furthermore, westerners and Africans should not be included in the force. According to Sprigg, it was "a waste of power, and money, and time to muster for drill and discipline the inhabitants in the neighbourhood of Cape Town, because there is no enemy here to contend with. You have not got a swarming population of barbarians who know that their land has been taken away from them."[76] Capetonians were soft, while Africans were barbarians. And he claimed that there was an immediate threat to the frontier, allowing no time for lengthy consideration. Sprigg made a motion in the Legislative Assembly to dismiss the government bill, claiming that a vote against the government would in fact be a vote of no confidence in the ministry. He lost, 32 to 25. Molteno remained in charge.

In describing the debate in the Legislative Assembly, the *Cape Argus*, owned by the liberal member Saul Solomon, commented that the legislature "confirmed the true doctrines of constitutional government" and "reaffirmed the unity of the country." Deciding who might bear arms was a central constitutional issue. It allowed Sprigg and the easterners the opportunity to raise a broad range of questions about "native" policy. Sprigg singled out Brownlee for especially harsh criticism, accusing him of "personal rule" over the chiefs and "endless palavers" with them. According to Sprigg, it was "not befitting the dignity of a member of the Government to argue and wrangle with these barbarians: let that be left to the agent." And contrary to what Merriman had said about the

[74] *Cape Argus*, June 28, 1877, suppl.; June 30, 1877, p. 3 and suppl.
[75] *Cape Argus*, June 28, 1877, suppl.
[76] *Cape Argus*, June 28, 1877, suppl.

progressive "civilization" of the Africans, Sprigg believed that "the mass of the natives do live like wild beasts. . . . They are not like civilized human beings." On the floor of the house, Saul Solomon restated the old principles of Cape liberalism – that a militia should incorporate all loyal citizens, regardless of race.[77] Such principles were easier to enunciate at a time when Africans were unlikely to own guns or desire to participate in the militia duties of citizens. Eastern Cape settlers feared the real prospect of newly prosperous and armed Africans, such as the Mfengu, attempting to fulfill the duties of citizenship by serving in the militia and by voting. Their concerns were shared by many Europeans in the Western Cape, too, although westerners had less reason to fear violent attacks. The historian Vivian Bickford-Smith has written in his study of Victorian Cape Town that "the ideological foundations of Cape liberalism would only be seriously tested when Blacks in considerable numbers came to demand equal treatment according to its principles, and when this endangered White political as well as social supremacy."[78] The spread of guns among Africans posed just such a threat to liberals who allowed – in theory but not in practice – the equality of Africans and Europeans.

The Legislative Assembly voted to send the Burgher Bill to a subcommittee, on which Sprigg was invited to serve. Yet he and his supporters refused to serve, which is where the matter rested when the assembly adjourned in August. Sprigg still succeeded in achieving a number of the goals of the commission. The Legislative Assembly voted to increase the numbers of the Frontier Armed and Mounted Police. Gun-control laws were tightened, too. The governor was given the authority to restrict the distribution of gunpowder and ammunition in any district where it might seem expedient. Justices of the peace were allowed to continue to sign permits for guns within the colonial boundaries, but dealers were required to obtain a permit from the prime minister or the secretary of native affairs in order to sell guns or ammunition across the colonial boundary.[79]

Sprigg's efforts to form an armed militia of white easterners and to regulate the possession of arms by Africans were stymied only for a moment. Over the next few months, an outbreak of fighting on the eastern frontier caused many Cape politicians to reconsider their commitments to

---

[77] *Cape Argus*, June 28, 1877, suppl.; June 30, 1877, p. 3 and suppl. Solomon's opinions were reiterated in editorials in the *Cape Argus* on July 21 and 24, 1877.

[78] Bickford-Smith, *Ethnic Pride and Racial Prejudice*, 27.

[79] Cape Statute No. 15, August 1877.

liberalism. Just as the legislative session was coming to a close in August 1877, a quarrel broke out along the border of the Eastern Cape between some Mfengu and Gcaleka Xhosa. A group of Gcaleka were attending an Mfengu wedding on land formerly possessed by the Gcaleka. A fight broke out between Gcaleka and Mfengu, followed by skirmishing and cattle rustling. The Cape government instructed the colonial police to support the Mfengu. On October 5, the Cape governor, Sir Bartle Frere, demanded that Sarili, the Gcaleka chief, cease hostilities, relinquish his chieftainship, and forfeit his territory. This gave Sarili little choice but to fight.

Frere himself took command of colonial forces and sent police units to support the Mfengu, but they were defeated. Then the hostilities escalated. Frere dispatched regular British troops to the frontier, while some Tembu and Ngqika Xhosa joined the Gcaleka. Most of the rebels were associated with the cattle killers of 1856–7, while those who had not killed cattle remained loyal. On February 7, 1878, combined British and Cape forces defeated the Xhosa in battle at Centane. The Xhosa fighters were mostly armed with weapons acquired during the previous decade. Once again, Xhosa forces failed to use firearms effectively in warfare. At Centane, the Xhosa formed a close formation and attacked British and Cape forces. Four hundred Xhosa men died, as compared to two on the British side. All Ngqika Xhosa, even those who supported the government, were forced to move out of the Ciskei, where their land was sold to settlers. Some Ngqika remained as farmworkers, while others went to Cape Town to work as indentured laborers, or moved to lands reserved for them across the Kei in Gcalekaland. A small Xhosa force withdrew to the Amatolas to fight a guerrilla war, which concluded on July 2, 1878, when Frere offered an amnesty to any remaining fighters.[80]

The Gcaleka War brought the problems of colonial defense to the surface. The Cape prime minister, John C. Molteno, jealously guarded the quasi-independence of the Cape Colony and disputed the right of Gov. Frere to control the colony's police and militia forces. Molteno and Merriman also pushed for the distribution of Ngqika lands among the colonists, a policy that was not endorsed by Frere. Molteno instructed the commander of Cape forces to wage war independently from the British, a decision that Frere considered to be insupportable and insubordinate. On February 2, 1878, Frere dismissed Molteno and Merriman from the

[80] Saunders, *The Annexation of the Transkeian Territories*, 59–72. Switzer, *Power and Resistance*, 74–5.

ministry. This was the prerogative of British governors ruling colonies, even those that had a measure of self-government, yet it was such a slap in the face to colonists that it was hardly ever done. In protest, the rest of the cabinet resigned. Frere responded by appointing Sprigg prime minister and calling a general election. In the general election, Frere's gambit paid off: voters confirmed Sprigg and his coalition in power. Now Sprigg had a freer hand to carry out his proposals for colonial defense. Frere had a Cape prime minister who could be relied on to support confederation and African disarmament.[81]

Just at the moment when the aggressive partners, Sprigg and Frere, were gaining the upper hand in the Cape Colony, support from the Conservative government in London was weakening. Disraeli was considering going to war against Russia in order to maintain Ottoman control of the Dardanelles. The possibility of a conflict in another part of the world inclined him toward moderation in South Africa. Carnarvon advocated British neutrality in Eastern Europe and resigned as secretary of state on January 24, 1878. He was replaced by Sir Michael Hicks Beach, who, like Disraeli, was not inclined toward an aggressive policy in South Africa.[82]

Frere still tried to bring about confederation – by provoking the Zulu into war. Frere remained consistently imperialistic, while Sprigg became even more so. Sprigg continued to pursue the establishment of an all-European defense force, but around the time of his appointment by Frere to the premiership, Sprigg began to advocate the disarmament of Africans, going one step further than the controls recommended by his frontier commission. The first efforts at disarmament were made among the Gcaleka and Ngqika Xhosa, who were required by Frere's proclamation to surrender their weapons. Frere could take such measures in his capacity as high commissioner, because the Transkei had still not been fully incorporated into the Cape Colony. It was also not unusual for a colonial governor to disarm a newly conquered group of people. But as historian Christopher Saunders indicates, it was at this point that Frere and Sprigg decided to make disarmament a cornerstone of the new "native policy."[83] In the session of 1878, it fell to Sprigg to steer disarmament legislation and militia legislation through the Cape parliament.

[81] Saunders, *The Annexation of the Transkeian Territories*, 59–72.
[82] Cope, *Ploughshare of War*, 207–8.
[83] Saunders, *The Annexation of the Transkeian Territories*, 72–3.

Sprigg introduced several bills that created an all-European armed force for the Cape. The bills were quite similar to the Burgher Force Bill of 1877, which had been rejected on the grounds that there was no rush to change the colony's defenses and that the bill should be considered more extensively. Since then the Gcaleka War had started and ended. The Xhosa had been heavily defeated, but colonial legislators had a greater sense of urgency about defense. According to Sprigg's revised plan, the Frontier Armed and Mounted Police were to be supplemented and renamed the Cape Mounted Rifles, a name that reflected their increasing orientation to fighting. A "yeoman force" was created, comprising young reservists who were to train regularly. They were supplemented by a "burgher force" made up of the rest of the colony's able-bodied men. Sprigg also proposed a bill to encourage the formation of volunteer units. All these military units were to be exclusively European. And all this was to be paid for by an excise tax on wine and spirits.

The farmers of the Western Cape disliked the excise tax but they were unable to block the bill. The fighting on the eastern frontier lent added legitimacy to the idea of a reformed militia. The climate made it easier to take cheap shots at westerners. The *Cape Times*, a pro-Sprigg newspaper founded in 1875, editorialized that "there are unfortunately representatives of Western communities whose sole idea of patriotic obligation is to let the inhabitants of the exposed districts fight their own battles."[84] The rest of Sprigg's military proposals sailed through the parliament with very little negative commentary. A few critics questioned the necessity for a yeomanry, or hoped for smaller or larger numbers of troops to be allocated to the different branches of the service, but on the whole Sprigg faced little immediate opposition.

One of the hallmarks of Sprigg's defense bills was that military service was to be restricted to Europeans. On introducing the bill, Sprigg said that "the defence of the colony ought to depend on the European inhabitants alone, for otherwise there was great danger of giving rise to a feeling on the part of the natives that the white men could not do without them. I do not wish for a moment to disparage the coloured inhabitants, but it would be a good day for them when they felt that there was no chance for them against the European race (hear, hear)."[85]

Only one member, Saul Solomon, mentioned that it was problematic to restrict service to Europeans, yet he did so only in jest. During

---

[84] *Cape Times*, May 18, 1878, p. 3.
[85] *Cape Argus*, May 21, 1878, p. 3.

the debate on the Burgher Force Bill, he rebuked John X. Merriman for taunting "others with inconsistency, when he was so extremely and egregiously inconsistent himself (hear, hear). What the Government last year proposed, and what they took their stand upon, was this, that in their Burgher Bill there was to be no distinction of colour." Merriman retorted, "That was last year," to the laughter of the house.[86] The Gcaleka War had changed many minds. Solomon only really had pragmatic concerns about the racial restriction. He mentioned that "it could be shown that during this war [the Gcaleka War] the native forces had rendered good service, and we ought not to appear ungrateful for it." Even the Irish were trusted to police Ireland, and "the Kafirs, bad as they were, were not, according to the hon. member for Wodehouse, worse than the Irish (laughter)."[87] In spite of these reservations, Solomon supported the armed forces bills.

From Liberalism to Utilitarianism

Even among old-school liberal humanitarians like Solomon, there was an increasing willingness to tolerate minor injustices for the sake of orderly governance. The Gcaleka War had certainly been an influence. Another influence is likely to have been the novelist Anthony Trollope, who visited South Africa from July 1877 to January 1878. Before his journey, Trollope made himself familiar with South African politics by reading books, articles, and parliamentary papers, and also by meeting with key imperial politicians. In London, Trollope met with his friend, Lord Carnarvon, and also with Sir Henry Barkly – the retired governor sent Molteno an unenthusiastic letter of introduction.[88] Trollope came away from his London meetings with Carnarvon and Barkly supporting the annexation of the Transvaal, even though, by 1878, the Zulu War had made him skeptical about confederation. In late July Trollope arrived in Cape Town, which he described as a "poor, niggery, yellow-faced, half-bred sort of a place, with an ugly Dutch flavour about it." During his stay, Trollope attended a session of the Legislative Assembly and also socialized with the Cape's leading politicians. He then embarked on a four-month tour that took him to the Eastern Cape, Kimberley, Natal, and the Transvaal. In Pretoria, he stayed at Government House with Shepstone, who lodged

[86] *Cape Argus*, May 21, 1878, p. 3.
[87] *Cape Argus*, May 18, 1878, p. 3.
[88] Trollope, *South Africa*, "Introduction" by J. H. Davidson, pp. 4–5.

him in the room that belonged to his young lieutenant Rider Haggard. Haggard entered his room to find Trollope sleeping in his bed. He later described Trollope as "obstinate as a pig."[89]

In *South Africa*, Trollope espoused some views that were conventionally liberal. He supported voting rights for black and white alike, arguing that the franchise should be based on education. He also formed a positive impression of the Zulu, thanks in part to the efforts of the Colensos, whom he met in Pietermaritzburg. Even so, he reported unfavorably on a delegation of Xhosa chiefs that came to see him. Trollope's views on Africans were not simple. His best-known argument about South Africa echoed the utilitarians: small injustices, such as the coercion of Africans, had to be tolerated in the interest of the greater good, which was the spread of civilization. While reflecting on the Langalibalele case, Trollope wrote that

The white man who has to rule natives soon teaches himself that he can do no good if he is overscrupulous. They must be taught to think him powerful or they will not obey him in anything. He soon feels that his authority, and with his authority the security of all those around him, is a matter of "prestige." Prestige in a highly civilized community may be created by virtue, – and is often created by virtue and rank combined. The Archbishop of Canterbury is a very great man to an ordinary clergyman. But, with the native races of South Africa, prestige has to be created by power though it may no doubt be supported and confirmed by justice. Thus the white ruler of the black man knows that he must sometimes be rough. There must be a sharp word, possibly a blow. . . . The Savage, till he has quite ceased to be a savage, expects to be coerced, and will no more go straight along the road without coercion, than will the horse if you ride him without reins. And with a horse a whip and spur are necessary, – till he has become altogether tamed.[90]

Trollope believed that indigenous people were bestial savages who might be led to improve themselves eventually. Their second-class status justified their rough treatment, which was necessary if regrettable. He went on by saying,

The white ruler of the black man . . . knows that without some spur or whip he cannot do his work at all. His is a service, probably, of much danger, and he has to work with a frown on his brow in order that his life may be fairly safe in his hand. In this way he is driven to the daily practice of little deeds of tyranny which abstract justice would condemn. . . . I am inclined to think

---

[89] A. Trollope to H. M. Trollope, July 23, 1877, in *Letters of Anthony Trollope*, 664–5. Glendinning, *Anthony Trollope*, 454–7. Hennessy, *Anthony Trollope*, 353–5.
[90] Trollope, *South Africa*, 1:238–9.

that the philanthropist at home when he rises in his wrath against some white ruler of whose harshness to the blacks he has heard the story forgets that the very civilization which he is anxious to carry among the savage races cannot be promulgated without something of tyranny, – some touch of apparent injustice.[91]

Trollope thus reflected on the Langalibalele case, and on "native administration" more generally, even after meeting with Colenso in Pietermaritzburg and with Langalibalele at Uitvlugt. Trollope was famous for disliking philanthropists, whom he regarded as hypocrites.[92] In South Africa and in Great Britain, this kind of thinking was beginning to gain ground, thanks in part to Trollope's influence – his book was widely read in both countries.[93]

With many liberals becoming inclined to tolerate apparent injustices, Sprigg's plan to disarm the Cape's Africans sailed through the parliament. The act, called the Peace Preservation Act, allowed the governor to proclaim that in certain districts all weapons had to be surrendered to a magistrate. The magistrate would then decide who might be allowed to continue keeping the weapons and who might not. Those who lost their weapons would be compensated. According to Sprigg, this measure was necessary "for getting arms out of the hands of disloyal natives. . . . It was the intention of the Government to disarm the Fingoes as well as the Kafirs, for this was absolutely necessary for the security of the black population themselves." Saul Solomon supported the measure, even though he "objected to regarding in a wholesale way all the coloured classes as disloyal." Later, he claimed that he believed the act would only be applied to disturbed districts in times of unrest.[94]

Solomon's qualified support represented a major switch for South Africa's most famous liberal, who was congratulated by the openly bigoted *Cape Times* for changing from "the aboriginal's friend" and adopting a stance that was critical "of the uncouth and nasty persons who exhibit the properties of the missing link in remote parts of the South African colonies."[95] The only member to object strenuously to the bill was Charles Fairbridge, a Cape Town attorney who was a well-known benefactor of the South African Library and the South African Museum. Fairbridge stated that "the Bill was very little better than a sham and

[91] Trollope, *South Africa*, 1:239.
[92] Hall, *Trollope*, 426–7.
[93] Dubow, *Commonwealth of Knowledge*, 131–4.
[94] BPP [C.2755] 1881, Appendix, "Debate in the House of Assembly," p. 320.
[95] *Cape Times*, August 8, 1879, p. 3.

a delusion . . . for years past we had allowed the sale of arms to go on unchecked, and now, in the midst of a war, when we had so many loyal allies among the coloured classes, it was proposed to deprive all the natives of their arms." He thought that "such a policy would be attended with a great deal of difficulty, and most probably danger, also."[96]

The Peace Preservation Act was written by the new attorney general Thomas Upington, who was Irish by birth. Upington stated, in a speech to the House of Assembly on May 15, that the act itself was based on the numerous "coercive acts," "arms acts," and "peace preservation acts" that Britain had imposed on Ireland during the nineteenth century. The first Peace Preservation Act of 1814 empowered the governor of Ireland, known as the Lord Lieutenant, to proclaim a district to be in a state of disorder and to dispatch magistrates and police there to govern it. Subsequent "coercive acts" passed on an almost annual basis restricted the possession of arms by the Irish in various ways. A similar act, the Seizure of Arms Act, had been passed in England in 1819 in the wake of the Peterloo Massacre. The act empowered justices of the peace to confiscate weapons in disturbed districts. Many thought the act to be contrary to the spirit of English laws, in particular the Bill of Rights of 1689, which guaranteed Protestants a right to bear arms. The Seizure of Arms Act was allowed to lapse in 1821.[97]

Some members of the Legislative Assembly questioned the practicalities of peace preservation acts. After all, the repeated application of repressive acts in Ireland implied that they did not work. Merriman, now in the opposition, quipped that "in spite of such repressive legislation, when an Irishman wanted to commit an agrarian outrage he had no difficulty in getting hold of a rusty blunderbuss." Merriman had doubts about the practicality of disarming large numbers of people, but he actually hoped for a more repressive piece of legislation that singled out the Mfengu for disarmament and increased the size and powers of the police.[98]

In passing the Peace Preservation Act, and in creating a new structure for the armed forces, the Cape parliament had passed a new type of discriminatory legislation. Discriminatory legislation had been prohibited by Ordinance 50 of 1828, which required all legislation to avoid racial distinctions, but Ordinance 50 had been modified in 1841 by the Masters and Servants Ordinance, which did not contain direct racial references but

[96] *Cape Argus*, May 21, 1878, p. 3.
[97] Malcolm, *Guns and Violence*, 96. Squires, *Gun Culture or Gun Control*, 26–7.
[98] *Cape Argus*, May 18, 1878, p. 3.

permitted ex-slave laborers who broke contracts to be punished harshly. Everybody recognized that the ordinance was aimed specifically at ex-slaves, none of whom were white. In 1878, when Upington, the attorney general, introduced the Peace Preservation Bill, he followed the example of the authors of the Masters and Servants Ordinance. Upington commented that "the only possible objection to the Bill that I think is likely to be raised, namely, that its provisions should be applicable to coloured persons only, I can only answer that, as a cardinal principle of legislation, anything approaching to distinctions of race, creed, or colour, ought to be avoided."[99] Yet everyone knew that these measures were to be applied to Africans alone. As one Wesleyan missionary wrote to the *Grahamstown Journal*, "Ashamed to acknowledge the principal of class legislation, our Government brings in a Bill, by the provisions of which no man is to have right (the natural right I call it) of carrying arms, only as the magistrate of other Government officer of his district may grant him special permission – but this with the tacit understanding that no black man shall have it granted!" According to the author, Africans thus deprived of their guns would resent being made a "nation of women." European citizens ought to worry lest these laws eventually be extended to them, too.[100] In this way, the practice of enacting discriminatory legislation under the cover of nondiscriminatory language, first used in the Masters and Servants Ordinance of 1841, was extended from the regulation of laborers to the regulation of firearms.

The government moved quickly to take weapons from Africans in the Eastern Cape. Even before the Peace Preservation Act became law, on August 2, 1878, the Cape initiated disarmament in the Transkei and Tembuland and among defeated Xhosa warriors. The governor, Frere, did not actually proclaim the eastern frontier districts of the Cape Colony to be subject to the act until April 21, 1879.

In some districts, disarmament provoked disgruntlement. William Cumming, a magistrate in Tembuland, reported that disarmament inspired the chiefs to circulate "preposterous rumours." Many Tembu now believed that after disarmament, "the Government intended to allow them to keep only a limited number of cattle; that their country was to be taken from them; that their wives and children were to be seized and conveyed to the Western Province and be there enslaved." Disarmament would lead to the collapse of their entire society. Cumming

[99] *Cape Argus*, May 18, 1878, p. 3.
[100] Reprinted in *Cape Argus*, June 11, 1878, suppl.

was not surprised that many Tembu believed these rumors. According to him, "From time immemorial, arms have been regarded as the insignia of manhood; and to part with, or be deprived of them, is, in the eyes of a native, an indelible disgrace." Tembu people asked, too, "what offence have we committed against Government that this should be done to us?" Disarmament hardly repaid their loyalty. How, then, did Cumming persuade them all to surrender their arms peacefully? He suggested to them "that Government had no sinister object in view in carrying out this measure, and that it was being done solely for their own good." We are left to wonder how he persuaded them and why they listened.[101]

We know very little about the Xhosa and Mfengu reaction to disarmament. We do know that many Xhosa and Mfengu protested, in spite of the fact that the *Blue Book on Native Affairs for 1878* reported that "disarmament has been carried out in the Transkei with the most satisfactory results; the arms were handed in by the natives in the most ready and praiseworthy manner."[102] The *Blue Book* also reported that the Mfengu handed over their guns and assegais peacefully, to be "registered," "ticketed," and "kept in serviceable order." Only one Mfengu evaded the law, "and he now no doubt wishes that he had not tried to do it."[103]

This rosy view was not supported by the *Cape Argus*, which pointed out that the *Blue Book on Native Affairs for 1878*, released in July 1879, contained obvious silences on the subject of disarmament. The newspaper pointed to one such omission by Major Elliott, the chief magistrate of Tembuland, and by his subordinate, J. W. Morris, the acting magistrate for Engcobo. According to the *Blue Book*, the chief Stokwe Tyali and his Vundhla followers rebelled against the government. They were defeated and dispersed.[104] By contrast, the *Cape Argus* reported that "Stockwe Inhlehla" "deliberately shot at the magistrate who demanded his arms." This resulted in "a great show of compulsion . . . but it all ended in smoke, for the Government desisted, and Stockwe Inhlehla and his people, and

[101] CPP [G.33] 1879, W. G. Cumming, "Xalanga District," *Blue Book on Native Affairs for 1878*, pp. 91–2.

[102] CPP [G.33] 1879, M. Blyth, "Report on the Social and Political Condition of the Transkei for the Year 1878," *Blue Book on Native Affairs for 1878*, p. 96.

[103] CPP [G.33] 1879, F. P. Gladwin, "Nqamakwe District," *Blue Book on Native Affairs for 1878*, p. 98.

[104] CPP [G.33] 1879, *Blue Book on Native Affairs for 1878*, p. 86.

all the surrounding tribes who were not minded to surrender, remain in possession of their guns to this day."[105]

The dissatisfaction of the Mfengu and Xhosa was raised several times during the 1879 session of parliament. On July 1, Andries Stockenstrom, Jr., the member for the Eastern Cape district of Albert, mentioned that there was "great dissatisfaction" on the part of Africans in the vicinity of Queenstown, which he attributed to "the way in which guns had been taken away from loyal natives."[106] From Queenstown, two separate memorials made their way to the government in Cape Town. One was signed by "Frederick Tabata (and twenty-one others)," the other by Petrus Mohongo, representing his own views and "the men under his supervision." Both memorialists claimed that they and their followers had bought weapons either to defend themselves from the Xhosa or to fight for the government. They received permits and bought guns, but when the war ended they were disarmed and had yet to receive compensation. Both memorials asked that the guns be restored to their owners. Both memorialists reiterated their loyalty to the queen. And from nearby Kamastone and Oxkraal, a petition came from "Joshua (And 441 others)," who protested that they were being disarmed in spite of being loyal. Joshua wrote that "our pride and joy has been that we were honoured and trusted by the queen's government, and anything that takes away our self-respect is likely to lead, sooner or later, to our ruin." Tellingly, Joshua noted that "up to the present time we have been most happy to see that there was one law for black and white, and that, as God is no respecter of persons, so the Lord's servants who governed us were just all alike."[107]

Joshua was correct when he observed that disarmament implied a broader change in government thinking about race and citizenship. Another African man from the Eastern Cape, "Tengo-Jilly," wrote to the *Cape Argus* that "restlessness" as well as "distrust and uncertainty" were resulting from the new Cape government's policies. He blamed mistaken policies on Sprigg and the new secretary for native affairs, William Ayliff: "Messrs. Ayliff and Sprigg, who evidently know nothing of natives except from hearsay; or if they know anything, they have certainly missed the method of dealing with them." He was particularly incensed by

[105] *Cape Argus*, July 22, 1879, p. 2.
[106] *Cape Argus*, July 3, 1879.
[107] *Cape Argus*, August 9, 1879, p. 3.

government insistence that Africans were acquiescing in disarmament. He wrote, "Many natives have expressed themselves in English, through the press or by petitions against disarmament; but in the face of all these remonstrances it appears that the Government still clings to the false and nonsensical assertions of its officials to the effect that the guns were voluntarily surrendered, and consequently no notice has been taken of all these remonstrances."[108]

Other Africans questioned the wisdom of disarmament. One chief, Siwani, and forty of his men wrote to their magistrate, pleading their loyalty and asking, "Will it become a good thing to take away from us our arms? The enemy is yet in the bush. It is not yet subdued; that we know very well, and these people in the bush hate us with a deep hatred, for we fought against them." Indeed, Siwani and his men claimed to have been "good servants of the government" and wondered how they had "sinned against our father, the Government."[109] They were using the rhetoric of paternalism to support their case. Mission-educated Africans protested too. Their newspaper, *The Christian Express*, opined that disarmament had done "more to create anger, disaffection, and a sense of injustice among the natives than any single thing of the kind has ever done.[110]

Since the Gcaleka War of 1877–8, Cape liberals had gone along with Sprigg on much of the legislation that pertained to Africans. Now some Cape liberals had second thoughts. Throughout the 1879 session of parliament, Saul Solomon and his allies fought a rearguard action against disarmament as part of a broader attack on Sprigg's "native policies." On June 26, 1879, during the course of a discussion about possible ammunition restrictions, Sprigg mentioned that in the Eastern Cape disarmament had proceeded peacefully. He argued that a "considerable number of arms had come in, and the measure had created no disturbance." Solomon retorted that African people were dissatisfied with disarmament. Solomon even claimed that when he had voted for the Peace Preservation Bill, he had not been "giving the Government power" to initiate "an indiscriminate process of disarmament . . . of friends and foes. . . ." Instead, Solomon had thought that the Peace Preservation Act was only to be directed against rebels in "disturbed" districts. Sprigg pointed out correctly

---

[108] *Cape Argus*, August 12, 1879, p. 3.
[109] *Cape Argus*, August 30, 1879, p. 3.
[110] As quoted by Switzer, *Power and Resistance*, 138.

that Solomon must have known that the law would be applied to all Mfengu and Xhosa. He had said as much during the course of debate.[111] *The Cape Times* took Solomon at his word, but speculated that the "little giant" had supported the act only because he assumed that it would prove ineffectual. Solomon had been wrong. *The Cape Times* took pleasure, once again, in explaining why universal African disarmament was necessary: "The frontier black man is essentially a savage. Whether Fingo or Kafir, Christian or heathen, he is a savage none the less. . . . And such being the case, it would be an odd philanthropy whereby one large section of barbarism were left in possession of the instruments of destruction, while another large section of barbarism, having a blood feud with the former, were deprived of every gun and assegai, and left naked to the fury of their enemies."[112] Not to be deterred, Solomon's newspaper, the *Cape Argus*, editorialized that "apart from the proceedings in Parliament, the Government must have already learned that their vaunted policy of depriving every coloured man in South Africa of his arms, irrespective of every consideration save that of colour, is little better than a madman's dream."[113]

It may have been a madman's dream to disarm Africans in the Eastern Cape, but it worked, even though many Mfengu and Xhosa expressed their dissatisfaction. It is hard to explain why a rebellion did not happen, although it might be inferred that the Gcaleka War was too devastating for any Ngqika or Gcaleka Xhosa to contemplate another fight with the Cape Colony. It might also be inferred that so many Mfengu had such extensive ties to the Cape, and such a vested interest in producing for the colonial market, that it would have been foolish for them to risk a war over disarmament. As Saul Solomon's *Cape Argus* put it, "The man who retained his arms was to incur the suspicion of hostile intent towards the white man, and rather than incur that suspicion, upon which loss of land and cattle was at that time wont to follow without much delay, it is not difficult to imagine that loyal and disloyal alike would throw down their arms as though they were red-hot."[114]

Solomon was right about some sectors of white opinion, judging by the words of Thomas Upington, the attorney general who had authored the

---

[111] *Cape Argus*, June 28, 1879. See also similar statements made by Sprigg on August 7, 1879, reported in the *Cape Argus*, August 9, 1879, suppl., as well as the long speech by Solomon on August 25, 1879, reported in the *Cape Argus*, August 28, 1879, p. 3.

[112] *Cape Times*, August 28, 1879, p. 3.

[113] *Cape Argus*, September 2, 1879, p. 2.

[114] *Cape Argus*, August 9, 1879, p. 2.

Peace Preservation Act. In late August, during the course of a parliamentary debate he blurted out that "natives" ought to be disarmed because they were the "natural enemies" of the colony. While some members of parliament expressed outrage at Upington's statement, clearly many supported him. The *Cape Times* explained that "to the white man the black man is naturally a foe. This may be a mistaken impression of the Attorney-General; but it is nevertheless consistent with enlightened policy, and with genuine philanthropy. In dealing with the black man we should not account of him as one who does not love our race and who, being a barbarian, is subject to dangerous impulses." Xhosa and Mfengu did well to mark Upington's words. As the *Cape Times* said, "The Attorney-General said what we all think, even probably Mr. Saul Solomon himself."[115] If they kept their arms, they were certain to be suspected of disloyalty by many Cape Europeans.

In this way, it was in the interest of the Mfengu and Xhosa to comply with disarmament. Sprigg had his own explanation for their compliance. When the debate over disarmament erupted again in late August 1879, Sprigg claimed that the Peace Preservation Act had been implemented very carefully and the government had explained the law thoroughly. According to Sprigg, Africans had responded by groveling that "we are children, and the government is our father; what is the word of the government?" The word of the government, in this case, was "that we intended, according to law, to disarm them for their own good." There was no "disgrace and discredit," simply an order that African "children" would have to obey. It was certainly for their own good, because "so long as you allow these people to possess arms, you encourage a warlike spirit." Africans were "much more likely to yield [to the warlike spirit] if they have offensive weapons in their hands." Guns actually had an effect on African consciousness. Thankfully for Sprigg, "There are at this moment large numbers of natives, Fingoes and others upon the frontier who are what are commonly called loyal; that is, they are well content to sit quietly under Her Majesty's Government." Even so, loyalty was not a consideration when disarming Africans. It "was for the good of the people themselves that their arms should be taken away; and that is the principle alone on which the Government have proceeded as regards what are commonly called loyal natives." He claimed that most Africans were loyal and were happy to be disarmed, because then "they had no

---

[115] Speech by Saul Solomon, August 29, 1879, *Cape Argus*, September 2, 1879, suppl. See also p. 3. Editorial in *Cape Times*, September 2, 1879, p. 3.

power of resistance, and could not fight the Government." Any resistance he blamed on the instigation of missionaries, traders, and liberals.[116]

To Sprigg loyalty was not the crux of disarmament. Instead, disarmament was to become a theater of paternalism, with government playing its proper fatherly role and Africans playing their proper childlike role. All Africans should be disarmed as quickly as practicable, because it was good for them. Sprigg's dream was to disarm all Africans. Solomon hoped to disarm only disloyal Africans. Solomon lost and Sprigg won in the Eastern Cape, where Xhosa and Mfengu protested but handed in their guns. Between August 1878 and March 1880, the Cape collected 10,860 guns and 15,764 assegais.[117] Gun control in the Eastern Cape appeared to be successful. By contrast, when the Cape attempted to implement disarmament uniformly and tried to disarm the Sotho, the Sotho did not hand in their guns. At first they tried to use the rhetoric of paternalism to negotiate with Cape officials. When that failed, they fought a war against the Cape, defeated Cape forces, and secured direct administration from England.

[116] Speech by J. Gordon Sprigg, August 29, 1879, *Cape Argus*, September 2, 1879, suppl.
[117] BPP [C.2569] 1880, Encl. 4, "Arms Returns," in No. 13, Frere to Hicks Beach, March 15, 1880, pp. 24–6.

9

Guns, Empire, and Political Culture in Basutoland, 1867–78

After disarming the Xhosa and the Mfengu, the Cape government took the next step and attempted to disarm the Sotho. The Sotho chiefs resisted the Peace Preservation Act more strenuously than did the Xhosa and Mfengu leaders. The Sotho chiefs' resistance was made easier by the mountainous, easily defended terrain of Basutoland. Sotho resistance was also helped by the 1879 Zulu defeat of the British army at Isandlwana, which made the British public wary of imperialist adventures in South Africa. The Sotho chiefs who resisted gun control also received support from liberals in the Cape Colony and in Britain who believed in the "civilizing mission" of colonialism. Liberal humanitarian activists helped the Sotho resist the imposition of gun-control laws, even though those laws were designed, in part, to diminish the level of violence in African societies.

The intercolonial regulation of guns became a topic of discussion in 1873, in the final months of Gladstone's government. It continued to be discussed throughout Benjamin Disraeli's government (1874–80) and into Gladstone's next government (1880–5). Two distinct networks formed to support or oppose discriminatory gun control. Proponents included Conservative politicians in Britain, who were becoming more nationalist and more racist, along with settler politicians from the Eastern Cape Colony, who wanted to make Africans into easily exploited subjects. Conservatives and settlers were opposed by old-school liberal humanitarians in Britain and South Africa, whose ranks included merchants and free traders as well as missionaries. In debating the relationship between gun control and citizenship, each group continually evaluated the risks of guns in order to strengthen appeals to the public in Britain and South

Africa. In South Africa, each group tried to trump the other by appealing to politicians and advocates in Britain.

Basutoland and the Cape Colony

In the decades before the imposition of Cape rule, Sotho men and their neighbors on the High Veld armed themselves heavily. The 1840s, the 1850s, and the 1860s were not only years of conflict between Africans, Boers, and Britons, in which people sought to increase their security through gun purchases. Those years also witnessed the initial migration of labor from the High Veld into the Cape Colony. Laborers returned home with guns and ammunition, which were trading briskly in these uncertain times. Historian Peter Delius has shown that in these years, men who were identified as Pedi, Sotho, Tsonga, and Ndebele migrated to engage in farmwork and railway construction, especially in the Eastern Cape. Basutoland became an important staging area for migrants. It even appears that Moshoeshoe and the Pedi chief, Sekhukhune, had formed an alliance for the purposes of shepherding labor through to the Cape safely. There was a strong demand for guns because of the region's insecurity and also because of opportunities for hunting in the north.[1] And yet even with these opportunities, Sotho chiefs did not require entire units of men to migrate and purchase guns for the purpose of forming armed regiments, as has sometimes been thought. The available evidence suggests that migration and also purchases of arms were largely individual decisions reached by Sotho men and that these men tended to support the chiefs. The chiefs generally ruled by consent of their subjects, unlike in later years, when their authority became more despotic.[2]

In March 1868, the Sotho paramount chief, Moshoeshoe, saved Basutoland from being taken over by the Orange Free State, by persuading the Cape governor, Sir Philip Wodehouse, to proclaim that "the Basuto shall be...British Subjects; and the Territory of the said Tribe shall be...British territory."[3] This proclamation left much to be clarified, including the nature of Basutoland's government. Moshoeshoe and his successors interpreted the proclamation to mean that Basutoland was

---

[1] Delius, "Migrant Labour and the Pedi, 1840–80," in *Economy and Society in Pre-Industrial South Africa*, 296–7, 306–7.

[2] Eldredge, *A South African Kingdom*, 169–71.

[3] Proclamation No. 14, March 12, 1868. As cited by Machobane, *Government and Change in Lesotho*, 42.

a British protectorate. As Moshoeshoe's successor, Letsie, put it, "We were told that the Government leaves a man to govern his country, with his sheep, his cattle, and his gun."[4] This view was supported by the Sotho chiefs' key European advisors, the French Protestant missionaries, and it appears to have been the understanding of Wodehouse himself. In this view, the British were allies who guaranteed the peace, while the chiefs would rule the country as they had done before.[5]

The Cape governor, Wodehouse, in his role as high commissioner, put in place a system of government that resembled, in its broadest outline, the system of "indirect rule" through chiefs that Shepstone was developing in neighboring Natal. Wodehouse divided Basutoland into three districts; a fourth was added in 1871. Each district was to be ruled by a senior chief who consulted with a resident British magistrate. The magistrate convened a court of appeals and supervised land sales and distributions. A senior magistrate, called the High Commissioner's Agent (or, less formally, the "governor's agent"), consulted with the paramount chief. Under the paramount chief and the senior chiefs, the Sotho were allowed to rule themselves, more or less, from 1868 to 1871, a period marked by the death of Moshoeshoe and the succession of Letsie.

In 1871, the new Cape governor and high commissioner, Sir Henry Barkly, modified the system. He reasoned that the Cape should be allowed to administer Basutoland, since the Cape was responsible for paying the costs of policing the vicinity. For the Sotho, this was an ominous development. The Cape was about to achieve "responsible government," or a greater degree of independence from Britain, which meant that settlers would have greater influence over the fate of Basutoland. It appears that at first, in spite of a meeting between Barkly and Letsie, the chiefs did not apprehend the significance of the change in government to the quasi-independent Cape Colony. In fact, later on, the French missionaries stationed in Basutoland made the claim that the Sotho received no formal notification. Their contention was confirmed by the Colonial Office in December 1880.[6] Even so, soon after annexation occurred in 1872, the

---

[4] CPP [G.26] 1882, *Report of the Honourable the Secretary for Native Affairs on His Visit to Basutoland in June, 1881*, p. 25. "Report of Proceedings of Meeting in School Room of the Morija Mission Station on the 23rd June, 1881." Letsie's speech as cited by Machobane, *Government and Change in Lesotho*, 43.

[5] Machobane, *Government and Change in Lesotho*, 41–3.

[6] BPP [C.2821] 1881, Mabille to Frere, March 24, 1880, Encl. 7 in No. 1, p. 12; Frere to Mabille, May 11, 1880, Encl. 8 in No. 1, p. 13. BPP [C.2754] 1881, Kimberley to Robinson, December 30, 1880, p. 6, para. 17.

chiefs took the advice of their European friends and petitioned for Sotho representation in the Cape parliament. The colonial secretary, Richard Southey, responded that representation in the parliament would require the Sotho to adopt all Cape laws. This argument from political principle scared the chiefs, who were wary of losing clients and wealth. They retracted their petition.[7]

The Sotho chiefs were put in a difficult position by administrators from the Cape. Since Sir George Grey's governorship in the 1850s, it had been the Cape's policy to undermine the traditional authority of African chiefs and to transform rural South Africa in the direction of a market economy. When the next governor, Sir Philip Wodehouse, negotiated the terms of British annexation with Moshoeshoe, the authority of the Sotho chiefs was not directly challenged. Yet soon after the annexation in 1868, Wodehouse used Cape forces to guard the boundaries of Basutoland, to regulate trade, and to resettle migrants. Shortly after Moshoeshoe's death in 1870, the governor put in place rule by magistrates. A hut tax was instituted to pay the costs of administration, including a "salary" to Letsie, the new paramount chief, and salaries to the other major Sotho chiefs too. Women could no longer be forced to marry against their will, boys could refuse to be circumcised, and Christian marriage received equal status to "pagan" marriage. All marriages had to be registered with resident magistrates, who were empowered to make numerous interventions in Sotho family law. Witchcraft was no longer considered a crime and the killing of witches was prohibited. Widows could take custody of their children and infanticide was prohibited. Chiefs who resisted these changes could be tried and imprisoned. Chiefs could even be sued by commoners.

The introduction of these and other legal concepts to the Sotho produced some annoyance among senior chiefs like Molapo and Masopha, the brothers of Letsie. Yet they needed British and Cape protection against the Orange Free State. Ties became even closer with the British and the Cape. In August 1871, with the permission of the new governor, Sir Henry Barkly, Basutoland was formally annexed by the Cape parliament. The Annexation Act stipulated that Cape laws would not extend to Basutoland, except in cases when laws were passed that made specific mention of the territory. While the Sotho were British subjects, they were not considered civilized enough to live under most Cape laws. The governor had the authority to make and repeal new laws in Basutoland.

---

[7] Machobane, *Government and Change in Lesotho*, 47–9.

The governor's new chief magistrate, Charles Duncan Griffith, set about administering the new mountain colony.[8] Griffith was a settler from the Eastern Cape who had led troops in the wars of 1846–7 and 1851–3. Afterward, he served as magistrate in several key Eastern Cape districts. In 1871, he became the governor's agent, or chief magistrate, attached to Letsie, the paramount Sotho chief. The advent of "responsible government" at the Cape made it possible for Griffith to bring the Sotho closer to "civilization."

The administration of Basutoland was created in late 1872, when the Cape Colony achieved responsible government. The Cape cabinet now had a secretary for native affairs, Charles Pacalt Brownlee, whose experience on the eastern frontier and knowledge of the Xhosa and Zulu languages made it possible for him to enjoy considerable latitude in his dealings with African leaders from the Eastern Cape. Yet he did not speak the Sotho language or have much direct experience of the northern frontier. For this reason, after 1874 he delegated much of the responsibility for Basutoland to his clerk, H. E. R. Bright. From 1871 to 1874, Bright had served as clerk to the governor's agent in Basutoland, where he befriended many people, African and European. Friendly relations were also the hallmark of administration under Griffith, who had a reputation for evenhandedness and appears to have earned the respect of chiefs, missionaries, and traders alike. While he sympathized with the mission's goal of changing Sotho customs, he respected the hesitancy of many Sotho. Griffith's evenhandedness is explained by Burman, who argues that the magistrates agreed with missionary goals, although they hoped that changes would unfold on a more gradual timetable.[9]

Sotho political culture was in a state of flux during the 1860s and 1870s, just like the rest of South Africa. Rulers were struggling to adapt to the emerging capitalist economy, which was causing the region's colonies, republics, and chiefdoms to become ever more closely intertwined, whether they liked it or not. At the same time, the exercise of power was being transformed by new ideologies and new technologies. As the *Cape Times* explained some years later, "whatever ministry is in power, the Basutos will be regarded as legitimate plunder until they are properly represented in Parliament. . . . But so long as the revenues of Basutoland are available for appropriation, the Basutos will have no

---

[8] Bradlow, "Cape Government's Rule," 124–5. Burman, *Chiefdom Politics and Alien Law*, 35–48.
[9] Burman, *Chiefdom Politics and Alien Law*, 49–60.

voice in the counsels of the nation.... Some day when the Basutoland balance appears on the wrong side of the national ledger, the territory will be invited to appear by proxy in order to advise in its more complete taxation."[10] Taxation without representation was not a sure foundation for relations between the Cape and the Sotho.

The advent of Cape administration raised significant issues in chiefly politics. Chiefs needed to decide how "loyal" they would be to the Cape administration and how they would express their loyalty. They developed new ideologies of chiefly rule, as did other South African chiefs who were coming under magisterial rule. William Beinart and Colin Bundy argue in *Hidden Struggles in Rural South Africa* that new loyalist ideologies "stressed the benevolence of the Queen" because she guaranteed the individual rights of her subjects against the predations of opportunistic settlers. The chiefs used the language of individual rights to uphold their own customary prerogatives over the community. And while abstract rights formed the basis of their claims, as Beinart and Bundy write, "loyalism emerged in attachment to particular officials, and was reflected in the elaborate language and codes of those purveying and receiving a benevolent, though firm paternalism."[11] By the 1870s, many Sotho had already adopted western dress and material goods, such as guns, bought with the money they earned as commercial farmers. Many Sotho men had also migrated to dig on the Kimberley diamond fields. When the Sotho adapted to capitalism and western ways, they also began to graft related western ideas, such as rights to private property, onto older political ideas about the authority of chiefs. When the Cape attempted to disarm the Sotho, few of the Sotho chiefs handed in their guns.

Why did the Sotho resist the Peace Preservation Act so strenuously, while others reluctantly acquiesced in it? By the 1870s, gun ownership had become deeply embedded in the newly emerging political culture of the Sotho. For Sotho men and for Sotho leaders, guns had become linked to the authority of chiefs. Ironically, chiefly authority was increasingly bound up with ideas about sovereignty, a sovereignty that derived partly from male dominance and partly from the support of the queen of England. And sovereigns, in theory, granted rights to Sotho subjects, including a right to earn and hold property. Disarmament, and especially disarmament that originated in the Cape, was not persuasive. Resistance

---

[10] *Cape Times*, September 8, 1879, p. 3.
[11] Beinart and Bundy, *Hidden Struggles in Rural South Africa*, 10. See also Thompson, "Languages of Loyalty," 635.

to the Peace Preservation Act underwrote the founding of a new form of government among the Sotho. In this way, resistance to one regime's policies with regard to technology helped produce another regime entirely. Movements that resist a new technological regime can be involved in coproducing their own new political order. This was the case in Basutoland in the late 1870s, just as it was the case in colonial Mauritius, where anticolonial nationalism coalesced as a mass movement during the 1937 riots against the introduction of a new sugar-cane variety.[12]

The ironies of Sotho resistance are manifold. The Sotho chiefs who resisted gun control received support from liberals in the Cape Colony and in Britain who believed in the "civilizing mission" of colonialism. Liberal activists helped the Sotho resist the imposition of gun-control laws, even though those laws were designed, in part, to diminish the level of violence in African societies. Liberal activists, most notably a group of French Protestant missionaries who lived among the Sotho, made crucial interventions in the dispute between the Sotho and the Cape. Their ability to circumvent the Cape government and appeal to London greatly contributed to the strength of Sotho resistance.

There are already several good accounts of Sotho relations with the Cape and the British, written by Edna Bradlow, Sandra Burman, Elizabeth Eldredge, and L. B. B. J. Machobane. Yet no historian has thoroughly explored the significance of gun ownership for Sotho political culture. Was it simply a coincidence that disputes over gun control prompted a war for independence? It is entirely possible that other legal impositions would have led to revolt, too, but it is difficult to say if some other issue would have been as significant to the Sotho as that of gun control. What we do know is this: Cape efforts at gun control did prompt a war of anticolonial resistance. For this reason it is important to examine the role of gun ownership in the creation of a new Sotho political culture and in the creation of a new, separate colony, Basutoland.

Sotho Loyalty and the New Push for Disarmament

During Griffith's first few years in Basutoland, he expressed serious concern about the arming of Sotho men at the Kimberley diamond mines and also at Cradock in the Eastern Cape. In 1873, when there was widespread official concern about the arming of African migrant workers, he wrote to the prime minister that "nothing, in my opinion, could be more

---

[12] Storey, *Science and Power in Colonial Mauritius*, 141–53.

subversive to all our efforts at civilizing these people and promoting among them habits of peace and order." He expressed his "great regret" at the "open traffic in firearms which has lately sprung up at the diamond fields." The guns were "of inferior construction and imperfect finish," yet "produced upon the natives" an "underlying moral effect." The "natives" were "essentially warlike and turbulent by disposition and character" and "as soon as they are well supplied with firearms, they invariably, as all past experience shows, become restless and agitated.... The desire for a struggle, whether against each other or against the white man becomes irresistible to them. Councils of peace and labors of years in the direction of industry, order and civilization are soon thrown to the winds, and the missionary, the magistrate and other friends of native progress and improvement have liked to lament the pulling down in a few months of all that it has cost so much energy and effort to build upon in the past."[13]

Griffith was introducing a key regulatory argument: that the possession of guns changed the thinking of African people about themselves and their place in society. The very consciousness of African people was being changed by firearms possession, which caused regression back to a savage state of being. This was the opposite of civilization, the goal of "missionaries, magistrates, and other friends of native progress." As Jean and John Comaroff have argued in *Revelation and Revolution*, overt efforts at "civilization" had a way of being rejected. Subtle colonialism, through the introduction of new material goods, could produce shifts in consciousness more effectively. Yet some material goods, like firearms, were now suspected of producing "savagery," not civilization. This argument stands in stark contrast with the argument made by Burchell in the early part of the nineteenth century: that the spread of guns would advance civilization. It resembles arguments made in the Boer republics that abetted the legal subjection of Africans.

Griffith admitted that while gun control was desirable, it would be difficult to achieve. In an 1873 letter to the secretary for native affairs, Charles Brownlee, he wrote that "I am quite unable to suggest any effectual remedy for it other than that which is now too late to enforce, namely the suppression of the sale of guns to the natives at the diamond fields

---

[13] CTAR, NA 272/28, Griffith to Molteno, March 12, 1873. Griffith complained about the Cradock arms trade in 1875: CTAR, NA 273/87 Griffith to Molteno, July 9, 1875; NA 273/90, Griffith to Molteno, July 14, 1875; NA 273/101, Griffith to Molteno, August 19, 1875; NA 273/10, April 18, 1876, Griffith to Brownlee; NA 273/16, Griffith to Brownlee, May 10, 1876.

and elsewhere." He opposed confiscation, wondering if it would be "fair or just to take these arms from the Basutos after their having procured them openly and honestly? And what sort of an opinion would they form of the British government if such a thing were attempted?" Instead of confiscation, Griffith proposed restrictions on sales of lead and powder, but even these steps were not taken.[14]

Gun regulation presented administrative difficulties. It was in other areas that Griffith was able to implement significant changes. From 1872 to 1876, he and the Cape magistrates under him were engaged in the project of building the colonial administration and undermining the chiefs' authority, in significant part through the enforcement of the new laws. As a consequence of the courts' evenhandedness toward Sotho commoners, more and more people brought their cases to the magistrates' courts. Numbers of magistrates were increased, as well as numbers of police officers and district medical officers. More missionaries arrived, and their increasingly numerous converts received government protection. The government even subsidized mission schools. To add insult to injury, magistrates supported commoners who did not wish to participate in the compulsory gardening, or *letsema*, that they performed on the chiefs' plots. And public national meetings, or *pitso*, were now to be hosted by the chief magistrate and not by the chiefs.[15]

A number of prominent Sotho men supported Griffith in the process of civilization. Among the most prominent was Tsekelo Moshoeshoe, a son of Moshoeshoe's sixth wife. Tsekelo had a western education, which enabled him to play an important role in the negotiations between the Sotho and the Cape in 1867. In 1873, Tsekelo wrote to Griffith warning him that the spread of guns was hindering the creation of Basutoland's new regime. Tsekelo called for a ban on the sale and importation of guns, claiming that "everything will progress forward but these guns will beget insubordination, disputes, arrogance, a refusal to conform to the laws, a defying of the summonses which summons people before the courts. They will beget a desire to get rid of this government of peace under which we live so happily." Tsekelo was making the same sort of argument as Griffith: guns produced a defiant way of thinking. In the same letter to Griffith, he even suggested that "the chiefs of Basutoland are the obstacles to progress of every kind."[16] Tsekelo probably stood to

---

[14] CTAR, NA 272, Griffith to Brownlee, August 30, 1873.
[15] Burman, *Chiefdom Politics and Alien Law*, 75–99.
[16] CTAR, NA 272/21, Tsekelo to Griffith, June 27, 1873.

benefit from colonialism more than most of his half brothers, nephews, and cousins.

At an early *pitso*, in 1873, Griffith laid out his understanding of the relationship between the government and the chiefs, particularly on the subject of guns. "Now understand me!" he announced. "The government of the Queen is not in the least afraid that you intend on using these guns against it." The loyalty of the Sotho was not in doubt. "For itself the government has no fear of these guns of yours but for you and the people of Basutoland; namely that by these guns you will bring great and it may be ruinous troubles upon your own selves . . . the government did not take this country under its wing for any gain or profit. . . . It did so simply to protect the Sotho people and nation from being utterly eaten up and your country from being entirely confiscated by enemies whom you are quite powerless to resist." According to Griffith, the Cape ruled Basutoland out of paternal concern. Out of gratitude, the Sotho expressed their loyalty, or at least they were not openly hostile. The Sotho received protection from their enemies (presumably the Boers). This protection was strong enough to warrant abandoning guns. Griffith said, "Now let me plainly tell you, I cannot see what possible use you can have for guns in Basutoland at all. You have no enemies to attack."[17] Everybody knew that Basutoland did, indeed, have uneasy relations with the Orange Free State and that there were few Cape or British forces visibly protecting the Sotho. Griffith's arguments must have seemed completely hollow to the major Sotho chiefs, who were all present at the meeting. None of them contradicted Griffith, agreeing, in principle, that guns were not good. None of them proposed a plan for regulating guns.

Burman points out that the principal Sotho chiefs were uneasy with Cape rule and that they expressed their uneasiness in different ways. The most important chiefs were Moshoeshoe's first wife's three sons: Letsie, Molapo, and Masopha. Letsie, who succeeded Moshoeshoe as paramount chief, was generally thought to be indolent. Instead of active opposition, he preferred to resist Cape impositions by stalling and delaying, a tactic that annoyed Griffith, who had to work closely with him. By contrast, Letsie's younger brother, Molapo, was inclined to more open forms of resistance. He presided as senior chief over the northern district of Basutoland, which was more remote from the Cape than were the other districts. On several occasions in 1872 and 1873, the resident

[17] CTAR, NA 272/85, Griffith's report on the *pitso* of August 20, 1873.

magistrate in his district, Major Charles Harland Bell, felt that Molapo was inciting the local people against British rule. Then, in 1873, when Langalibalele and the Hlubi were fleeing Natal by crossing the Drakensberg into Basutoland, Molapo decided to help the government. Griffith offered the Hlubi cattle as a reward to the chief who captured Langalibalele, while the Natal government was also offering cattle – 150 head – if Langalibalele were taken alive. Molapo's son, Jonathan, discovered the Hlubi and betrayed them to the British. When Molapo collected the reward, he garnered the distrust of many Sotho as well as many other Africans, making it imperative for him to forge a closer alliance with the Cape administration.

The most consistent resistance to Cape rule came from Masopha, a veteran of the wars with the Orange Free State. Masopha defied the government in a number of ways: first, by refusing for several years to move from Thaba Bosiu to Berea, where the government had assigned him to rule as the senior chief, and second, by obstructing important legal decisions of the Berea resident magistrate, William Henry Surmon.

Surmon also supervised Letsie's heir apparent, Lerotholi (Lerothodi), whose loyalty was bought by his economic dependence on his father. Three other sons of Moshoeshoe – Nehemiah, George, and Sofonia – were impoverished because they were born to lesser wives in an era when there was no more open space on the High Veld. They were educated in Cape Town and so found a different way to express their loyalty to the crown. They were loyal, but when they learned of the Cape annexation in 1871, they insisted that the Sotho be given representation in the Cape parliament, together with the full rights and responsibilities of British subjects, and that Cape law be fully extended to Basutoland, a move that would have significantly diminished the power of the chiefs. In any event, the loyalty of these junior chiefs and others was purchased through scholarships for their children to study in Cape Town and through their appointment to the colonial police force.[18]

Griffith was comfortable enough with a colonial police force built through chiefly patronage that in 1873 he proposed that the government should arm them with a hundred Snider breechloaders, a decision that was reversed by the Cape prime minister, J. C. Molteno. Molteno wrote to Griffith, telling him that "I cannot agree with you in thinking that in order that the government should be respected and

---

[18] Burman, *Chiefdom Politics and Alien Law*, 61–9.

carried on efficiently in Basutoland, the native police force must of necessity be armed with breechloaders or on the other hand disbanded." He urged, instead, that unarmed Sotho police officers be supplemented with armed Europeans.[19]

Loyalty was bought not only through scholarships and appointments, but also through the administration of the hut tax. On the basis of thin evidence, Burman makes a likely argument about the way in which Cape magistrates relied on the chiefs to collect taxes. Not only did chiefs receive a percentage of the take, but they could employ a new instrument of patronage: underassessment. The tax was based on the number of huts in the taxpayer's possession. A chief collecting taxes could underassess the number of huts in exchange for favors.[20] Thus, did the chiefs and the Cape build a new political culture.

Introducing the Idea of Disarmament to the Sotho

Even as Cape rule made inroads in Basutoland, it appears that the Sotho chiefs retained considerable respect among the commoners. Griffith and his fellow administrators from the Cape recognized that they could only gradually change Sotho political culture. The loyalty of the chiefs was secured with patronage, paternalism, and the greatest tact. This was no more evident than when the system began to fail. In 1877, the tactless behavior of one magistrate, Hamilton Hope, precipitated the rebellion of one of the more difficult chiefs, Moorosi. Moorosi led the Phuthi, a group that lived on the far southern boundary of Basutoland. The Phuthi spoke their own language, which was akin to the Swazi language. They thought of themselves as distinct from their Sotho and Xhosa neighbors. During the 1820s, the Phuthi became vassals of Moshoeshoe. In 1869 and 1870, Moorosi successfully petitioned the governor to include the Phuthi in Basutoland. Moorosi had preserved close ties to the Sotho chiefdom, in significant part by marrying his daughter to Letsie's son, Lerotholi. The Cape did not appoint a magistrate to the Phuthi until 1877, when Hope arrived in Quthing at the beginning of the Gcaleka War.[21]

---

[19] CTAR, CO 5488, Mills to Griffith, April 9, 1873; Molteno to Griffith, March 5, 1874.
[20] Burman, *Chiefdom Politics and Alien Law*, 69–71.
[21] Burman, *Chiefdom Politics and Alien Law*, 108–10. Atmore, "The Moorosi Rebellion: Lesotho, 1879," 2–6.

Almost immediately, Hope intervened in a land dispute and interpreted the law incorrectly. Moorosi protested by bringing five hundred armed men to visit, requesting a *pitso*. Hope granted the *pitso* provided that Moorosi's men lay down their arms, which they did. Moorosi asked Hope to read the laws out loud, which he did, and then the chief began a harangue against the administration. Hope recorded that Moorosi asked the crowd, "Are you my people, or are you the Government people? If you are Government people you are fools. Do you obey this man (pointing to me) or do you obey me? They all with one voice cried out, we obey Morosi."[22] Over the course of several days, Moorosi and Hope debated back and forth over their respective powers to administer justice, with Moorosi's armed followers making their presence felt. In the end, after threats from Hope, Moorosi agreed to allow the young magistrate to judge a case. When Hope judged the case harshly, Moorosi once again protested. By January 1878, it was clear that significant numbers of the Phuthi were not accepting Hope's judgments and were looking to Moorosi instead. Their loyalty was far from being displaced from the chief to the British.[23]

Phuthi – and Sotho – alienation from Cape rule began with Sprigg's assumption of the premiership. Sprigg's denigration of "uncivilized" Africans produced significant changes in Cape "native" policy. Under the previous prime minister, J. C. Molteno, and his secretary for native affairs, Charles Brownlee, Cape policy was to slowly and gradually undermine the Sotho chiefs and their supporting legal and administrative structures. When opportunities arose to make changes, they were made, but the government did not go too far out of its way to create these opportunities. It was thought that sudden wrenching changes might provoke the Sotho into rebellion. Sprigg did not fear rebellion. Together with his new secretary for native affairs, William Ayliff, he pushed for rapid change.[24]

One significant change was to be disarmament. In October 1878, Griffith returned to Basutoland as the governor's agent, having spent the previous year commanding the Frontier Armed and Mounted Police against the Ngqika and Gcaleka Xhosa. Griffith returned with instructions from Sprigg, who wrote to him from King William's Town near the scene of the war. Sprigg reported that the disarmament of the Xhosa

---

[22] Burman, *Chiefdom Politics and Alien Law*, 112.
[23] Burman, *Chiefdom Politics and Alien Law*, 110–21. Atmore, "The Moorosi Rebellion: Lesotho, 1879," 6–18.
[24] Burman, *Chiefdom Politics and Alien Law*, 132.

and Mfengu "is proceeding very successfully from the Sea right up to Wodehouse" and then wrote that "I want you now to commence with the Basutos. Assemble the leading men & acquaint them with the native policy of the present Government."[25]

These heavy-handed instructions presented a problem for Griffith, whose relations with the Sotho chiefs were marked by caution and tact. Caution and tact were necessary, at least in part because the Sotho chiefs had mastered the art of frontier warfare in recent conflicts with the Orange Free State. The chiefs could still summon thousands of skilled veterans to defend their rugged country. This situation stood in stark contrast to the Eastern Cape, where the Xhosa leadership had failed as tacticians and where the terrain was better suited to offensive operations. For these reasons, Sprigg's provocative call to disarm the Sotho presented a major challenge to Griffith. Sprigg's rationale for disarmament could not, as such, be presented to the Sotho, as it was founded on an insulting view of their capabilities – and on an overly optimistic view of colonial capabilities. In the letter, Sprigg called the Sotho "barbarous people," who "are not to be allowed to ruin themselves & every body else – but that our superior intelligence is to be beneficially excised [*sic*] on their behalf – that they are to be held in hand & guided & trained with the view of raising them out of barbarism into civilization. That the proof of manhood is not the possession of a gun but the capacity to observe & maintain order & to assist in advancing the moral & material prosperity of the community."[26] It is interesting to note that Sprigg considered guns to be no proof of manhood, as he himself had spent much of 1876 and 1877 urging Eastern Cape settlers to arm themselves and form militia units. Even more striking, though, is Sprigg's view of the Sotho, which was laden with paternalism.[27]

---

[25] CTAR, NA 279, Griffith to Sauer, June 5, 1881, No. 1, "Copies of Semi-Official Letters," Encl. Sprigg to Griffith, October 5, 1878. At the end of Sprigg's premiership, May 8, 1881, Griffith took the opportunity to forward the new secretary for native affairs, J. W. Sauer, copies of all "semiofficial" correspondence and telegrams that he had with Sprigg from 1878 to 1880.

[26] CTAR, NA 279, Griffith to Sauer, June 5, 1881, No. 1, "Copies of Semi-Official Letters," Encl. Sprigg to Griffith, October 5, 1878.

[27] It is unfortunate to note that it is difficult for historians to explore the development of Sprigg's thinking on these issues beyond what is contained in official reports and newspapers. Sprigg took copious notes and engaged in voluminous correspondence, but after his death his family burned most of his papers, including many official documents that had been in his personal possession. For details of the destruction, see the introduction to Vanstone's "Sir John Gordon Sprigg."

Sprigg, who was an immigrant from England, represented a new kind of white ruler: racially arrogant and impatient with diplomacy. His approach to gun control defined his premiership, which in itself marked a watershed in Cape history, when the old humanitarian liberalism started to be eclipsed by the new liberalism that was simultaneously utilitarian and racial. At a *pitso* on October 24, 1878, Griffith shied away from announcing full-blown racialism, while trying his best to make the case for disarmament to the chiefs in a more familiar way, weaving the concept of loyalty into his presentation. At the meeting, Griffith recounted the death, destruction, and dispossession that the Cape Colony had visited on the rebel Xhosa, commenting that "from all that I have told you I hope you will learn as a lesson, and see what the result of rebellion is. . . . The [Xhosa] chiefs listened to bad advisers, and thus brought themselves and their people to destruction. And thus will it ever be with people who rebel against the just and mild rule of the Queen."[28] Next, Griffith commented briefly on his "astonishment" at Moorosi's recent behavior and then moved on to disarmament:

I have no doubt that many of you have heard, that it is the intention of the Government to call upon all its people to disarm. The Tembus, the Fingoes, and all other tribes in the Colony and under British rule will have to do so. Many of these people have already shown their loyalty by giving up their arms at once when called upon to do so. It is the intention of the Government to compensate all the people who give up their arms. This policy has been adopted by the Government because it wishes the country to be at peace. The Government says the people have no use for guns, as there is no game in the country to shoot, that if they are allowed to keep their guns they will only fight with each other – the Government will protect all its subjects. I mention these matters to you to-day, because you Basutos will also be called upon to give up your arms, and I hope you will all do so willingly; and you will suffer no loss by doing so, as it is the intention of the Government, to pay you the value of your guns.[29]

In announcing the likelihood of disarmament, Griffith avoided Sprigg's racial ideology completely. Griffith spoke as a diplomat floating a trial balloon – a weak statement on the likelihood of disarmament, rather than a proclamation that disarmament would now commence. His weak claims were followed up with rhetoric that was not racial but vaguely utilitarian. Guns were to be given up because they no longer had a use, because the government would guarantee the peace, and because "all" the people were being disarmed. "All" the people seemed to mean "all" the

[28] CPP [G.33] 1879, *Blue Book on Native Affairs for 1878*, 30.
[29] CPP [G.33] 1879, *Blue Book on Native Affairs for 1878*, 30.

African people, given the mention of only "the Tembu, the Fingo, and all other tribes in the Colony." Handing in guns would be a demonstration of loyalty, which implied that not handing in guns would be an act of disloyalty. Griffith anticipated the counterargument that Sotho guns had been earned through hard work, in his offer of government money for guns.

At the *pitso*, reaction was muted. Much of the meeting was devoted to a petition by Tsekelo Moshesh that would have had the effect of weakening the authority of local chiefs and strengthening the hand of the principal chiefs, Letsie, Masopha, and Molapo.[30] Only occasionally did the conversation turn to guns. Ntho registered his disappointment, claiming that "when we were made British subjects we selected the Colony because we heard that in Natal the Queen's subjects were disarmed.... We like our guns as playthings." George Moshoeshoe spoke up, saying that "I am not a Gcaleka; so I say woe to him who cries that he is being killed when he is being disarmed. God disposes and appoints all things. Who can stay his will?" He echoed Ntho's claim that the Sotho preferred to be annexed to the Cape rather than Natal, citing the Cape's more liberal gun laws, but said, "I will be satisfied if I am disarmed. I will look upon it as a proof of loyalty. We will be tried like Abraham, but our guns are not precious as Isaac was." And Ramabidikue commented that "with regard to our being disarmed, we do not know what to say, but we cannot be classed with the other tribes who have given up their guns. Perhaps we have been deceived by the Government leading us to believe that it trusts us." To him, uniform "native" policy on disarmament was unfair.[31]

At this *pitso* of October 24, 1878, there was some dissatisfaction with Griffith's suggestion of disarmament. After the *pitso*, as word of possible disarmament spread among the Sotho, more protests were recorded by the Cape magistrates. At the end of 1878, Major Bell reported from Leribe that disarmament would be unpopular and difficult to enforce. Besides, the government did not have the revenue to grant compensation for the guns. He estimated that there were ten thousand rifles in Basutoland, with a total value of £75,000. Instead of paying such a large sum, he instead proposed that guns be licensed and taxed, a measure that would provide more revenue and that would also ensure their continued "loyalty and respect." Major Bell's son, Charles, wrote from his magistrate's post in

---

[30] Burman, *Chiefdom Politics and Alien Law*, 72–4.
[31] CPP [G.33] 1879, *Blue Book on Native Affairs for 1878*, 32–5.

Berea that the people in his district were "loyal and peaceably inclined," although they would consider disarmament to be "a very serious matter, a gun in the eyes of a Mosutho, being the most valuable article he possesses, and the possession of which he considers it his duty to retain at any sacrifice." It would be "premature" to disarm the Sotho, wrote Bell. His colleague in Quthing, John Austen, urged that disarmament "be very cautiously approached, and that some distinction should be made between all staunch loyal natives." And from Thaba Bosiu, Henry Davies reported that the Sotho were divided over disarmament. Some Sotho would obey any order of the government, while others felt aggrieved about giving up expensive weapons that the government had been encouraging them to buy.[32]

Guns and War in Zululand

As Sotho grumbling mounted, colonial attention shifted to the northeast, to the Transvaal and Zululand. In 1877, Theophilus Shepstone, acting as Lord Carnarvon's agent, had overthrown the government of the Transvaal and taken control of the country himself. In August 1878, to better reconcile the Afrikaners to British rule, he restored the rights of Europeans to buy arms and ammunition, which had been suspended after the occupation. The government monopolized sales of arms and ammunition while also keeping in force the Transvaal's ban on Africans buying arms and ammunition.[33] To solidify white rule in the Transvaal, Shepstone began a war against Sekhukhune, the paramount chief of the Pedi, in October 1878. And Shepstone once again curried favor with Transvaal Afrikaners, this time by claiming part of Zululand for white settlement. He made such a claim in spite of the fact that the boundary had already been confirmed by a Natal commission. Shepstone also conveniently overlooked the way in which five years earlier he himself had engineered an alliance between Natal and the Zulu.

The Zulu posed a considerable threat to Shepstone's claims on behalf of the Transvaal. The Zulu also stood in the way of Carnarvon and Frere's plans for confederation. Zulu claims were backed by an army that was increasingly armed with modern weapons, thanks to John Dunn, who was, in the words of Theophilus Shepstone, "partly English and partly

---

[32] CPP [G.33] 1879, *Blue Book on Native Affairs for 1878*, 6, 12, 15, 20.
[33] PRO CO 879/17 Conf. Print Africa No. 222, 1880, "Trade in Arms," Enclosures in No. 1, Wolseley to Hicks Beach, January 2, 1880, pp. 2–6.

Zulu, the former by birth, the latter by choice and long residence."[34] Dunn was, in fact, a European who, through extensive cattle acquisitions and forty-two marriages into twenty-one Zulu clans, had become one of the most powerful chiefs in Zululand. This was thanks in part to his alliance with Cetshwayo, the heir apparent to the Zulu king, Mpande. In 1857, Cetshwayo granted Dunn land. Dunn then went about acquiring firearms for Cetshwayo as part of his extensive involvement in trade with Delagoa Bay. Dunn went there for guns, which he sold exclusively to Cetshwayo up until 1873, when Shepstone installed Cetshwayo as paramount. After that, other chiefs were less of a threat. Ironically, Shepstone allowed them to become Dunn's customers for firearms, too. Dunn also used guns to form a band of two hundred hunters who roamed Natal and Zululand during the 1860s, when they killed off most of the area's large, valuable elephants as well as many other spectacular quadrupeds. Dunn's trips to Delagoa Bay also involved the recruitment of Tsonga laborers to work on Natal's farms and railways. By the 1870s, his influence over migrant labor was so great that the colony appointed him Protector of Immigrants, which was like asking the fox to guard the henhouse. According to Shepstone, Dunn was motivated "by his own great desire to make money," but his motives seem to have been more complex. He did indeed make money, but he also made shrewd political moves to become both a chief and a colonial official.[35]

After Cetshwayo's installation as paramount, the Zulu did purchase more firearms. Between 1873 and the outbreak of the Anglo–Zulu War in 1878, colonial officials estimated that twenty thousand guns entered Zululand from Delagoa, two-thirds of which were imported by Dunn. Shepstone believed that the "traffic in firearms... tended more than any other circumstance to bring about the Zulu war."[36] Some shared his concern, including Hicks Beach and his assistant, William Malcolm, who exchanged notes on the subject of punishing Dunn for arms smuggling.[37]

34 PRO CO 879/17 Conf. Pr. Africa No. 209, "Memorandum by Sir Theophilus Shepstone on Sir General Wolseley's [sic] Scheme for the Settlement of Zululand," October 14, 1879, p. 1.
35 Ballard, "John Dunn and Cetshwayo." For Dunn's version of events, see "John Dunn's Notes," in Moodie, *John Dunn, Cetywayo, and the Three Generals*.
36 Cope, *Ploughshare of War*, 221–49. Knight, *Anatomy of the Zulu Army*, 213–15. Quotations by Shepstone from PRO CO 879/17 Conf. Pr. Africa No. 209, "Memorandum by Sir Theophilus Shepstone on Sir General Wolseley's [sic] Scheme for the Settlement of Zululand," October 14, 1879, p. 1.
37 PRO CO 291/1 Transvaal No. 815, minutes by Malcolm and Hicks Beach, January 28, 1878.

Most historians believe that it was Shepstone and Frere's machinations, more than any other factor, that brought about the Zulu War, but at the time the British consul and vice-consul in Mozambique also attributed the conflict to the proliferation of guns. In correspondence circulated to the Cape and British governments in 1879, the Mozambique consul provided evidence that the Zulu were heavily involved in the gun trade at Delagoa Bay and English River, a nearby waterway. The consul admitted to some uncertainty: "the remarks I am able to make upon the gun and powder trade of the Coast are somewhat uncertain in tone," but he did not hesitate to make claims anyway. He and his colleague, the vice-consul, reported that during the years 1875–7, local traders sold an average of twenty thousand guns with percussion caps, together with ten thousand barrels of gunpowder. Most of the guns were older models. They reported that "the Zulus themselves are thoroughly dissatisfied with the description of gun sold to them." They were valued at eight shillings, but sold for one pound and four shillings, or the equivalent in cattle or other forms of barter. The consul continued, "Having discovered to their cost how ineffectual they are when met with rifles such as our troops possess ... I am told that in consequence a strong demand has arisen for breech-loading rifles." During 1875–7, the consuls estimated that traders sold about five hundred breechloaders with cartridges. Large numbers of Zulu were involved in the trade, along with some Pedi – about one-eighth were Pedi and the rest were Zulu, according to the vice-consul. In August 1876, the consul observed that "2,300 Zulus have just arrived on the southern bank of English River for the purpose of carrying away arms into their country" and that "Delagoa Bay is being turned into an armoury in the flank of Zululand, rendering the restrictions on the supply in Natal quite nugatory." One Dutch trader based in Lourenço Marques indicated that he had sold eight hundred guns, together with lead and powder, on one day.[38]

In spite of official concerns about the gun trade between Delagoa and Zululand, the lieutenant governor of Natal, Sir Henry Bulwer, persuaded the officials in the Colonial Office in London that Shepstone was exaggerating the importance of the gun trade.[39] There were reasons for Bulwer to be skeptical of Shepstone and to be supportive of Dunn. Confederation, as well as Shepstone's own personal power, would be advanced by

[38] PRO CO 879/17 Conf. Pr. Africa, No. 28: O'Neill to Salisbury, Encl. in No. 3, August 5, 1879, pp. 4–6; Thompson to O'Neill, Encl. 2 in No. 4, September 22, 1879, pp. 6–7.
[39] PRO CO 179/126 Natal No. 7405, "Importation of Firearms," Bulwer to CO, with minutes by CO, April 30, 1878.

portraying the Zulu as armed and risky, while the development of Natal's farms and railways relied heavily on Dunn's recruitment of migrant laborers. Bulwer took the official position that Natal's gun regulations were strict enough and simply needed to be enforced more effectively. Licensing was the best approach because, in the words of a receptive Colonial Office staffer, a new tax would encourage Africans to work harder, "which is the great thing needed to raise them out of savage habits."[40] Natal could not yet regulate gun possession in Zululand, which was still independent, but the British government convinced the Portuguese authorities to restrict gun sales in Mozambique. This did not completely stop smuggling, but the restrictions were tight enough that in October 1878 Cetshwayo was reported to be complaining about them.[41]

By that time, relations between the British and the Zulu kingdom were tense. In December 1878, Frere, working with Shepstone, issued an extraordinary ultimatum to Cetshwayo, demanding that he hand over several fugitives from Natal, change the Zulu legal system, and demobilize the Zulu army. Cetshwayo responded by mobilizing even more troops. In January 1879, a force of British soldiers, colonial settlers, and African allies invaded Zulu territory, only to be outfought and almost completely annihilated by a Zulu army at Isandlwana. After this embarrassment, the British spent several months regrouping. Disraeli ordered Sir Garnet Wolseley to return to Natal and take command. By July 1879, Wolseley, helped by Dunn, defeated the Zulu. By and large, the Zulu did use traditional weapons and tactics, although some British officers noted that on occasion, Zulu forces opposed them with breech-loading rifles. It appeared that while individual Zulu shot well, the Zulu as a whole did not make a concerted effort to adapt their battlefield tactics to the new weapons, except on rare occasions. On March 27, 1879, Colonel Evelyn Wood reported that his column "came under a well-directed fire" from a force of concealed Zulu. "The enemy," he wrote, "well-supplied with Martini-Henry rifles and ammunition, occupied a hill not seen from the laager, and opened so accurate an enfilade fire, though at long range, that I was obliged to withdraw a company."[42]

---

[40] PRO CO 179/126 Natal No. 7403, "Importation of Arms and Ammunition," minutes by Antrobus and Malcolm, June 25–26, 1878.

[41] PRO CO 179/127 Natal No. 14354, Frere to CO, October 4, 1878, with minutes by Pearson and Meade, November 13, 1878.

[42] PRO WO 132/1, Buller Papers, Letter of Wood to the Deputy Adjutant General, March 30, 1879, published in the supplement to the *London Gazette*, May 6, 1879.

Notwithstanding such incidents of Zulu marksmanship with modern weapons, the Zulu relied mainly on traditional battlefield tactics. These worked at Isandlwana but not in any subsequent battles. As a result of the tactical and strategic mismatch, the British captured Cetshwayo and torched his capital, Ulundi. As Wolseley subjected Zululand, he and Dunn together destroyed Cetshwayo's reserve of gunpowder, which they estimated at 1,100 pounds, some of which had been taken from British troops at Isandlwana. Captured British rifles tended to be kept by individuals. Wolseley and Dunn also destroyed a hut at Ulundi that belonged to Sotho gunsmiths, who were apparently working for Cetshwayo. Three miles away they discovered and burned a magazine containing supplies of powder, sulfur, and lead that had belonged to "Christian Kaffirs" who worked for Cetshwayo.[43] Cetshwayo's technical support had come from a wide variety of Africans and Europeans.

While Wolseley began the work of dividing and administering Zululand, he also turned his attention to Sekhukhune. Using a combined force, including British regulars and Swazi auxiliaries, Wolseley sacked the Pedi capital of Maroteng, captured Sekhukhune, and laid waste to the surrounding countryside. The defeat of the Pedi and the Zulu would appear to have advanced the cause of confederation. And yet public attention in Britain tended to focus on the defeat at Isandlwana, the worst defeat inflicted on the British army since the Crimean War. Many people in Britain came to view the Anglo–Zulu War as unnecessary, needlessly provoked by Frere's ultimatum to Cetshwayo. Disraeli and most of the cabinet wanted to recall Frere, who was saved only by his friendship with Queen Victoria and by his ties to powerful colonists at the Cape. Disraeli decided not to recall Frere, but when he sent Wolseley to Natal, the general was appointed "Governor of Natal, Governor of the Transvaal, Commander-in-Chief, and High Commissioner for South East Africa."

The appointment of Wolseley to these posts effectively stripped Frere of his powers as high commissioner. He kept the title, although now it meant little more than simply governor of the Cape Colony. Frere would have done well to resign, as the historian Richard Cope points out. Instead, Frere clung to power, hoping to redeem himself by somehow bringing about confederation. Cope writes that "the result of this decision was that he died a slow and agonizing political death in public."[44] Frere's wish

---

[43] PRO WO 147/7, Journal of G. Wolseley, August 12, 1879, pp. 106–7; August 18, 1879, p. 116. On captured rifles, see *James Stuart Archive*, 3:318.

[44] Cope, *Ploughshare of War*, 254.

to redeem himself through confederation helps explain why he chose to become so deeply committed to the extension of a uniform "native policy," including disarmament, to Basutoland.

Sprigg's New Approach

While British and Cape attention was focused on Natal and the Transvaal, a small but significant rebellion was developing in Basutoland. The Phuthi chief Moorosi's disagreements with Cape administrators deteriorated to the point where open conflict broke out. After months of tension and hostility in Quthing, Hope was replaced as resident magistrate by the more experienced John Austen, who then proceeded to antagonize Moorosi even further by imprisoning his son and threatening to deport the angry chief. Threats of disarmament did not help. On the contrary, Saul Solomon's *Cape Argus* newspaper editorialized that it was disarmament, more than anything else, that inspired Moorosi's actions against the government.[45] In February 1879, just after the Zulu defeated the British at Isandlwana, Moorosi forced Austen to flee the Quthing District. Moorosi and the Phuthi were now in open revolt. Griffith invaded Moorosi's territory with a force of about a thousand reluctant Sotho together with two hundred Cape militiamen and a contingent of one hundred Cape Mounted Rifles. From March to November they besieged Moorosi's residence on "Moorosi's Mountain," where the Phuthi defenders dug well-positioned trenches. Moorosi's force of several hundred well-armed followers put up a stout resistance, showing that well-armed and motivated soldiers could use the rough terrain of Basutoland to their advantage. Even so, they had no hope of reinforcement over a long winter's fighting and their numbers dwindled to sixty. Moorosi held on because he refused to accept the Sprigg's terms: unconditional surrender.[46]

Sprigg's terms for Moorosi, and his approach to disarmament, indicated a certain rigidity in thinking. Sprigg failed to appreciate that after Isandlwana, another shift in imperial policy was beginning to take place. Under public pressure, the British government was becoming wary of military commitments in South Africa. Public wariness led policymakers to debate two different approaches: trusting loyal Africans to protect and govern themselves more extensively or not trusting Africans at all.

---

[45] *Cape Argus*, July 9, 1879, p. 2.
[46] Burman, *Chiefdom Politics and Alien Law*, 121–31. Atmore, "The Moorosi Rebellion: Lesotho, 1879," 18–35.

The latter approach grew in part out of London's frustration with the inability of the South African colonies and republics to arrive at uniform gun laws. By April 1878, the secretary of state for the colonies, Hicks Beach, was so frustrated after a discussion of improving South African gun regulations that he wondered, in a minute to his junior colleagues, that maybe the high commissioner should be empowered to take unilateral action in the name of the empire.[47] This never came to pass but increased frustration was, indeed, reflected in an internal Colonial Office document from the next year, "Confidential Print, African No. 200" of July 1879, which proposed further restrictions on the arms trade in South Africa. The author recognized that Wolseley, Shepstone, and other local officials were recommending the wholesale disarmament of Africans, yet recognized that the trade could also be suppressed relatively cheaply through negotiations with Portugal, whose government in Mozambique had previously allowed a brisk trade in weapons bound for the Transvaal, as well as the for entire region between the Limpopo and the Zambezi. At the very least, by 1879 the Portuguese agreed to impose the same rules on gun importation as the ones that existed in the Cape and Natal.[48]

The author of the Colonial Office confidential print preferred Frere's recommendation to empower magistrates to license gun owners selectively, along the lines of Natal's existing policy. The *Cape Argus*, probably unaware of the Colonial Office documents and discussions, took a different tack, noting that Natal's regulations had not worked well. This premise led the editors to make a broader argument about government: "We have now an experience in native management extending to considerably more than half a century. And if that experience proves one thing more than another, it is the indubitable truth that good government and honorable dealing are more to be relied upon than large armaments and restrictive legislation."[49] The *Cape Argus*, the bellwether paper for Cape liberal humanitarians, did not oppose disarmament. In August 1878, the editors wrote, "No man in his sober senses would complain of steps being taken to render the natives within and about our borders powerless from mischief. The thing could be done effectually without any straining of justice, and without creating evils worse than the possession

---

[47] PRO CO 291/1 Transvaal No. 3697, "Sale of Firearms to Natives at the Diamond Fields," with minutes by Antrobus, Malcolm, and Hicks Beach, April 2–6, 1878.
[48] PRO CO 879/16, Conf. Pr. Africa, No. 200, July 21, 1879, pp. 4, 8.
[49] *Cape Argus*, June 28, 1879, p. 2.

of firearms."[50] If disarmament could be done in a just way, they would support it.

Wariness was quickly apprehended by the allies of the Sotho in London, who wanted to alleviate public concern by asking the British and Cape governments to allow loyal Africans under British rule to do more to assist the empire. This was the recommendation of Rev. Eugène Casalis, director of the Paris Evangelical Missionary Society, who wrote to F. W. Chesson, secretary of the Aborigines Protection Society, one of England's most famous humanitarian organizations, asking him to press the British government to cement alliances with "loyal tribes" such as the Sotho – and not to further alienate them by more talk of disarmament.[51] Casalis persuaded the Aborigines Protection Society to forward a letter to Hicks Beach. In the letter, Casalis urged the Cape "to show confidence in the tribes who have given proof of loyalty." When the Cape government pressed for disarmament in Basutoland and the Eastern Cape, "no distinction [was] made between the tribes which have fought for, and those which have fought against the British Government."[52] The government's response to the Aborigines Protection Society, written by Hicks Beach's undersecretary of state, Robert Herbert, was testy. Herbert wrote that the humanitarians "fail to appreciate the nature and object of this policy, which was adopted for the security and welfare of Her Majesty's subjects in the Cape Colony, whether European or coloured, and was never intended or represented as a punishment for disloyalty."[53] The secretary of the Aborigines Protection Society, F. W. Chesson, replied that he understood that the government did not intend disarmament as a punishment for disloyalty. The problem was that the Sotho and others perceived it as punishment, a perception that would not enhance security on the Cape's borders.[54]

The secretary of state for the colonies, Sir Michael Hicks Beach, notified Frere that he was being lobbied directly by the Sotho's French missionaries. All the correspondence was forwarded to Frere at the

---

[50] *Cape Argus*, August 28, 1879, p. 2.

[51] RHL Anti-Slavery Papers, Mss. Brit. Emp. C128/61, Casalis to Chesson, March 21, 1879.

[52] BPP [C.2569] 1880, No. 1, Aborigines Protection Society (Chesson) to CO, April 5, 1879, pp. 1–2.

[53] BPP [C.2569] 1880, No. 3, CO (Herbert) to Aborigines Protection Society, April 17, 1879, pp. 2–3.

[54] BPP [C.2569] 1880, No. 4, Aborigines Protection Society (Chesson) to CO, May 14, 1879, p. 3.

Cape. Frere responded by recommending "caution in dealing with the Basutos." He believed that "in Basutoland there are circumstances not met with elsewhere, which modify the question considerably." According to Frere, the Sotho were keen to keep their arms because they believed that there was a chance of the British abandoning the colony. Even though this belief was "absurd," it still needed to be taken into account. Frere recommended that in Basutoland, "gun licenses might be granted, as in England, to respectable people on payment of an annual sum for the permit."[55] But gradually, as Frere was losing support in England, he came to support a harder line.

Sprigg's 1879 Pitso

After the Zulu defeat of the British at Isandlwana, Frere began to grasp at straws. Sprigg provided one in the form of Sotho disarmament. Sprigg set himself the task of persuading the Sotho chiefs that uniform African disarmament was necessary for security. Sprigg traveled personally to Basutoland to speak with Moorosi and to address the Sotho *pitso* of October 16–17, 1879, at Maseru. His talks with Moorosi failed to bring any resolution to the crisis. His presentation to the *pitso* – the first by a Cape premier – was received coolly by a large number of men. The official report estimated that on the first day, between six thousand and ten thousand Sotho men attended, including the principal chiefs, plus missionaries, magistrates, and traders, and even farmers from the Orange Free State. Before this tremendous audience, Sprigg made a poor impression. One witness wrote that Sprigg "being of insignificant stature, having a short staccato manner of speech, and dressed in a tweed suit and a straw-hat furnished with a long puggaree [neck-shade], he looked anything but an important powerful personage, while his general manner was fussy and wanting in dignity, and in no way impressed the people."[56]

Sprigg began by thanking the Sotho for their loyal support during the Moorosi rebellion. He followed these expressions of gratitude with an announcement: that the government would be doubling the hut tax from ten shillings to one pound. According to Sprigg, the new revenue was to

---

[55] BPP [C.2482] 1880, No. 106, Frere to Hicks Beach, September 22, 1879, p. 299. Frere's recommendation referred to Britain's Gun Licence Act of 1870. See Malcolm, *Guns and Violence*, 119–23.

[56] Taylor, *Doctor to Basuto, Boer & Briton*, 56.

support school construction, public works, and a larger police force.[57] This may have been Sprigg's intention, but at no point in his speech did he address the Sotho concern, expressed in the missionary newspaper since 1877, that significant amounts of Basutoland revenues were being expropriated to the Cape.[58]

Having warmed up his audience by announcing a tax increase, Sprigg moved on to the next topic: disarmament. Sprigg confirmed Griffith's statement at the 1878 *pitso*, that the Cape government would require the Sotho to disarm, just as it had asked "the natives in the lower part of the Colony, totally irrespective of the side which they took in the late and previous wars."[59] Bearing arms was no longer to be linked to loyalty.

The Government feel sure, as it has told you already, that you are already loyal to it, and that it is your intention to be faithful in the future, as you have been in the past, but the Government ... knows that there have been tribes thoroughly as loyal and faithful to the Government as you are this day, who have yet gone into rebellion, when they had at one time no intention of fighting against the Government.[60]

He was echoing recent arguments in favor of gun control that stressed the presumed ways in which guns changed the consciousness and behavior of Africans. Unintentional rebellions might be caused by gun possession. "It is the belief of the Government that if Morosi and his people had not possessed guns they would never have gone into rebellion...."[61] It seemed to Sprigg that Moorosi and other Africans with guns lacked the capacity to make mature judgments. He had the nerve to say to thousands of Sotho men that

The Government feels, that, like the rest of the natives in South Africa, you possess very much the character of children, and the Government knows that children cannot at all times trust even themselves; that they are led away by excitement, and that when the war fever is abroad in the land, the natives often become infected by it, and without the slightest intention of going into rebellion, they are drawn into it, and then they use these guns, which they had no intention of using, for the purpose of fighting against the Government and their fellow-creatures.[62]

---

[57] BPP [C.2482] 1880, pp. 489–91. The official report of the *pitso* is also published in CPP [G.13] 1880, *Blue Book on Native Affairs*, pp. 38–65.

[58] *Little Light of Basutoland* (August 8, 1877), pp. 1–2; (October 10, 1877), p. 2; as cited by Burman, *Chiefdom Politics and Alien Law*, 135.

[59] BPP [C.2482] 1880, p. 491.

[60] BPP [C.2482] 1880, p. 492.

[61] BPP [C.2482] 1880, p. 492.

[62] BPP [C.2482] 1880, p. 492.

Sprigg's use of the "child" metaphor had a special resonance for European imperialists. Earlier in the nineteenth century, Hegel had described Africa as "the land of childhood."[63] And at the end of the century, Kipling wrote famously in his poem, "The White Man's Burden," that colonial subjects were "New caught, sullen peoples/Half devil and half child." The theme was carried forward into the twentieth century by eminent South African segregationists like J. C. Smuts, who classified "the African" as a "child-type, with a child-psychology and outlook."[64] The vision of Africans as childlike exhibited some of the contradictions of colonialism, as the anthropologists Jean and John Comaroff have pointed out. When Europeans described Africans as children, they recognized the possibility for Africans to grow up and be like them. Even so, the process of growing up could last indefinitely.[65]

According to Sprigg, since the Sotho were "children" who lacked self-control, "the government thought it desirable for the good of the people themselves that the arms should be surrendered.... This is not a harsh, or unjust, or unkind measure on the part of the Government; it is done simply for the good of the people themselves." Government would ensure the good of all the people, black and white. According to Sprigg, the Peace Preservation Act "applies to black and white alike." This was technically true, although as we have seen already, the Cape parliament clearly intended to disarm only Africans. Africans needed to become "like the white man, and not to regard it as a proof of manhood that you possess guns." In the better parts of London and Cape Town, carrying arms in public was no longer acceptable. Sotho gun ownership should be restricted only to the police and a local militia.[66]

Sprigg noted that he had heard that the Sotho would resist disarmament. He claimed not to believe these rumors, citing Sotho loyalty to the Queen and to the Cape's magistrates. (Loyalty was invoked only when discussing responsibilities, not rights.) Besides, Sprigg reminded the Sotho that "you know that the tribes that have gone to war with the Government in the Colony have been destroyed." Sprigg cited the recent defeats of the Ngqika, Gcaleka, and Zulu, and mentioned that only two days

---

[63] Fyfe, "Race, Empire, and the Historians," 22.
[64] Mamdani, *Citizen and Subject*, 4.
[65] Comaroff and Comaroff, *Revelation and Revolution*, 2:396.
[66] BPP [C.2482] 1880, p. 492. The public carrying of arms in England is discussed in Malcolm, "The Nineteenth Century," in *Guns and Violence*, 90–132.

before leaving Cape Town for Basutoland, he had seen Cetshwayo in chains.[67]

The sheer effrontery of Sprigg's speech is impressive. Standing before thousands of Sotho men, he lied, dissembled, and made threats. He represented a new kind of imperialism: forceful, racist, and patronizing. In this view, Africans were like children and if they disobeyed new laws they would be punished severely. While speaking in this way about Africans, Sprigg appealed to the ideals that the previous generation of imperialists had articulated: the Sotho should behave because they were subjects of the queen. In appealing thus to the older and the newer theories of imperialism, Sprigg did not seem to understand that loyalty to the queen had been articulated by his humanitarian predecessors as part of a social contract. In return for loyalty to the queen, she guaranteed her subjects' political rights.

The Sotho men who attended the 1879 *pitso* remained attached to the older approach to empire. They believed that their loyalty was reciprocated by rights and liberties. One by one they rose to defend the old social contract. One of the most eloquent statements was made by Tsekelo Moshesh, the son of Moshoeshoe's sixth wife, who had represented his father during the negotiations establishing Cape administration in Basutoland. Tsekelo invoked the memory of Moshoeshoe and the history of the agreement, saying that "Moshesh was not simply brought to accept the Queen's Government by the pressure of circumstances." He deliberately chose British rule over rule by the Orange Free State, knowing "that by coming to the Queen's Government we should have full liberty.... We are highly delighted with the administration of justice in the Queen's dominions, and with the way in which your trials are conducted, and we wish to be like the English." And like the English, Tsekelo noted that the Sotho would not "accept any measure without discussion."[68]

In accepting English justice the Sotho accepted the possibility of punishment by English standards. They also knew that under the common law, they had a right to know why they were being punished. The paramount chief, Letsie, was one of several speakers who asked Sprigg and Griffith to tell the Sotho what they had done wrong.[69] They were not giving in to Sprigg's idea that disarmament was good for them: it

---

[67] BPP [C.2482] 1880, pp. 492–3.
[68] BPP [C.2482] 1880, p. 498.
[69] BPP [C.2482] 1880, p. 497.

was surely punishment, punishment for some misdeed. Ramalseatsana insisted that "as the Queen's subjects we have a right before our guns are taken away that our fault should be pointed out to us, otherwise we shall be very much alarmed if we have not heard what we are accused of. . . . "[70] Makotoko, "a Christian of Leribe," asked Sprigg directly if he thought the Sotho were planning to rebel. "Designs" to rebel would be grounds for disarmament. The audience responded, "We have no designs."[71]

If the Sotho had acted like disobedient children, they would accept punishment. As Lerotholi stated, "If we have broken the peace of the Queen, then let it be said right out to us, and let us be told that we are naughty boys."[72] Some of them even tentatively accepted Sprigg's paternalistic rhetoric toward them, provided that the government treated them fairly. Tsita Mofoka, described as a "hereditary chief," called himself and the Sotho "children" and "dogs." In his words, "When a parent takes away a sharp knife from a child he takes it away because he sees that the child has stuck himself with it, and we could see that Morosi had used this sharp knife and stuck himself, and it was right to take it away from him."[73] Even Letsie, the paramount chief, followed this line of reasoning to some extent, saying that "the Government wants to cut off our claws. The women cut off the nails of a little baby when they grow too long and it scratches at its face, and I want you, Colonel Griffith, to ask whether we scratch out our own eyes or whether we scratch out the eyes of the Government with these nails of ours?" Then, referring to the Boers who were disarmed by the British after the battle of Winburg, Letsie stated that "these were children of the Government who had scratched their eyes, and we saw it was quite right that they should be disarmed."[74]

There had already been one case, in 1877, in which two hundred Sotho men had willingly surrendered their guns to a magistrate. The magistrate at Thlotsi ended a fight between the supporters of two Sotho chiefs by requiring them to appear before his court. The local doctor, Henry Taylor, reported that "the next morning over 200 men rode in to the court-house, each carrying a rifle. . . . When the charge of fighting was read out to them, they all pleaded 'Guilty' in a unanimous shout; they were fined £2 each for the offence, and every man's rifle was confiscated

---

[70] BPP [C.2482] 1880, p. 500.
[71] BPP [C.2482] 1880, p. 495.
[72] BPP [C.2482] 1880, p. 499.
[73] BPP [C.2482] 1880, p. 496.
[74] BPP [C.2482] 1880, p. 497.

for three months. The whole 200 deposited their guns on the floor of the court-room without a word, each gun was labeled with the owner's name, and they were told they could come and fetch them in three months' time. The fines were duly paid, some in money and some in cattle, and the incident ended."[75] It was plausible for the men at the *pitso* to suggest that they would turn over their guns if they were charged with a specific offense.

Disarmament was a serious matter because the Sotho had come to believe that guns were held at the pleasure of the queen. Several men at the *pitso* reminded Sprigg that their guns "belong to the Queen." Tsita Mofoka stated that "[t]here is no question about these guns; they belong to the Queen, and they are there to serve the Queen." Makotoko restated this point, "As for the guns they belong to the Queen. (Cheers: 'They belong to the Queen.') We will follow the Queen with these guns." According to Lerotholi, Letsie's son, "the custom with us is that when a boy begins to run about he sharpens a stick and calls it an assegai, and stabs field mice with it, and now we have grown up and we have got guns, and these guns we say belong to the Queen." Guns "belonged" to the queen rhetorically and ideologically, even at the same time as they belonged to people. Lerotholi explained, "All that I have got to say is, that my gun belongs to the Queen, and that I will follow the Queen about with this gun wherever she goes and I will stick to it. I have got a gun that my father lent me, but there is also one of my own private property that I worked for."[76] Earning private property was one of the hallmarks of "civilization," under the older model of imperialism. In the newer model, represented by Sprigg, a benevolent government would deprive African workers of property.

The Sotho men pointed out that as citizens they were entitled to hold property like any Englishman. The property in question, guns, even received special sanction from the queen. These were the main ideological claims that they put up against Sprigg's attempt to introduce race-based disarmament. Tsekelo said, "And now what would become of our great confidence in the justice of the Queen's Government if now we are to be disarmed, not because we have done evil, but just because our colour is black." He continued, telling Sprigg that "the fault you have to find with us is our black colour; or, perhaps, it is true, as Mr. Upington said in

---

[75] Taylor, *Doctor to Basuto*, 21–2.
[76] BPP [C.2482] 1880, pp. 496, 499.

Parliament, we were the natural enemies of the white men because we were black."[77]

The shift to race-based restrictions was perhaps best summed up by Tsita Mofoka, who said that "I am only sorry that I am black to-day; I think that being black is a very great misfortune. The reason why I say it is a misfortune is that although you may be following the Government ever so faithfully, it turns round upon you, and says, 'You do not belong to me,' just because I have a black skin." Alas, in resisting racism, he showed that he too was coming to perceive Africans as "ethnic subjects" in much the same way as the colonial administrators were starting to do. He hoped for special status for the Sotho under disarmament laws. Sprigg had claimed that disarmament had been good for the Africans of the Eastern Cape. Tsita Mofoka responded by saying, "As for these tribes that have been mentioned, these Kafirs, we are not Kafirs, we are Basutos, we do not change our minds every day as the Kafirs do (cheers)."[78] As Jean and John Comaroff have written, missionaries and other agents of colonialism encouraged Africans to become two different sorts of people: modern citizens, holding property and obeying laws, and ethnic subjects, following special traditions ascribed to their groups.[79] This point has no better illustration than in the responses of the Sotho men at the *pitso*.

Sotho arguments against discrimination and in favor of continued protections from the queen were morally and legally convincing by the standards of the late 1870s. And legally, as Tsekelo pointed out, there was not yet a disarmament law for Basutoland. As he said, "if we are now being informed of a law that has been already established, then we must be told so distinctly." Technically, the governor had to proclaim that a district was to be disarmed and he had not yet added Basutoland to the list. Tsekelo also hoped that "then we will have a right to ask whether it is a law that is already irrevocably passed or not, and if so we will ask whether we were represented when this law was discussed. Now this is our Parliament, although it is a very disorderly Parliament."[80] He articulated a right to discuss the law while suggesting that the Sotho ought to have been represented during parliamentary discussion of a law that would affect them. It fell to Sprigg to articulate a response to these persuasive arguments.

[77] BPP [C.2482] 1880, pp. 498–9.
[78] BPP [C.2482] 1880, p. 496–7.
[79] Comaroff and Comaroff, *Revelation and Revolution*, 2:367–8.
[80] BPP [C.2482] 1880, p. 498.

Night fell before he could do so. The next day, Griffith invited the "principal chiefs" to meet with Sprigg in a Maseru schoolroom. The most influential chiefs – Letsie, Molapo, and Masopha – all claimed that they were too ill to attend. Only Tsekelo and several other Sotho leaders attended. Sprigg spoke first to Tsekelo's point that there was not yet an official governor's proclamation putting the Peace Preservation Act into effect in Basutoland. Sprigg claimed that on the previous day, "[n]o speaker appeared to me to understand the reasons which influenced the Government in shaping the [disarmament] policy which it proposes to carry out." He then explained to Tsekelo the way in which the Peace Preservation Bill became law, which was already perfectly clear. In the face of Tsekelo's concern that Sotho opinion should somehow be taken into consideration, Sprigg claimed that "[w]hen the Act was being discussed in the Cape Parliament, the Basutos were well represented by members of that Legislature who take a great interest in the affairs of Basutoland, and none of them more than myself." Not only did Sprigg and his colleagues claim to represent Basutoland, but he was now visiting Basutoland because he wanted "an opportunity of conferring with the people of Basutoland and gathering their opinions."[81]

Sprigg explained once again that race had nothing to do with disarmament. The Sotho would be disarmed "not because you are black, but because you are children." "You" plainly meant black people, an element of Sprigg's argument that had not been lost on the Sotho the day before. Sprigg continued, linking paternalist practice to claims about consciousness and behavior:

when the excitement of war is in the air you are hurried away in spite of all your good intentions. You call the Government your father, and it is as your father that I speak to-day. Yesterday I asked if you could tell me what good a gun was; I got no reply then, and I shall be glad if you can give me an answer to-day. I find that the possession of a gun on your part is a mere sentiment; some of you think it makes a man of you to have a gun. The Government, your father, does not think so. The past history of the native races has shown that it makes wild beasts of them; and it is because the Government thinks only of your good and advancement that it puts the question, whether it is not desirable for you, at the call of the Government, to give up your arms?[82]

In making this insulting argument, Sprigg hoped that the Sotho could be persuaded that it was in their own interests to give up their guns.

[81] BPP [C.2482] 1880, p. 502.
[82] BPP [C.2482] 1880, p. 502.

Sofonia, a son of Moshoeshoe who had been educated in Cape Town, rose to tell Sprigg that "[w]e have a proverb which says a man who makes a mistake in a public assembly cannot be killed, and we know that the Government of the Queen is freedom." This was a statement that could be understood in a number of ways, depending on whether the "man" in question meant Sprigg or Sofonia. Sofonia reiterated what other speakers had already said about how the Sotho had preferred Cape administration to administration by Natal or the Orange Free State, because the Cape more strongly guaranteed Sotho liberties and permitted the ownership of guns. For these reasons, Sofonia said that "I have no desire except to be a subject of the Queen, and therefore I say with boldness that a black man is not accorded equal rights with a white man." To Sofonia, and to others, it seemed that the Cape was reneging on its pledge of color blindness. The Cape was known for reneging on other pledges too. Sofonia reminded Sprigg that when the Cape abandoned the Orange River Sovereignty in 1854, the Sotho were placed in a difficult position vis-á-vis the land-hungry settlers of the Orange Free State.[83]

The Sotho men who attended this meeting made many of the same arguments that were made on the previous day. They asked many of the same questions, some based on their sense of entitlement to earned possessions and on their sense of "ethnic" superiority. What had they done wrong to deserve losing their guns? Had they not earned their guns? Were they not better than the Xhosa and the Mfengu? In response, Sprigg summarized Tsekelo's earlier point about guns and the roots of conflict: "Tsekelo says that taking away guns will not lessen the chances of war; that we must remove the causes of dissatisfaction and discontent." Sprigg dismissed this claim. The Sotho would be better off without guns, because the possession of guns caused conflict. According to Sprigg, the recent Zulu and Gcaleka wars had been caused by gun possession. He said, "It was the possession of those guns by the Zulus that led them to try the issue of war with the English Government." And in the case of the Ngqika, "they got possession of guns, and they thought they were strong enough at last to beat the English Government." Even France "thought she was strong enough by the possession of improved guns to beat the soldiers of the German Empire, and so she forced on a war mainly because she thought she was prepared for it by the possession of those

---

[83] BPP [C.2482] 1880, p. 503.

guns."[84] Putting an end to gun possession would diminish the likelihood of conflict.

Sprigg's reasoning seems awkward and flawed. The Zulu, Ngqika, and Gcaleka all acquired more guns during the 1870s, yet there is not a single reputable historian today who would argue that their conflicts with the Cape and the British Empire were caused by wider gun possession. Guns almost certainly made these conflicts more deadly but they had underlying economic, political, and social causes. Sprigg's claims were not convincing to the Sotho men who attended the 1879 *pitso*. They argued instead that they had earned their guns and that the guns were protected by the queen until it was proved that they had done something wrong. They rejected Sprigg's arguments as racist; Cape laws were supposed to be race blind. This was not simply a case of "resistance," as is commonly thought to have happened during imperialist expansion in Africa. The responses of the Sotho men demonstrate their clear concern not to be disarmed or dispossessed and yet to preserve ties to the British Empire. If anything, British settlers and a British governor pushed the Sotho into rebellion, at a time when many Sotho were attempting to articulate loyalism within the political culture that had begun to evolve under Moshoeshoe.

It was difficult for the Sotho to work constructively with a Cape government that seemed bent on antagonizing them. Any possibility for conciliation or trust seemed remote. Several months later, when the *pitso* transcript was published, the missionary Adolphe Mabille noted that "the official report of the Pitso does not contain a sentence of which all present say Mr. Sprigg made use of, namely, that he would not enforce disarmament, but that persuasion and advice would be the means used by the magistrates." This omission was noted in Basutoland as further evidence of the Cape government's untrustworthiness. As Mabille noted, "All these matters, small in themselves, but following each other, have made the people distrustful of the government."[85]

[84] BPP [C.2482] 1880, p. 507.
[85] BPP [C.2821] 1881, Mabille to Frere, February 17, 1880, p. 9.

The Origins of the Cape–Sotho Gun War, 1879–80

The Cape government of Gordon Sprigg was slowly but surely alienating Sotho loyalists. Shortly after Sprigg's *pitso*, on November 20, 1879, Cape forces brought their siege of Moorosi's mountain to a bloody conclusion. The Cape Mounted Rifles stormed the mountain and killed Moorosi and his sons. The chief's head was severed and his body parts were put on display – accounts vary as to the grisly details. The power of Cape forces and the results of resistance were made plain for all the residents of Basutoland to see. The Phuthi were scattered to work on Cape farms, except for a small minority of Christians who had remained loyal.[1] Sprigg began to arrange for the Cape government to auction Phuthi land in the Quthing district to European settlers, in the face of embarrassed protests from Griffith, who reminded Sprigg that the former Cape governor, Sir Philip Wodehouse, had promised Moshoeshoe that the British would never alienate any part of Basutoland from the Sotho paramount chief's domain.[2]

The chiefs' allies in the Aborigines Protection Society lobbied effectively in London. As a result, the Colonial Office increased its scrutiny of Sprigg's government. Just after Sprigg's *pitso*, on November 18, 1879, delegates of the society met with Lord Kimberley, the former secretary of state for the colonies. Even though Kimberley no longer held

---

[1] Atmore, "The Moorosi Rebellion: Lesotho, 1879," 31–5. Atmore's account of the mutilation is somewhat at odds with a report in the *Christian Express*, entitled "Mutilation of Morosi's Body," printed in the *Cape Argus*, February 10, 1880, supplement.

[2] BPP [C.2569] 1880, Encl. in No. 14, Governor's Agent, Griffith to Ayliff, November 27, 1879, pp. 34–5. Burman, *Chiefdom Politics and Alien Law*, 135–6.

a cabinet position, he remained the Liberal party's leader in colonial matters. He was particularly interested in the issue of disarmament in Basutoland.

When it came to disarmament, Kimberley was in a curious position. He had served as Lord Lieutenant of Ireland from 1864 to 1866, when he himself had imposed a Peace Preservation Act. He was also the cousin of Sir Philip Wodehouse, and was well acquainted with his cousin's dealings with Moshoeshoe. The Aborigines Protection Society hoped to find more favor in Kimberley than in the Conservative secretary of state, Sir Michael Hicks Beach, who declined to meet with them. In doing so, Hicks Beach did solicit more information, which was ultimately published in parliamentary command papers.[3]

Much information from Basutoland bypassed Sprigg and Frere and went by a circuitous route to London. The Sotho chiefs and other influential Sotho men spoke to their French Protestant missionaries. The missionaries corresponded with their headquarters in Paris, and also with the Aborigines Protection Society in London. There, the Aborigines Protection Society laid the concerns of the missionaries, and, indirectly, of the Sotho, at the doorstep of the Colonial Office. Eugène Casalis, director of the Paris Evangelical Missionary Society, used this circuitous system to hammer home his point about the need to trust loyal Africans. "They [Sprigg and his ministers] mistrust the Basutos," Casalis wrote to the Aborigines Protection Society, "which is the origin of their mistaken policy. . . . The disarmament will cause much discontent and division among the people, destroy every vestige of confidence in & attachment to the British government to whom they have proved so submissive & faithful." According to Casalis, the Sotho might naturally have given up guns over time as they became more "civilized," but that process of civilization was about to be disrupted by conflict. Casalis was so concerned to preserve the Sotho missions that he asked Frederick Chesson, the secretary of the society, to withhold his name from any publications, even as Chesson was sharing Casalis's letters with Hicks Beach, the secretary of state for the colonies.[4]

The Sotho, supported by a network of French and British sympathizers, proved more adept at manipulating the imperial government than the Cape premier, Sprigg, who was issuing threats that were not likely

---

[3] PRO, CO 48/498, Chesson to CO, January 21, 1880; CO to Chesson, February 4, 1880.
[4] RHL Anti-Slavery Papers, Mss. Brit. Emp. S18 C128/62, Casalis to Chesson, January 13, 1880; S18 C128/63, Casalis to Chesson, January 27, 1880.

to be backed up by an imperial government that was becoming wary of military adventures in South Africa. To weaken Sprigg's position further, the Gcaleka War, the Zulu War, as well as smaller disturbances in Griqualand East, Tembuland, and Pondoland were making settlers weary of fighting, especially since a drought was in full swing during the summer of 1879–80. The *Cape Argus* even noted that Sprigg's aggressive, posturing correspondence with the Sotho – in which he referred to himself as "the master of the Colony," – was "like a tale told by an idiot, full of sound and fury, signifying nothing."[5]

Negotiating Sotho Disarmament

In spite of such *ad hominem* attacks in Saul Solomon's newspaper, Sprigg's message was gaining ground in powerful circles. It appears that Sprigg was collaborating closely with Frere, who had real talent for rhetoric and diplomacy. Possibly on account of Frere's influence, Sprigg began to moderate his tone somewhat in late 1879. In his letters to Griffith, he urged diplomacy – what Griffith had been doing all along. In December Sprigg wrote, "I feel sure that if the Disarmament business is managed with discretion we shall have a great success there – and we shall be able to meet Parl^t & show the opposition...that all their gloomy predictions are falsified."[6] Again, in January 1880, Sprigg requested moderation, advising Griffith that "the thing has to be done *gradually* & *carefully* & with *all consideration* for the *circumstances of the hour*, while at the same time you will need to be firm."[7] Firmness involved putting pressure on Letsie, who Sprigg thought needed to be reminded that "a man who draws such large incomes as he does from the public treasury is expected to aid the Gov^t and not oppose it."[8]

While Sprigg learned about diplomacy, Frere was an old hand who held a broader, imperial perspective on disarmament. Diplomacy and knowledge made it possible for him to articulate the policy of imperialist disarmament based on experiences in other colonies. Frere took on

---

[5] *Cape Argus*, January 13, 1880, p. 2; January 20, 1880, p. 2. In the Cape parliament, Sprigg's nickname was the "Master of the Colony." This was a double entendre, referring to his political mastery and also to his manner, which resembled that of a schoolmaster.

[6] CTAR, NA 279, Griffith to Sauer, June 5, 1881, No. 1, "Copies of Semi-Official Letters," Encl. Sprigg to Griffith, December 9, 1879.

[7] CTAR, NA 279, Griffith to Sauer, June 5, 1881, No. 1, "Copies of Semi-Official Letters," Encl. Sprigg to Griffith, January 19, 1880.

[8] CTAR, NA 279, Griffith to Sauer, June 5, 1881, No. 1, "Copies of Semi-Official Letters," Encl. Sprigg to Griffith, February 3, 1880.

the missionaries directly. On January 17, 1880, Frere wrote to Adolphe Mabille, the obstreperous French missionary to the Sotho, advising him to stop encouraging the Sotho to resist disarmament. Mabille protested that the Sotho were loyal. Frere responded that many loyal nations under British rule had been disarmed, including Scotland and Ireland. According to Frere, initial reluctance to disarm soon gave way to gratitude: "within a second generation you would have found it difficult to meet with a dozen sensible Highlanders who did not in their hearts applaud the measure." In India, disarmament after the rebellion of 1857 "was only one of many measures, often very unpalatable at first to the people affected, but so evidently for their good in the long run, that the people at length recognized the spirit which enacted it."[9] Frere's service in India and his wide knowledge of imperial affairs made it possible for him to build a comparative case. The constitution of a new kind of order in South Africa was related to new orders elsewhere, in spite of local differences. Colonial governors often had a comparative perspective, on account of their prior service as administrators. Their perspective allowed them to make comparative arguments that colonists, lacking such experience, could not easily refute. Yet the comparative perspective opened up the possibility that laws that were suitable to one colonial milieu might be introduced to places where they would not be well received.

Frere trusted that "meantime you and your fellow missionaries will take the parent's side." Like Sprigg, Frere conceived of relations between Europeans and the Sotho in terms of parents and children. He argued through parental metaphors and analogies. "Do I 'doom' my child 'to destruction,' or do him any wrong, if I take from him the sharp knife which has just been given to him as a birthday present.... The child thinks he is quite able to use the knife without risk to his own fingers. I, as his parent, think differently, and I insist upon my right, or in other words, I tell him my might, my parental authority, must override his right to have his own knife."[10]

Frere sought disarmament out of paternalistic concern for African development. He also made the related argument that guns fostered negative developments in African consciousness. According to Frere, new owners of guns thought themselves to be more powerful than they really were.

---

9 BPP [C.2821] 1881, Frere to Mabille, January 17, 1880, Encl. 2 in No. 1, pp. 4–6.
10 BPP [C.2821] 1881, Encl. 2 in No. 1, Frere to Mabille, January 17, 1880, pp. 4–6.

Many Natives, and Europeans also, and I might say the greater number of Natives, are encouraged by the possession of arms to form inordinate ideas of their own prowess and importance. You see the same with children of all races. A lad who has never had a gun thinks himself a man directly he is entrusted with it, but in the case of Natives this weakness is carried to an unusual extent, and I have no doubt whatever in my own mind that the facilities with which guns have been obtained by Natives of all classes in all parts of the country has [*sic*] been one main cause of the war fever of which we have had of late so many and such distressing symptoms.[11]

Frere linked guns to changes in African behavior toward the state. According to this argument, guns promoted a premature masculinity that was associated with rebellion. But Sotho men perceived the relation between guns and order differently. They associated guns with the broader rights of citizenship that came with British rule. Letsie skillfully sought redress by applying to Frere and the queen, in separate but identical petitions submitted on January 21, 1880. In doing so, Letsie was following the correct procedure for forwarding a complaint. To make the complaint more powerful, the letter was co-signed by Jonathan and Lepoyo, the delegates of Molapo and Masopha, and forwarded by Adolphe Mabille, the French missionary to the Sotho.[12] Ironically, Mabille had played a key role in instructing Letsie in the ways of British political culture. Later, Mabille wrote that he taught Letsie "that he was a British subject, and that, as such, he had certain rights. Starting from the point that, in a general way, the British Government was founded on justice and equity, I told the chiefs that they were allowed certain privileges, such as to draw up petitions, and to send deputations, always adding that, after they had tried *all constitutional means*, if they failed to get what they thought were their rights, they were bound to obey; that resistance would be useless, and life and existence were better than death and ruin."[13] It is apparent that Griffith, too, had instructed Letsie on petitioning the government. On April 11, Letsie wrote to Griffith, stating, "What makes me glad in your letter is that you say that, as all British subjects, I have the right to petition the Colonial Parliament... but I am deeply grieved to find that we are, as it were, deprived of the right to place our complaints before the Queen." He addressed a petition to the queen.[14]

---

[11] BPP [C.2821] 1881, Frere to Mabille, January 17, 1880, Encl. 2 in No. 1, p. 5.

[12] BPP [C.2569] 1880, Encl. 1 in No. 10, "Petition of Basuto Chiefs and People," p. 10.

[13] BPP [C.2755] Encl. in No. 10, Mabille to Sprigg, June 22, 1880, pp. 13–15; also published as an open letter in the *Cape Argus*, June 30, 1880.

[14] BPP [C.2755] Encl. in No. 25, Letsie to Griffith, April 11, 1880, p. 92.

Griffith's and Mabille's instructions about privileges and petitions touched the core of English (if not British) political culture. In the English tradition "petition" has a specific and powerful meaning. It is a document in which subjects ask the monarch or the parliament for something. The most dramatic petition is a Petition of Right, addressed to the monarch, often for the recognition of a right that the monarch had taken away. When a king or queen accepts a petition of right, this implies that the right is now officially recognized and restored. There are a number of famous petitions in English history. For example, the 1628 Petition of Right asked Charles I to stop collecting taxes that had not been approved by parliament, one of several rights that he had knowingly violated. There are also hundreds of lesser known petitions made by obscure people concerning local problems. These are significant for another reason. Ordinary subjects could petition the government, even if they did not have the vote – which few people had before the Reform Act of 1832. Even without a vote, the petition allowed ordinary subjects to represent their views to the government.[15]

The petition suited the Sotho, who had been denied representation in the Cape parliament. Letsie's petition, like other historic petitions, reiterated the complaints made by the chiefs at the October 1879 *pitso*, when they insisted that Sprigg could only justify disarmament by showing that the Sotho were not loyal. Letsie argued that the Sotho had done their "utmost to obey" the Cape's magistrates. This was noted by the previous Cape governor, Sir Henry Barkly, who had written that he had "never had reason to doubt the loyalty of the chiefs or people." Many Sotho had even become Christians. "Therefore may we not confidently ask, what have we done that the Government should disarm us."[16]

The format of the petition allowed resistance to be articulated with the language of loyalty. According to Letsie, the loyalty of the people was enough to guarantee the peace. It was not guaranteed by disarmament, as Sprigg had argued. Letsie wrote, "Our guns will never precede us, nor teach us to do anything which may be at variance with the Queen's will." Only people could do that. "A gun is a dead thing, only a piece of wood with a piece of iron attached to it. Had they a will of their own to do mischief, then we could understand that the Government has a right to disarm us." Letsie went on to use the issue of disarmament to question the validity of the Cape's jurisdiction over Basutoland, and reiterated

---

[15] Colley, *Britons*, 51–2. Maier, *American Scripture*, 50.
[16] BPP [C.2569] 1880, Encl. 1 in No. 10, "Petition of Basuto Chiefs and People," p. 10.

Sotho demands for an explanation for disloyalty. There had to be a reason for the Sotho to be disarmed disgracefully. Letsie concluded by saying that "disarmament to us is as if we were being disgraced in our own eyes and in the eyes of all our neighbours. It is just as if an animal was deprived of its natural means of defence." Such a disgrace could only be explained by one thing: "Have we not a right to suppose that we are to be disarmed because we are black, and are therefore not trusted by the Government," which was ironic, because "this Government has been sought by ourselves."[17] Sprigg accepted Letsie's petition and asked the governor, Frere, to forward it to the queen. While the colony waited for a response from the British government, Sprigg postponed Sotho disarmament. As Sprigg awaited a decision, he gave a speech to an Eastern Cape audience in which he denounced the petition as "twaddle."[18] As the Sotho people awaited a decision, they expressed the hope that they might be separated from the Cape, and governed directly by Britain through a high commissioner.[19]

Meanwhile, the French missionaries resumed lobbying the Colonial Office in London. Like Letsie, the missionaries focused on the issue of loyalty. The Sotho had just "given the Government the most satisfactory proof of their loyalty by assisting in subduing the Chief Morosi" and did not understand why they should now be disarmed. To the Sotho, "the possibility of being called to give up their arms . . . is, in their opinion, the most irrational and opprobrious treatment that can be inflicted on man." After disarmament, they feared oppression. All this was disastrous from a missionary perspective. The mission was fostering an "increasing taste for civilisation," which made the Sotho "more and more averse to everything resembling war. The very men who may now consider the disarmament as an insult and a threat, suffered their guns to rust in a corner."[20] That was not entirely true: many enterprising men had just bought new guns. The missionaries had great faith in the idea that "civilization" would gradually bring with it a natural aversion to warfare and weapons.

---

[17] BPP [C.2569] 1880, Encl. 1 in No. 10, "Petition of Basuto Chiefs and People," pp. 10–11.

[18] *Cape Argus*, February 17, 1880, p. 2.

[19] *Cape Argus*, "Basutoland: From Our Special Correspondent," February 7, 1880, p. 2.

[20] BPP [C.2569] 1880, Encl. in No. 7, Casalis et al. to Hicks Beach, February 25, 1880, pp. 4–6. See also the letters of Coillard, Mabille, and the board of the Paris Evangelical Mission Society enclosed in BPP [C.2821] 1881, "Correspondence Respecting the Affairs of Basutoland."

Although the missionaries believed in civilization and progress, all advanced by Christianity, they criticized Frere and Sprigg for conceiving of the Sotho as metaphorical children who might eventually grow to civilizational adulthood. In a letter to Mabille, Frere responded by adding some nuance to his statements about "children." According to him, "I never said and never meant that they were more 'childish' in any other respect than the great British people to which they belong, who are all the children of the British Government, and who in England are liable to punishment for carrying arms without a licence or other legal authority."[21] He had, in fact, said "Many Natives, and Europeans also, and I might say the greater number of Natives, are encouraged by the possession of arms to form inordinate ideas of their own prowess and importance. You see the same with children of all races."[22] And Sprigg had told the *pitso* that they were children.

While missionaries corresponded with the governor and lobbied the Colonial Office, the governor's agent in Basutoland, Charles Griffith, also communicated his deep reservations about policy to Cape Town. A few days after Letsie sent his petition, Griffith sent an anguished letter to William Ayliff, the secretary for native affairs, complaining about the new Basutoland policies. These included the threat of disarmament, together with the threat to expropriate Moorosi's territory in Quthing; the doubling of hut taxes; and the appropriation of £12,500 in surplus revenue from the chiefs. These measures, taken together, provoked Griffith to respond in the strongest possible terms for a civil servant:

I cannot but feel that I have been placed in an equivocal position, one which must naturally create a wide gap in that good feeling which has hitherto existed between the whole nation and myself as their "Father" and the Government Representative.... I have now had the honour to serve Her Majesty in different positions of difficulty and trust with an *unsullied reputation* for *thirty-two* years, and therefore I am loth to run the risk of losing this hard-won reputation without raising one warning note.[23]

As Griffith saw it, paternalism was being undermined. Colonial officials perceived that loyalty had a personal dimension. If the chiefs could not trust Griffith, broader policy aims, such as civilization and citizenship, could not be carried out. Yet Sprigg remained bent on disarming the

---

[21] BPP [C.2821] 1881, Encl. 6 in No. 1, Frere to Mabille, March 7, 1880, p. 11.
[22] BPP [C.2821] 1881, Encl. 2 in No. 1, Frere to Mabille, January 17, 1880, p. 5.
[23] BPP [C.2755] Griffith to Ayliff, January 26, 1880, pp. 73–4.

Sotho and his response to Griffith was stern. He sent a telegram on February 9, saying, "Meanwhile I may tell you for your guidance that there will be no wavering, and you can inform the Magistrates and the Chiefs and headmen that the Govt is aware of the purport of the petition and that it intends to enforce your notice and if they wish to stand well with the Government they will listen to what you say."[24] Sprigg also began to wonder about Griffith's loyalty. On February 13, Sprigg wrote to Griffith, "*I don't doubt your Allegiance for a moment,* but you might imagine that the Gov^t would be influenced by the malignant advice to which they are exposed. It is not so, we are going through with the business."[25]

Proclaiming Disarmament in Basutoland

Sprigg and Frere decided to act – before receiving instructions from London. Frere read Letsie's petition and consulted with Sprigg and his ministers. Frere mailed Letsie's petition to the Colonial Office in London on February 20, then followed up on March 2 with a letter in which he criticized Letsie's petition. Before that, though, on February 26, the Cape Colony's undersecretary for native affairs, H. E. R. Bright, wrote to Griffith, advising him that the governor had received and rejected the petition. Bright informed Griffith that the colonial government intended to enforce the Peace Preservation Act in Basutoland.[26] Sprigg also wrote to Griffith, "I am not going to do anything that will give just cause for a rising of the people. I expect a large number of guns will be surrendered, and those that are concealed will become worthless."[27] The government would not conduct house-to-house searches because hidden weapons would fall into disuse, or so went the theory.

The Cape government's decision was made without reference to the queen and the British government, who were still considering the petition. This raised several political questions at once: constitutionally, the governor answered to the queen and the British government, while personally, Frere owed his continuing employment to Victoria, who had supported

---

[24] CTAR, NA 279, Griffith to Sauer, June 5, 1881, No. 2, "Copies of Telegrams," Encl. Sprigg to Griffith, February 9, 1880.

[25] CTAR, NA 279, Griffith to Sauer, June 5, 1881, No. 1, "Copies of Semi-Official Letters," Encl. Sprigg to Griffith, October 5, 1878.

[26] BPP [C.2755] Bright to Griffith, February 26, 1880, pp. 70–3.

[27] CTAR, NA 279, Griffith to Sauer, June 5, 1881, No. 1, "Copies of Semi-Official Letters," Encl. Sprigg to Griffith, February 26, 1880.

him even as he ruined his reputation in the Zulu War. To complicate matters, the Sotho, like many South Africans under British rule, were thought to conceive of loyalty to Britain as personal loyalty to the queen. As the *Cape Argus* put it, in the language of the day, "Personal attachment is a powerful factor in the loyalty of a savage or semi-civilized people, and if Mr. Sprigg has calculated upon a transfer of Basuto affections from the Great Queen to himself, he whom they have dubbed 'the forgetful one,' he has unquestionably reckoned without his head. What the Basutos have seen and heard of the Colonial Secretary [Prime Minister Sprigg] is not calculated to inspire them with devotion, reverence, or any kindred qualities."[28] The Sotho would never trust Sprigg; nor was Sotho trust being repaid in any British officials. Griffith, who had served as governor's agent since 1872, and who had even been called "father" by some Sotho, was now condemned. He had promised the Sotho, in exchange for their help against Moorosi, they could keep their guns and also have a share in Moorosi's land, which was now being divided amongst settlers.[29]

In London the Colonial Office began to move in the opposite direction of Sprigg and Frere. The concerns of the missionaries coupled with the British public's reluctance to support aggressive imperial designs in South Africa persuaded Sir Michael Hicks Beach, the secretary of state for the colonies, to send an important message to Frere on March 10, 1880. Hicks Beach now urged that disarming the Sotho would probably lead to "serious trouble." "I strongly recommend caution," he continued. While he hesitated to "interfere with the responsibility of your ministers," he wanted them to "clearly understand that no Imperial troops can be furnished."[30] The importance of this message was underlined by the fact that it was sent by telegraph, which had only just connected Britain to South Africa via submarine cable. In the wake of Isandlwana, the British government hoped that rapid communication would bring closer control over Cape affairs, although as Daniel Headrick has argued it may have only helped colonial administrators to further manipulate London.[31] In any event, the message did not arrive in time, and the simultaneous reliance on shipboard mail and telegraphy complicated communications. Frere received Hicks Beach's telegram on March 11; while Hicks

---

[28] *Cape Argus*, March 6, 1880, pp. 2–3.

[29] "Basutoland: Not One Question, but Many: From our Special Correspondent," *Cape Argus*, March 23, 1880, p. 3 and suppl.

[30] BPP [C.2569] 1880, No. 8, Hicks Beach to Frere, March 10, 1880, p. 6.

[31] Headrick, *Tentacles of Progress*, 106–7.

Beach received Letsie's petition on March 18 and Frere's response on March 25.[32]

The embattled Frere began to shift his own position. Initially he had recommended a more flexible approach to Basutoland gun regulation than Sprigg wanted. Now, after the *pitso*, Frere supported Sprigg's position that uniform African disarmament was necessary, including the disarmament of the Sotho. Frere probably sensed that his supporters in London were wavering, while local, settler support might be courted fruitfully. Frere appears to have been persuaded of the need for stricter gun control by Bright, the undersecretary for native affairs, who recorded his advice to Frere in a memorandum to Griffith. From this, it seems that all Bright did was to reiterate the statements that Sprigg had already made to the Sotho. Bright wrote to Griffith, the governor's agent in Basutoland, telling him that Letsie knew full well the government's reasons for disarmament. Letsie and the Sotho had been informed of them by Sprigg personally when he visited the *pitso*. The transcript of the *pitso* was even translated into the Sotho language, published as a pamphlet, and sent to Sotho leaders. Bright quoted the part in which Sprigg urged the Sotho to consider how disarmament would bring peace to South Africa. Bright quoted Sprigg, who had remarked to the Sotho that disarmament "is for your own advantage, and that you will willingly accede to the order of the Government." Sprigg forwarded the petition, and Bright's response, to the governor's office, minuting to Frere that he completely agreed with Bright's assessment.[33]

Frere consulted with the Cape government and decided to deny Letsie's petition against disarmament. Frere outlined his reasons in the dispatch that he sent to Hicks Beach on March 2, 1880. Frere made what was, for the time, a strong critique of Letsie's petition, calling it "groundless" and filled with "fallacies which have been industriously inculcated upon the Basutos." He believed that the petition had actually been drawn up by "an accomplished European." The document was not authentically Sotho, even though the author used "the local colours of Basuto imagery." The author was trying to make a sentimental appeal, not a reasoned argument. According to Frere, reasoned discourse was not likely when "dealing with a people like the Basutos, so much more guided by their feelings than by their reason." Frere's own reasoned argument

[32] BPP [C.2569] 1880, Nos. 8–10, p. 6.
[33] BPP [C.2569] 1880, Encl. 4 in No. 10, Bright to Griffith, February 26, 1880, pp. 13–15. Sprigg's minute of March 2, 1880, is attached as Encl. 5 in No. 10.

was that people did not carry arms in Britain and other "civilized coun-tries." Disarmament was a "precautionary measure, to prevent casual and sanguinary breaches of the peace, such as constantly occur in a popula-tion which habitually goes armed." Disarmament was "also intended to remove an obvious temptation to resistance to lawful authority and even to rebellion." Even so, disarmament was "not to be taken as evidence of 'suspicion of disloyalty,' nor as a punishment nor as a measure which involves any humiliation." In England, people were generally disarmed, yet nobody doubted the loyalty of the English. Nobody called the English children, either, but Frere continued to compare the Sotho to children: "A parent of course takes mischievous weapons out of the hands of his own children, not because he fears that the children may use them against their parents, but because he knows it is well for the children that they should not always be handling weapons which may destroy themselves or their friends, without any previous ill-will or malice." There was now only one point on which Frere felt the need for some flexibility. First, disarmament would be voluntary, and then, after the Peace Preservation Act was proclaimed, there would still not be widespread house-to-house searches. The police would pay a fair price for weapons and prevent the public carrying of arms. This measure would get people out of the habit of carrying arms and would encourage general disarmament.[34]

After he sent this letter to Hicks Beach, Frere received the secretary of state's telegram of March 10, 1880, urging caution and threatening to withhold imperial troops. Hicks Beach began his message by saying, "It has been represented to me that, if disarmament is enforced on the Basutos, serious trouble is possible."[35] Frere was referring to another letter that he had just received from the Aborigines Protection Society, who reported that the most famous missionary in South Africa, Robert Moffat, was concerned about the hypocrisy of disarming Africans who had been encouraged to buy guns.[36] Three days after receiving the tele-gram from Hicks Beach, Frere responded by informing Hicks Beach of the "caution and firmness" of Sprigg and his cabinet, "who were fully alive to their responsibility, but who also felt the danger of leaving arms in the hands of a population able to defy the law." Frere expanded on this telegram in a letter that he mailed to Hicks Beach on March 15, 1880.

[34] BPP [C.2569] 1880, No. 10, Frere to Hicks Beach, March 2, 1880, pp. 6–10.
[35] BPP [C.2569] 1880, No. 8, Hicks Beach to Frere, March 10, 1880, p. 6.
[36] BPP [C.2676] 1880, No. 1, Aborigines Protection Society (Chesson) to Colonial Office, March 6, 1880, pp. 1–2.

In this letter, he made the most sweeping case for disarmament that any official had yet made in a public document, although much had already been rehearsed in his January 17 letter to Mabille.[37]

Frere summarized the principal arguments against disarmament. Before his arrival at the Cape, "It had become the fashion . . . to say that 'Kaffir wars were things of the past.'" Traders and "even men of high principle" argued that the availability of guns in the Cape Colony would attract African laborers. Traders and "even sensible missionaries" argued that a free trade in guns would bring with it desirable economic developments. They argued "that the better the natives were supplied with guns the more rapid would be the destruction of game, and the necessity which would thence be imposed upon the native tribes to take to habits of stricter industry than those of the hunter." This argument did indeed have a long pedigree in South Africa. We have already seen William Burchell making the same case as early as 1812. Frere disagreed. Migrant laborers to the Cape came from the north; on their way home, they passed through the Boer republics with their guns, even though the republics prohibited Africans from carrying arms. Yet it was unclear how Frere saw his summary as a refutation.[38]

Frere mocked humanitarian arguments about skill: that "a native tribe armed with firearms [is] less formidable than one armed after their own fashion with assegais." According to Frere, the Zulu War and Moorosi's rebellion had amply demonstrated that Africans could shoot well. Similar evidence was available from the Gcaleka War and from engagements with rebels along the border of Griqualand West. Frere was like the settlers in that he perceived a threat from African skill. To bolster his argument further, he added that a majority of settlers now favored African disarmament. And he claimed that disarmament was not only supported by Sprigg's ministry, but by the previous ministry of Molteno, too.[39]

Frere then moved beyond local circumstances to make general arguments in favor of disarmament. In the first place, the possession of guns changed the behavior of "natives." "The general possession of firearms by natives" tended "to increase their martial pride and conceit in their

[37] BPP [C.2569] 1880, No. 13, Frere to Hicks Beach, March 15, 1880, p. 17. BPP [C.2821] 1881, Encl. 2 in No. 1, Frere to Mabille, January 17, 1880, pp. 4–6. The letter to Mabille was made public only in 1881.
[38] BPP [C.2569] 1880, No. 13, Frere to Hicks Beach, March 15, 1880, p. 17.
[39] BPP [C.2569] 1880, No. 13, Frere to Hicks Beach, March 15, 1880, pp. 17–19.

prowess." "In a vain uncivilised race," Frere continued, "the possession of a gun is apt to encourage the most pernicious amount of self conceit and belief in the invincibility of the owner. It is a direct incentive to insubordination and war."[40] There were connections between guns, thoughts, and deeds.

In fact, according to Frere, the rare sight of guns in England was a sign of civilization. And "To a man accustomed to the usages of civilised society, the question [of disarmament] requires little argument." Violent crime was more likely in places where arms were habitually carried – in seaport towns, in Albania and Montenegro, and even in America and Australia. Frere claimed, "It is self-evident that persons who do not carry arms professionally, or for purposes of sport, can have no legitimate use for them, or need of them, except for self-defence. In a well-ordered community where the police protects the unarmed, the carrying of arms is entirely superfluous." Englishmen had come to believe that security was the concern of the state, not the individual. Orderly communities did not need individuals to carry guns. It was the duty of the state to protect people from criminals as well as from external enemies. The Sotho feared that if they were disarmed they would be attacked by the Orange Free State. Frere urged calm, stating, "This of course is an argument which cannot be admitted by any government really intending to protect the life and property of its subjects."[41]

Communities that were coming under English "order" needed to be disarmed. Frere wrote that "a wise government cannot permit any portion of the population, whose attachment to the government is in the least doubtful, to remain generally possessed of arms." In the eighteenth century, this had been government policy in Scotland, and in the nineteenth century, it was policy in Ireland. In India during the rebellion of 1857, Lord Canning had disarmed sepoys suspected of disloyalty. It did not matter if the loyal and the disloyal were treated alike, because the government could not determine, at any given point, exactly who was loyal and who was disloyal. General disarmament was the only practicable policy. Even if it proved difficult to confiscate all the

---

[40] BPP [C.2569] 1880, No. 13, Frere to Hicks Beach, March 15, 1880, pp. 18–19.
[41] BPP [C.2569] 1880, No. 13, Frere to Hicks Beach, March 15, 1880, pp. 19–20. Frere's dispatch arrived at the Colonial Office on April 7, 1880. Two more letters by Frere, dated March 17 and May 6, and covering much of the same ground, arrived on April 15 and June 5. See BPP [C.2569] 1880, No. 16, Frere to Hicks Beach, March 17, 1880, pp. 38–41. BPP [C.2676] 1880, No. 23, Frere to Secretary of State for the Colonies, May 6, 1880, pp. 42–4.

guns, if people got out of the habit of carrying guns in public, disarmament would eventually be achieved. And proposing universal African disarmament would not inspire universal African revolt. He derided this possible counterargument as "difficult of proof or disproof, save by experience." This, of course, was also true of much of his own argument.[42]

Frere's argument persuaded some, but not all, in the Colonial Office. The assistant undersecretary, Edward Wingfield, minuted, "I am afraid that the answer of the Cape Ministry will not convince the Basutos – that disarmament is not a sign of want of confidence in them and there can be little doubt that it will lower them in the eyes of the other native races." He went on to recommend that the Cape carry out a modest climb-down from their strict policy of disarmament, including a grace period for the voluntary surrender of arms, and a ban on searches of houses. Yet Hicks Beach was inclined to agree with Frere, at least initially. He minuted that the Peace Preservation Act was not like the act of the same name in Ireland, where it was directed at rebellious communities. Hicks Beach followed Frere, writing that the law was aimed at getting the Sotho out of the habit of carrying arms, "in accordance with the custom of civilized nations."[43]

At around the same time as Hicks Beach was receiving Frere's dispatches, he also received two seemingly contradictory dispatches from Wolseley, written in Pretoria on March 10 and received in London on April 15. In the first letter, which was circulated only to the British cabinet as a "confidential print," Wolseley reiterated his concerns about the gun trade in Africa. He condemned the gun trade as one of the most important factors contributing to the continued existence of the slave trade. He advocated a complete ban on gun sales to Africans, for the reason "that to completely prevent the supply of fire-arms and ammunition to its people would be to kill the slave trade, and at the same time to put an end to all serious wars between the European settlers and the Natives." He hoped that parliament would pass an act banning British subjects from engaging in the arms trade in Africa and that other countries would follow suit.[44]

---

[42] BPP [C.2569] 1880, No. 13, Frere to Hicks Beach, March 15, 1880, pp. 19–20.

[43] PRO CO 48/494, Frere to Hicks Beach, confidential, March 2, 1880, with minutes of April 1 by Wingfield and April 9 by Hicks Beach.

[44] PRO CO 879/17 Conf. Pr. Africa No. 222, Wolseley to Hicks Beach, March 10, 1880, pp. 7–8.

On the same day, Wolseley wrote another letter to Hicks Beach, criticizing Frere's efforts at gun control in Basutoland. Hicks Beach published this one as a command paper and circulated it to the entire parliament, perhaps hoping to use it as a way to pressure Frere to step down. Wolseley wrote that he still believed that "nearly all the danger to which our position in South Africa exposes us, arises from the indiscriminate possession of firearms by the Kafirs in and around the several British colonies." He sought to end the gun trade, but thought it would be impossible to disarm Africans who already had guns. According to Wolseley, "any general attempt to disarm them [Africans in South Africa] would be a most dangerous experiment." It was neither practical nor ideal to suggest disarmament. Wolseley picked up on the arguments already put forward by some humanitarians and Africans about political culture. He wrote to Hicks Beach that Africans might ask, "Is this the manner in which the Government rewards our loyalty?" Wolseley pointed out that many Africans had been loyal to Britain during the wars of the 1870s, and that the British government and British merchants had taken a permissive attitude to the gun trade, hoping that it would encourage migrant laborers to come to the Cape and Griqualand West. A general order for African disarmament would be so provocative that it might cause a "general rising of the natives against the white man in South Africa," something that had never happened before "because we have never yet adopted any line of policy that was calculated to unite them generally against us." If a "Basuto war" were to break out, "every native from the Zambesi to Cape Agulhas will feel that every shot fired in it against us, has been fired in his interests." He predicted that other Africans would join the Sotho, that the Cape did not have "military forces capable of dealing effectually with the Basutos," and that a war with the Sotho could only be won with regular troops from Britain, which meant that the British government should pay close attention to the Cape's scheme for disarmament.[45]

Frere did not wait for a response to his March 1880 letters. On April 6, 1880, he proclaimed that the Peace Preservation Act would be in force in Basutoland, effective May 21, 1880.[46] His position entitled him to make such proclamations, without permission from the Colonial Office, because Act 12 of 1871, under which Basutoland came under Cape administration, empowered the governor to make and enforce proclamations there, so long as the Cape parliament was willing to pay the expense.

45 BPP [C.2569] 1880, No. 15, Wolseley to Hicks Beach, March 10, 1880, pp. 36–7.
46 BPP [C.2569] 1880, No. 17, Frere to Hicks Beach, April 6, 1880, pp. 43–5.

The *Cape Argus* estimated that to buy 18,000 guns it would cost the government £100,000, a large sum of money that the Sotho might then use to buy guns again, albeit from smugglers.[47] The question of Sotho disarmament became closely related to the question of how independent a "responsible" colonial government could be. Did the Cape's legislators have enough money to foot the bill for independent actions? Could settlers act responsibly with regard to indigenous populations? These were the key points of reference in debates about the varying degrees of independent government in Britain's colonies of settlement.

Implementing Disarmament in Basutoland

In the midst of these changes in the British and Cape governments, the Sotho responded in several different ways to the imposition of disarmament. A handful of Sotho were willing to comply. One chief, Masopha, contemplated rebellion. And the paramount chief, Letsie, on the advice of the French missionaries, continued to articulate resistance with loyalty, seeking lawful means of redress. The missionaries opposed disarmament because they feared that war would ruin their missions. Instead, they advocated levying a tax on guns to reduce the popularity of gun ownership.

Rev. Adolphe Mabille, who had helped Letsie to draft the petitions to the governor and the queen, fired the first shot against disarmament. He owned Basutoland's only printing press, at Morija, and he refused to translate or print the government's proclamation of the Peace Preservation Act. This forced a two-week delay in enforcing the act. Sprigg badgered Griffith by telegram: "*Let there be no more delay. I am vexed that the proclamation has not been published already.*"[48] Sprigg wrote to Frere that Mabille "refused at the last moment to fulfil his engagement."[49] Later, in a speech to the Cape parliament, Sprigg derided Mabille's action as "childish" – a familiar enough metaphor. Mabille saw things differently. He responded in an open letter to Sprigg, published in the newspapers. Mabille had not acted childishly, but only in accord with British custom. He refused to publish the proclamation until the governor and

---

[47] *Cape Argus*, April 16, 1880, p. 2. On May 25, 1880, Sprigg confirmed that the Cape government had sufficient funds to pay more than £100,000 for Sotho weapons, as reported in the *Cape Argus*, May 26, 1880, p. 3.

[48] CTAR, NA 279, Griffith to Sauer, June 5, 1881, No. 2, "Copies of Telegrams," Encl. Sprigg to Griffith, March 30, 1880.

[49] BPP [C.2755] 1881, Encl. in No. 2, Minute of Sprigg to Frere, April 9, 1880, p. 5.

the queen had responded to Letsie's petition. Mabille was dismayed that he had spent years teaching the Sotho about the rights and duties of British citizenship, and months advising Letsie on the proper ways to seek legal redress against disarmament, only to witness the government acting before hearing an important petition. He wrote: "Sir Bartle Frere wants no missionaries...to explain the law to the natives." He told Sprigg, "you wanted those poor people to obey your dictates blindfold; you did not care about their understanding what it is to be a British subject.... Yes, a despotic sway is all you wished to have." Then, in a wicked twist of the knife, Mabille wrote, "I glory in this, that I, a Frenchman, should have been more English than an Englishman."[50]

Mabille's defiance was highly symbolic and it seemed, at first, that it could be easily overcome. Griffith simply had the proclamation translated and printed elsewhere. Another set of issues came to a head in April 1880 that introduced significant changes in the politics of South African disarmament and confederation. During that month, Wolseley's and Frere's letters sat on Hicks Beach's desk at the Colonial Office while the secretary of state was involved in the Conservative Party's campaign to gain reelection. He put off major decisions for a while and did not respond immediately. He did not have to because the Liberals won. On April 23, 1880, Gladstone became prime minister again and the Earl of Kimberley once again became secretary of state for the colonies. Five days later a dispatch arrived from Frere, informing the Colonial Office that he was proclaiming the Peace Preservation Act in Basutoland.

At that very moment, colonial policy was adrift. For years the Liberals had been divided over the expansion of the British Empire. Old-style humanitarian Liberals like W. E. Forster supported the extension of Crown Rule to African chiefdoms and opposed the devolution of power onto settler governments, which had gradually fallen out of fashion with the public over the course of the previous decade. Radical Liberals like Joseph Chamberlain, as well as the Liberal Party's allies among the Irish Home Rulers, were opposed to expenditures on imperial expansion and supported the independence of the Transvaal. Gladstone had sided with the Radicals in his campaign speeches, most famously in his Midlothian speech, in which he stated that Disraeli had extended British rule to the Transvaal "unwisely" and "insanely." But when he came into

<hr>

[50] BPP [C.2755] 1881, Encl. in No. 10, "The Colonial Secretary and Mr. Mabille," *Cape Argus*, June 30, 1880, pp. 13–15.

office, Gladstone started to favor the view held by Liberal peers like Kimberley, who believed that Britain had to maintain its prestige in the eyes of the world so that free trade could succeed. This view was pragmatic and opportunistic, and at first it greatly resembled the policy of Disraeli, Carnarvon, and Hicks Beach. In fact, now that both Natal and the Transvaal were under direct rule from London, and now that the Xhosa, the Zulu, and the Pedi were defeated, it even seemed that Carnarvon's plan for confederation might be brought to fruition with minimal additional expense. They did not realize the depth of opposition that was developing among the Afrikaners and the Sotho.[51]

Gladstone and Kimberley began to put in place their policy of pragmatic confederation. Gladstone reneged on his campaign pledge to grant independence to the Transvaal. Kimberley wrote to Frere, informing him that the queen had read Letsie's petition and endorsed Frere's policy of disarming the Sotho, as a mark of "the progress of the Basuto people towards civilization." Kimberley also wrote that since "the disarmament has now been some time in progress...I do not see that I could now discuss this question with any advantage." Yet Kimberley, in putting in place an inexpensive, pragmatic colonial policy, did not completely embrace Sotho disarmament. He informed Frere that he agreed with Hicks Beach's decision not to send British troops to Basutoland. Kimberley cautioned Frere to treat the Sotho with "consideration" because they were "distinguished for their loyalty." To give the Sotho a vehicle for expressing their loyalty, Kimberley advised Frere to raise a "native militia" in Basutoland "as soon as possible."[52] And to ameliorate hard feelings among the Sotho chiefs, Kimberley rebuked Frere and Sprigg for planning to auction Moorosi's land in Quthing. Kimberley sided with Griffith, who had been arguing that Kimberley's cousin, the Cape governor Sir Philip Wodehouse, had promised that all parts of Basutoland would remain in the hands of the Sotho paramount. The question was once again to be taken up by the Cape parliament, which convened in May for its annual session.[53]

The 1880 session of the Cape parliament focused extensively on the disarmament of Basutoland. As Saul Solomon's newspaper, the *Cape Argus*, wrote at the beginning of the session, there was a reason for

---

[51] Robinson, Gallagher, and Denny, *Africa and the Victorians*, 63–5.

[52] BPP [C.2569] 1880, Nos. 18–19, Kimberley to Frere, May 13, 1880, pp. 46–7.

[53] BPP [C.2569] 1880, No. 21, Kimberley to Frere, May 20, 1880, pp. 49–51.

the parliament to pay such close attention to the question of Sotho disarmament.

The discussion of Letsie's petition will be watched with great interest both here and in England. It will have a special interest for all of us apart from the main issue. We shall learn from it the real level of our political morality, and the point of tension at which the good faith of the community will or will not hold against an applied strain.

The debate was a moral test of the colony's newly "responsible" government because of the specific circumstances attaching to the regulation of the gun trade. In the words of the *Cape Argus*,

It will not be forgotten, we hope, under what urgent circumstances we were induced to make our bargain with the Basutos and others, whereby they obtained the much-coveted symbol of manhood. Our necessity was great. Unbounded wealth lay awaiting the labour that should pour it into the white man's lap.... We got what we wanted; we use up the labour without much scruple. Whatever the niggers would tolerate, we put upon them.... It was not a merry life for them at the Fields; but they got their guns and were content.... We got the diamonds, and we could not have got them otherwise. We would have made any terms for this object. Those we made were made in the name of the Queen of England. They were made by a British government. Did we mean to keep them? The "niggers" believed we did. They believed us – that is a point we cannot get over.

In all honesty let us admit that to black arms we owe in the main the prosperity that lifted this Colony from the lowest depths of despair. And we owe it to them, as the price of a small privilege, which in the first joy of our happy rescue we were willing enough to pay, the right which stamped them as free men, and worthy of our confidence. We gave it frankly, unhesitatingly, and without reserve. And so they received it, never doubting our honour and singleness of purpose. This trust of theirs is the political talisman by which we govern. It secures a facile acquiescence, very unlike the submission of fear and compulsion. Spite of the "natural enemy" theory, they take our will as implying fatherly care and good intent.[54]

Good paternal government was based on mutual trust as well as benevolent behavior and peaceful acquiescence. Accordingly, the proper regulation of labor as well as guns involved relations of trust between rulers and ruled. A government that took back gun "rights" or "privileges" as well as "symbols of manhood" – all three terms were used by the *Cape Argus* – would undermine its credibility.

[54] *Cape Argus*, May 18, 1880, p. 2.

With the stakes so high, debate in the Cape parliament's House of Assembly became heated. Debate opened on May 20, 1880 when Thomas Fuller, legislator for Cape Town and manager of the Union Steamship Company, introduced a motion of censure on Sprigg's government. Specifically, the motion criticized the government for making a major, emergency expenditure on disarmament without consulting the Cape parliament. Fuller considered this to be unconstitutional. He and members of the opposition claimed that they supported stricter gun control measures, including licensing. Fuller himself supported strict controls on Africans who were "uncivilized," but "if he has come out of savagery, so as to be able to earn for himself a respectable name and a material competence, and has behaved, year by year, in an orderly manner, so as to become a good citizen, I would treat that man in no one respect in anywise different from the way I would treat him if he were a white man."[55] This was to be more than a debate about the constitutionality of an expenditure – Africans were being disarmed; Europeans were not; and the opposition sought to reverse the new policies of the government. The policies were not legally discriminatory, but in practice everybody knew that only Africans were affected.

The debate occupied the House of Assembly for eight days between May 20 and June 1, 1880. The proceedings were followed closely in the Cape and also in Britain, where the *Cape Argus* debate transcript was forwarded by Frere to the Colonial Office and later printed as part of a parliamentary command paper.[56] The Sotho also followed the debate closely. A deputation of six Sotho dignitaries, including Letsie's son, Joseph Mojela Letsie, attended the debates. They watched and listened in the gallery, having had their request to address the House of Assembly denied by Sprigg. They carried with them two more petitions from Letsie, which they presented to Frere and also to members of the opposition, who received them at a supper at Saul Solomon's home.

For some, the visit of the deputation and the supper at Solomon's house called up all the contradictions of Cape liberalism. Solomon hoped to show that he and his allies were "friends of the natives." "Philanthropic

[55] BPP [C.2755] Appendix, "Debate in the House of Assembly," p. 296. See also *Cape Times*, May 14, 1880, p. 3.

[56] BPP [C.2755] "Correspondence Regarding the Affairs of Basutoland," January 1881. See Nos. 3, 5, and 7, Frere to Kimberley, May 22, June 1, and June 8, 1880, pp. 6, 8, 9, which forwarded the debate transcripts. The transcripts were received at the Colonial Office on June 15, June 28, and July 5, 1880.

flashes in the pan," the government newspaper, the *Cape Times*, gleefully remonstrated. "The man and brother who has the honour of dining with Saul Solomon and his parliamentary friends on one single day out of a lifetime would most certainly be consigned to the outer kitchen" were he to visit again later. Solomon had gone on record in favor of the "parallel development" of Africans and Europeans, implying that they would develop along "lines which can never possibly meet." The *Cape Times* had, instead, "a higher opinion of the capacity of the African races and of the future opened to them by the slow education of civilization and just government." For imperialists in the late nineteenth century, "slow" meant very slow while "just" meant European. As the *Cape Times* stated, "The point at issue ... is in fact whether the land shall be that of the civilized man or of the barbarian." "Savages" had to "submit to laws made for the protection of a civilized community."[57]

Seeking just government from the Cape, in the first Sotho petition Letsie demanded that Moorosi's land be retained by the Sotho. In the second petition, he reiterated his position on disarmament. He complained that loyal Sotho were being disarmed like rebels and that the arms were the fruit of hard work. He made the dramatic claim that "we feel it to be our duty to lift up our voices and let our cry come before your Honourable House for deliverance from this harsh and humiliating law. We feel that by this law we are disgraced in our own eyes, and in the eyes of all our neighbors."[58]

During the debate in the House of Assembly, most members of the opposition followed Fuller and argued that it was unconstitutional to impose the Peace Preservation Act on Basutoland. Saul Solomon questioned the legality of the act and complained that many laws, including "Pass Laws, Cattle Removal Laws, Vagrancy Laws," and the Peace Preservation Act, treated Africans badly. He quoted a letter written to him by an African: "It is singular that every law which is intended for the natives now-a-days is stamped with coercion and repression on its brow. This, it is needless to observe, will make the aborigines detest the much-longed-for British rule."[59]

While criticizing the government for unconstitutional acts and for alienating Africans, opponents made a number of supplemental arguments. Solomon and John X. Merriman presented the stock argument

[57] *Cape Times*, May 18, 1880, pp. 3, 5.
[58] BPP [C.2755] 1881, "The Petition of Letsie," Encl. 2 in No. 8, pp. 10–11.
[59] BPP [C.2755] 1881, Appendix, "Debate in the House of Assembly," pp. 324–5.

against gun control: as Merriman said, "you cannot shut out the means of ingress for guns."[60] This pragmatic claim was followed by another more hypothetical argument. Thomas C. Scanlen, a rising star in Cape politics and law, argued against Frere's claim that guns inspired warlike behavior among Africans, calling it a "radical error." Taking away guns was more likely to cause war. "What if you do remove the guns?" asked Scanlen. "You have, on the one hand, the almost worthless guns; and, as the price of those guns, you have sown a feeling of discontent, and instilled into the mind of the natives a feeling that we are afraid of their possessing these arms; and have also instilled into their minds a craving to possess them, greater than they knew before." This was not only a policy of "inutility." It was bound to produce the opposite of its intended effect, because it completely misunderstood the mentality of gun owners. Scanlen observed:

When the future historian came to write the history of our country, he thought that he would say that this policy, which was now so ardently pursued, was one of the greatest delusions which South Africa had ever witnessed; and only to be compared to that of the natives which led them to slaughter their cattle, so as to raise such a feeling in their people as to lead them to rush upon the white man, and clear him off this Continent for ever.... This policy was one which was likely to irritate the natives, and to sink deep into their hearts for years to come.[61]

In defense of the policy, Sprigg and his supporters denied that the disarmament of Basutoland was unconstitutional. The members of the opposition who had voted for the Peace Preservation Act should have known that it could be used in this way. Sprigg echoed Frere, making the general claim that civilized countries did not "permit its peasantry to about with arms in their hands."[62] Some Sprigg supporters made more exceptional arguments. Bernardus Johannes Keyter argued, following Frere, that all Africans should be disarmed because "the only effect of leaving arms in the hands of the natives was to foster a warlike spirit and lead them one day to defy the Government."[63] James Kirkwood agreed, saying that "men who had guns had a natural disposition to use them," and that hopefully the "whole native population would be disarmed."[64] The secretary for native affairs, William Ayliff, claimed that if Africans were to

---

[60] BPP [C.2755] 1881, Appendix, "Debate in the House of Assembly," p. 303. Solomon's remarks on the impossibility of gun control are on p. 326.

[61] BPP [C.2755] 1881, Appendix, "Debate in the House of Assembly," p. 330.

[62] BPP [C.2755] 1881, Appendix, "Debate in the House of Assembly," p. 350.

[63] BPP [C.2755] 1881, Appendix, "Debate in the House of Assembly," p. 329.

[64] BPP [C.2755] 1881, Appendix, "Debate in the House of Assembly," p. 331.

be disarmed in the Eastern Cape, then out of fairness they needed to be disarmed in Basutoland. And now that government policy in Basutoland had been announced, it "would be suicidal in the extreme" to withdraw it. The respect of Africans would be lost, which would prove the likely cause of expensive conflicts in the future. This was an important justification of the continuation of the policy. According to Ayliff the real reason to have the policy in the first place was that Africans could not be trusted. In spite of any material progress the Sotho had made, "In dealing with savage nations they must look upon them with distrust and suspicion." Members of the opposition cried "oh!" but Ayliff continued. "They knew how Governments in the past had distrusted these people, and the cry of peace had been constantly raised where there was no peace. He wished the people could see that it was to their advantage to give up their allegiance to their chiefs, and then a great difficulty would be overcome."[65] Disarmament was meant to support the long-standing Cape policy of undermining the chiefs' authority.

The Sprigg government survived censure by a margin of nine votes. Even so, Frere's days in Cape Town were numbered. When Frere opened the new session of the Cape parliament on May 7, 1880, he announced that he would be working with Sprigg and his government to convene a new intercolonial conference on confederation. The Dutch members of the Cape parliament opposed the idea completely, insisting that the Transvaal would have to regain its independence first, so that it might reach an independent decision about confederation. This was a significant development. Previously the Cape Dutch had identified more closely with their British rulers and trading partners than with the Transvaal trekboers. Now, a unified Afrikaner front began to emerge, led by Jan Hendrik Hofmeyr, elected to the House of Assembly in 1879. Hofmeyr and the Cape Afrikaners had several grievances. Sprigg's cabinet contained no westerners and no Afrikaners, and in 1878, Sprigg financed the Xhosa war and railway construction by imposing an excise tax on brandy, which was produced mainly by Afrikaners in the Western Cape. Going beyond this specific tax, there was general resentment among Cape Afrikaners toward the British, whose policy of free trade hurt Cape vineyards and wheat farms. At the same time, during the 1870s a new cultural trend was emerging: pride in Afrikaner culture

[65] BPP [C.2755] 1881, Appendix, "Debate in the House of Assembly," p. 311.

and in the Afrikaans language. Budding national pride caused many Cape Afrikaners to be suspicious of British imperialism in the form of South African confederation. A closer identity came to be sensed between Cape Afrikaners and the Afrikaners who lived in the Transvaal and the Orange Free State, as evinced in an April 1880 visit to Cape Town by leading Transvaal Afrikaners.[66] They opposed a failed, last-ditch effort by Sprigg to achieve a confederation that included the Transvaal. Some Cape Afrikaners suspected, too, that the Peace Preservation Act might eventually be applied to them. One wrote from Grahamstown to the *Cape Argus* under the pseudonym "Afrikander," claiming that with Sprigg and Frere in power, "The disarmament of the Boers may, of course, come all in good time. . . . Having disarmed the Fingoes, they say, we must serve the Basutos the same, and when all the natives have been subjected to the castrating process, a beginning will doubtless be made with the irreconcilable farmers [Afrikaners]. Finally, Mr. Sprigg and his friends will be left alone with shooting-irons in their hands, and we may then look for fine doings."[67] The author echoed older, republican ideals of an armed citizenry, which had been present at the Cape since the days of the VOC, while rejecting the notion of the state monopolizing the possession of arms as the metaphorical mutilation of a man.

Cape Afrikaner disaffection threatened to torpedo the new plans of Frere, who concocted yet another plan for achieving confederation: grant the Transvaal independence quickly, before the Boers became completely alienated from British dominion. Then the Boers would be allowed to vote, presumably in favor of union. Frere was grasping at straws. Kimberley took a longer view of confederation. He decided that Britain should hang on to the Transvaal, in the hope that over time, gold discoveries would lure enough British migrants to outnumber the Boers. Kimberley eventually dismissed Frere in a telegram sent on August 1, 1880. Even then Frere felt the need to write a long letter back defending his policies, including the disarmament policy in Basutoland, which he felt would be undermined by his dismissal.[68]

In June and July of 1880, just after the Cape House of Assembly concluded its debate, strife broke out in Basutoland surrounding the linked

---

[66] Giliomee, *The Afrikaners*, 212–20.
[67] *Cape Argus*, May 19, 1880, p. 3.
[68] BPP [C.2695] 1880, No. 40, Frere to Kimberley, August 3, 1880, pp. 79–81. Lehmann, *The First Boer War*, 81–4.

problems of disarmament and loyalty. Letsie himself urged compliance but his own sons prevented him from turning in his guns. The loyal principal chief Molapo died, while the other principal chief, Masopha, was urging disobedience. Lesser loyal chiefs sought to give up their arms by the new deadline of July 12, while rebel chiefs threatened them with violence if they did. The loyal chiefs sensed that if they gave up their weapons, they could not protect themselves. To allay these concerns, Sprigg allowed the magistrates to license any loyalists who wished to bear arms. Griffith used them to form a loyal Sotho militia, yet held out little hope that disarmament would take place. Many powerful chiefs, including Masopha and Letsie's son, Lerotholi, were openly defiant at a public meeting hosted by Letsie on July 3, 1880, in which the delegates to Cape Town discussed their reception. Griffith summarized their views with characteristic understatement: "the Basutos as a tribe are averse to surrendering their arms and do not intend to do so."[69] Anticipating trouble, four thousand Sotho workers left the diamond mines and returned home, leaving the mine owners clamoring for labor.[70]

Griffith's analysis was correct. Reports from different parts of Basutoland indicated that many chiefs were keeping their weapons and even building fortifications. Chiefs who were disloyal were "eating up" or removing cattle and belongings from chiefs who were loyal. Loyal chiefs and their followers were fleeing to the residences of Cape magistrates, who had few resources for providing food and shelter. Even the paramount chief, Letsie, was not being obeyed. Letsie set out with a thousand men to arrest Masopha and Lerotholi, who flatly defied him, supported by their own armed force. Bands of rebel fighters patrolled the countryside, making the loyalists' position impossible. The credibility of the Cape, along with the credibility of the loyal chiefs, was diminishing. Sprigg made a final, incredible offer: rebel chiefs would be forgiven if they would only appear before a magistrate, admit wrongdoing, return stolen property, and pay a fine.[71]

---

[69] BPP [C.2755] 1881, Griffith to Sprigg, June 23, 1880, Encl. 2 in No. 9, pp. 12–13; Sprigg to Griffith, June 26, 1880, Encl. 3 in No. 9, p. 13; Griffith to Sprigg, July 7, 1880, Encl. 4 in No. 13, p. 30; Frere's Minute to Ministers, July 11, 1880, Encl. 5 in No. 13, pp. 30–1; "Minutes of Meeting Held by the Chief Letsie" in Griffith to Ayliff, July 14, 1880, Encl. 2 in No. 22, pp. 51–7.

[70] *Diamond Fields Advertiser*, August 18, 1880, p. 3.

[71] Burman, *Chiefdom Politics and Alien Law*, 141–5.

Last-Ditch Efforts to Maintain Cape Rule in Basutoland

There was no longer any hope of peaceful disarmament in Basutoland. Griffith began to see the situation as desperate. He requested arms and ammunition from the Cape, so that Europeans and loyalists might group together at each magistracy and defend themselves until relief came. Sprigg rejected Griffith's request for arms and ammunition, adding, in a telegram, "You know that you have all the sympathy of the Govt with you at this very anxious time."[72] This was the last straw for Griffith. On July 14, 1880, he replied to Sprigg acidly,

"You who are comfortably settled at Cape Town *out of all danger*, no doubt take a very calm view of the situation up here, but we who have our families here with us and so many people looking to us for advice & protection cannot take the same view as you do, and I cannot help feeling that I am being cruelly treated by you. My request for arms & ammunition &c. was pooh-poohed in the coolest manner as I was the most ordinary of alarmists, whereas the history of my thirty two years service will prove to the contrary.[73]

Griffith accused Sprigg of acting recklessly during the implementation of the Peace Preservation Act in Basutoland, in spite of repeated warnings from himself and other Europeans. As a result of Sprigg's heedless actions, "The very worst feelings of the Basutos have now been roused, and the state of the Country cannot be better described than as an armed truce." The arrival of Cape forces "will be the signal for a general rising and massacre of all the Whites & Loyal people." For this reason, Griffith recommended the evacuation of all Europeans before initiating any military action. He also urged the Cape government to arrange for loyalists "to hire a few farms in the Free State," as "Loyal people are looking up to me for advice & protection, and what can I do for them!" Having been put in an impossible position by Sprigg, Griffith had reached the point of exasperation: "You say the Gov^t sympathize with me, but that is poor consolation at a time when you are just waiting to see a mine sprung at your feet. Sympathy won't assist you to protect the lives & property of the people around you." In spite of all these frustrations, Griffith concluded by reaffirming his commitment, writing that "God only knows that I *have done & will continue* to do everything in my power to prevent

[72] CTAR, NA 279, Griffith to Sauer, June 5, 1881, No. 2, "Copies of Telegrams," Encl. Sprigg to Griffith, July 1, 1880.

[73] CTAR, NA 279, Griffith to Sauer, June 5, 1881, No. 1, "Copies of Semi-Official Letters," Encl. Griffith to Sprigg, July 14, 1880.

a disturbance. I know the horrors of war too well, and look upon it as the greatest curse that can befall a country." Even so, he hated the prospect of leaving Basutoland, after years of working to undermine the authority of the chiefs and introduce European laws and customs. He wrote, "I cannot help feeling what an ignominious thing it will be if we have to fly out of the Country and abandon our property to these rascals."[74]

To overcome resistance, Sprigg himself traveled to Basutoland to meet with key chiefs, hoping that they might persuade rebels to disarm. Letsie assured Sprigg of his personal loyalty but refused to persuade other chiefs to hand in their weapons. Letsie argued that Masopha could not be persuaded because his resistance came from his "sheer stupidity and ignorance." Lerotholi could not be persuaded, either, because his own disloyalty came from being "mad from drinking." He continued: "There are two madmen here who run about the country and threaten the people, but no child ever would think of punishing a madman for being mad."[75] Another government ally, the chief George Moshoeshoe, painted a grim picture for Sprigg. The actions of the Cape government were not only generating resistance to disarmament but undermining all aspects of colonial government, including the collection of the hut tax. According to him, "the magistrates have ceased to exercise their authority, and the people no longer respect the Government." Only the appearance of large numbers of European and African troops could persuade them otherwise. There was a strong impression that disarmament would lead to oppression. According to George Moshoeshoe, "Langalibalele was first disarmed and then taken prisoner and sent to Cape Town, and from this Masopha may infer that he will be treated in a similar manner, and may refuse to give up his arms, and taking his arms by force can only be done with great difficulty."[76]

With Cape rule unraveling over the issue of disarmament, war seemed inevitable. Adolphe Mabille sensed that the way to effect change was to bypass the local administration and appeal directly to public opinion outside of South Africa. Mabille wrote to Frederick Chesson, secretary of the Aborigines Protection Society in London, hoping that the society would mobilize its membership in support of the Sotho. He was not the

---

[74] CTAR, NA 279, Griffith to Sauer, June 5, 1881, No. 1, "Copies of Semi-Official Letters," Encl. Griffith to Sprigg, July 14, 1880.

[75] BPP [C.2755] Encl. 1 in No. 42, "Interview between the Colonial Secretary and Letsea," with interpreter Emile Rolland, August 26, 1880, pp. 156–7.

[76] BPP [C.2755] Encl. 2 in No. 42, "Interview between the Colonial Secretary and George Moshesh," summarized by Lyon Cowper, August 30, 1880.

only pro-Sotho activist to write to the society. Chesson received a letter from Joseph Orpen, too, who questioned the constitutionality of Cape actions in Basutoland, and called for the society to pressure the queen to exercise her royal veto over colonial legislation, a highly unlikely proposition.[77] Mabille was more practical. He crafted his appeal so that it fit the new objectives of the Aborigines Protection Society, which had, since the 1870s, given up its goal of changing indigenous societies wholesale, in favor of the more modest goal of better administration in British colonies.[78] Mabille wrote to Chesson that the Cape government was bent on economic development at any cost. The French missionary made the further point that "tribes which had already expressed their ardent wish to come under British rule have drawn back from fear of being treated as the Basutos." Violations of "constitutional rights" could be blamed on Sprigg's "headstrong line of conduct." Mabille hoped that the Aborigines Protection Society would mobilize its membership against Sprigg. The missionary then embarked on a two-year tour of France, Britain, and the United States where he denounced the policies of Sprigg's government.[79]

Sprigg made one last attempt to preserve the peace. In late August 1879, he traveled to Basutoland to confer with Letsie and several of the other loyal chiefs. One chief, George Moshoeshoe, recommended strict punishment for those who resisted disarmament, but this was a minority position. It appears that most of the chiefs – and most of the Sotho who attended a *pitso* on September 3 – believed that Sprigg should scale back his plan for disarmament. Sprigg indicated that he would be satisfied if the chiefs turned over their weapons in a symbolic gesture and that he was willing to wait to implement full disarmament until matters in Basutoland settled down. The opposition chiefs, led by Lerotholi, sensed weakness on Sprigg's part and rejected his proposal.[80]

Now Sprigg believed that only force could restore order and loyalty to Basutoland. Sprigg lacked support from the British army, but decided to use existing Cape forces against the rebel chiefs. He ordered the Cape

[77] RHL Anti-Slavery Papers, Mss. Brit. Emp. S18 C144/60, Orpen to Chesson, June 29, 1880.

[78] Porter and Low, "Trusteeship and Humanitarianism," *Oxford History of the British Empire*, 4:215–7.

[79] RHL Anti-Slavery Papers, Mss. Brit. Emp. S18 C140/211, Mabille to Chesson, July 27, 1880. The next letter, C140/212, Mabille to Chesson, August 11, 1880, reminded Chesson of the way in which Cape forces mutilated Moorosi and raised questions about possible improprieties in Sir Philip Wodehouse's acquisition of Basutoland.

[80] Bradlow, "Cape Government's Rule," 164–5.

Mounted Rifles to take the field. From September 1880 to February 1881, they engaged the separate forces of Joel Molapo, Masopha, and Lerotholi in different locations. In some instances, Sotho forces besieged magistracies, which Cape forces attempted to relieve. In other fighting, Sotho soldiers, particularly those under Lerotholi, waged a guerilla war, using their mobility and knowledge of the mountainous terrain to their advantage against the Cape Mounted Rifles and Cape Yeomanry. Cape forces suffered two thousand casualties and yet little progress was made. By April 1881, the war had cost the Cape Colony £3 million and Sprigg still demanded that the Sotho chiefs comply with disarmament. The chiefs refused, even though their losses were great, too. Cape forces killed approximately eight thousand Sotho soldiers and confiscated significant amounts of property. Even so, the rebel chiefs still controlled the country. They were helped by their former enemies from the Orange Free State. The Orange Free State prohibited the trade in guns and ammunition to Africans, but several enterprising Boers sold ammunition to the chiefs who fought the Cape. Sprigg remained inflexible, which led members of the House of Assembly to entertain a motion of "No Confidence." Sprigg's government fell, to be replaced by a government led by the liberal Thomas Scanlen. Jacobus Sauer, who had friendly relations with some Sotho chiefs, replaced Ayliff as secretary for native affairs.[81]

This was a moment of transition in the Cape parliament, as well as in the Cape governor's office. Frere was replaced by an interim governor, Sir George Strahan, who had previously governed territories in West Africa and the Caribbean. He relieved Frere in September 1880 and served only until January 1881, when he left the Cape to become governor of Tasmania. In that short time, Strahan oversaw the retrocession of Griqualand West to the Cape Colony, while acting as an intermediary between a Cape government at war in Basutoland and a British government reluctant to support any further military efforts in South Africa. Strahan may have been reluctant about the war himself. In December 1880, he forwarded to Kimberley a letter from a Sotho, Letha Matete, who urged a moratorium on disarmament, thinking that a moratorium would work to the disadvantage of the rebels, Lerotholi and Masopha,

---

[81] Bradlow, "Cape Government's Rule," 168–72. Burman, *Chiefdom Politics and Alien Law*, 148–53. On ammunition from the Orange Free State, see BPP [C.2866] 1881, Brand to Strahan, January 6, 1881, Encl. in No. 24, Strahan to Kimberley, February 7, 1881, p. 42.

especially if professional soldiers from Britain were not to be used. Letha Matete's letter made the further point that Sir Bartle Frere "began this disturbance about the guns; this evil is his."[82]

The new governor, Sir Hercules Robinson, took the initiative to make peace. He offered an "Award" to the chiefs which they accepted. The terms included an amnesty for rebels and the reinstatement of Cape magistrates. Magistrates would not confiscate guns, but would instead license their use. Loyalists and European traders who had lost property would be compensated, while a fine of five thousand cattle would be paid to the Cape. Letsie, who played both sides during the war, and the rebel Lerotholi accepted the offer, but Masopha continued to resist from his fort at the top of a mountain. The Cape administration was imposed once again, with significant changes. Griffith retired, ostensibly on account of illness, but probably also because he felt that the Sotho associated him with disarmament. The other experienced magistrates lacked credibility, too. Over the course of late 1881 and early 1882, the Cape replaced most of its Basutoland magistrates. Lacking experience, and with the Cape's credibility significantly undermined, they failed to reestablish Cape rule. The Cape, backed by humanitarians, negotiated with Britain for Basutoland to be separated from the Cape and ruled directly by London as a Crown Colony. By 1883, the principal chiefs, but not Masopha, accepted this new arrangement as a way to preserve and extend their power, as the British intended to rule only indirectly through the chiefs. This followed the pattern of India's princely states, where British residents were appointed to advise the ruler.[83]

As the chiefs worked to build their authority under the new regime of indirect rule, the memory of the Gun War became a cornerstone of Sotho pride. Some of the best evidence of this comes from the *lithoko*, or praise poems, of the Sotho chiefs who were involved in the Gun War. Many poems brag about defying the Cape and defeating Cape forces. The praise poem of Lerotholi contains the most defiant lines about the Gun War. Lerotholi, who succeeded Letsie as paramount chief in 1891, is said to have composed the following lines himself:

---

[82] PRO CO 48/496, Matete to Governor's Agent, August 23, 1880, Encl. in Strahan to Kimberley, December 13, 1880.

[83] Bradlow, "Cape Government's Rule," 168–204. Burman, *Chiefdom Politics and Alien Law*, 153–80. Details of the negotiations between the Sotho chiefs, the Cape, and the Colonial Office may be found in BPP [C.2964] 1881; [C.3112] 1882; [C.3493] and [C.3708] 1883.

He burned the house of his friend. [Frere]
He started a row with the Sparkling Soldier. [Frere]
It was then that he said: "Stop cattle-raiding, Sprigg,
You'll see me raiding yours."
    Since you eat in your house, you miser,
Against whom do you think you can turn your shield?
Do you think you can turn it against the people's provider?
Haha!
You've eaten a dog, while I ate a cow![84]

The Sotho chiefs appeared to have won a victory. With hindsight, though, it appears that they achieved sovereign independence at a cost. The rebel chiefs asserted their rights to guns as private property. Their new, quasi-independent status was based on resistance to a colonial law that would have taken away their property. Such notions of property arrived in Basutoland with the French Protestant missionaries, who encouraged the Sotho to embrace European material goods as well as the Enlightenment notions of rights that went along with them. In North America and Europe, these notions of rights were guaranteed by emerging nation-states that hoped to establish communities of language, religion, and morality. In South Africa, African nations such as the Tswana, the Swazi, and the Sotho, paid a steep price for their nationhood. Relations with their European neighbors were asymmetrical. The quasi-independent nation-states of Bechuanaland (Botswana), Basutoland (Lesotho), and Swaziland that were invented at the end of the nineteenth century instead became rural slums that supplied labor to settler-owned farms and mines in the rest of South Africa. As the Comaroffs have argued for the Tswana, the appearance of sovereignty masked a reality in which Europeans classified and subjected a group of people who were thought to be marginal and separate.[85] In the case of the Sotho, their marginalization was a direct result of their rebellion, while their rebellion was a direct result of the Cape's heedless efforts at gun control. The rebellion derived partly from a belief, articulated by Letsie and Mabille, that Sotho men had the rights of British citizens. Citizenship appeared to be attainable by the Sotho in the years before the Gun War. But by the time of the Gun War, shifts in British and Cape thinking made full citizenship unlikely.

[84] Damane and Sanders, *Lithoko*, 144.
[85] Comaroff and Comaroff, "New Persons, Old Subjects," in *Of Revelation and Revolution*, 2:365–404.

II

Conclusion

During the 1870s and 1880s, South Africans became more deeply enmeshed in a capitalist economy that had been emerging since mid-century. Commercial farming and mining boomed during this period, allowing African wage laborers to buy guns. The ownership of guns by Africans concerned both British and Boer settlers, who saw guns not only as instruments of civilian life on the frontier, but also as instruments that brought political power. The ties between guns and power increased during this period, thanks to the development of the breech-loading rifle. Breech-loading rifles became available to wealthy buyers, while redundant – yet still effective – muzzle-loading rifles flooded the subcontinent at cut-rate prices. British and Boer officials incorporated disarmament into their plans to deprive Africans of land and citizenship. While developing a plan to disarm, dispossess, and disenfranchise Africans, British settler politicians promoted the creation of all-white militias, arguing that whites should maintain their skills with arms, not lose them, even as hunting declined in importance. Skills were to be preserved in order for settlers to defend against attacks by Africans.

Disarmament became closely related to the efforts of the British government to confederate all the various British colonies, Boer republics, and African chiefdoms into one state. In this state, Africans were to be treated as second-class citizens under a uniform "native policy." In order to build this regime, politicians in London and Cape Town created and managed a discourse about the risks of African skills with guns that justified more extensive interventions in the lives of Africans. Within this wider discourse, an important role was played by ideological descriptions of African skills with guns. Depictions of guns shifted their emphasis. At

the start of the century, settlers described guns as ordinary frontier artifacts, but by the 1870s, they depicted them as dangerous tools that, in
skilled hands, could be used either to support or to undermine the emerging colonial order.

Guns and Confederation, 1881–1910

The Sotho Gun War made politicians in London and Cape Town reluctant to pursue the project of confederation any further. So did conflict
with the Boers in the Transvaal. In 1877, Theophilus Shepstone orches-
trated the annexation of the Transvaal by Britain, with the support of
Carnarvon. The annexation was not initially resisted by the Boers of the
republic, whose government was bankrupt and whose military had just
been defeated by the Pedi. When the unrepresentative nature of administration by Britain became apparent, Boer republicans signed petitions
against annexation. The Transvaal's former military commander, Paul
Kruger, led two delegations to London, both of which were rebuffed by
the Colonial Office. Back home, Kruger and other Boer leaders stoked
anti-British xenophobia and began to organize armed resistance underground. In December 1880, a tax dispute in Potchefstroom between the
British administration and a Boer farmer and his neighbors widened into
a full-scale armed rising.

The administrator of the Transvaal, Sir Owen Lanyon, called on British
troops from Natal to suppress the rebels. British regular troops, including battalions of infantry, cavalry, and artillery, together with the Natal
Mounted Police, marched toward the Transvaal. Along the Transvaal–
Natal border, they were defeated in several small, sharp engagements
by Boer commandos. On February 27, 1881, in the culminating battle of the war, 150 Boer fighters dislodged 400 British regulars from a
position on top of Majuba Hill, killing 92 of them, including their commander, the governor of Natal, Sir George Pomeroy Colley. The success
of amateur Boer soldiers against British regulars came as a surprise. The
Transvaal commandos had been defeated by the Pedi in 1876, while
Orange Free State commandos had difficulty against the Sotho during
the 1860s. Surely, British regulars were better soldiers than the Boers,
Pedi, and Sotho? In fact, as the historian John Laband has pointed out,
the Boer commandos of the 1860s and 1870s were masters of movement
and marksmanship, which suggests that the Sotho and Pedi had become
masterful, too. The Boer commandos of 1880–1 were armed with the
Westley-Richards breech-loading rifle, which was similar in design to the

Martini-Henry used by the British. The Boers fired accurately, according to all accounts, yet that alone could not ensure victory. Laband demonstrates in his recent book, *The Transvaal Rebellion*, that in each significant engagement of the war of 1880–1, Boer commandos used better tactics, providing better supporting fire for moving troops. They read the terrain more effectively, combining human skill with environmental awareness and technological capacities in such a way that they defeated their British adversaries. Faced with defeat in the Transvaal, the new Liberal administration of Gladstone granted independence to the Transvaal, even though the Transvaal was known to contain significant deposits of gold. Five years later, miners would discover the massive gold reef at the Witwatersrand. The gold rush that followed introduced many foreigners to the republic, while the boomtown of Johannesburg grew up around the mines.

For the purposes of the present study, it is worth noting that the Boer commandos of the 1880–1 war were highly skilled marksmen and trackers. These were skills that were becoming increasingly difficult to sustain. Fewer game animals were left, affording Boer men less practice in shooting and tracking. By the 1890s, as young Boers were moving to the city and as Britain was once again coveting the Transvaal, citizens had to be encouraged to practice shooting by State President Paul Kruger. Shooting targets did not require the same level of skill as shooting animals did but it was better than nothing. As the Transvaal government prepared for war in the mid-1890s, Kruger learned something else about Boer marksmen. Of the 24,238 Transvaal men eligible to be called up for militia service, 9,996 did not own a rifle. The ones who did own a rifle tended to own Martini-Henrys, which were outclassed by the British army's new magazine rifles, the Lee-Metford and the Lee-Enfield. Boer marksmanship during the war of 1899–1902 owed mainly to Kruger's wise decision, shortly before the war, to buy thirty-seven thousand Mauser magazine rifles that were superior to the Lee-Metford and Lee-Enfield.[1]

The Lee-Metford was adopted by the British army in 1889. Its name comes from James Lee, who designed the action. The rifle had a magazine that held ten 0.303-caliber (7.7-mm) bullets in cartridges containing black powder. The shooter raised and pulled a bolt to extract the spent cartridge and to raise up a new cartridge. The shooter closed the

---

[1] Bryden, *With Gun and Camera*, 197. Pakenham, *The Boer War*, 35. Breytenbach, "The Military Preparations and Weaponry of the Republics," 8–9. Nasson, *The South African War*, 57.

firing chamber by pushing and then lowering the bolt. The barrel's rifling was shallow, following the Metford pattern, but when the British army switched to smokeless – and more powerful – cordite powder during the early 1890s, shooters found that the new powder damaged the rifling. The army switched the rifling to a deeper Enfield pattern, while keeping Lee's design for the magazine and bolt action. Hence the new rifle was called the Lee-Enfield. This became the British army's rifle during the South African War (or Anglo–Boer War) of 1899–1902. The early "Mark I" Lee-Enfields were inferior to the Mauser in several ways. The Mauser also used a bolt action and magazine, but the magazine could be loaded with a clip of bullets, while the Lee-Enfield had to be loaded one cartridge at a time. The Enfield cartridge had a rim, while the Mauser cartridge did not, which suited it better for repeated firing. Finally, a significant number of the Lee-Enfields brought to South Africa in 1899 were sighted poorly and had to be shipped back to England for factory adjustments.

The two decades leading up to the South African War of 1899–1902 have received attention from numerous historians. The period is marked by continued efforts on the part of imperialist politicians to unify South Africa under one Anglophone government. Imperialist ideologies persisted, supported by the development of mining capitalism, as well as by the spread of railroads and telegraphs. Towering political figures appear to dominate the period, such as Sir Hercules Robinson, Joseph Chamberlain, and Cecil Rhodes. The period saw the proclamation of a British protectorate over Bechuanaland, the institution of Cape rule over Pondoland, and the conquest of Ndebeleland and Mashonaland by Rhodes's British South Africa Company. And during the South African War, the British army defeated the commandos of the Boer republics by implementing a policy of total war. The unification of South Africa was achieved through the expenditure of much blood and gold.

Guns were certainly part of this story. In 1878, Frere was concerned enough about the gun trade in the independent enclave of Pondoland that he deposed a Pondo chief, Mqikela, and arranged for the Cape to buy portions of the coast and the interior from the successor chief, Nqwiliso. During the 1880s, colonists in the Cape and Natal noted that Mpondo men were heavily armed. Officials also believed that Pondoland's Port St. John's was still a conduit for gun smuggling into the interior. In one incident that was actually documented, in 1884 the British resident in Port St. John's reported that German arms traders had delivered three hundred rifles, plus ammunition, to Mpondo arms traffickers. The regulation of the gun trade persuaded the British government to declare a protectorate over Pondoland in 1885. One chief who continued to value his independence mobilized fifteen thousand Mpondo warriors and raided the Cape. The Cape decided to temporarily rearm select "native levies" along the border in order to provide a measure of security. It proved impossible for Mpondo holdouts to resist the Cape, which took over the administration of the chiefdom.[2]

In the late 1880s, guns were part of the story of settler expansion to the north. In 1888, Rhodes's partner Charles Rudd obtained a concession from the Ndebele chief, Lobengula, by promising him a thousand Martini-Henry rifles and one hundred thousand rounds of ammunition, plus £100 every month and an armed steamboat for the Zambezi. Rudd bore a letter of support from the governor, Sir Hercules Robinson, and was accompanied by Bechuanaland's British administrator, Sir Sidney Shippard, during the final stages of the negotiations, even though sending guns across the colonial border to arm Africans was still against Cape policy. The Cape government, with Sprigg serving again as prime minister, asked Robinson for a certificate absolving it from any responsibility for the arms deal.

The arms deal attracted the attention of Khama, the Tswana chief, who had recently come under British "protection." Khama insisted that the British government should provide him with Martini-Henry rifles, too. Robinson agreed to send eight hundred rifles to Khama and then put the matter of further arms trading before the British government for its consideration. The secretary of state for the colonies, Lord Knutsford, indicated to Robinson's successor, Sir Henry Loch, that the Tswana should be allowed enough arms and ammunition to hunt game and to defend themselves.[3]

Britain pursued a policy of pragmatism in southern Africa, revealing a degree of continuity with earlier decades of the nineteenth century, when the Cape Colony's government supplied guns to allies on the northern frontier. In the 1880s and 1890s, state dealing in firearms was used to support diplomatic efforts among chiefs such as Khama and Lobengula. This was a tiny part of a global pattern that has been described by

---

[2] *Cape Argus*, May 18, 1880, p. 3. *Cape Times*, May 3, 1880. CPP [A.70] 1880, "Copy of Statement (on Oath) of a Detective Policeman on Gun-Running." BPP [C.4590] 1885, Oxland to Sec'y for Native Affairs, March 29, 1884, Encl. in No. 10, Robinson to Derby, April 29, 1884, pp. 10–11. For a broader discussion of the role of traders in the politics of Pondoland, see Beinart, "European Traders and the Mpondo Paramountcy."
[3] PRO CO 879/31 Conf. Pr. (Africa) No. 381, No. 39, Robinson to CO, October 18, 1889, pp. 38–40; No. 42, Knutsford to Loch, November 19, 1889, pp. 41–2.

Jonathan Grant in his book, *Rulers, Guns, and Money.* Western European governments provided arms as a way to turn states into clients in Eastern Europe, East Asia, South America, and the Horn of Africa. By this time in southern Africa, few independent chiefdoms remained, and there was even pressure to impose regulations on colonists and private merchants. In 1889 and 1890, representatives of the European colonial powers met at Brussels to discuss regulating the trade in slaves, liquor, and firearms in Africa. The powers agreed to allow flintlock muskets and black powder to be traded in any area where slaving did not occur. Traders were allowed to sell "precision arms," such as breech-loading rifles, to individuals who needed them for personal defense. These individuals had to receive a government license and the weapon was to be registered and stamped. French and Portuguese diplomats argued that the restrictions would work only if the entire African continent were subject to the agreement. The British successfully negotiated for the exemption of southern Africa, citing settler quasi-independence and chiefly diplomacy. The treaty would apply only to sub-Saharan Africa above Bechuanaland.[4]

Khama and the Tswana chiefs succeeded in protecting themselves against the Transvaal and also against Rhodes's ambitions by encouraging the British government to form a protectorate over them in 1885. Lobengula had no such protection. In exchange for the controversial rifles, Lobengula knowingly signed away the mineral rights to his dominion, without realizing that he was also signing away his entire sovereignty. Rhodes's British South Africa Company (BSAC) received a charter from Queen Victoria to rule Ndebeleland and Mashonaland. The company introduced miners, settlers, and administrators into the territory. Lobengula repudiated the concession. Over the course of 1893–7, many Ndebele and Shona rebelled against BSAC rule, only to be cut down by troopers firing breechloaders and machine guns.

The "arms gap" between Africans and Europeans was a feature of many confrontations during the era of "high imperialism" and the "scramble for Africa." In South Africa, the time had passed for rich discussions about which citizens could own guns and which could not. As we have seen, those issues were settled by the Boer republics at their founding. Natal laws empowered the magistrates and governor to choke off the supply of guns to Africans. And during the late 1870s, the Cape implemented racially discriminatory disarmament. More racially discriminatory

---

[4] The zone's northern boundary was set at 20° north and 22° south. Miers, *Britain and the Ending of the Slave Trade*, 262–4.

legislation followed in the 1880s and 1890s, when Rhodes, Sprigg, and their supporters crafted various laws that restricted African landownership and voting in various ways.

Gun ownership remained a marker of both citizenship and race in the Cape and also in the more intensely discriminatory political systems of the republics and Natal. In 1889, a Natal investigation into the application of firearms laws revealed that Africans were substantially disarmed. The secretary for native affairs, Henrique Shepstone – son of Theophilus Shepstone – actually complained to the investigating commission that too few Africans knew how to shoot. When asked if Natal's firearms laws were working, he said that they worked too well. He pushed, instead, for arming a select number of Africans, who could help defend the colony. He stated that "my idea is that we should allow a certain number of them to hold guns. Whenever we have got into trouble, we have always called our Natives out and armed them. Many of them who have been called out have never had a firearm in their hand before, and have been of no use for the purpose they were called out. The Natives themselves say, 'You call us out, arm us, and we do not know how to use the guns; in fact, they are useless to us.'" Select Africans might be armed, but Shepstone recommended against the widespread possession of guns, because "it would give them confidence to resist any order given by the Government." In this way, Shepstone echoed Frere's earlier argument about the effects of guns on Africans.[5]

The issue of arming Africans appeared to be settled until a brief flare-up during the South African War of 1899–1902. The conventional story of firearms in the South African War is that British rifles in the hands of British soldiers were inferior to German rifles in the hands of Boer commandos. The ultimate Boer surrender owed to many other factors, as numerous studies have demonstrated.[6] The war is conventionally portrayed as a "white man's war" that was watched by Africans from the sidelines. In recent years, historians have shown that significant numbers of Africans helped both sides. Boer commandos rode off to war with African and mixed-race male servants, called *agterryers*, following the practice that had developed in the first commandos two centuries

---

[5] Colony of Natal, *Gunpowder Laws' Committee, 1889*, pp. 74, 79.
[6] For an introduction, see Nasson, *The South African War*, and Pakenham, *The Boer War*. After the war, the British army learned its lesson. The Lee-Enfield was improved and soldiers received more training in marksmanship. When British and German troops faced each other for the first time in 1914, it was the British who outshot the Germans.

ago. The *agterryers* took care of horses and livestock while attending to camp chores. In battle, they carried extra weapons and ammunition. The British, for their part, hired one hundred thousand Africans as assistants. They attended to support duties, too, but at least ten thousand were armed and fought for the British. More clamored to fight, particularly in parts of the Cape that were threatened by Boer commandos. In one famous case, a Calvinia blacksmith, Abraham Esau, pressed Cape government officials to arm "coloured" loyalists. These efforts to form a militia were rebuffed because British officials hesitated to alienate rural Cape Afrikaners. This would lead to bad publicity, but nearby British army intelligence officers encouraged Esau to gather information about disloyal Afrikaners. When Cape Afrikaner rebels and Orange Free State commandos took control of Calvinia in January 1901 and proclaimed republican "native law" to be in force, Esau resisted. For doing so, the Boer magistrate had him tortured and executed.[7]

Incursions into the Cape by commandos from the Boer republics raised the possibility of a widespread rebellion against British rule by Cape Afrikaners. There was even talk that Boer commandos might take Cape Town. The governor, Sir Alfred Milner, called on Cape citizens to volunteer to serve with the Town Guards, local militia units for men who could not leave home. Thousands of men volunteered, although only whites were allowed to join.[8] In January 1901, Milner took the related steps of proclaiming martial law throughout the Cape and also of proclaiming that the Peace Preservation Act of 1878 would be put into effect. The proclamation applied to all citizens, except for civil servants and members of the armed forces, including the Town Guards, who were exempted. All other citizens were required to apply for licenses to keep their weapons. Different rules applied to different types of weapons. Rifles were to be surrendered. According to Milner's proclamation, "It is not desirable that any person not belonging to one of the exempted classes should under present circumstances be allowed to retain a rifle." Rifles were deemed riskier than revolvers, which could be licensed to "all persons in regard to whom there is no reasonable ground for suspecting that they will put them to an improper use." Other weapons, such as shotguns, swords, and assegais, were to be licensed freely.[9]

---

[7] Nasson, "Martyrdom, Myth, and Memory," in *Abraham Esau's War*, 120–41.
[8] Bickford-Smith, Van Heyningen, and Worden, *Cape Town in the Twentieth Century*, 14–15.
[9] *Government Gazette*, January 22, 1901, p. 142.

Milner's proclamation of the Peace Preservation Act technically applied to all residents of the Cape Colony equally. And yet, as in previous cases, the act was used to restrict the rights of particular groups of citizens. By 1901, the Cape Colony's non-European population was substantially disarmed. Out of the European population, Afrikaners made up a majority, but their emerging national identity, coupled with resentment toward the British government for its wartime ruthlessness, made it unlikely that they would wish to join Cape forces and fight their Boer brethren – although there were exceptions.

Once again, the Peace Preservation Act introduced de facto discrimination, yet the political context of 1901 was quite different from the political context of 1878. In January 1901, Milner had actually hoped to proclaim martial law throughout the Cape Colony, but he was advised against taking this step by the Cape cabinet – led by the elderly John Gordon Sprigg, who was serving for the fourth and last time as prime minister. Sprigg and his ministers advised Milner to take a lesser step and proclaim the Peace Preservation Act to be in force throughout the Cape Colony. Milner compromised. He proclaimed the Peace Preservation Act throughout the colony and proclaimed martial law everywhere in the Cape, except for areas under "tribal" law as well as the port cities of Cape Town, Port Elizabeth, and East London. But in October, the ports too came under martial law. This was part of a wider crackdown on individual liberties, as General Kitchener pursued total war against Boer commandos and civilians in the interior. The British government considered suspending the Cape's constitution, but Sprigg prevented this by making a successful appeal to the Dominion prime ministers at the 1902 Colonial Conference. This victory for parliamentary rights did not immediately affect individual rights. The war ended with the Treaty of Vereeniging, signed on May 31, 1902, but in September 1902, the new Cape governor, Sir Walter Hely-Hutchinson, amended the Peace Preservation Act by requiring all weapons – even revolvers, shotguns, and assegais – to be licensed or surrendered.[10] After that point, restrictions on weapons were eased gradually, until June 6, 1905, when Hely-Hutchinson repealed the Peace Preservation Act altogether.

When the South African War ended, Britons and Boers negotiated the shape of the future Union of South Africa. While they were doing so, the British appointed Sir Godfrey Lagden, a former administrator

---

[10] *Government Gazette*, September 19, 1902, p. 753.

from the Transvaal, to lead an official review of "native policy." The Lagden Commission, also known as the South African Native Affairs Commission, heard testimony from magistrates on a broad range of topics. Many magistrates spoke about firearms policy, but none devoted substantial attention to it. The ownership of firearms by Africans was no longer perceived to be a problem, because discriminatory policies, coupled with an expansion of state powers, had made it nearly impossible for Africans to own modern firearms. Magistrates still believed that gun ownership changed the thought processes of Africans. G. M. Rudolph, who had served in Natal since the 1850s, indicated that he thought that gun ownership caused Africans to rush into rebellion. Another career magistrate, H. W. Struben, who had served in the Cape, Natal, and the Transvaal, noted that "whenever the natives become possessed of firearms it tends to give them a feeling of unrest. They must let off the gun at something; and there is a tendency on the part of the natives when they feel themselves well armed to become more or less impudent, I might say aggressive, and afterwards they are prepared to try conclusions with the white people." Even so, only old muzzle-loaders and shotguns remained in circulation.[11] These no longer presented a problem for the colonial order. Other threats to orderliness were perceived to be more important: the commission's recommendations focused mainly on ways of controlling Africans through new policies pertaining to land, voting, and education. These recommendations paved the way for further acts of discrimination that are beyond the scope of this study. For present purposes, it is worth noting that the possession of firearms – and the absence of firearms – continued to mark who was a citizen, and who was not, in South Africa.

Perspectives on Firearms Proliferation in South Africa

To put colonial South African gun control in a wider perspective, it is useful to reflect on the argument that the sociologist Ulrich Beck made in his book, *Risk Society*. According to Beck, debates about regulating technological risk became increasingly important to politics when European and

---

[11] *South African Native Affairs Commission*, testimony by G. M. Rudolph, 3:322; testimony by H. W. Struben, 2:306–7. The following witnesses also addressed the possession of firearms by Africans: E. Dower, 2:68; N. A. Low, 2:113–14; J. B. Moffatt, 2:141; W. Brownlee, W. Liefeldt, and N. O. Thompson, 2:980, 988, 991; W. Leary, 2:1214; H. Sprigg, 2:1246; S. Harrison, 3:3; D. C. Uys, 3:328; G. Hulett, 3:926; W. S. Taberer, 4:40, W. Edwards, 4:49; W. Windham, 4:451–2; J. Ellenberger, 4:243–4, 248.

North American societies made the transition to industrialization. Risk could no longer be attributed to events beyond the control of people, but to human technological choices. This argument rings true when we examine the early industrialization of South Africa in the 1870s, when arguments about order began to focus on the choices that surrounded ownership of a gun. Other scholars who write about technology and public policy, particularly Sheila Jasanoff, have argued that politicians, scientists, and regulators have manipulated discourses about technological risk in culturally specific ways to create new kinds of order. New technologies, such as the computers of today and the breech-loading rifles of the 1870s, help throw into question older modes of sovereignty and authority. Rulers who reformulate technology policies must often reformulate other aspects of governance too.[12]

The promotion of skill and the exaggeration of risk were two sides of the same coproduced technical and political coin. To understand colonial discourse about the risks of guns, it is important to recall that the colonies of South Africa had different "native" policies. The two independent Boer republics across the Orange River – the Orange Free State and the South African Republic (also known as the Transvaal) – restricted citizenship to European men and deprived Africans of all civic rights, including any right to possess weapons. The republics were relatively weak states, though, which meant that enforcement was inconsistent. To the east of the republics, in the British colony of Natal, guns had to be registered with British magistrates who supervised African chiefs. (African chiefdoms remained substantially intact so that chiefs might administer "customary" law under the supervision of the colony's government.) Chiefs retained a degree of autonomy in certain other regions along the Cape Colony's borders, such as the Transkei, Basutoland, and Griqualand East, while the Mpondo remained independent.

The Cape Colony, which the British had taken from the Dutch during the Napoleonic wars, had a unique set of regulations and practices. Guns had been subject to a variety of sporadically enforced regulations ever since the seventeenth century. In the 1870s, permits to purchase firearms could be issued by unsalaried justices of the peace as well as by salaried resident magistrates. Rules for issuing permits were spelled out in the Cape Colony's "Circular Number 4" of 1874, which instructed resident

---

[12] Beck, *Risk Society*, 183; Jasanoff, *Fifth Branch*; Brickmann, Jasanoff, and Ilgen, *Controlling Chemicals*; Wynne, "Public Understanding of Science."

magistrates to issue gun permits only to Africans who were "fit" to possess guns, without defining how, exactly, to determine fitness. Justices of the peace received no such instructions. As a consequence, many settlers felt that justices of the peace were too liberal in issuing permits.[13] Even so, permissive policies were defended by prominent liberals. The Cape Colony's secretary for native affairs, Charles Brownlee, stated that Africans wanted to know "why if they are really British subjects we should be so anxious that they should not possess guns."[14]

Discussions about skill with weapons helped launch a new, openly discriminatory form of governance at the Cape. In the 1870s, the antiliberal architects of confederation argued that liberal "native" policies of the Cape had to be brought in line with the restrictive policies of British Natal and the Boer republics. Depriving Africans of firearms and full citizenship was intended to make the Boers and the Natal settlers comfortable with confederation. It would also simplify labor relations in an emerging capitalist economy in which European settlers hoped to turn Africans into mineworkers and farmhands.[15]

The racial politics of skill appear to have continued through the Boer War and into the twentieth century, although this matter has not been the subject of much study. Under the Union government, formed from the various colonies and republics in 1910, one of the hallmarks of segregation legislation was to reserve skilled jobs for whites and assign unskilled jobs to blacks. This was especially controversial in mines, where white workers sought to preserve segregation so as to keep their skilled jobs, even when many blacks had acquired the same skills. The history of race, labor, technology, and skill in the twentieth century falls beyond the scope of this book. Substantial scholarly efforts have focused on the social history of labor in the technologically driven mining industry. Other areas of South African industrial history have attracted scholarly attention, such as the country's dependency on foreign countries for technical expertise, capital investment, and resource inputs. Less attention has been paid to the history of other technologies.

For future historians of technology in South Africa, it is perhaps worth noting that the book has highlighted the overlap between technological discourse and political discourse. This overlap can easily be found in the

---

[13] CPP [A. 23] 1877, Brownlee to Chalmers, October 4, 1876, pp. 23–4.
[14] CPP [A. 23] 1877, Brownlee to Chalmers, November 8, 1876, pp. 27–8.
[15] Marks and Atmore, "Imperial Factor"; Etherington, "Labour Supply"; Cope, "C. W. de Kiewiet."

correspondence of chiefs, magistrates, and governors from the nineteenth century. But the most eloquent illustration of the way in which racial thinking about skill became embedded in political consciousness comes from the autobiography of Nelson Mandela. In *Long Walk to Freedom*, he describes an airplane trip that he took in 1962 out of South Africa and into newly independent Africa:

> We put down briefly in Khartoum, where we changed to an Ethiopian Airways flight to Addis. Here I experienced a rather strange sensation. As I was boarding the plane I saw that the pilot was black. I had never seen a black pilot before, and the instant I did I had to quell my panic. How could a black man fly an airplane? But a moment later I caught myself: I had fallen into the apartheid mind-set, thinking that flying was a white man's job. I sat back in my seat and chided myself for such thoughts.[16]

If even Mandela found it hard to believe that an African could have sufficient skills to fly an airplane, then an ideological "construction" of technological skill had entered into the thinking of the leader who would do the most to "deconstruct" the apartheid regime. Ideological descriptions of skill are that pervasive. This presents a challenge for historians, who must rely on past witnesses to describe skill's empirical characteristics.

The construction of apartheid was closely related to another technological issue: the issue of technology as property. The Sotho chiefs who resisted the imposition of the Peace Preservation Act did not articulate a right to bear arms, such as the ones that are enshrined in the British and American bills of rights. Instead, the Sotho chiefs protested that guns were property and that in the British system, property owners had rights. Rights to private property anchored capitalist ventures in mining and farming. Sotho farmers and merchants understood correctly that these rights to property were guaranteed by the queen. And guns were not only property, but were also capital investments that could be easily moved, sold, and used. In the late 1870s, the Peace Preservation Act seemed remarkable to liberals because it extended the scope of discriminatory legislation. With greater hindsight, the act also seems significant because it restricted the even spread of capitalism. The Cape government, like the governments of Natal and the Boer republics, made a pact with the devil that had profound consequences for South Africa's economic development. When the colonial government dispossessed African farmers and merchants, racial

---

[16] Mandela, *Long Walk to Freedom*, 254–5.

ideology was allowed to trump full capitalist development. Uneven economic development became the Achilles heel of modern South Africa.[17]

By contrast, a different model prevailed in New Zealand. There, the Maori began to make extensive contacts with European merchants at the end of the eighteenth century, at around the same time as substantial numbers of Boers were beginning to cross the Cape's eastern and northern frontiers. Like the Xhosa, Zulu, and Sotho, many Maori obtained guns. In New Zealand, the results were nothing short of appalling. From 1806 to 1845, the acquisition of weapons – together with the rapid acquisition of European crops and trade goods – is thought to have intensified long-standing conflicts between different groups of Maori. The ensuing "Musket wars" were especially intense from 1818 to 1833. Warfare resulted in widespread migration and enslavement. Approximately one-third to one-half of the Maori population died.[18] The rapid mortality associated with the spread of guns was quite different from that in South Africa, where guns spread more slowly, giving indigenous societies more time to make adjustments. The slower spread of guns in South Africa probably had much to do with geography. The Southern African interior is extensive compared with the interiors of the North and South Islands, whereas New Zealand's coastline is extensive, making its markets relatively more accessible.

As in South Africa, liberalism and dispossession characterized the British approach to the Maori. New Zealand's Maori policies were founded on – and complicated by – the 1840 Treaty of Waitangi, which guaranteed Maori all the rights of British subjects. The English text gave the queen sovereignty, while the Maori text allocated to her the government but not necessarily the sovereignty. The English text provided for European settlement as well as for protections for the Maori, but the Maori version confirmed that the Maori would retain control over the land. While land disputes regarding the treaty's two versions still carry on today, the English version goes much farther to protect the rights of people subject to British colonialism than any document produced in South Africa. In the Cape Colony, Ordinance 50 of 1828 and the Masters and Servants Ordinance of 1841 prohibited de jure racial discrimination but allowed plenty of leeway for de facto discrimination. By contrast, the Treaty of Waitangi made it plainer that indigenous people had the rights

---

[17] I am indebted to Keith Breckenridge for this insight.
[18] Crosby, *Musket Wars.*

of British subjects, but these guarantees did not prevent the Maori from being subjected to de facto discrimination.

De facto discrimination was especially notable in land transactions. It also occurred in the regulation of firearms. The first discriminatory measure to control guns was enacted by Sir George Grey, who governed New Zealand from 1845 to 1854 before moving on to the Cape Colony.[19] Grey enacted the Arms Importation Ordinance of 1845, which empowered the governor to regulate the sale of firearms and gunpowder in proclaimed districts. The ordinance was aimed directly at the Maori. The preamble states, "Whereas certain tribes of the Native race of New Zealand have taken up arms against the Queen's sovereign authority...."[20] In 1846, Ordinance 18 required anybody trading in arms and ammunition to be licensed. The ordinance did not mention the Maori, but it is unlikely to have been passed had there not been concerns about Maori arms purchases. Loyal Maori objected to the inconvenience of the regulations, but a government board that investigated the state of "native affairs" in 1856 concluded that "the natives generally do not look upon either of these laws as oppressive or unjust."[21] Government investigators believed that Maori continued to buy arms anyway.[22] As a consequence, the arms acts were allowed to lapse in 1857. Shortly afterward, Maori were said to be buying significantly greater quantities of arms. The Arms Act of 1860 updated the licensing of dealers by also requiring them to record the names of all buyers and to stamp each gun sold, so that it would be easy to trace sales.

The Arms Act of 1860 does not mention the Maori, but when it was under consideration by the lower house of New Zealand's parliament, the House of Representatives, the debate focused mainly on the best ways in which to restrict Maori gun purchases and on whether or not such restrictions were constitutional. One opponent of the measure argued

---

[19] Grey governed the Cape from 1854 to 1861. He returned to New Zealand as governor from 1861 to 1868. Afterward, he settled in New Zealand and was elected to the parliament. He served as prime minister from 1877 to 1879.

[20] *New Zealand Statutes*, 9 Vict., Sess. 6, No. 1.

[21] BPP [492] Vol. XLVII 1860, pp. 96–7. Reprinted from New Zealand Parliamentary Papers A.3 – 1856, "Report of a Board Appointed by H. E. the Gov. to Inquire into and Report upon the State of Native Affairs." The same assessment of Maori opinions on the subject of firearms regulations is given in BPP [2747] Vol. XLVII 1860, "Memorandum" Encl. in No. 100, Gore Brown to Labouchere, July 23, 1856, p. 243.

[22] BPP [2747] Vol. XLVII 1860, "Memorandum" Encl. in No. 100, Gore Brown to Labouchere, July 23, 1856. This is indicated in the summaries on pp. 248 and 257 as well as in the specific testimonies that follow.

that such a law was "far more stringent and has more inquisitorial and meddling powers than the most stringent of the Irish Acts passed when Ireland was in rebellion" and that it would "prevent a man from doing that which, under his birthright, he is entitled to do – to keep arms for his own protection." Another opponent of the measure argued that it would deprive only "friendly natives" of their weapons: rebels would not obey laws that were unenforceable.[23] Such idealism was met with utilitarian arguments in favor of regulation. A proponent of stricter gun control responded by saying that "the principal ingredient of the opposition to this measure was its inconvenience and occasional injustice rather than that the Maoris should be supplied with arms to the danger of loss of life and property." And as for the rights of British subjects, surely they did not really apply to Maori:

No one entertained a profounder respect than he did for British rights and institutions, but, as applied to intercourse with uncivilized and semi-savage tribes, the argument was somewhat out of place. It was absurd to apply the refinements of British constitutional rights, which had been centuries in growing, to a national the commencement of whose civilization dated but from yesterday.[24]

This argument prevailed in spite of any guarantees contained in the Treaty of Waitangi. The laws became stricter in 1869, when an amendment to the Arms Act allowed the governor to proclaim districts in which individuals who owned firearms would have to apply for a government license. In this way, New Zealand's firearms laws were truly starting to resemble the peace preservation acts that had been passed in Ireland throughout the century. An Arms Act of 1880 continued the same system in force while providing more detailed regulations.

From the 1860s to the 1880s, the arms acts were proclaimed in different parts of New Zealand as part of the colony's efforts to combat Maori rebels. Settlers believed that many Maori continued to buy arms. Significant numbers were confiscated from rebel Maori, although one official return from 1864 indicated that only 165 of the 578 men surrendering were also giving up a gun.[25] New Zealand's extensive coastline and rugged interior gave smugglers a geographical advantage. In instances

[23] *New Zealand Parliamentary Debates*, October 9, 1860, pp. 638–9; October 25, 1860, pp. 755–66. Quotation is from the speech by Brandon, pp. 757–8.
[24] *New Zealand Parliamentary Debates*, October 25, 1860, speech by Brown, pp. 760–1.
[25] *New Zealand Parliamentary Papers*, AJHR (1864) E.6, "Return of Arms Surrendered by Natives." See also AJHR (1864) E.3, "Further Papers Relative to the Native Insurrection."

when arms traders were caught, juries hesitated to convict them because the penalties – including capital punishment for Europeans who traded arms to Maori – were thought to be too severe. In any case, by the 1880s the rebellions were over and settlers did not believe that the Maori posed a major threat any longer. In 1882, all the regulations were suspended in the South Island. In the North Island, where the Maori population was denser, most regulations were suspended after 1885, but Maori were required to apply for licenses to buy arms and ammunition.

While Maori did experience instances of de facto discrimination, government policy toward them was rather different than the policies of the colonial governments of South Africa. In New Zealand, it was official policy to "amalgamate" Maori as citizens of the colony, and while this policy was often violated, it was still significant for New Zealand political culture. In 1862, the New Zealand House of Representatives held an extensive debate on the amalgamation of Maori and European colonists. A resolution passed that reaffirmed the desirability of making New Zealanders into "one people." In practice, many settlers still took advantage of Maori and did not live up to the colony's lofty humanitarian goals. Even so, the historian Alan Ward has written that official commitments to amalgamation helped Maori avoid the level of slaughter that indigenous people experienced at the hands of settlers in Africa, Asia, Australia, and the Americas. Amalgamation restrained the hands of settlers. It also made it possible for interracial schools and interracial marriages to receive official sanction. Settlers and Maori were in the habit of interacting socially, informally and formally as members of sporting clubs and trade unions. Maori also participated in civic institutions. In 1867, the New Zealand House of Representatives enacted a law that reserved four seats for Maori members. Granted, these were set aside on the basis of race, but the existence of these seats indicated that the government took amalgamation seriously.[26]

The architects of amalgamation made room for Maori to participate in civic culture, while in South Africa, humanitarian liberals kept Africans at arm's length. In both countries, laws were passed, restricting access to arms. In South Africa, the disarming of Africans was extended to the armed forces. Africans sometimes joined colonists on campaigns as part of separate irregular units called "native levies." One regular unit, the Cape Mounted Rifles, was made up predominantly of Khoi or Coloured

[26] Ward, "Myths and Realities," in *A Show of Justice*, 308–15.

troopers. Still, South African militia units were formed exclusively from settlers, be they the Boer commandos or the Cape Colony's militia forces. Africans who rode with these forces did so as servants. In the 1870s, as the Cape Colony debated gun control, a related question about arms and civic duties came up: how best should the colony organize the militia? It would be all white, as Africans were not considered to be worthy. In New Zealand, the opposite was true. During the Anglo–Maori wars of the 1860s, Maori who were loyal to the British formed irregular units that supported colonial forces. From 1865 to 1868, loyal Maori received 3,609 firearms from the British, mainly Enfield rifles. A further 282 firearms were issued in 1868 and 1869.[27] In 1886, at a time when racial exclusion was becoming more intense in South Africa, the New Zealand parliament enacted a law that required all able-bodied men, including Maori, to serve in the militia, although some Maori districts could be proclaimed to be excluded. When the bill was considered by the parliament, it was not debated extensively. One member objected to including Maori in the militia, but he was countered by another member, who stated that "I am convinced that there are no people in the country more true to the colony than the Maori race, and if to-morrow I were to be engaged with a foreign enemy in this country I should like uncommonly well to act with the Maoris. They are loyal, honest, and brave. It is misunderstanding that has led to the troubles which have existed between us; and I am quite certain that there are no better subjects of the Queen, or people who are more Anglo-Saxon in their heart for all practical purposes, than are the Maoris." One of the Maori members agreed, saying that "should any danger arise from outside of this colony, the Natives would at once join with their European friends here to resist any such attack."[28]

New Zealand policies toward Maori were headed in a direction that was rather different from the colonies and republics of South Africa. The coproduction of ideas about bearing arms and ideas about order are clear in the case of nineteenth-century New Zealand and South Africa. As the Comaroffs have shown, the imposition of colonial rule was also about the gradual spread of European ideologies, epistemologies, and commodities, all of which were linked. Guns were useful commodities that people linked

---

[27] *New Zealand Parliamentary Papers*, AJHR (1868) D.21, "Return of Arms, Accoutrements, and Ammunition Issued to Friendly Natives during the Years 1865, 1866, 1867, and 1868." AJHR (1870) D.13, "Return of Arms and Ammunition Issued to Friendly Natives."

[28] Speeches by Scotland, Grace, and Ngatata, in *New Zealand Parliamentary Debates*, June 2, 1886, pp. 204–5.

to new ways of thinking and behaving. As such, they became a potently symbolic part of New Zealand and South African history.

As the present study indicates, the story of guns in nineteenth-century South Africa cannot be understood apart from the story of representations of guns, representations that derived from the process of imperial expansion and closely related shifts in South African political culture. Historians must recognize that when they connect ideology to material culture, they must somehow also appreciate the differences between the ideological, the material, and the cultural. In this study, the story of local South African experiences with guns proved inextricably linked to the history of colonial descriptions and analyses of these experiences. The pairing of the material and the discursive appears to be inescapable. New power arrangements that blend ideological, environmental, and technological practices may require a new historical analysis that draws from methods that are simultaneously empirical and discursive. Of course, it is the historian's duty to recognize that representations of reality may be different from what really happened. The formation and elaboration of such representations may themselves constitute a story. That has certainly been the case in the present study.

The links between ideology and technology have been observed by numerous historians. In the case of South Africa, pseudoscientific racism had taken hold among European policymakers by the time the "Gun War" started between the Cape and the Sotho. As the historian Michael Adas points out in *Machines as the Measure of Men*, colonial officials and settlers increasingly believed that it would be difficult to transfer technical skills to colonial subjects. Colonial rulers agreed that transfers of skills would not be warranted, at the same time as the image of unskilled Africans and Asians became a central element of imperialist ideology.

Ideas about technology, as well as the breechloaders, quinine, and steamships themselves, were central to Europe's "new imperialism."[29] As European empires expanded, technical knowledge and practices circulated in complex ways; they were not simply transferred from the European "core" to the colonial "periphery." As Daniel Headrick and others have shown, the new "tools of empire" were debated extensively in many different locations.[30]

---

[29] Adas, *Machines as the Measure of Men*; Drayton, *Nature's Government*; Headrick, *Tools of Empire* and *Tentacles of Progress*.

[30] Some representative works on science, technology, and imperialism that take local, colonial knowledge into account are Arnold, *Science, Technology, and Medicine in Colonial*

How important were these technologies? How important were these ideas about technologies? For many years, historians and social scientists debated the origins of the "new imperialism" of the late nineteenth century. Theories of imperialism were associated with strains of various ideologies, particularly liberalism and Marxism. All relegated technology to an important yet subordinate role. The strongest proponent of the technological approach to the history of the new imperialism, Daniel Headrick, wrote in 1981 that "to advance the claims of technology – which many still associate with the concept of matter over mind – seems at first to defy an axiom of Western historiography: that history results from the interaction of human decisions."[31] Historians hesitate to admit the possibility that geography and technology cause things to happen. Yet the subjects of our research reveal the influence of inanimate things with some frequency. So do our readers: witness the market success, in recent years, of accounts such as Jared Diamond's *Guns, Germs, and Steel*, which place geographical and technological explanations at the forefront of global history.

To bridge the gap between the public understanding of the role of technology and the professional historian's aversion to "technological determinism," Headrick divided the history of technology and imperialism into motives and means. The motives for imperialism came from human society, while technology provided the means. The new imperialism occurred during the 1870s and 1880s because Europeans of that era had a temporary technological advantage over most other people in the rest of the world.

Headrick's diplomatic solution to this historiographical problem nonetheless produced a predictable result. His book, *The Tools of Empire*, was a hit with students and general readers, but quite a few professional historians dismissed it, along with Headrick's follow-up study, *The Tentacles of Progress*, as technological determinism, in spite of Headrick's best efforts not to make such an argument.

Academic scorn for technological determinism is in proportion to the public's fascination with it, which in turn is related to widespread belief in progress. As historian Michael L. Smith has written about the role of

India; Dubow, *Science and Society in Southern Africa*; Fairhead and Leach, *Misreading the African Landscape*; Grove, *Green Imperialism*; Richards, *Indigenous Agricultural Revolution*; Storey, *Science and Power in Colonial Mauritius*; Todd, *Colonial Technology*.

[31] Headrick, *Tools of Empire*, 9.

technology in United States history, "About technological determinism we could also argue that the issue is not really technology at all but rather a curious cultural and political fetishism whereby artifacts stand in for technology, and technology in turn signifies national progress."[32] Assigning causation to technology is a way of hiding human decisions that are political and controversial. Public weddedness to the idea of "technology as progress" is easily punctured by academic skepticism. A new technology is readily shown to be a conduit for ideology, while technological progress is often shown to have its costs. Costs and benefits vary from person to person and place to place. If the history of technological imperialism shows anything, it is that different people in different regions experience the same technologies in different ways.

Discussions about the influence of technology have a peculiar economy. For academic historians, criticizing technological determinism is light work that produces a wonderful result: the confirmation of one's sense of intellectual superiority. For nonacademic readers, continued belief in determinism shores up continued belief in progress – in spite of the wonders of technology exhibited at Verdun, Auschwitz, and Hiroshima. In the face of modern history, continued belief in technological determinism is a triumph of hope over experience. Yet such a belief, when it is held widely, helps individuals claim unfounded expertise in a world in which technological expertise often results in power.

For all these reasons, I have tried to push beyond the issue of whether or not technologies influence societies and societies influence technologies. In telling the story of guns in colonial South Africa, it has proved impossible to tell a story in which "structure," or persistent human and material conditions, mediates "agency," the ability of people or things to change the course of events. Instead of telling a story of causes and effects, I have told a story about people and guns in South Africa that follows the historian William Cronon's injunction to environmental historians: "An ecological history begins by assuming a dynamic and changing relationship between environment and culture, one as apt to produce contradictions as continuities."[33] I have assumed that a technological history assumes a dynamic and changing relationship between technology and culture. This has, indeed, produced as many contradictions as continuities.

[32] "Recourse of Empire," in Smith and Marx, *Does Technology Drive History?*, 39.
[33] Cronon, *Changes in the Land*, 13.

Bibliography

Archival Sources

Cape Town Archives Repository (CTAR)

Colonial Office: Correspondence: CO 242–5488
Griqualand West: Correspondence: GLW 45–188
Government House: Correspondence: GH 10–14
Napier Collection: A 1415
Native Affairs Department: NA 272–84
Southey Papers: A 611

Public Record Office (PRO), Kew

Carnarvon Papers, PRO 30 / 6

Colonial Office (CO)

Original Correspondence: Cape: CO 48 / 154–506
Original Correspondence: Natal: CO 179 / 16–135
Original Correspondence: Transvaal: CO 291 / 1
Supplementary Correspondence: CO 537 / 124
Confidential Prints: Africa: CO 879 / Vol. 1, No. 19; Vol. 5, No. 37; Vol. 6, No. 59; Vol. 7, Nos. 64, 67; Vol. 9, Nos. 89, 96; Vol. 10, Nos. 102, 105; Vol. 13, No. 151; Vol. 14, Nos. 161, 162; Vol. 15, Nos. 173, 190; Vol. 16, No. 200; Vol. 17, Nos. 208, 209, 222, 225; Vol. 31, No. 381; Vol. 37, No. 441

War Office (WO)

Buller Papers, WO 132
Wolseley Papers, WO 147

Rhodes House Library (RHL), Oxford

Anti-Slavery Papers, Mss. Brit. Emp. S18
J. C. Molteno Papers, Mss. Afr. S23

Official Publications

British Parliamentary Papers (BPP)

These documents are known informally as Parliamentary Blue Books, as they were bound in blue covers. Formally they are known as "Command Papers" – technically they were commanded by the monarch to be presented to the parliament.

1802–3: [76] Vol. VII
1837: [503] Vol. XLIII
1847: [786] Vol. XXXVIII
1851: [424] Vol. XXXVIII, [635] Vol. XIV, [1352] Vol. XXXVIII
1852: [57] Vol. XXXIII
1860: [492] Vol. XLVII, [2747] Vol. XLVII
1868–9: [4140] Vol. XLIII
1870: C.18, C.99
1874: C.1025
1875: C.1119, C.1121, C.1141, C.1158
1876: C.1342, C.1399, C.1631
1877: C.1681, C.1732, C.1883
1878: C.1961, C.2000, C.2079, C.2100, C.2144
1879: C.2220, C.2374, C.2454
1880: C.2482, C.2505, C.2569, C.2584, C.2655, C.2676, C.2695
1881: C.2754, C.2755, C.2821, C.2866, C.2964
1882: C.3112, C.3175, C.3381, C.3410, C.3419
1883: C.3486, C.3493, C.3686, C.3708
1884: C.3841, C.4205, C.4265
1885: C.4589, C.4590

Cape Parliamentary Papers (CPP)

These documents are formally titled: Colony of the Cape of Good Hope, *Annexures to the Votes and Proceedings of the House of Assembly*. Excerpts from many of these documents were subsequently included in the British Parliamentary Papers. In such cases, I have given citations to the British Parliamentary Papers, which are more widely accessible.

1865: A.34, C.16
1868: A.25, A.37, G.32
1870: A.8
1873: G.27
1874: G.27
1875: A.20, G.21

1876: A.13, G.16, G.52
1877: A.23, G.1, G.12
1878: G.17
1879: G.33, G.43, G.58
1880: A.12, A.56, A.67, A.70, A.105, G.13, G.72, G.74
1881: A.29, A.35, A.44, A.68, G.20
1882: A.2, A.8, A.26, A.31, A.52, A.71, A.90, G.26, G.33, G.47, G.74
1883: G.6, G.8, G.9, G.10, G.54

New Zealand Parliamentary Papers (AJHR)

These documents are formally titled: Colony of New Zealand, *Appendices to the Journals of the House of Representatives.* Excerpts from many of these documents were subsequently included in the British Parliamentary Papers. In such cases, I have given citations to the British Parliamentary Papers, which are more widely accessible.

1856: A.3
1864: E.3, E.6
1868: D.21
1870: D.13

General

Colony of Natal. *Blue Books.* Pietermaritzburg: Government Printer, 1867–99.
Colony of Natal. *Gunpowder Laws' Committee, 1889: Evidence and Annexures.* Pietermaritzburg: Government Printer, 1889.
Colony of Natal. "Petition of the Natal Chamber of Commerce Regarding Restrictions on the Gun Trade." *Legislative Council Sessional Papers,* L.C. no. 14, 1874.
Colony of the Cape of Good Hope. *Blue Books.* Cape Town: Government Printer, 1857–86.
Colony of the Cape of Good Hope. *Government Gazette.* Cape Town: Government Printer, 1803–1905.
South African Native Affairs Commission, 1903–1905. 5 vols. Cape Town: Government Printer, 1905.
Statute Law of Griqualand West. Cape Town: Government Printer, 1882.
Statutes of Natal. Comp. and ed. R. L. Hitchins. Pietermaritzburg: P. Davis & Sons, 1900.
Statutes of the Cape of Good Hope, 1652–1900. 4 vols. Ed. Hercules Tennant and Edgar Michael Jackson. Cape Town: J. C. Juta, 1871–1900.

Newspapers and Periodicals

Anti-Slavery Reporter
Cape Argus
Cape Frontier Times
Cape Monitor

Cape Monthly Magazine
Cape Times
Diamond Field
Diamond Fields Advertiser
Diamond News and Griqualand West Government Gazette
Diamond News and Vaal Advertiser
Eastern Province Herald
Friend of the Orange Free State
Friend of the Orange River Sovereignty
Gold Fields Mercury
Grahams Town Journal
Natal Witness
Port Elizabeth Mercury
South African Commercial Advertiser
Times (London)

General

Adams, Buck. *The Narrative of Private Buck Adams*. Ed. A. Gordon-Brown. Cape Town: Van Riebeeck Society, 1941.

Adas, Michael. *Machines as the Measure of Men: Science, Technology, and Ideologies of Western Dominance*. Ithaca and London: Cornell University Press, 1989.

Agar-Hamilton, J. A. I. *The Native Policy of the Voortrekkers: An Essay in the History of South Africa, 1836–1858*. Cape Town: Maskew Miller, 1928.

Agar-Hamilton, J. A. I. *The Road to the North: South Africa, 1852–1886*. London: Longmans, 1937.

Ajayi, J. F. Ade, and Robert Smith. *Yoruba Warfare in the Nineteenth Century*. 2nd ed. Cambridge: Cambridge University Press; Ibadan: Ibadan University Press, 1971.

Alberti, Ludwig. *Ludwig Alberti's Account of the Tribal Life and Customs of the Xhosa in 1807*. Trans. William Fehr. Cape Town: A. A. Balkema, 1968.

Alexander, James. *Narrative of a Voyage of Observation*. 2 vols. London: Colburn, 1837. Repr. Cape Town: C. Struik, 1967.

Ambler, Charles, and Jonathan Crush, eds. *Liquor and Labor in Southern Africa*. Athens: Ohio University Press, 1992.

Andersson, Karl Johann [Pseud. C. J. Anderson.]. *Notes of Travel in South Africa*. Ed. Llewellyn Lloyd. London: Hurst & Blackett, 1875.

Appadurai, Arjun, ed. *The Social Life of Things: Commodities in Cultural Perspective*. Cambridge: Cambridge University Press, 1986.

Arbousset, Jean Thomas, and F. Daumas. *Narrative of an Exploratory Tour of the North-East of the Colony of the Cape of Good Hope*. Trans. John Croumbie Brown. Cape Town: Robertson, 1846. Repr., Cape Town: C. Struik, 1968.

Arnold, David. *The New Cambridge History of India*. Vol. 3.5, *Science, Technology and Medicine in Colonial India*. Cambridge: Cambridge University Press, 2000.

Ashe, Waller, and E. V. Wyatt-Edgell. *The Story of the Zulu Campaign.* London: S. Low et al., 1880.

Atmore, Anthony. "The Moorosi Rebellion: Lesotho, 1879." In *Protest and Power in Black Africa.* Eds. Robert I. Rotberg and Ali A. Mazrui. New York: Oxford University Press, 1970: 2–35.

Atmore, Anthony, and Peter Sanders. "Sotho Arms and Ammunition in the Nineteenth Century." *Journal of African History* 12, no. 4 (1971): 535–44.

Atmore, Anthony, J. M Chirenje, and S. I. Mudenge. "Firearms in South Central Africa." *Journal of African History* 12, no. 4 (1971): 545–56.

Bailey, DeWitt, and Douglas A. Nie. *English Gunmakers: The Birmingham and Provincial Gun Trade in the 18th and 19th Century.* London: Arms and Armour Press, 1978.

Bain, Andrew Geddes. *Journals of Andrew Geddes Bain: Trader, Explorer, Road Engineer and Geologist.* Ed. Margaret Hermina Lister. Cape Town: Van Riebeeck Society, 1949.

Baines, Thomas. *Explorations in South West Africa.* London: Longman, Green, 1864.

Baines, Thomas. *The Northern Goldfields Diaries of Thomas Baines.* 3 vols. Ed. J. P. R. Wallis. London: Chatto & Windus, 1946.

Baker, Clyde. *Modern Gunsmithing: A Manual of Firearms Design, Construction, and Remodeling for Amateurs and Professionals.* 2nd ed. Marines, N.C.: Small Arms Technical Publishing, 1933.

Baldwin, William Charles. *African Hunting and Adventure from Natal to the Zambezi.* London: Richard Bentley, 1894.

Ballard, Charles. "John Dunn and Cetshwayo: The Material Foundations of Political Power in the Zulu Kingdom, 1857–1878." *Journal of African History* 21, no. 1 (1980): 75–91.

Beachey, R. W. "The Arms Trade in East Africa in the Late Nineteenth Century." *Journal of African History* 3 (1962): 451–67.

Beck, Roger B. "Bibles and Beads: Missionaries as Traders in Southern Africa in the Early Nineteenth Century." *Journal of African History* 30, no. 2 (1989): 211–25.

Beck, Roger B. "The Legalization and Development of Trade on the Cape Frontier, 1817–1830." Ph.D. dissertation, Indiana University, 1987.

Beck, Ulrich. *Risk Society: Towards a New Modernity.* Thousand Oaks, CA: Sage, 1992.

Becker, Peter. *Rule of Fear: The Life and Times of Dingane, King of the Zulu.* London: Longmans, 1964.

Beinart, William. "Empire, Hunting, and Ecological Change in Southern and Central Africa." *Past and Present* 128 (August 1990): 162–86.

Beinart, William. "European Traders and the Mpondo Paramountcy, 1878–1886." *Journal of African History* 20 (1979): 471–86.

Beinart, William. "Political and Collective Violence in Southern African Historiography." *Journal of Southern African Studies* 18, no. 3 (September 1992): 455–86.

Beinart, William. *The Political Economy of Pondoland, 1860–1930.* Cambridge: Cambridge University Press, 1982.

Beinart, William. *The Rise of Conservation in South Africa: Settlers, Livestock, and the Environment, 1770–1950.* Oxford: Oxford University Press, 2003.

Beinart, William, and Colin Bundy. *Hidden Struggles in Rural South Africa: Politics & Popular Movements in the Transkei & Eastern Cape, 1890–1930.* London: James Currey; Berkeley and Los Angeles: University of California Press; Johannesburg: Ravan, 1987.

Beinart, William, and JoAnn McGregor, eds. *Social History & African Environments.* Oxford: James Currey, Athens: Ohio University Press; Cape Town: David Philip, 2003.

Beinart, William, and Peter Coates. *Environment and History: The Taming of Nature in the USA and South Africa.* London and New York: Routledge, 1995.

Belich, James. *The Victorian Interpretation of Racial Conflict: The Maori, the British, and the New Zealand Wars.* Quebec: McGill-Queen's University Press, 1989. First published in 1986 by Auckland University Press under the title *The New Zealand Wars and the Victorian Interpretation of Racial Conflict.*

Bellesiles, Michael A. *Arming America: The Origins of a National Gun Culture.* New York: Alfred A. Knopf, 2000.

Bentley, Trevor. *Pakeha Maori: The Extraordinary Story of the Europeans Who Lived as Maori in Early New Zealand.* Harmondsworth, Middlesex, England: Penguin Books, 1999.

Berg, Gerald M. "The Sacred Musket. Tactics, Technology, and Power in Eighteenth-Century Madagascar." *Comparative Studies in Society and History* 27, no. 2 (1985): 261–79.

Berkovitch, Barry M. "The Westley Richards Centre-Fire 'Monkey-Tail' Carbine." *Journal of the Historical Firearms Society of South Africa* 6, no. 3 (June 1973): 6–8.

Berkovitch, Barry M. *The Cape Gunsmith: A History of the Gunsmiths and Gun Dealers at the Cape of Good Hope from 1795 to 1900, with Particular Reference to Their Weapons.* Stellenbosch: Museum, 1976.

Beyers, C. J., and J. L. Bassou, eds. *Dictionary of South African Biography.* 5 vols. Pretoria: Human Sciences Research Council, 1987.

Bhila, H. H. K. *Trade and Politics in a Shona Kingdom: The Manyika and Their Portuguese and African Neighbors, 1575–1902.* London: Longman, 1982.

Bickford-Smith, Vivian. *Ethnic Pride and Racial Prejudice in Victorian Cape Town.* Cambridge: Cambridge University Press, 1995; Johannesburg: Witwatersrand University Press, 2001.

Bickford-Smith, Vivian, Elizabeth van Heyningen, and Nigel Worden. *Cape Town: In the Twentieth Century.* Claremont, South Africa: David Philip, 1999.

Bijker, Wiebe E. *Of Bicycles, Bakelites, and Bulbs: Toward a Theory of Sociotechnical Change.* Cambridge, Mass.: MIT Press, 1995.

Bijker, Wiebe, Harry Collins, and G. H. de Vries. "Ways of Going On: An Analysis of Skill Applied to Medical Practice," *Science, Technology, and Human Values* 22, no. 3 (Summer 1997): 267–85.

Bijker, Wiebe E., and John Law, eds. *Shaping Technology/Building Society: Studies in Sociotechnical Change.* Cambridge, Mass.: MIT, 1992.

Bird, John. *The Annals of Natal, 1495 to 1845.* 2 vols. Cape Town: Maskew Miller, 1888. Repr. Cape Town: C. Struik, 1965 and 1968.

Bissett, John. *Sport and War, or Recollections of Fighting and Hunting in South Africa from the Years 1834 to 1867.* London: Murray, 1875.

Blackmore, Howard L. *British Military Firearms, 1650–1850.* London: Jenkins, 1961. Rev. ed. London: Greenhill, 1994.

Blanch, H. J. *A Century of Guns: A Sketch of the Leading Types of Sporting and Military Small Arms.* London: J. Blanch & Son, 1909.

Bonner, Philip. "Factions and Fissions: Transvaal/Swazi Politics in the Mid-Nineteenth Century." *Journal of African History* 19, no. 2 (1978): 219–38.

Booth, Bradford Allen, ed. *The Letters of Anthony Trollope.* Westport: Greenwood, 1979.

Bowker, Thomas Holden. "War Journal." In *Comdt. Holden Bowker.* Ed. Ivan Mitford-Barberton. Cape Town: Human & Rousseau, 1970: 97–165.

Boyle, Frederick. *To the Cape for Diamonds: A Story of Digging Experiences in South Africa.* London: Chapman & Hall, 1873.

Braddock, John. *A Memoir on Gunpowder.* Madras: Church Mission Press, 1827. Repr. London: Richardson, 1832.

Bradford, Helen. "Women, Gender and Colonialism: Rethinking the History of the British Cape Colony and Its Frontier Zones, c. 1806–70." *Journal of African History* 37, no. 3 (1996): 351–70.

Bradlow, Edna. "The Cape Government's Rule of Basutoland, 1871–1883." In *Archives Year Book for South African History.* Vol. 2. Johannesburg: Government Printer, 1969.

Braverman, Harry. *Labor and Monopoly Capital: The Degradation of Work in the Twentieth Century.* New York: Monthly Review Press, 1974.

Breckenridge, Keith. "'We Must Speak for Ourselves': The Rise and Fall of a Public Sphere on the South African Gold Mines, 1920 to 1931." *Comparative Studies in Society and History* 40, no. 1 (January 1998): 71–108.

Breytenbach, J. H. "The Military Preparations and Weaponry of the Republics." Extract from *Geskiedenis van Tweede Vryheidsoorlog, 1899–1902.* Vol. 1. Pretoria: Government Printers, 1972. In *Journal of the Historical Firearms Society of South Africa* 6, no. 3 (June 1973): 8–10.

Breytenbach, J. H., et al. *South African Archival Records.* Cape Town: Government Printer, 1949–64.

Brickmann, Ronald, Sheila Jasanoff, and Thomas Ilgen. *Controlling Chemicals: The Politics of Regulation in Europe and the United States.* Ithaca: Cornell University Press, 1985.

Brookes, E. H. *The History of Native Policy in South Africa.* 2nd rev. ed. Pretoria: Schaik, 1927.

Brooks, Peter, and Paul Gewirtz, eds. *Law's Stories: Narrative and Rhetoric in the Law.* New Haven and London: Yale University Press, 1996.

Brown, M. L. *Firearms in Colonial America: The Impact on History and Technology, 1492–1792.* Washington, D.C.: Smithsonian Institution Press, 1980.

Brownlee, Charles Pacalt. *A Chapter on the Basuto War: A Lecture.* Lovedale: Mission Press, 1889 [Pamphlet, 35 pp.].

Brownlee, Charles Pacalt. *Reminiscences of Kafir Life and History and Other Papers.* Ed. Christopher Saunders. Lovedale: Lovedale Press, 1916. Facs. repr. Pietermaritzburg and Durban: University of Natal Press and Killie Campbell Africana Library, 1977.

Bryant, A. T. *Olden Times in Zululand and Natal.* London: Longmans, 1929. Repr. Cape Town: C. Struik, 1965.

Bryden, H. A. *With Gun and Camera in Southern Africa.* London: E. Stanford, 1893.

Bunn, David. "Comaroff Country." *Interventions: International Journal of Post-colonial Studies* 3, no. 1 (2001): 5–23.

Burchell, William J. *Travels in the Interior of Southern Africa,* 2 vols. Ed. Isaac Schapera. London: Longman, 1822. Facs. repr. London: Batchworth, 1953.

Burman, Sandra. *Chiefdom Politics and Alien Law: Basutoland under Cape Rule, 1871–1884.* London: Macmillan, 1981.

Campbell, John. *Travels in South Africa.* London: Black, Parry, 1815.

Carnegie, David. *Among the Matabele.* London: Religious Tract Society, 1894.

Casalis, Eugène. *The Basutos, or Twenty-Three Years in South Africa.* London: Nisbet, 1861. Facs. repr. Cape Town: C. Struik, 1965.

Caulk, R. A. "Firearms and Princely Power in Ethiopia in the Nineteenth Century." *Journal of African History* 13, no. 4 (1972): 609–30.

Chanock, Martin. *Law, Custom, and Social Order: The Colonial Experience in Malawi and Zambia.* Cambridge: Cambridge University Press, 1985.

Chanock, Martin. "Paradigms, Policies, and Property: A Review of the Customary Law of Land Tenure." In *Law in Colonial Africa.* Ed. Kristin Mann and Richard Roberts. Portsmouth, NH: Heineman, 1991: 61–84.

Chapel, Charles Edward. *The Complete Guide to Gunsmithing: Gun Care and Repair.* New York: A. S. Barnes, 2nd rev. ed. 1962.

Chapman, James. *Travels in the Interior of South Africa, 1849–1863.* Ed. Edward C. Tabler. Cape Town: Balkema, 1971.

Chase, Kenneth. *Firearms: A Global History to 1700.* Cambridge: Cambridge University Press, 2003.

Clements, W. H. *The Glamour and Tragedy of the Zulu War.* London: John Lane, 1936.

Cline, Walter Buchanan. *Mining and Metallurgy in Negro Africa.* Menasha, Wisc.: Banta, 1937.

Coates, Peter, comp. *The Cape Town English Press Index.* 6 vols. Cape Town: South African Library, 1980–96.

Cobbing, Julian. "The Mfecane as Alibi: Thoughts on Dithakong and Mbolompo." *Journal of African History* 29 (1988): 487–519.

Cohen, David William. *The Combing of History.* Chicago: University of Chicago Press, 1994.

Cohen, David William, and E. S. Atieno Odhiambo. *Burying SM: The Politics of Knowledge and the Sociology of Power in Africa.* Portsmouth, N.H.: Heinemann, 1992.

Colenso, Frances Ellen, with Lt. Col. Edward Durnford. *History of the Zulu War and Its Origin.* London: Chapman & Hall, 1880.

Colenso, John William. *Defence of Langalibalele, with Additional Evidence and an Appendix Bringing Down the History of the Case to the Latest Date.* London: n.p., 1874.

Colley, Linda. *Britons: Forging the Nation, 1707–1837.* New Haven: Yale University Press, 1992.

Comaroff, Jean, and John Comaroff. "Revelations upon Revelation: After Shocks, Afterthoughts." *Interventions: International Journal of Postcolonial Studies* 3, no. 1 (2001): 100–26.

Comaroff, Jean, and John Comaroff. *Of Revelation and Revolution.* Vol. 1, *Christianity, Colonialism, and Consciousness in South Africa.* Vol. 2, *The Dialectics of Modernity on a South African Frontier.* Chicago: The University of Chicago Press, 1991 and 1997.

Cooper, John S. *For Commonwealth and Crown: English Gunmakers of the Seventeenth Century.* Gillingham: Wilson Hunt, 1993.

Comaroff, John. "Foreward." In *Contested States: Law, Hegemony, and Resistance.* Ed. Mindie Lazarus-Black and Susan F. Hirsch. London: Routledge, 1994.

Cope, Richard L. "C.W. de Kiewiet, the Imperial Factor, and South African 'Native Policy.'" *Journal of Southern African Studies* 15, no. 3 (April 1989): 486–505.

Cope, Richard L. "Local Imperatives and Imperial Policy: The Sources of Lord Carnarvon's South African Confederation Policy." *The International Journal of African Historical Studies* 20, no. 4 (1987): 601–26.

Cope, Richard L. "The Origins of the Anglo-Zulu War of 1879." Ph.D. dissertation, University of the Witwatersrand, 1995.

Cope, Richard L. *Ploughshare of War: The Origins of the Anglo-Zulu War of 1879.* Pietermaritzburg: University of Natal Press, 1999.

Cope, Richard L. "Shepstone, the Zulus, and the Annexation of the Transvaal." *South African Historical Journal* 4 (November 1972): 45–63.

Cope, Richard L. "Strategic and Socio-Economic Explanations for Carnarvon's South African Confederation Policy: The Historiography and the Evidence." *History in Africa*, 13 (1986): 13–34.

Cope, Richard L. "Written in Characters of Blood? The Reign of King Cetshwayo Ka Mpande, 1872–9." *Journal of African History* 36 (1995): 247–69.

Cory, George. *The Rise of South Africa.* 6 vols. London: Longmans, 1910–40.

Crais, Clifton C. *White Supremacy and Black Resistance in Pre-Industrial South Africa: The Making of the Colonial Order in the Eastern Cape, 1770–1865.* Cambridge: Cambridge University Press, 1991.

Cronon, William. *Changes in the Land: Indians, Colonists, and the Ecology of New England.* New York: Hill and Wang, 1983.

Crosby, Ron D. *The Musket Wars: A History of Inter-Iwi Conflict, 1806–45.* Auckland: Reed, 1999.

Crowder, Michael. *West African Resistance: The Military Response to Colonial Occupation.* London: Hutchinson, 1978.

Cunynghame, Sir Arthur. *My Command in South Africa, 1874–1878.* London: Macmillan, 1879.

Currey, J. B. "The Diamond Fields of Griqualand West and Their Probable Influence on the Native Races of South Africa." *Journal of the Society of Arts* 24 (1876): 373–81.

Curtin, Philip D. *Economic Change in Precolonial Africa: Senegambia in the Era of the Slave Trade.* Madison: University of Wisconsin Press, 1975.

Damane, M., and Peter Sanders. *Lithoko: Sotho Praise-Poems.* Oxford: Clarendon, 1974.

Davenport, T. R. H. "The Cape Liberal Tradition to 1910." In *Democratic Liberalism in South Africa: Its History and Prospect.* Ed. Jeffrey Butler, Richard Elphick, and David Welsh. Middletown, Conn.: Wesleyan University Press; Cape Town: David Philip, 1987: 21–34.

Davenport, T. R. H. "The Consolidation of a New Society: The Cape Colony," in *A History of South Africa to 1870.* Ed. Monica Wilson and Leonard Thompson. Originally published as *The Oxford History of South Africa.* Oxford: Oxford University Press, 1969; rev. ed. Cape Town: David Philip; London: Croom Helm, 1982: 272–333.

Davenport, T. R. H., and Christopher Saunders. *South Africa: A Modern History.* 5th ed. London: Macmillan, Ltd.; New York: St. Martin's, 2000.

De Kiewiet, C. W. *A History of South Africa: Social and Economic.* London: Oxford University Press, 1957.

De Kiewiet, C. W. *The Imperial Factor in South Africa: A Study in Politics and Economics.* London: Frank Cass, 1937. Repr. 1965.

Deacon, H. J., and Janette Deacon. *Human Beginnings in South Africa: Uncovering the Secrets of the Stone Age.* Walnut Creek, CA: Altamira, 1999.

Delius, Peter. *The Land Belongs to Us: The Pedi Polity, the Boers and the British in the Nineteenth-Century Transvaal.* Berkeley and Los Angeles: University of California Press, 1984.

Delius, Peter. "Migrant Labour and the Pedi, 1840–80." In *Economy and Society in Pre-Industrial South Africa.* Ed. Shula Marks and Anthony Atmore. London: Longman, 1980: 293–312.

Diamond, Jared. *Guns, Germs, and Steel: The Fates of Human Societies.* New York: Norton, 1997.

Dictionary of South African Biography. 5 vols. Ed. W. J. De Kock. Cape Town: National Council for Social Research, 1968–87.

Doke, C. M., et al. *Zulu-English Dictionary.* Johannesburg: University of the Witwatersrand Press, 1990.

Dolman, Alfred. *In the Footsteps of Livingstone: Being the Travel Notes Made by Alfred Dolman.* Ed. J. Irving. London: John Lane, 1924.

Doughty, Oswald. *Early Diamond Days.* London: Longmans, 1963.

Dovers, Stephen, Ruth Edgecombe, and Bill Guest, eds. *South Africa's Environmental History: Cases & Comparisons.* Athens: Ohio University Press; Cape Town: David Philip, 2002.

Dower, William. *The Early Annals of Kokstad and Griqualand East.* Port Elizabeth: Kemsley, 1902. Facs. repr. ed. Christopher Saunders, Pietermaritzburg: University of Natal Press, 1978.

Dracopoli, J. L. *Sir Andries Stockenstrom, 1792–1864.* Cape Town: Balkema, 1969.

Drayton, Richard. *Nature's Government: Science, Imperial Britain, and the 'Improvement' of the World*. New Haven: Yale University Press, 2000.

Du Toit, André, and Hermann Giliomee. *Afrikaner Political Thought: Analysis and Documents*. Vol. 1. *Analysis and Documents, 1780–1850*. Berkeley and Los Angeles: University of California Press, 1983.

Dubow, Saul. *A Commonwealth of Knowledge: Science, Sensibility, and White South Africa, 1820–2000*. Oxford: Oxford University Press, 2006.

Dubow, Saul, ed. *Science and Society in Southern Africa*. Manchester: Manchester University Press, 2000.

Duminy, Andrew, and Bill Guest, eds. *Natal and Zululand from Earliest Times to 1910*. Pietermaritzburg: University of Natal Press, 1989.

Echenberg, Myron J. "Late Nineteenth-Century Military Technology in Upper Volta." *Journal of African History* 12, no. 2 (1971): 241–54.

Eldredge, Elizabeth A. "Sources of Conflict in Southern Africa, c. 1800–30: The 'Mfecane' Reconsidered." *Journal of African History* 33 (1992): 1–35.

Eldredge, Elizabeth A. *A South African Kingdom: The Pursuit of Security in Nineteenth-Century Lesotho*. Cambridge: Cambridge University Press, 1993.

Ellenberger, D. F. *History of the Basuto: Ancient and Modern*. London: Caxton, 1912.

Ellis, John. *The Social History of the Machine Gun*. Baltimore: The Johns Hopkins University Press, 1975.

Elphick, Richard. *Kraal and Castle: Khoikhoi and the Founding of White South Africa*. New Haven: Yale University Press, 1977.

Elphick, Richard, and Rodney Davenport, eds. *Christianity in South Africa: A Political, Social, and Cultural History*. Oxford: James Currey; Cape Town: David Philip, 1997.

Elphick, Richard, and Hermann Giliomee, eds. *The Shaping of South African Society, 1652–1840*. Cape Town: Maskew Miller Longman (Pty) Ltd, 1989.

Elphick, Richard, and V. C. Malherbe. "The Khoisan to 1828." In *The Shaping of South African Society, 1652–1840*. Ed. Elphick, Richard, and Hermann Giliomee. Cape Town: Maskew Miller Longman (Pty) Ltd, 1989: 3–65.

Etherington, Norman. *The Great Treks: The Transformation of Southern Africa, 1815–1854*. London: Pearson Education, 2001.

Etherington, Norman A. "Labour Supply and the Genesis of South African Confederation in the 1870s." *Journal of African History* 20, no. 2 (1979): 235–53.

Etherington, Norman. "Natal's Black Rape Scare of the 1870s." *Journal of Southern African Studies* 15, no. 1 (October 1988): 36–53.

Etherington, N. A. "Why Langalibalele Ran Away." *Journal of Natal and Zulu History* 1 (1978): 1–24.

Evans, Christopher. *"The Labyrinth of Flames": Work and Social Conflict in Early Industrial Merthyr Tydfil*. Cardiff: University of Wales Press, 1993.

Evans, Julie, Patricia Grimshaw, David Philips, and Shurlee Swain. *Equal Subjects, Unequal Rights: Indigenous Peoples in British Settler Colonies, 1830–1910*. Manchester: Manchester University Press, 2003.

Eybers, G. W. *Select Constitutional Documents Illustrating South African History 1795–1910*. London: Routledge, 1918.

Fairhead, James, and Melissa Leach. *Misreading the African Landscape: Society and Ecology in a Forest-Savanna Mosaic.* Cambridge: Cambridge University Press, 1996.

Feierman, Steven. "The Comaroffs and the Practice of Historical Ethnography." *Interventions: International Journal of Postcolonial Studies* 3, no. 1 (2001): 24–30.

Ferguson, James. *The Anti-Politics Machine: "Development," Depoliticization, and Bureaucratic Power in Lesotho.* Cambridge: Cambridge University Press, 1990.

Fisher, Humphrey J., and Virginia Rowland. "Firearms in the Central Sudan." *Journal of African History* 12, no. 2 (1971): 215–39.

Foltz, William J., and Henry S. Bienen. *Arms and the African: Military Influences on Africa's International Relations.* New Haven: Yale University Press, 1985.

"Fossor." *Twelve Months at the South Africa Diamond Fields.* London: E. Stanford, 1872.

Fraser, John George. *Episodes in My Life.* Cape Town: Juta, 1922.

Fyfe, Christopher. "Race, Empire, and the Historians." *Race and Class* 33, no. 4 (1992): 15–30.

Fynn, Henry Francis. *The Diary of Henry Francis Fynn, 1803–1861.* Ed. J. Stuart and D. Malcolm. Pietermaritzburg: Shuter and Shooter, 1950.

Garavaglia, Louis, and Charles Worman. *Firearms of the American West, 1803–1865.* Albuquerque: University of New Mexico Press, 1984.

Gardiner, Allen F. *Narrative of a Journey to the Zoolu Country.* London: William Crofts, 1836. Facs. repr. Cape Town: Struik, 1966.

Gemery, Henry A., and Jan S. Hogendorn. "Technological Change, Slavery and the Slave Trade." In Clive J. Dewey and A. G. Hopkins, ed. *The Imperial Impact: Studies in the Economic History of Africa and India.* London: Athlone, 1978: 243–58.

George, J. N. *English Guns and Rifles.* Plantersville, S.C.: Small-Arms Technical Publishing, 1947.

Geschiere, Peter. "Historical Anthropology: Questions of Time, Method and Scale." *Interventions: International Journal of Postcolonial Studies* 3, no. 1 (2001): 31–9.

Geyer, Michael, and Charles Bright. "Global Violence and Nationalizing Wars in Eurasia and America: The Geopolitics of War in the Mid-Nineteenth Century." *Comparative Studies in Society and History* 38, no. 4 (October 1996): 619–57.

Gibson, James Young. *The Story of the Zulus.* London: Longmans, 1911.

Giliomee, Hermann. *The Afrikaners: A Biography of a People.* Cape Town: Tafelberg; Charlottesville: University of Virginia Press, 2003.

Given, Brian J. *A Most Pernicious Thing: Gun Trading and Native Warfare in the Early Contact Period.* Ottawa: Carleton University Press, 1994.

Glass, Stafford. *The Matabele War.* London: Longmans, 1968.

Glendinning, Victoria. *Anthony Trollope.* New York: Knopf, 1993.

Glynn, Henry T. *Game and Gold: Memories of over 50 Years in the Lydenburg District, Transvaal.* London: Dolman, 1938.

Goodfellow, Clement Francis. *Great Britain and the South African Confederation, 1870–1881.* Cape Town: Oxford University Press, 1966.

Goodman, J. D. "The Birmingham Gun Trade." In *The Resources, Products, and Industrial History of Birmingham and the Midland Hardware District.* Ed. Samuel Timmins. London: Robert Hardwicke, 1866.

Grant, Jonathan A. *Rulers, Guns, and Money: The Global Arms Trade in the Age of Imperialism.* Cambridge, Mass.: Harvard University Press, 2007.

Gray, Richard. "Portuguese Musketeers on the Zambezi." *Journal of African History* 12, no. 4 (1971): 531–3.

Greener, W. O. *A Bibliography of Guns and Shooting.* Westminster: Roxburghe, 1894.

Greener, W. O. *The Science of Gunnery.* London: Longmans, 1841.

Greener, W. O., and C. E. Greener. [Pseud. "Artifex and Opifex"]. *The Causes of Decay in a British Industry.* London: Longmans, 1907.

Griffin, B. S. "The Gun Flint." *Journal of the Historical Firearms Society of South Africa* 1. Repr. ed. of 1958–1960: 7–10. Cape Town: C. Struik, 1963.

Griffin, B. S. "Muzzle Loaders in Bechuanaland." *Journal of the Historical Firearms Society of South Africa* 2, no. 5 (December 1962): 20–3.

Grove, Richard H. *Green Imperialism: Colonial Expansion, Tropical Island Edens and the Origins of Environmentalism, 1600–1860.* Cambridge: Cambridge University Press, 1995.

Grundlingh, M. A. S. "The Parliament of the Cape of Good Hope, with Special Reference to Party Politics, 1872–1910." *Archives Year Book for South African History.* Vol. 2. Johannesburg: Government Printer, 1973.

Grundy, Kenneth W. *Soldiers Without Politics: Blacks in the South African Armed Forces.* Berkeley and Los Angeles: University of California Press, 1983.

Guelke, Leonard, and Robert Shell. "Landscape of Conquest: Frontier Water Alienation and Khoikhoi Strategies of Survival, 1652–1780." *Journal of Southern African Studies* 18, no. 4 (Dec. 1992): 802–24.

Guest, William R. "Colonists, Confederation, and Constitutional Change." In *Natal and Zululand from Earliest Times to 1910: A New History.* Ed. Andrew Duminy and Bill Guest. Pietermaritzburg: University of Natal Press and Shuter & Shooter, 1989: 146–69.

Guest, William R. *Langalibalele: The Crisis in Natal, 1873–1875.* Durban: University of Natal, 1976.

Guy, Jeff. *The Destruction of the Zulu Kingdom: The Civil War in Zululand, 1879–1884.* Pietermaritzburg: University of Natal Press, 1994.

Guy, Jeff. "Ecological Factors in the Rise of Shaka and the Zulu Kingdom." In *Economy and Society in Pre-Industrial South Africa.* Ed. Shula Marks and Anthony Atmore. London: Longman, 1980: 102–19.

Guy, Jeff. *The Heretic: A Study of the Life of John William Colenso, 1814–1883.* Johannesburg and Pietermaritzburg: Ravan and the University of Natal Press, 1983.

Guy, J. J. "A Note on Firearms in the Zulu Kingdom with Special Reference to the Anglo-Zulu War, 1879." *Journal of African History* 12, no. 4 (1971): 557–70.

Guy, Jeff. *The View Across the River: Harriette Colenso and the Zulu Struggle against Imperialism.* Charlottesville: University Press of Virginia, 2001.

Hacker, Barton C. "Military Institutions, Weapons, and Social Change: Toward a New History of Military Technology." *Technology and Culture: The International Quarterly of the Society for the History of Technology* 35, no. 4 (October 1994): 768–834.

Haggard, H. Rider. *King Solomon's Mines.* Oxford World's Classics. Oxford: Oxford University Press, 2006.

Hall, N. John. *Trollope: A Biography.* Oxford: Clarendon, 1991.

Hamilton, Carolyn Anne. "'The Character and Objects of Chaka': A Reconsideration of the Making of Shaka as 'Mfecane' Motor." *Journal of African History* 33 (1992): 37–63.

Hamilton, Carolyn. *Terrific Majesty: The Powers of Shaka Zulu and the Limits of Historical Invention.* Cambridge, Mass.: Harvard University Press, 1998.

Harper, Douglas. *Working Knowledge: Skill and Community in a Small Shop.* Berkeley and Los Angeles: University of California Press, 1987.

Harris, Clive, ed. *The History of the Birmingham Gun-Barrel Proof House, with Notes on the Birmingham Gun Trade.* Birmingham: Guardians of the Birmingham Proof House, 1946; 2nd ed. 1949.

Harris, William Cornwallis. *The Wild Sports of Southern Africa.* London: Bohn, 1852. Facs. repr. Cape Town: Struik, 1963.

Headrick, Daniel R. *The Tentacles of Progress: Technology Transfer in the Age of Imperialism, 1850–1940.* New York: Oxford University Press, 1988.

Headrick, Daniel R. *The Tools of Empire: Technology and European Imperialism in the Nineteenth Century.* New York: Oxford University Press, 1981.

Hennessy, James Pope. *Anthony Trollope.* Boston: Little, Brown, 1971.

Herd, Norman. *The Bent Pine: The Trial of Chief Langalibalele.* Johannesburg: Ravan, 1976.

Hertslet, Sir Edward. *The Map of Africa by Treaty.* 3rd ed. Vol 2. London: H.M.S.O., 1909. Facs. repr. London: Frank Cass, 1967.

Hibbard, M. G. "The Arms of the Cape Mounted Riflemen, 1806–1926." *The Journal of the South African Muzzle Loaders Association* [later to become *Journal of the Historical Firearms Society of South Africa*] 2, no.3 (December 1961): 6–16.

Hinchley, Bernard T. "Notes on the Connection between the Birmingham Gun Trade and the South African Market in the Early Nineteenth Century." *Journal of the Historical Firearms Society of South Africa* 3, no. 5 (June 1965): 18–20.

Historical Dictionary of South Africa. 2nd ed. Comp. Christopher Saunders and Nicholas Southey. Lanham, Md.: Scarecrow, 2000.

Hodgson, Thomas Laidman. *Journals of the Rev. T. L. Hodgson, Missionary to the Seleka-Rolong and the Griquas, 1821–1831.* Ed. Richard L. Cope. Johannesburg: Witwatersrand University Press, 1977.

Hofmeyr, Jan Hendrik. *The Life of Jan Hendrik Hofmeyr (Onze Jan).* Cape Town: De Villiers, 1913.

Holden, Rev. William C. *History of the Colony of Natal, South Africa.* London: Alexander Heylin; Grahamstown: Godlonton White, 1855. Facs. repr. Cape Town: Struik, 1963.

Hole, Hugh Marshall. *The Passing of the Black Kings.* London: P. Allan, 1932.

Holub, Dr. Emil. *Seven Years in South Africa.* 2 vols. London: Sampson, Low, 1881.

Hulme, J. J. "The Minie Rifle: Its Development and Use in South Africa." *Journal of the Historical Firearms Society of South Africa* 1. Repr. ed. Cape Town: C. Struik, 1963: 49–55.

Immelman, R. F. M. *Men of Good Hope: The Romantic Story of the Cape Town Chamber of Commerce.* Cape Town: Cape Town Chamber of Commerce, 1955.

Inikori, J. E. "The Import of Firearms into West Africa 1750–1807: A Quantitative Analysis." *Journal of African History* 18, no. 3 (1977): 339–68.

Isaacman, Allen F., and Barbara S. Isaacman. *Slavery and Beyond: The Making of Men and Chikunda Ethnic Identities in the Unstable World of South-Central Africa, 1750–1920.* Portsmouth, NH: Heinemann, 2004.

Isaacs, Nathaniel. *Travels and Adventures in Eastern Africa.* 2 vols. Ed. L. Hermann. Cape Town: The Van Riebeeck Society, 1936–7.

Jasanoff, Sheila. *The Fifth Branch: Science Advisers as Policymakers*: Cambridge, Mass.: Harvard University Press, 1990.

Jasanoff, Sheila. *Science at the Bar: Law, Science, and Technology in America.* Cambridge, Mass.: Harvard University Press, 1995.

Jasanoff, Sheila, ed. *States of Knowledge: The Co-Production of Science and Social Order.* London and New York: Routledge, 2004.

Jasanoff, Sheila, Gerald E. Markle, James C. Petersen, and Trevor Pinch, eds. *Handbook of Science and Technology Studies.* Thousand Oaks: Sage, 1995; 2nd ed., 2001.

Jeffreys, M. K., et al. *Kaapse Plakkaatboek.* Cape Town: Cape Times, 1944.

John Wright and Andrew Manson. *The Hlubi Chiefdom in Zululand-Natal: A History.* Ladysmith: Ladysmith Historical Society, 1983.

Kea, R. A. "Firearms and Warfare on the Gold and Slave Coasts from the Sixteenth to the Nineteenth Centuries." *Journal of African History* 12, no. 2 (1971): 185–213.

Keck, Margaret E., and Kathryn Sikkink. *Activists beyond Borders: Advocacy Networks in International Politics.* Ithaca: Cornell University Press, 1998.

Keegan, Timothy. *Colonial South Africa and the Origins of the Racial Order.* Cape Town: David Philip, 1996.

Keegan, Timothy. "Dispossession and Accumulation in the South African Interior: The Boers and the Tlhaping of Bethulie, 1833–61." *Journal of African History* 28, (1987): 191–207.

Keegan, Timothy. "Trade, Accumulation and Impoverishment: Mercantile Capital and the Economic Transformation of Lesotho and the Conquered Territory, 1870–1920." *Journal of Southern African Studies* 12, no. 2 (April 1986): 196–216.

Keegan, Timothy. *Rural Transformations in Industrializing South Africa: The Southern Highveld to 1914.* London: Macmillan, 1987.

Kilpin, Ralph. *The Romance of a Colonial Parliament: Being a Narrative of the Parliament and Councils of the Cape of Good Hope.* London: Green, 1930.

Kirkland, Turner, and Toby Bridges. "Africa: Black Powder Hunting Paradise." *Journal of the Historical Firearms Society of South Africa* 6, no. 6 (December 1974): 25–9.

Kitchingman, James. *The Kitchingman Papers: Missionary Letters and Journals, 1817 to 1848, from the Brenthurst Collection.* Ed. and comp. Basil Le Cordeur and Christopher Saunders. Johannesburg: Brenthurst, 1976.

Knight, Ian. *The Anatomy of the Zulu Army: From Shaka to Cetshwayo 1818–1879.* London: Greenhill Books, 1995.

Kopel, David B. *The Samurai, The Mountie, and the Cowboy: Should America Adopt the Gun Controls of Other Democracies?* Amherst, N.Y.: Prometheus, 1992.

Kunene, D. P. *Heroic Poetry of the Basotho.* Oxford: Clarendon, 1971.

Kuper, Adam. "The 'House' and Zulu Political Structure in the Nineteenth Century." *Journal of African History* 34 (1993): 469–87.

Laband, John. *Kingdom in Crisis: The Zulu Response to the British Invasion of 1879.* Pietermaritzburg: University of Natal Press, 1992.

Laband, John. *The Transvaal Rebellion: The First Boer War, 1880–1881.* Harlow, U.K.: Pearson, 2005.

Lacy, George. *Pictures of Travel, Sport, and Adventure.* London: Pearson, 1899.

Lamar, Howard, and Leonard Thomson, eds. *The Frontier in History: North America and Southern Africa Compared.* New Haven: Yale University Press, 1981.

Lambert, John. "Chiefship in Early Colonial Natal, 1843–1879." *Journal of Southern African Studies* 21, no. 2 (June 1995): 269–85.

Lancaster, J. C. S. "The Governorship of Sir Benjamin D'Urban at the Cape of Good Hope." *Archives Year Book for South African History.* Vol. 2. Pretoria: Government Printer, 1991.

Lategan, Felix V. *Die Boer se Roer: Die Groot Geweerboek van Suid-Afrika.* Cape Town: Tafelberg, 1974.

Lategan, Felix V. "Fire-Arms, Historical." *Standard Encyclopedia of Southern Africa* 4 (1971): 515–36.

Laurence, Perceval. *The Life of John Xavier Merriman.* London: Constable, 1930.

Law, Robin. "Horses, Firearms and Political Power in Pre-Colonial West Africa." *Past and Present* 72 (August 1976): 112–52.

Le Cordeur, Basil. *The Politics of Eastern Cape Separatism, 1820–1854.* Cape Town: Oxford University Press, 1981.

Leask, Thomas. *The Southern African Diaries of Thomas Leask, 1865–1870.* Ed. J. P. R. Wallis. London: Chatto & Windus, 1954.

Legassick, Martin. "Firearms, Horses and Samorian Army Organization 1870–1898." *Journal of African History* 7, no. 1 (1966): 95–115.

Legassick, Martin. "The Griqua, the Sotho-Tswana, and the Missionaries, 1780–1840: The Politics of a Frontier Zone." Ph.D. dissertation, University of California at Los Angeles, 1969.

Lehmann, Joseph. *Echoes of War: The First Boer War.* London: Jonathan Cape, 1972. Repr. London: Buchan & Enright, 1985.

Lerman, Nina. "'Preparing for the Duties and Practical Business of Life': Technological Knowledge and Social Structure in Mid-19th-Century Philadelphia." *Technology and Culture* 38, no. 1 (1997): 31–59.

Lester, Alan. *Imperial Networks: Creating Identities in Nineteenth-Century South Africa and Britain.* London: Routledge, 2001.

Lewsen, Phyllis. "The First Crisis in Responsible Government." *Archives Year Book for South African History.* Vol. 11. Pretoria: Government Printer, 1942.

Lichtenstein, Henry. *Travels in Southern Africa in the Years 1803, 1804, 1805, and 1806.* Trans. Anne Plumptre. London: Henry Colburn, 1812. Repr. ed. Cape Town: Van Riebeeck Society, 1928.

Livingstone, David. *Livingstone's Missionary Correspondence, 1841–1856.* Ed. Isaac Schapera. Berkeley and Los Angeles: University of California Press, 1961.

Livingstone, David. *Missionary Travels and Researches in South Africa.* New York: Harper, 1858.

Livingstone, David. *South African Papers, 1849–1853.* Ed. Isaac Schapera. Cape Town: The Van Riebeeck Society, 1974.

Lord, William Barry, and Thomas Baines. *Shifts and Expedients of Camp Life, Travel, and Exploration.* London: 1876. Facs. Repr. Johannesburg: Africana Book Society, 1975.

Lye William F. "The Ndebele Kingdom South of the Limpopo River." *Journal of African History* 10, no. 1 (1969): 87–104.

Lye, William F. "The Difaqane: The Mfecane in the Southern Sotho Area, 1822–24." *Journal of African History* 8, no. 1 (1967): 107–31.

Machobane, L. B. B. J. *Government and Change in Lesotho, 1800–1966: A Study of Political Institutions.* London: Macmillan, 1990.

Mackenzie, John. *Ten Years North of the Orange River, 1859 to 1869: A Story of Everyday Life and Work among the South African Tribes.* Edinburgh: Edmonston & Douglas, 1871. Repr. London: Frank Cass, 1971.

Mackenzie, John M. *The Empire of Nature: Hunting, Conservation, and British Imperialism.* Manchester: Manchester University Press, 1988.

Macmillan, W. H. *Bantu, Boer, and Briton: The Making of the South African Native Problem.* London: Faber & Gwyer, 1929. Rev. ed., Oxford: Clarendon, 1963.

Maier, Pauline. *American Scripture.* New York: Knopf, 1997.

Malcolm, Joyce Lee. *Guns and Violence: The English Experience.* Cambridge, Mass.: Harvard University Press, 2002.

Malcolm, Joyce. *To Keep and Bear Arms: The Origins of an Anglo-American Right.* Cambridge, Mass.: Harvard University Press, 1994.

Malone, Patrick. *The Skulking Way of War: Technology and Tactics among the New England Indians.* Lanham, Md.: Madison Books, 1991.

Mamdani, Mahmood. *Citizen and Subject: Contemporary Africa and the Legacy of Late Colonialism.* Princeton: Princeton University Press, 1996.

Mandela, Nelson. *Long Walk to Freedom.* Boston: Little, Brown, 1994.

Manson, Andrew. "A People in Transition: The Hlubi in Natal, 1848–1877." *Journal of Natal and Zulu History* 2 (1979): 13–26.

Marais, J. S. *Maynier and the First Boer Republic.* Cape Town: Maskew Miller, 1944.

Marks, Shula. "From *Of Revelation and Revolution* to From Revelation to Reconciliation: A Comment." *Interventions: International Journal of Postcolonial Studies* 3, no. 1 (2001): 55–64.

Marks, Shula. "Khoisan Resistance to the Dutch in the Seventeenth and Eighteenth Centuries." *Journal of African History* 13, no. 1 (1972): 55–80.

Marks, Shula, and Anthony Atmore, eds. *Economy and Society in Pre-Industrial South Africa.* London: Longman, 1980.

Marks, Shula, and Anthony Atmore. "Firearms in Southern Africa: A Survey." *Journal of African History* 12, no. 4 (1971): 517–30.

Marks, Shula, and Anthony Atmore. "The Imperial Factor in South Africa in the Nineteenth Century: A Reassessment." *Journal of Imperial and Commonwealth History* 3, no. 1 (1974): 105–39.

Martineau, John. *Life and Correspondence of the Right Hon. Sir Bartle Frere.* 2 vols. London: John Murray, 1895.

Matthews, J. M. *Incwadi Yami, or Twenty Years Personal Experience in South Africa.* New York: Rogers & Sherwood, 1887. Facs. repr., Johannesburg: Africana Book Society, 1976.

Mavhunga, Clapperton. "Firearms Diffusion, Exotic and Indigenous Knowledge Systems in the Lowveld Frontier, South Eastern Zimbabwe, 1870–1920." *Comparative Technology Transfer and Society* 1, no. 2 (August 2003): 201–32.

McClendon, Thomas. "The Man Who Would Be *Inkosi*: Civilising Missions in Shepstone's Early Career." *Journal of Southern African Studies* 30, no. 2 (June 2004): 339–58.

McClendon, Thomas. "You Are What You Eat Up: Deposing Chiefs in Early Colonial Natal, 1847–1858." *Journal of African History* 47, no. 2 (2006): 259–79.

McCracken, J. L. *The Cape Parliament, 1854–1910.* Oxford: Clarendon, 1967.

McCracken, J. L. *New Light at the Cape of Good Hope: William Porter, the Father of Cape Liberalism.* Belfast: Ulster Historical Foundation, 1993.

McNaughton, P. R. *The Mande Blacksmith: Knowledge, Power, and Art in West Africa.* Bloomington: Indiana University Press, 1988.

McNeill, William H. *The Pursuit of Power: Technology, Armed Force, and Society since A.D. 1000.* Chicago: University of Chicago Press, 1982.

McPherson, James M. *Battle Cry of Freedom: The Civil War Era.* New York: Oxford University Press, 1988.

Men of the Times: Old Colonists of the Cape Colony and Orange River Colony. Johannesburg: The Transvaal Publishing Co., 1906.

Mentzel, O. F. *A Geographical and Topographical Description of the Cape of Good Hope.* Trans. Harry J. Mandelbrote. 3 vols. Cape Town: Van Riebeeck Society, 1921–44.

Methuen, Henry H. *Life in the Wilderness, or, Wanderings in South Africa.* London: Richard Bentley, 1846; 2nd ed., 1848.

Miers, Sue. *Britain and the Ending of the Slave Trade.* London: Longman, 1975.

Miers, Sue. "The Brussels Conference of 1889–1890: The Place of the Slave Trade in the Policies of Great Britain and Germany." In *Britain and Germany in Africa: Imperial Rivalry and Colonial Rule.* Ed. Prosser Gifford and William

Roger Louis, with Alison Smith, 83–118. New Haven: Yale University Press, 1967.

Miers, Sue. "Notes on the Arms Trade and Government Policy in Southern Africa between 1870 and 1890." *Journal of African History* 12, no. 4 (1971): 571–7.

Moffat, John S., et al. *The Matabele Mission: A Selection from the Correspondence of John and Emily Moffat, David Livingstone, and Others.* Ed. J. P. R. Wallis. London: Chatto & Windus, 1945.

Moffat, Robert. *Missionary Labours and Scenes in Southern Africa.* London: John Snow, 1842.

Moffat, Robert, and Mary Moffat. *Apprenticeship at Kuruman: Being the Journals and Letters of Robert and Mary Moffat.* Ed. Isaac Schapera. London: Chatto & Windus, 1951.

Mohr, Edward. *To the Victoria Falls of the Zambezi.* Trans. A. G. Bell. London: Sampson et al., 1876.

Molteno, Percy Albert. *The Life and Times of Sir John Charles Molteno.* 2 vols. London: Smith, Elder, 1900.

Mönnig, H. O. *The Pedi.* Pretoria: Schaik, 1967.

Moodie, Donald, comp., trans., ed. *The Record, or a Series of Official Papers Relative to the Condition and Treatment of the Native Tribes of South Africa.* Cape Town: n.p., 1838–41. Facs. repr. Amsterdam: Balkema, 1960.

Moodie, Duncan Campbell Francis. *John Dunn, Cetywayo and the Three Generals.* Pietermaritzburg: Natal Printing and Publishing Co., 1886.

Moore, S. F. *Social Facts and Fabrications: Customary Law on Kilimanjaro, 1880–1980.* Cambridge: Cambridge University Press, 1994.

Morris, Donald R. *The Washing of the Spears: A History of the Rise of the Zulu Nation under Shaka and Its Fall in the Zulu War of 1879.* New York: Simon and Schuster/Touchstone Books, 1965.

Mostert, Noël. *Frontiers: The Epic of South Africa's Creation and the Tragedy of the Xhosa People.* New York: Knopf, 1992.

Moyer, Richard A. "The Mfengu, Self-Defence and the Cape Frontier Wars." In *Beyond the Cape Frontier: Studies in the History of the Transkei and Ciskei.* Ed. Christopher Saunders and Robin Derricourt, 101–26. London: Longman, 1974.

Muller, C. F. J. *Leiers na die Noorde: Studies oor die Groot Trek.* Cape Town: Tafelberg, 1976

Muller, C. F. J. "Robert Scoon, 'n Vroeë Suid-Afrikaner." *South African Historical Journal* 4 (November 1972): 3–28.

Nasson, Bill. *Abraham Esau's War: A Black South African War in the Cape, 1899–1902.* Cambridge: Cambridge University Press, 1991.

Nasson, Bill. *The South African War, 1899–1902.* New York: Oxford University Press, Inc., 1999.

Natal Ordinances, Laws, and Proclamations. Vol. 1. *1843–1870.* Comp. Charles Fitzwilliam Cadiz with Robert Lyon. Pietermaritzburg: Government Printer, 1879.

Neumark, S. D. *The Economic Influences of the South African Frontier, 1652–1836.* Stanford: Stanford University Press, 1956.

Newton-King, Susan. *Masters and Servants on the Cape Eastern Frontier, 1760–1803.* Cambridge: Cambridge University Press, 1999.

Nicholson, George. *Fifty Years in South Africa: Being Some Reflections and Recollections of a Veteran Pioneer.* London: Greener, 1898.

Oates, Frank. *Matabele Land and the Victoria Falls: A Naturalist's Wanderings in the Interior of South Africa.* Ed. C. G. Oates. London: Kegan Paul, 1881.

Okoye, Felix N. C. "Dingane: A Reappraisal." *Journal of African History* 10, no. 2 (1969): 221–35.

Omer-Cooper, J. D. "Has the Mfecane a Future? A Response to the Cobbing Critique." *Journal of Southern African Studies* 19, no. 2 (June 1993): 273–93.

Orpen, Joseph M. *Some Principles of Native Government Illustrated; and the Petitions of the Basuto Tribe Regarding Land, Law, Representation, and Disarmament, to the Cape Parliament, Considered.* Cape Town: Saul Solomon, 1880.

Ortner, Sherry B. "Specifying Agency: The Comaroffs and Their Critics." *Interventions: International Journal of Postcolonial Studies* 3, no. 1 (2001): 76–84.

Oxford History of the British Empire. 5v. Ed. William Roger Louis. Oxford: Oxford University Press, 1999.

Pakenham, Thomas. *The Boer War.* New York: Random House, 1979.

Parsons, Neil. *King Khama, Emperor Joe, and the Great White Queen: Victorian Britain through African Eyes.* Chicago: University of Chicago Press, 1998.

Pearse, R. O., et al. *Langalibalele and the Natal Carbineers: The Story of the Langalibalele Rebellion, 1873.* Ladysmith: Ladysmith Historical Society, 1973.

Peires, J. B. *The Dead Will Arise: Nongqawuse and the Great Xhosa Cattle-Killing Movement of 1856–7.* Johannesburg: Ravan, 1989.

Peires, J. B. *The House of Phalo: A History of the Xhosa People in the Days of Their Independence.* Johannesburg: Ravan, 1981.

Peires, J. B. "Paradigm Deleted: the Materialist Interpretation of the Mfecane." *Journal of Southern African Studies* 19, no. 2 (June 1993): 295–313.

Penn, Nigel. *The Forgotten Frontier: Colonist and Khoisan on the Cape's Northern Frontier in the 18th Century.* Athens: Ohio University Press; Cape Town: Double Storey Books, 2005.

Perrin, Noel. *Giving Up the Gun: Japan's Reversion to the Sword, 1543–1879.* Boston: David R. Godine, 1979.

Phillips, Lionel. *Some Reminiscences.* London: Hutchinson, 1924.

Piot, Charles. "Of Hybridity, Modernity, and Their Malcontents." *Interventions: International Journal of Postcolonial Studies* 3, no. 1 (2001): 85–91.

Pocock, J. G. A. *The Machiavellian Moment: Florentine Political Thought and the Atlantic Republican Tradition.* Princeton: Princeton University Press, 1975.

Porter, Andrew, and Alaine Low, eds. *The Oxford History of the British Empire.* Vol. 3, *The Nineteenth Century.* Oxford: Oxford University Press, 1999.

Pretorius, J. G. "The British Humanitarians and the Cape Eastern Frontier, 1834–1836." *Archives Year Book for South African History.* Vol. 1. Pretoria: Government Printer, 1988.

Pringle, Thomas. *Narrative of a Residence in South Africa.* Ed. A. M. Lewin Robinson. London: Edward Moxon, 1835. Repr. Cape Town: C. Struik, 1966.

Procida, Mary A. "Good Sports and Right Sorts: Guns, Gender, and Imperialism in British India." *Journal of British Studies* 40 (October 2001): 454–88.

Reitz, Deneys. *Commando: A Boer Journal of the Boer War.* 2nd ed. London: Faber & Faber, 1931.

Richards, Paul. *Indigenous Agricultural Revolution: Ecology and Food Production in West Africa.* London: Hutchinson, 1985.

Richards, W. A. "The Import of Firearms into West Africa in the Eighteenth Century." *Journal of African History* 21 (1980): 43–59.

Roads, C. H. *The British Soldier's Firearm, 1850–1864.* London: Herbert Jenkins, 1964.

Roberts, Richard, and Kristin Mann. "Introduction: Law in Colonial Africa." In *Law in Colonial Africa.* London: James Currey, 1991: 3–58.

Robinson, A. M. L. "Newspapers and Periodicals." *Standard Encyclopedia of Southern Africa.* Ed. D. J. Potgieter. Cape Town: NASOU Ltd., 1973: 187–97.

Robinson, Ronald, John Gallagher, and Alice Denny. *Africa and the Victorians: The Official Mind of Imperialism.* 2nd ed. London: Macmillan, 1981.

Ross, Robert. *Adam Kok's Griquas: A Study in the Development of Stratification in South Africa.* Cambridge: Cambridge University Press, 1976.

Ross, Robert. *Cape of Torments: Slavery and Resistance in South Africa.* London: Routledge & Kegan Paul, 1983.

Ross, Robert. *A Concise History of South Africa.* Cambridge: Cambridge University Press, 1999.

Ross, Robert. *Status and Respectability in the Cape Colony, 1750–1870: A Tragedy of Manners.* Cambridge: Cambridge University Press, 1999.

Rotberg, Robert I., and Miles F. Shore. *The Founder: Cecil Rhodes and the Pursuit of Power.* New York: Oxford University Press, 1988.

Russell, Carl P. *Guns on the Early Frontiers: A History of Firearms from Colonial Times through the Years of the Western Fur Trade.* Berkeley and Los Angeles: University of California Press, 1957.

Rydén, Göran. "Skill and Technical Change in the Swedish Iron Industry, 1750–1860." *Technology and Culture* 39, no. 3 (1998): 383–407.

Samkange, Stanlake. *Origins of Rhodesia.* London: Heinemann, 1968.

Sanders, Peter. *The Last of the Queen's Men: A Lesotho Experience.* Johannesburg: Witwatersrand University Press, 2000.

Saunders, Christopher. "The Annexation of the Transkeian Territories." In *Archives Year Book for South African History.* Pretoria: The Government Printer, 1978.

Saunders, Christopher. *The Making of the South African Past: Major Historians on Race and Class.* Cape Town: David Philip, 1988.

Saunders, Christopher, Colin Bundy and Dougie Oakes. *Illustrated History of South Africa: The Real Story.* Pleasantville, New York: The Reader's Digest Association, 1988.

Schama, Simon. *Citizens: A Chronicle of the French Revolution.* New York: Knopf, 1989.

Schama, Simon. *The Embarrassment of Riches: An Interpretation of Dutch Culture in the Golden Age.* New York: Knopf, 1987.

Schapera, Isaac, ed. and trans. *Praise Poems of the Tswana Chiefs*. Oxford: Clarendon, 1965.

Schapera, Isaac, and B. Farrington, ed. and trans. *The Early Cape Hottentots, Described in the Writings of Olfert Dapper (1668), Willem ten Rhyne (1686), and Johannes Gulielmus de Grevenbroek (1695)*. Cape Town: Van Riebeeck Society, 1933.

Schmidt, Peter R. *The Culture and Technology of African Iron Production*. Gainesville: University of Florida Press, 1996.

Scott, Joan W. *The Glassworkers of Carmaux: French Craftsmen and Political Action in a Nineteenth-Century City*. Cambridge, Mass.: Harvard University Press, 1974.

Scully, Pamela. "Liquor and Labor in the Western Cape, 1870–1900." In *Liquor and Labor in Southern Africa*. Ed. Jonathan Crush and Charles Ambler, 56–77. Athens: Ohio University Press, 1992.

Scully, William Charles. *Reminiscences of a South African Pioneer*. London: T. F. Unwin, 1913.

Sedgwick, C. E. C. "Frontier Flintlocks – Cape Colony." *Journal of the South African Muzzle Loaders Association*, [later renamed *Journal of the Historical Firearms Society of South Africa*] 2, no. 1 (December 1960): 6–10.

Selous, Frederick Courteney. *A Hunter's Wanderings in Africa*. 4th ed. London: Bentley, 1895.

Selous, Frederick Courteney. *Sunshine and Storm in Rhodesia*. London: Rowland & Ward, 1896. Facs. repr. New York: Negro Universities Press, 1969.

Shapin, Steven, and Simon Schaffer. *Leviathan and the Air-Pump: Hobbes, Boyle, and the Experimental Life*. Princeton: Princeton University Press, 1985.

Shineberg, Dorothy. "Guns and Men in Melanesia." *Journal of Pacific History* 6 (1971): 61–82.

Showers, Kate B. *Imperial Gullies: Soil Erosion and Conservation in Lesotho*. Athens: Ohio University Press, 2005.

Smaldone, Joseph P. "Firearms in the Central Sudan: A Revaluation." *Journal of African History* 13, no. 4 (1972): 591–607.

Smaldone, Joseph P. *Warfare in the Sokoto Caliphate: Historical and Sociological Perspectives*. Cambridge: Cambridge University Press, 1977.

Smith, Andrew. *Andrew Smith's Journal of His Expedition into the Interior of South Africa, 1834–36*. Ed. William F. Lye. Cape Town: Balkema, 1975.

Smith, K. W. "The Fall of Bapedi of the North-Eastern Transvaal." *Journal of African History* 10, no. 2 (1969): 237–52.

Smith, Merritt Roe, and Leo Marx, eds. *Does Technology Drive History? The Dilemma of Technological Determinism*. Cambridge, Mass.: MIT Press, 1994.

Smith, Robert Sydney. *Warfare and Diplomacy in Pre-colonial West Africa*. 2nd ed. Madison: University of Wisconsin Press, 1989.

Smith-Dorrien, Horace. *Memories of Forty-Eight Years' Service*. New York: Dutton, 1925.

Solomon, W. E. G. *Saul Solomon: The Member for Cape Town*. Cape Town: Oxford University Press, 1948.

Solway, Jacqueline, and Michael Lambek. "Weber in Southern Africa? Reflections on John and Jean Comaroff's *Of Revelation and Revolution*, Volume II."

Interventions: International Journal of Postcolonial Studies 3, no. 1 (2001): 92–9.

South African Archival Records (SAAR). Transvaal, Nos. 1–7, 1844–68. *Orange Free State*, Nos. 1–4, 1854–59. *Natal*, Nos. 1–5, 1838–59. Ed. J. H. Breytenbach et al. Cape Town: Government Printer, 1949–66.

Spring, Christopher. *African Arms and Armor*. London: British Museum; Washington, D.C.: Smithsonian Institution Press, 1993.

Squires, Peter. *Gun Culture or Gun Control? Firearms, Violence and Society*. London: Routledge, 2000.

Stanford, Walter. *Reminiscences*. 2 vols. Ed. J. W. Macquarie. Cape Town: Van Riebeeck Society, 1958 and 1962.

Stockenstrom, Andries. *The Autobiography of the Late Sir Andries Stockenstrom*. 2 vols. Ed. C. W. Hutton. Cape Town: Juta, 1887.

Storey, William Kelleher. "Guns, Race, and Skill in Nineteenth-Century Southern Africa." *Technology and Culture* 45, no. 4 (October 2004): 687–711.

Storey, William Kelleher. "Plants, Power, and Development: Founding the Imperial Department of Agriculture for the West Indies, 1880–1914." In *States of Knowledge: The Co-Production of Science and Social Order*, ed. Sheila Jasanoff, 109–130. London: Routledge, 2004.

Storey, William Kelleher. *Science and Power in Colonial Mauritius*. Rochester: University of Rochester Press, 1997.

Stow, George W. *The Native Races of South Africa*. Ed. George McCall Theal. New York: Macmillan, 1905; facs. repr. Cape Town: C. Struik, 1964.

Struben, Hendrik Wilhelm. *Recollections of Adventures: Pioneering and Development in South Africa, 1850–1911*. Ed. Edith Struben. Cape Town: Maskew Miller, 1920.

Stuart, James, comp. *The James Stuart Archive of Recorded Oral Evidence Relating to the History of the Zulu and Neighbouring Peoples*. 4 vols. Ed. C. de B. Webb and J. B. Wright. Pietermaritzburg and Durban: University of Natal Press and the Killie Campbell Africana Library, 1979.

Stuart, James, comp.; Anthony T. Cope, ed. *Izibongo: Zulu Praise-Poetry*. Oxford: Clarendon, 1968.

Switzer, Les. *Power and Resistance in an African Society: The Ciskei Xhosa and the Making of South Africa*. Madison: University of Wisconsin Press, 1993.

Tabler, Edward C. *The Far Interior: Chronicles of Pioneering in the Matabele and Mashona Countries, 1847–1879*. Cape Town: Balkema, 1955.

Taylor, Henry S. *Doctor to Basuto, Boer & Briton, 1877–1906*. Ed. Peter Hadley. Cape Town: David Philip, 1972.

Taylor, James Benjamin, with Henry O'Kelly Webber. *A Pioneer Looks Back*. London: Hutchinson, 1939.

Taylor, Stephen. *The Mighty Nimrod: A Life of Frederick Courteney Selous, African Hunter and Adventurer, 1851–1917*. London: Collins, 1989.

Taylor, Stephen. *Shaka's Children: A History of the Zulu People*. London: HarperCollins, 1994.

Theal, George M., comp. *Basutoland Records: Copies of Official Documents of Various Kinds, Accounts of Travellers, &c.* 3 vols. Cape Town: Richards, 1883. Repr. Cape Town: C. Struik, 1964.

Theal, George McCall. *History of Africa*. 11 vols. London: Allen and Unwin, 1889. Repr. Cape Town: C. Struik, 1964.

Theal, George McCall. *Records of the Cape Colony from February 1793 to April 1831: Copied from the Manuscript Documents in the Public Record Office, London*. 36 vols. London: William Clowes, 1897–1905.

Thompson, Andrew. "Languages of Loyalism in Southern Africa, c. 1870–1939." *English Historical Review* 118, no. 477 (June 2003): 617–50.

Thompson, George. *Travels and Adventures in Southern Africa*. 2 vols. Ed. Vernon S. Forbes. London: Henry Colburn, 1827. Facs. repr. Cape Town: Van Riebeeck Society, 1967–8.

Thompson, Leonard. *A History of South Africa*. New Haven: Yale University Press, 1990.

Thornton, R. W. *The Origin and History of the Basuto Pony*. Morija: Morija Printing Works, 1938.

Thunberg, Carl Peter. *Travels at the Cape of Good Hope, 1772–1775*. Ed. V. S. Forbes. London: n.p., 1793–5. Repr. Cape Town: Van Riebeeck Society, 1986.

Todd, Jan. *Colonial Technology: Science and the Transfer of Innovation to Australia*. Cambridge: Cambridge University Press, 1995.

Trollope, Anthony. *South Africa*. London: Chapman & Hall, 1878.

Turrell, Robert Vicat. "The 1875 Black Flag Revolt on the Kimberley Diamond Fields." *Journal of Southern African Studies* 7, no. 2 (April 1981): 194–235.

Turrell, Robert Vicat. *Capital and Labour on the Kimberley Diamond Fields, 1870–1890*. Cambridge: Cambridge University Press, 1987.

Tylden, Geoffrey. *The Armed Forces of South Africa*. Johannesburg: University Press, 1954.

Tylden, Geoffrey. "Identification and Classification of Firearms in South Africa." *Africana Notes and News* 1, no. 1 (December 1943): 4–8.

Tylden, Geoffrey. "The Problem of Barrel Fouling." *The Journal of the South African Muzzle Loaders Association* [later published as *The Journal of the Historical Firearms Society of South Africa*] 2, no. 3 (December 1961): 23.

Tylden, Geoffrey. "Shoulder Firearms in Southern Africa, 1652–1952." *Africana Notes and News*, no. 12 (June 1957): 198–219.

Tylden, Geoffrey. "The Shoulder Firearm on Horseback." *The Journal of the South African Muzzle Loaders Association* [later published as *The Journal of the Historical Firearms Society of South Africa*] 2, no. 4 (June 1962): 16–19.

Tylden, Geoffrey. "Swivel Guns, Elephant Guns – So-Called – and Large Bores." *The Journal of the South African Muzzle Loaders Association* [later published as *The Journal of the Historical Firearms Society of South Africa*] 2, no. 3 (December 1961): 17–18.

Uys, C. J. *In the Era of Shepstone: Being a Study of British Expansion in South Africa, 1842–1877*. Lovedale: Lovedale Press, 1933.

Van Onselen, Charles. *The Seed Is Mine: The Life of Kas Maine, a South African Sharecropper, 1894–1985*. New York: Hill & Wang, 1996.

Van Onselen, Lennox. "In Defence of the Muzzle Loader." *Journal of the Historical Firearms Society of South Africa* 1. Repr. ed. Cape Town: C. Struik, 1963: 14–16.

Van Sittert, Lance. "Our Irrepresible Fellow-Colonist: The Biological Invasion of Prickly Pear (*Opuntia ficus-indica*) in the Eastern Cape Colony c.1890–1910." In *South Africa's Environmental History: Cases and Comparisons*. Ed. S. Dovers, R. Edgecombe, and B. Guest. Cape Town: David Philip, 2002: 139–59.

Van Sittert, Lance. "To Live This Poor Life: Remembering the Hottentots Huisie Fishery, Cape Town, c. 1934–c1965." *Social History* 26 (2001): 1–21.

Vanstone, James Perry. "Sir John Gordon Sprigg: A Political Biography." Ph.D. diss. Queen's University, Kingston, Ont., 1974.

Vedder, Heinrich. *South West Africa in Early Times: Being the Story of South West Africa up to the Date of Maharero's Death in 1890*. Trans. and ed. Cyril G. Hall. Oxford: Oxford University Press, 1938; 2nd ed. London: Frank Cass, 1966.

Vijn, Cornelius. *Cetshwayo's Dutchman: Being the Private Journal of a White Trader in Zululand during the British Invasion*. Trans. and ed. J. W. Colenso. London: Longmans, 1880. Facs. repr. New York: Negro Universities Press, 1969.

Vimercati, Paul, as told to S. P. Berkemeyer. "The Mighty 8 Bore." *Journal of the Historical Firearms Society of South Africa* 8, no. 1 (June 1978): 17–20.

Wahl, Norman. "American Percussions in South Africa." *Journal of the Historical Firearms Society of South Africa* 4, no. 4 (December 1967): 5–6.

Walker, Eric A. *A History of South Africa*. London: Longmans, 1928; 2nd ed. 1940.

Ward, Alan. *A Show of Justice: Racial 'Amalgamation' in Nineteenth Century New Zealand*. Canberra: Australian National University Press, 1973; reprinted with corrections by Auckland University Press, 1995.

Watson, R. L. "The Subjection of a South African State: Thaba Nchu, 1880–1884." *Journal of African History* 21, no. 3 (1980): 357–73.

Welsh, Frank. *South Africa: A Narrative History*. New York, Tokyo, and London: Kodansha International, 1999.

White, Gavin. "Firearms in Africa: An Introduction." *Journal of African History* 12, no. 2 (1971): 173–84.

White, Landeg. "Power and the Praise Poem." *Journal of Southern African Studies* 9, no. 1 (October 1982): 8–32.

Wilmot, Alexander. *The Life and Times of Sir Richard Southey*. Cape Town: Maskew Millar; London: Sampson Low, Marston, 1904.

Winner, Langdon. "Do Artifacts Have Politics?" In *The Whale and the Reactor: A Search for Limits in an Age of High Technology*. Chicago: University of Chicago Press, 1986.

Woon, Harry Vernon. *Twenty-Five Years Soldiering in South Africa*. London: Andrew Melrose, 1909.

Worden, Nigel. *The Making of Modern South Africa: Conquest, Segregation and Apartheid*. Oxford: Blackwell, 1994.

Worden, Nigel, Elizabeth vanHeyningen, and Vivian Bickford-Smith. *Cape Town: The Making of a City*. Claremont, South Africa: David Philip, 1998.

Worger, William H. *South Africa's City of Diamonds: Mine Workers and Monopoly Capitalism in Kimberley, 1867–1895.* New Haven: Yale University Press, 1987.

Wright, John, and Andrew Manson. *The Hlubi Chiefdom in Zululand-Natal: A History.* Ladysmith: Ladysmith Historical Society, 1983.

Wynne, Brian. "Public Understanding of Science." In *Handbook of Science and Technology Studies.* Eds. Jasanoff et al. Thousand Oaks, CA: Sage, 1995: 361–88.

Index

BOOKS IN THE SERIES